RENEWALS 458-4574

DATE DUE

MAY 1 2			
GAYLORD			PRINTED IN U.S.A

Emerging Democracy in Late Imperial Russia

EMERGING DEMOCRACY
IN
LATE IMPERIAL RUSSIA

CASE STUDIES ON
LOCAL SELF-GOVERNMENT (THE ZEMSTVOS),
STATE DUMA ELECTIONS,
THE TSARIST GOVERNMENT,
AND
THE STATE COUNCIL BEFORE AND DURING WORLD WAR I

EDITED BY
MARY SCHAEFFER CONROY

UNIVERSITY PRESS OF COLORADO

Copyright © 1998 by the University Press of Colorado

International Standard Book Number 0-87081-470-2

Published by the University Press of Colorado
P.O. Box 849
Niwot, Colorado 80544

The University Press of Colorado is a cooperative publishing enterprise supported, in part, by Adams State College, Colorado State University, Fort Lewis College, Mesa State College, Metropolitan State College of Denver, University of Colorado, University of Northern Colorado, University of Southern Colorado, and Western State College of Colorado.

The paper used in this publication meets the minimum requirements of the American National Standard for Information Sciences — Permanence of Paper for Printed Library Materials. ANSI Z39.48–1984

Library of Congress Cataloging-in-Publication Data

Emerging democracy in late Imperial Russia : case studies on local
  self-government (the Zemstvos), State Duma elections, the Tsarist
  government, and the State Council before and during World War I /
  edited by Mary Schaeffer Conroy.
      p.   cm.
   Includes index.
   ISBN 0-807081-470-2 (hardcover : alk. paper)
      1. Russia—Politics and government—1894-1917.   2. Democracy—
Russia.   I. Conroy, Mary Schaeffer, 1937–   .
DK260.E44   1998
947.08'3—dc21   97-48794
                                                          CIP

This book was designed and
typeset in URW Bergamo
by Stephen Adams

10   9   8   6   5   4   3   2   1

ISBN 087081470-2
9 780870 814709
90000

CONTENTS

CONTRIBUTORS

MARY SCHAEFFER CONROY is Professor of History at the University of Colorado in Denver. She is author of *Peter Arkad'evich Stolypin: Practical Politics in Late Tsarist Russia* (Boulder: Westview Press, 1976), *In Health and In Sickness: Pharmacy, Pharmacists and the Pharmaceutical Industry in Late Imperial, Early Soviet Russia* (Boulder: East European Monographs; distributed by Columbia University Press, 1994), and chapters and articles on government, medical care, and women in late Imperial, early Soviet Russia.

DITTMAR DAHLMANN is Professor of East European History at Rheinische Friedrich-Wilhelms-Universität Bonn, Germany, and head of the Institute for Research on Culture and History of the Germans in Russia. His major publications include *Die Provinz wählt. Rußlands Konstitutionell-Demokratische Partei und die Dumawahlen 1906–1912* (Cologne, Welmar, Vienna: Böhlau Verlag GmbH & Cie, 1996).

WILLIAM GLEASON is Professor of History at Doane College. From 1995 to 1997 he served as professor and consultant at Peter Mogila University in Kiev, Ukraine. He is the author of *Alexander Guchkov and the End of the Russian Empire* (Philadelphia: The American Philosophical Society, 1983), coauthor (with John Thompson) of *A Vision Unfulfilled: Russia and the Soviet Union in the Twentieth Century* (Lexington, MA: D. C. Heath and Co., 1996), and numerous articles on the zemstvos in late Imperial Russia.

ALEXANDRA S. KORROS is Associate Professor of History at Xavier University, Cincinatti, Ohio. She is author of numerous chapters and articles on Stolypin and the State Council. She is currently researching and writing a book on the State Council, the upper chamber of the Russian legislature, before 1917.

ANTTI VELI KUJALA is Senior Lecturer in Finnish and Russian History at the University of Helsinki, Finland, and Senior Fellow of the Academy of Finland. His major publications include *Akashi Motojiro, Rakka ryusui: Colonel Akashi's Report on His Secret Cooperation with the Russian Revolutionary Parties during the Russo-Japanese War* (Helsinki: Finnish Historical Society, 1988), edited with Olavi K. Falt, and *Venäjänhallitus Ja Suomen Työväenliike, 1899–1905* (Helsinki: Finnish Historical Society, 1995).

KIMITAKA MATSUZATO is Associate Professor of History at Hokkaido University, Japan. A specialist on pre-Soviet Russian agriculture and the so-called Stolypin Land Reforms, his numerous publications include "Stolypinskaia reforma i rossiiskaia agrotekhnologicheskaia revoliutsiia," *Otechestvennaia istoriia*, no. 6, 1992, pp. 164–200, and "The Fate of Agronomists in Russia: Their Quantitative Dynamics from 1911 to 1916," *The Russian Review*, vol. 55, 1996, pp. 172–200.

THOMAS PORTER is Associate Professor of History at North Carolina Agricultural and Technical State University, Greensboro. He is the author of *The Zemstvo and the Emergence of Civil Society in Late Imperial Russia, 1864–1917* (San Francisco: Mellon Research University Press, 1991) and has published numerous articles on the zemstvos and the Union of Zemstvos before and during World War I.

CHARLES E. TIMBERLAKE is Professor of History at the University of Missouri. He has published numerous chapters and articles on education, religion and monasteries, and local self-government, particularly in Tver' Province, in late Imperial Russia. His major publications include his edited *Religious and Secular Forces in Late Tsarist Russia* (Seattle and London: University of Washington Press, 1992).

MAPS AND FIGURES

EMERGING DEMOCRACY IN LATE IMPERIAL RUSSIA

I

INTRODUCTION

The late 1980s to early 1990s has been a challenging and exciting period for historians of Russia, particularly those focusing on late Imperial Russia. On the one hand, political developments during First Party Secretary Mikhail Gorbachev's administration gave rise to renewed interest in the political system operating in Russia in the decades before the revolutions of 1917. On the other hand, Gorbachev's policy of *glasnost'* or openness gave historians the possibility to examine this era more fully. Prior to the late 1980s Soviet historians were forced to conform to Marxist paradigms, toe the Party line, and in general justify the Soviet regime and its policies.[1] The Soviet government presented a negative picture of late Imperial Russia and barred access to archives that would tell a different story. Glasnost unfettered Soviet historians and permitted general access not only to sensitive Party records but materials from regional archives.

Gorbachev's dismantling of the Soviet political system stimulated curiosity in the system that preceded it. The Soviet system was undemocratic from its inception and remained so for the seventy years of its existence. Immediately after seizing control of the imperial capital of Petrograd (as St. Petersburg was called during World War I) in October 1917, Lenin not only suppressed nonsocialist parties, but also refused to share power with other socialists, save for a half-year coalition with so-called Left Socialist Revolutionaries. In January 1918 he shut down a Constituent Assembly that had been elected in November, after his takeover, because it was dominated by rival socialists. From March 1921, only one party was legal, Lenin's Bolshevik or Communist Party as it came to be called. The party orchestrated elections to local soviets and the national parliament.[2] It controlled the media, the arts, and educational institutions. The government banned independent religious and social organizations.[3] Waves of repression —summary executions and exile to labor camps, often meted out extralegally—kept the population in line from October 1917 through the 1980s.[4]

Lack of democracy in Soviet Russia was closely linked with the economic system that the Bolsheviks installed. Save for a brief and tentative hiatus during the period of the New Economic Policy in the 1920s and collective farmers' limited rights to small-scale production and trade between 1935 and 1945 and after Stalin's death in 1953, the Soviet government concentrated the means of production in its hands.[5] Private enterprise was illegal until the late 1980s. Prohibition on independent economic activity deprived citizens of leverage against the government and precluded democracy from developing.[6] There could be no "power of the purse" in the Soviet Union. Despite the Soviet regime's economic and cultural achievements, despite citizens' ability to cope, despite the benefits enjoyed by some, Soviet citizens were expendable.[7] Their recourse against government excesses was limited to passive resistance and subterfuge.

Soviet leaders began to reform Russia's political and economic system after Stalin's death. However, civil rights remained fragile. Democracy only began to resurface when Gorbachev allowed genuine elections to the Soviet parliament in 1989, independent quasi-political groups, then non-Communist parties, and in 1991, genuine elections for the presidency of Russia. Finally, major national minorities were allowed to establish sovereign states, ending the Soviet regime.

As the transformation of the Russian political system proceeded in the 1990s, the questions that piqued both Russians and foreigners were whether democracy would be viable in post-Soviet Russia or whether authoritarianism was somehow inherent to Russia and, concomitantly, what sort of political system best suited Russia, in accordance with tradition, demography, and culture and in order to complete the transition to a market economy. Soviet political institutions, after all, at least in form, replicated tsarist political institutions.[8]

Whether post-Soviet Russia will establish viable democratic institutions will be determined by multiple contemporary factors. But because countries, like individuals, have behavior patterns, an examination of the political system existing in Russia before 1917, particularly in the late imperial period, provides perspective on the type of political system appropriate for post-Soviet Russia and gives insights into the likelihood of democracy emerging. Russians themselves are keen to know about their pre-Soviet political institutions, not for prescriptive purposes but for context in which to rebuild their post-Soviet political institutions. Foreigners too need accurate knowledge of pre-Soviet Russia if they are to avoid egregious errors and make genuine contributions to post-Soviet Russia.

Conventional wisdom has it that democracy cannot flourish in Russia because "Russia has never known democracy throughout its history." Pundits have dredged up the sixteenth-century ruler Ivan (or Ioann) the Terrible and the eighteenth-century Peter the Great, not to mention Stalin, to prove that Russians are accustomed to and indeed appreciate and need strong leaders. As if in confirmation, the independence and caprice of local officials and the anarchy encountered by foreign businesses in post-Soviet Russia cry for a strong hand at the helm. Is Russia, then, predestined never to enjoy authentic representative institutions—is the country doomed to choose between chaos and tyranny?

Especially instructive in answering this query is the era of the last two Romanovs, Alexander III and Nicholas II (1881–1917), when a political system approximating that in post-Soviet Russia prevailed. Russia had a strong executive branch that had been evolving from the fifteenth century. Tsars stood at the apex of Russian government. In the nineteenth and early twentieth centuries, they were assisted at the central level by ministers, who managed government departments and were loosely organized before 1906 in a Committee of Ministers; by the State Council, a body of some seventy-two men, appointed for life, who drafted laws that were then approved by the Tsar; and by the Governing Senate, which had administrative functions and also served as the highest court of the land. Governors appointed by the Tsar administered the provinces.

Although the Russian government was absolutist before 1906, there being no popularly elected national legislature to check it, there were mechanisms that enabled citizens to counter executive authorities and manage their own affairs. Citizens could sue in courts and appeal for redress of grievances to the Governing Senate; from the mid-1860s and 1870s many cities had popularly elected city councils, and in thirty-four provinces popularly elected provincial and county councils (zemstvos) operated as well. Male taxpayers could vote in both city and zemstvo elections; women could vote in city elections through male relatives. Finally, in 1906, a popularly elected lower legislative chamber, the State Duma, was established. Although Duma suffrage was not based on "one man, one vote" (women were excluded from voting), multiple political parties existed. In 1906 the Committee of Ministers was transformed into a Council of Ministers, but ministers were appointed by the Tsar and were individually responsible to him; thus the Russian "cabinet" had less cohesion than the British and the Chair of the Council or Ministers was not a Prime Minister in the British sense.

Popular books, films, and even purported documentaries paint late Imperial Russia in broad, simplistic brush strokes—the government was oppressive and inept, virtually crumbling away in World War I; Nicholas in particular was incompetent, Alexandra hysterical, and nobles wallowed in luxury while the masses were mired in ignorance and penury.

Some scholars have joined the chorus. Although the view that the revolutions of 1917 were inevitable because "government" and "society" were hopelessly estranged has been modified if not discarded, during the last two decades many historians have complained about the arbitrariness or *proizvol* of the tsarist government.[9] Geoffrey Swain epitomizes those disillusioned with the tsarist government. He trumpets of the February 1917 Revolution that toppled Nicholas's regime[10]—despite the fact that the successor Provisional Government was not elected, despite the chaos that ensued following the overthrow of the tsarist government,[11] despite the fact that socialist democrats' economic theories were deleterious for citizens and the economy[12]— "after a bitter struggle" begun "nearly fifty years earlier, democracy had triumphed."[13]

Since history is as much interpretation as fact, scholars are entitled to such views. Additionally, pessimistic pictures of the tsarist regime provide a convenient explanation for the February Revolution of 1917 that swept it away. However, are these depictions of Russia's political system prior to the revolutions of 1917 complete and accurate? Are they the whole story?

Well before Gorbachev's reforms, historians were assembling a mosaic of the political system of late Imperial Russia. In the 1960s and 1970s American historians began to study various aspects of the government of Nicholas II, the first three Dumas, which functioned between 1906 and 1912, and selected political figures and political parties.[14] Alfred Levin updated his pioneering work on the Second Duma[15] and published a monograph on the Third Duma.[16] Geoffrey Hosking focused on the moderately liberal (or moderately conservative, depending upon one's point of view) Octobrists or Party of October 17, which dominated the Third Duma, and their interaction with Peter Stolypin, Minister of Internal Affairs and Chairman of the Council of Ministers from 1906 until his assassination in 1911.[17] Howard Mehlinger's and John Thompson's examination of the elections for the First Duma moved forward our understanding of Nicholas's regime a great deal by showing that the Tsar and his government permitted fairly free elections to the Duma.[18]

Soviet historians also produced some insightful studies of prerevolutionary political institutions despite the strictures confining them prior to glasnost. Although Peter Zaionchkovsky's 1970s monograph on Alexander III to some extent stereotypically categorized his reign as one of unmitigated reaction, Zaionchkovsky's elaboration of the multiplicity of institutions and crosscurrents of opinion involved in policy making during Alexander's reign and the mixed impact this had on society, allowed the reader to infer that sweeping condemnation of the second-to-the-last Tsar's administration was not warranted.[19] V. A. Nardova's mid-1980s monograph on city self-government showed how vigorous municipal government had become by the late nineteenth century, particularly in St. Petersburg, and also how bureaucrats in the central government supported elected city officials when conflicts erupted between them and appointed governors.[20]

Marc Szeftel was sanguine that in the late imperial period representative institutions were being integrated into the absolutist political system. In the mid-1970s he averred that "the Duma period represents in the history of Russia, with one brief exception, the farthest point of progress in its institutional development in three respects." He noted, first, "the existence of a *national legislative assembly* elected on a competitive political basis where not only oppositional, but even revolutionary opinions could express themselves. Second," Szeftel remarked, in the late imperial period Russia had "a system of government based, more than at any other time, on the concomitant principles of *separation of powers* and of the rule of law and," finally, "a greater degree of *civil liberties* available to the population than ever before." He insisted that these conditions obtained "notwithstanding the survival of strong remnants of absolutism and legal inequality which greatly underscored the still existing distance between Russian institutions and those of other countries of Europe. Important above all," he contended, "were the prospects of further development offered by the so-called Duma system which allowed for reasonable expectations that on its basis the remnants of absolutism and the surviving inequality" would "be eliminated in the long term, while the separation of powers, the rule of law and the civil liberties" would "be developed considerably. These expectations were warranted, especially, by the rapid transformation ever magnifying the pluralistic features of Russian life."[21]

The opening of central and regional archives in Russia in the 1980s and 1990s has enabled historians to present the nineteenth-, early-twentieth-century tsarist government and political system in greater chiaroscuro. Additionally, realizing that by no means all political and economic developments were confined to the capital, historians have begun to explore local political institutions and the ties between the provinces and the center.

A post-Soviet compilation recently translated into English presents refreshingly unbiased vignettes of Russia's rulers from Peter the Great through Nicholas II.[22] W. Bruce Lincoln's account of progressive tsarist officials' preparation of the "Great Reforms" during the 1840s and 1850s,[23] Daniel Orlovsky's study of the Ministry of Internal Affairs between 1802 and 1881,[24] Thomas Pearson's and Francis Wcislo's studies of the tsarist government's program for local self-government in the late imperial period,[25] David Macey's review of the tsarist government's agrarian reform and relationship with the peasantry,[26] have added dimension to our profile of the government. For example, Macey emphasizes that tsarist officials did not entertain using undue force in their massive social engineering program, transforming communal peasants into owners of private farms.

Research on Russian business in the late imperial era has enhanced our knowledge of the tsarist government. Thomas Owen emphasizes that ministers' legalism and dilatoriness made the formation of joint-stock corporations difficult.[27] Nevertheless, this did not prevent the formation of noncorporate stock associations, businesses, or the development of the economy; Jo Ann Ruckman, Charles Ruud, Paul Gregory, Peter Gatrell, and other historians have shown that entrepreneurs consistently forged ahead, confronted government officials, and circumvented regulations.[28] These findings disprove the theory advanced by Theodore H. Von Laue, among others, that the tsarist government promoted Russian business and was in league with the Russian "bourgeoisie."[29] In fact, tariffs and other government policies often harmed Russian businesses and ministers often sympathized with laborers in their conflicts against business owners and managers.[30] Such findings, in turn, support research suggesting that a sizable portion of the laboring masses was not inherently committed to political and economic revolution in the late imperial period, thus abolishing one of the popularly proffered explanations for the revolutions of 1917.[31]

Anna Geifman's work on Russian revolutionaries puts a new spin on the tsarist government's repressive policies. Although her intent is to demythologize revolutionaries and show how their values shaped the Soviet regime, her description of revolutionaries' destructiveness and wanton violence validates the tsarist government's attempts to curtail them.[32]

Major contributions to our understanding of the political process in late Imperial Russia have been made by historians who have focused on the local scene. Richard Robbins's account of appointed governors in the nineteenth and early twentieth century shows the competency and concern for public welfare exhibited by many of these emissaries of the central government.[33] Our appreciation of the liveliness of municipal self-government has been furthered by the investigations of Walter Hanchett, Patricia Herlihey, Daniel Brower, and Joseph Bradley.[34] Charles Timberlake has begun to chronicle the robustness of provincial and county self-governing bodies—the zemstvos.[35] Robert Edelman's book on the Nationalist Party in the southwestern provinces of the empire sheds light on how political parties developed in the decade before 1917 and linked local and national members.[36] William Gleason's biography of Octobrist leader Alexander Guchkov illuminates the mentality of the party that stood in "loyal opposition" to the government in the late imperial period and helped govern briefly after the fall of tsarism in

1917.[37] Narratives of the initiative and assertiveness of various *sosloviia* or "classes" and grass-roots organizations document the vitality of civil society in late Imperial Russia.[38] They also emphasize that society was not homogeneous; moreover, many members of representative bodies—the zemstvos, city dumas and the State Duma—were hostile toward private enterpreneurs.[39] Yet, such pluralism is integral to democracy.

Studies on late Imperial Russia to date, of which the foregoing are but a sample, indicate that the political situation was complex and in flux.[40] Government officials, on both the central and local level, were domineering, intrusive, and at times moved with glacial slowness; many also were socially aware, progressive, and conscientious. Additionally, since Russia had a sizable bureaucracy, despite the fact that the Tsar had the final word, many power blocs and individuals participated in making policy. Moreover, civil society had a life of its own and representative instituitions were taking hold, tempering governmental policies. Democratic ingredients were leavening Russia's political system in the late imperial period. These signs of emerging democracy were linked with the prevailing economic system. A tripartite economic system, blending government ownership, and control over the economy with private enterprise and elements of socialism, not only resulted in economic growth but established a foundation for democracy. Private enterprise offered individual ctitizens opportunites for socioeconomic advancement and also a corner of independence, some measure of bargaining power, and a mechanism for protection against, on the one hand, the domination of govenrment officials and, on the other, the threat of mass tyranny by fellow citizens.

These findings notwithstanding, our picture of governance, representative institutions, and politics in late Imperial Russia is still a series of preliminary sketches rather than a finished portrait. Controversies and questions still abound. For example, during the last few years a debate has been raging about whether diverse viewpoints and agendas within the professional and industrial community retarded their concerted political action to such a degree that, even without war and revolution, democracy and representative institutions would have been stillborn in late Imperial Russia.[41]

Many aspects of the political process, particularly at the regional level, are still murky. Before Russia's national legislature was instituted and even afterward much that was important in politics took place in the provinces. Yet we know very little about how provincial and county councils—the zemstvos—actually operated. We know next to nothing about their elections, the mix of political and economic viewpoints to which delegates subscribed, alignments and compromise among zemstvo delegates, how effectively zemstvos spent funds at their disposal, how they related to city governments in provincial capitals and county seats, and how they related to central and local government officials before and during World War I.

Many key tsarist officials, such as V. K. von Pleve and B. V. Stürmer (or Shtiurmer) still appear as caricatures rather than real people. We still have much to learn about the day-to-day operations of the imperial ministries, the relationship of ministers to their staffs, and who exactly made policy in the Russian government before and especially during World War I. We need to learn more about government officials' interaction with the two chambers of the Russian legislature—the Duma and the State Council—the day-to-day operations of the chambers, their interaction with each other, and how various political parties operated.

Historians contributing to the present collection attempt to fill in some of these gaps, clarifying our picture of governance, representative institutions, and in some cases, assessing the degree of burgeoning democracy in late Imperial Russia. They focus on the political process in local and national institutions both before and during World War I, presenting case studies based on new archival sources and heretofore unexamined or cursorily examined published materials. Peter Arkad'evich Stolypin, who dominated Russian political life as Minister of Internal Affairs and Chairman of the Council of Ministers from 1906 until his untimely death in 1911, is the focal point for several of the chapters dealing with Russia prior to World War I. Soviet historians considered him a reactionary; he is now eulogized in Russia. The new information in this collection rounds out Stolypin and his policies. Three chapters also present new information on the controversial Pleve and B. V. Shtiurmer.

This book does not purport to be definitive—many more years of research are needed to achieve that goal. Nevertheless, the authors hope that by intensively probing a limited number of major subjects they will flesh out politics and the political system of late Imperial Russia, providing a work stimulating and seminal for scholars and informative for students and the public. Because the historians contributing to the present collection are international—American, Finnish, German, and Japanese—and have shared no common seminar, mentors, or school of thought, they have particularly varied viewpoints. They do not always agree with each other's interpretations. This underlines for the reader the complexity of late Imperial Russia and the fact that history is shaped both by information available and by the perceptions and biases historians bring to their task.

Chapters 2 and 3 in this collection discuss the degree to which zemstvos and zemstvo figures were a political force in late Imperial Russia. George Yaney surveyed the zemstvos in his work on the Russian government and representative institutions prior to 1905.[42] In chapter 3 of this collection William Gleason and Thomas Porter provide a more concrete and more kinetic portrayal of them; therefore, only a brief review is presented here.

The tsarist government established zemstvos in thirty-four provinces in 1864 to replace boards of welfare, instituted in the 1770s. The zemstvos operated in both the provincial capital and in county seats (there were approximately ten counties in each province). They were to care for the socioeconomic needs of the local populace. Property owners who paid zemstvo taxes, whether they were communal peasants, owners of immovable property, or owners of estates, were eligible to elect delegates to the zemstvos.

Although historians have lauded the achievements of the zemstvos in the areas of health and education, they have criticized the limitations the government placed on them. For instance, landowners voted in separate curiae; representation was not equal but rather was based on the amount and value of property held by each category. The Russian government considered zemstvos ancillary to the state structure; they were to fulfill "state functions," assisting salaried governors appointed by the Tsar. Indeed, the zemstvos were instituted partly because it was assumed that decentralization would cut administrative costs. In the late nineteenth century the government set a cap on zemstvo tax increases. It also extended loans to zemstvos, often not repaid. These financial measures lessened zemstvos' independence. Zemstvos were not supposed to discuss political issues or to combine with one another, so opposed was Tsar Nicholas to a parliament before 1905, and the central and local government further curbed zemstvo operations as the nineteenth century wore on.

In Chapter 2 Charles Timberlake tackles the question of how much and what kind of power zemstvos wielded. He examines one county zemstvo and the provincial zemstvo in Tver' Province during the 1890s and first years of the twentieth century. Three interrelated noble families, including that of the famous anarchist Mikhail Bakunin, formed the chief liberal group in both zemstvos.

In 1890 the central government issued new regulations that allowed governors to supervise zemstvo decisions more closely, particularly those related to expenditures, and to confirm chairmen of county zemstvo boards and members of provincial zemstvo boards. Timberlake's research in Tver' archives reveals that Tver' governors took these new responsibilities seriously. As a result there was a great deal of friction between Tver' zemstvo liberals and governors in the late nineteenth, and early twentieth century over expenditures and the zemstvo's hiring of professionals labelled "the Third Element." Clashes also erupted between the Tver' provincial zemstvo and the central government in St. Petersburg in the early twentieth century.

Nevertheless, Timberlake concludes that the provincial and county zemstvos in Tver' Province were political bodies. Although zemstvo delegates were not supposed to engage in politics, their deliberations were in fact politics and their activities akin to local government functions in any state, anywhere, at any time. Although local officials sometimes hampered them, zemstvo representatives formed political coalitions and flexed their political muscles. In part, the political power of the zemstvos was enhanced because of the complexity of zemstvo operations; outsiders appointed by the government to bring the zemstvos to heel found themselves relying on insiders, sometimes zemstvo liberals, as was the case with Shtiurmer in the Tver' provincial zemstvo, at the outset of his career. Thus, despite the fact that Russia had no national legislature before 1906 and despite the government's efforts to rein in popular political activity, the Tver' provincial and county zemstvos illustrate how liberals transformed limited local self-government into a real political force, which was both a counterweight and a supplement to nonelected officials.

Zemstvo figures were among the most vocal advocates for a national legislature, for their experiences in managing local affairs stimulated their desire to have more voice in policy making at the national level. In chapter 3 William Gleason and Thomas Porter depict how zemstvo activists moved from the provinces onto the national stage and brought the liberals' long-cherished goal of a national legislature to fruition by creating a General Zemstvo Organization to assist the military in the Russo-Japanese War of 1904–1905.

Gleason and Porter show that the sparring between central officials and zemstvo activists honed the activists' strategic and tactical skills. The formation and activity of the zemstvo union proved zemstvo activists possessed considerable political savvy. Minister of Internal Affairs V. K. von Pleve at first squelched the idea of a zemstvo union. Resourceful zemstvo leaders then appealed to Nicholas himself. The Tsar permitted representatives from fourteen zemstvos to form an organization for the front, a decision that mitigates Nicholas's antidemocratic image. Zemstvo activists showed further resolve in amassing sizable funds from their constituents for their war work.

Some zemstvo figures remained in opposition to the government and to Stolypin, in particular, after 1906. However, others cooperated with the government. Gleason and Porter confirm that, for his part, Stolypin welcomed zemstvo participation in famine relief and settling peasants in Siberia and was willing to cooperate with moderate zemstvo liberals. Gleason and Porter note that the government subsidized zemstvo efforts in famine relief and resettlement, institutionalizing zemstvo assistance but also tying zemstvos more closely to the state structure.

Gleason and Porter also address the issue of whether "government" and "society" (obshchestvo) were hopelessly alienated in the decades before 1917. They suggest that these terms are too general and the supposed cleavage between "government" and "society" too abstract to apply to Russia in the late imperial period. For, as does Timberlake, Gleason and

Porter remind us of the specificity of government officials, that individual bureaucrats had differing attitudes and policies toward representative government at different times. V. K. von Pleve, Minister of Internal Affairs between 1901 and 1904, though usually depicted as a reactionary and hostile to the zemstvo union, was as capable of cooperating with the zemstvos as Stolypin.

In the main, because of liberals' aggressiveness and capability and the cooperation between officials and liberals, Gleason and Porter offer grounds for cautious optimism that democracy was developing in late Imperial Russia.

Some fifty years of agitation for a national legislature on the part of liberals—zemstvos figures, professionals and intellectuals, and specialists hired by zemstvos—combined with revolutionary upheavals in 1904 and 1905, finally resulted in the establishment of a national legislature in Russia. Convinced he had no alternative, Nicholas II agreed in October 1905 to a popularly elected lower chamber, the Duma, and a revamped State Council, which served as an upper chamber. Half the 196 members of the latter body were appointed and half were elected by corporate groups. The Russian government, rechristened the Council of Ministers but still appointed by Nicholas and individually responsible to the Tsar alone, was now to share power with the legislature. The playing field was not level. Certain areas, like military spending, were outside the Duma's purview and the Duma could initiate bills, which had to pass both chambers, only in tandem with the government. Nevertheless, political parties, already in embryonic form, were legalized and, as noted, exuberant and free elections to the First Duma took place in the winter of 1905 and spring of 1906.

The relationship between the government and the first two Dumas, which met in the spring of 1906 and 1907, respectively, was rocky. Both sides were at fault. The Kadet or Constitutional Democratic Party, which dominated the First Duma, was eager to establish an English-style political system and was not disposed to negotiate with the government; the government was equally unwilling to compromise with the legislature or the Kadets. The Second Duma was torn asunder by radical socialist parties while the hapless Kadets and their splinter groups tried to establish order. The government dissolved both legislatures after a few months.

Stolypin tried to ensure a more tractable Third Duma by issuing a new electoral law June 3, 1907, which weighted representation in favor of owners of landed estates. This violated the Fundamental Laws of 1906, which required the legislature to sanction alterations to electoral regulations and earned Stolypin the epithet of "Bonaparte." However, the plurality that right-of-center Octobrists enjoyed as a result of the new electoral law enabled the Third Duma to last its full five-year term. Further, this Duma not only sanctioned but extended important social reforms that the government had begun in 1906 and, although concilia-tory, was not passive, attempting to enlarge its budget and legislative powers. The Fourth Duma, which began in 1912, was caught in the throes of World War I.

Chapters 4 through 7 examine the evolution of the new national legislature and its relationship with the authoritarian government. In chapter 4, Dittmar Dahlmann focuses on the formation of the Consti-tutional Democratic or Kadet Party in Saratov Province and analyzes Kadet activity and returns in elections from Saratov Province to each of the four Dumas. This party was extremely important because it was the haven of liberal democrats in the late imperial period that supplanted the tsarist government in February 1917. The chapter distills Dahl-mann's monumental, German-language tome on Kadet Party politics in five Russian provinces between 1906 and 1912.

Dahlmann describes the varied ethnic composition, economic activ-ity, and political views of Saratov's inhabitants, conveying the heteroge-neity of the Kadets' potential constituents. He describes how liberal landowners and zemstvo activists, on the one hand, and liberal intellec-tuals and professionals, on the other, coalesced during 1904 and 1905 to establish the Kadet Party in the spring of 1906. The diversity among the founding fathers soon caused the party to fragment. However, the Ka-dets' main problems in Saratov were their small numbers and the limited appeal of their program. Of necessity the Kadets had to proselytize workers and particularly peasants, who formed the bulk of the popula-tion in the province. The party attracted retail clerks, some workers, and Volga Germans, but despite the Kadets' radical agrarian program (expro-priation of landed estates), peasants were cool to them. The party's main base remained liberal urban professionals and intellectuals. For tactical reasons the Kadets in Saratov Province aligned with radical-left parties, but the coalition soon disintegrated.

Dahlmann depicts lively politics in Saratov. The Kadets had considerable organizational talents; pluralism and real voter choice were evident in elections to the Duma from Saratov Province. Nevertheless, in contrast to Gleason and Porter, Dahlmann ends on a pessimistic note: the Kadets simply had too small a base of support. Dahlmann stresses that the main indicator of a party's strength was not the number of delegates it sent to the Duma but the number of delegates the party won in the provincial zemstvo assembly. The Kadets' and their Progressist allies' proportion of delegates in the Saratov provincial assembly fluctuated between 20 and 30 percent in all four Duma elections.[43] Yet, there were only thirty active Kadets in the provincial party committee in Saratov on the eve of World War I. In Dahlmann's opinion, the Kadets' failure to gain a wider constituency and reconcile divergent political groups boded ill for the future of democracy in Russia.

Chapters 5 through 7 plunge into politics at the national level. In chapter 5, Mary Conroy examines political developments during the Third Duma period through the prism of pharmacy legislation.

Liberal members of the zemstvos and Kadet and Octobrist delegates to the Third Duma who appeared as sympathetic figures in earlier chapters now loom as bugbears for the owners of private pharmacies as well as for private armsmakers and shipbuilders.[44] Liberal zemstvo activists, radical pharmacists, and Octobrist and Kadet politicians considered privately owned pharmacies exploitative and hoped to curb them by expanding "public" pharmacies, that is, zemstvo- and city-owned pharmacies that sometimes practiced socialized medical care. Between 1907 and 1911 thirty-four Octobrists in the Duma from agrarian, urban, religious, and even business backgrounds forged a bill allowing zemstvo pharmacies to be freely established while private pharmacies were to remain restricted by government regulations. The bill, welcomed widely in the press, was passed by the Duma and the State Council and signed into law in 1912, impelling pharmacy owners negatively impacted by it to frantically petition the Governing Senate, Russia's supreme court, to squelch the law. Conroy argues that this indicates that socialism was pervasive in late Imperial Russia, but so was private enterprise.

This chapter also reveals that the Third Duma was lively and that the Octobrists and Kadets were stubbornly assertive. Although Octobrists worked productively with the government they also maintained their independence. Stung by Stolypin's dismissive behavior of the Third Duma in the Naval General Staff Crisis of 1909 and the Zemstvo Crisis of 1911,[45] the pharmacy bill put forth by Octobrists showed, in conjunction with several other bills, that they had no intention of capitulating to the government. They introduced the pharmacy bill without waiting for a tandem bill from the Minister of Internal Affairs, in violation of the Fundamental Laws. The Kadets similarly used pharmacy measures to display their self-confidence. Opposed to Stolypin's new Pharmacy Statute, the Kadets held caucuses on the bill, affirming their continued opposition to the government, their political sophistication, and their ability to coordinate diverse political groups for a common cause. The Octobrists' and Kadets' behavior signalled they did not intend to stop crusading for a legislature that had parity with the government. Additionally their activity calls into question the theory that the heterogeneity of civil society weakened society and impeded the progress of representative institutions and, ultimately, democracy in late Imperial Russia.

The dilemma of how the aspirations of national minorities could be reconciled with state requirements in late Imperial Russia, as significant as how representative institutions could be meshed with the absolutist government traditional to Russia, has been too little addressed by historians. Particularly crucial was the position of the semiautonomous Grand Duchy of Finland, with its proximity to the imperial capital, St. Petersburg. From the end of the nineteenth century, in contrast to earlier laissez-faire treatment, the Russian government attempted to integrate Finland more firmly within the empire, at times even contemplating military intervention. In chapter 6, Antti Kujala examines the Russian government's Finnish policies, mainly in the context of internal Russian politics but also from the vantage point of the Finns.

Chief elements of the government's plans for administrative integration included channelling Finnish matters through the Council of Ministers rather than permitting the Minister State Secretary for Finland to communicate directly with the Tsar; eliminating matters having significance for the whole empire from the competence of the Finnish parliament; establishing suffrage for Russians living in Finland commensurate with that enjoyed by Finns; insisting the Finns pay a fee in lieu of service in the Russian military (the Finns desired their own army but the Russian government considered arming them to be too dangerous); and, finally, annexing two Finnish parishes in the Vyborg Province of Finland—or the whole province—to Russia proper. Kujala describes the genesis of this policy, how and why plans for administrative integration escalated during Stolypin's administration, and the fate of the policy during the administration of his successor, V. N. Kokovtsov.

Through meticulously mining newly available archival sources and closely reading published materials, Kujala presents a revisionist interpretation of Russia's relationship with Finland in the late imperial era. In opposition to many historians, he opines that funnelling communication through the Council of Ministers did not, per se, harm Finland's autonomy. He acknowledges that the suffrage rights of Russians living in Finland were unequal to the suffrage rights of Finnish inhabitants, reminds that "russification" in Finland was administrative rather than cultural, and notes that Stolypin implemented measures curtailing Finland very slowly and hoped these measures would be ameliorated by the Duma.

Nevertheless, Kujala also contends that the Russian government's Finnish program alienated the Finns and that Russian authority over Finland was ultimately preserved by threat of force. Why then did the Russian government pursue these policies?

In part, according to Kujala, Russian policies were a response to revolutionary movements in Finland, real or perceived. The Russian government viewed the Finns as a threat to the empire, especially to the capital, St. Petersburg. Ironically, the Finns' anti-Russian attitude, radical nationalism, and agitation for separatism had been engendered by the Russian government's turn-of-the-century policy of administrative integration.

Further, according to Kujala, the Russian government's Finnish policies rested on faulty intelligence. In another work he has depicted the revolutionary activity of some Finnish groups during the Russo-Japanese War of 1904–1905.[46] In this chapter, Kujala claims that the

Finns ceased revolutionary activity after 1908. However, intelligence reports to the Russian government continued to depict them as a threat. Ironically, Russian intelligence downplayed Finnish revolutionary activity during the war, when some Finns actually were preparing for the independence they would achieve in 1917, because the Russian government feared that taking a strong stand against Finland would alienate Sweden.

But, at bottom, Kujala maintains that the status of Finland in the empire was more important to internal government politics than as an issue in itself. He argues that Stolypin knew little about Finland and relied on staff position papers. Although at one point Kujala calls Stolypin the father of Russia's Finnish policies, he also asserts that Tsar Nicholas II was the main architect of Finnish policy. Kujala believes that Nicholas was motivated mainly by dislike of the Finns. Stolypin and other ministers used the Finnish sword to curry favor with him and to achieve greater support from the Duma and the State Council.

Alexandra Shecket Korros has long been concerned about the role of the State Council, the upper chamber of the legislature, in the new representative political system of late Imperial Russia. Thus, although she reviews Stolypin's Finnish policies and his other nationality policies as well, her focus is the State Council's reaction to these policies. In so doing she adds to our store of information on the operation of this largely neglected political institution and its relationship with the Russian government.

Korros accepts the standard interpretation that Stolypin promoted nationalist policies in the State Council after the Naval General Staff Crisis of April 1909 not so much out of interior conviction but because he needed reliable political support in the upper chamber. He particularly needed to form a new coalition to counter the reactionary Right bloc which sought to discredit him.

In recounting the formation of the Center-Right group, Korros emphasizes how Stolypin neutralized the Far Right by his selective support of nationalist legislation—special curiae allowing Russians as well as Poles to be elected to the State Council from the nine western provinces; transfer of the Kholm section from Poland to the jurisdiction of the Governor General of Kiev; and the effort to put Finland more firmly within imperial control. Korros maintains that Stolypin presented himself as the author of the Russian government's Finnish policy, stressing how his position on Finland fit with other nationalist policies, for example, his opposition to a Kadet and Octobrist bill to extend the rights of the Old Believers as a threat to the authority of the Orthodox Church.

Korros's analysis of archival materials, State Council debates, and media coverage of nationalist issues during 1909 and 1910 conveys the dynamic of State Council politics and the importance of that body to the Stolypin administration. Stolypin's decision to play the nationalist card, according to Korros, forced new alignments within the Center, the largest group in the State Council. Although the upper chamber was not popularly elected, her analysis underscores that political alignments played a crucial role in determining the fate of legislation in the State Council. Korros shows us how increasing politicization in Russian society had indeed filtered upward into what had been intended to be a uniformly conservative "buffer" to a more broadly representative and therefore more radical State Duma.

Chapters 2 through 7 present a mixed picture of Russia on the eve of World War I. On the one hand, they reveal friction between representative institutions and governmental officials and controversies between political and economic groups. On the other hand, they indicate that participatory politics was becoming institutionalized on both the national and local levels on the eve of the war.

World War I created new problems for Russia. Severed trade links and transportation bottlenecks caused shortages, refugees flooding into Russia from the western borderlands competed for jobs and resources, and military losses were disheartening. Nevertheless, government agencies, businesses, popular and public organizations (cities and zemstvos, scientific and professional societies) hurled themselves into the war effort. These disparate bodies frequently cooperated although they also conflicted with and duplicated each others' efforts.

Most historians portray the Russian government as imploding during World War I due to frequent changes of ministers ("ministerial leapfrog") resulting from Empress Alexandra's and Rasputin's machinations and Nicholas's command of the troops at the front. Archival records, on the other hand, depict one ministry, that of Internal Affairs, conducting business as usual throughout the war and continuing to do so even after the tsarist government was superseded by the Provisional Government in February/March 1917. Further, archival records emphasize that the Russian government subsidized wartime activities of public organizations, indicating both that the government had financial resources and that public organizations could not have functioned without the government.[47]

However, revolution did occur in February 1917. One interpretation of the overthrow of the Romanov regime is that food shortages ignited longstanding frustrations on the part of the masses and liberal intellectuals, who had served in representative institutions and wartime organizations, fearing mass uprisings and lacking confidence in Nicholas's government, decided to take command.[48] The two final chapters in the present collection examine public organizations—city governments, zemstvos, and the Union of Zemstvos—during the war and touch upon these issues. The authors arrive at different conclusions.

In chapter 8 William Gleason and Thomas Porter discuss the contributions of the Union of Zemstvos to the war effort. They show how, as the war went from bad to worse for Russia, zemstvo activists lost confidence in Nicholas and his government. Meanwhile, the activists' successful wartime activity heightened their self-confidence. They concluded they would have to take over not only prosecution of the war but administration of the empire, an outlook that propelled them to February 1917.

Kimitaka Matsuzato's chapter 9 also looks at the zemstvos' and other local bodies' activities during World War I. However, he views the zemstvos' wartime efforts as counterproductive. He links zemstvo activists to the February Revolution but in a negative, rather than a positive, way.

Matsuzato rejects the theory that polarization between government and society generated the revolutions of 1917. He particularly repudiates the theory that deep-seated grievances spawned peasant disturbances during World War I and that peasant violence played a leading role in the fall of the tsarist regime in February. Instead he asserts that the overturn of the monarchy in February was the work of a minority and contends that peasant violence erupted *after* peasants were radicalized by the February Revolution of 1917.

From analyzing evidence in many regional archives, Matsuzato concludes that a tangled web of bureaucratic organs and an excess of parochialism, mainly on the part of zemstvos, resulted in poor use of food resources during World War I, exacerbated transportation bottlenecks, drained the power of the central government, and ultimately was greatly responsible for the collapse of the tsarist regime. Matsuzato maintains that, over all, there was an abundance of food in wartime Russia. However, a proliferation of national agencies and their local agents, some assigned to purchase food for the army, others to manage the food supply, and still others to purchase food for civilians, unduly complicated food-purchasing and transport facilities. Local agents, appointed by the central government to procure grain for the army, competed for grain purchases with local agents representing the Chairman of the Special Council on Food and with municipal agents attempting to acquire food for the civilian population. Local Grain-Purchasing Agents for the Army received considerable power to regulate railway food shipments; they used this power to block grain shipments for competitor agents and for civilians. Local Grain-Purchasing Agents for the Army from grain-producing areas established food embargoes, causing agents from grain-consuming areas to engage in panic buying.

Matsuzato contends that zemstvos were mainly responsible for the deteriorating food and transportation situation because, in most food-producing provinces, chairs of provincial zemstvo boards were appointed Local Grain-Purchasing Agents for the Army and it was they who initiated the restrictive railway regulations and food embargoes. They also eroded authority, clashing with governors, who, in grain-consuming provinces, usually were appointed Agents of the Chair of the Special Council on Food.

But the tsarist government helped dig its own grave. First, it allowed the formation of multiple agencies. Second, it gave Local Grain-Purchasing Agents for the Army quotas and delegated to them (and in some cases other agents and contractors) sizable amounts of power to acquire grain, regulate local production and business, and orchestrate railway shipments. These powers intensified natural autarkic tendencies. Finally, the central government committed grave financial errors by attempting to control prices and also by granting large nonrepayable loans to municipalities and zemstvos to purchase grain, thus encouraging purchasing.

Matsuzato's analysis of the economic situation in a number of provinces during World War I emphasizes the variegated topography and complexity of the Russian Empire. It also suggests the need for balance between central and local government. Finally, it reiterates the continuities between the tsarist and Soviet governments, for economic affinities forged in grain purchasing during World War I were retained in the Soviet period.

In sum, this collection portrays a more normal Russia than that in the popular media. It emphasizes that the political system in late Imperial Russia was multifaceted and constantly evolving. Important changes had taken place in Russia's political organization between the third quarter of the nineteenth century and World War I. The government remained in charge on the eve of the war. However, the "government" had many faces. Additionally, representative institutions had become entrenched and were modifying government policies. Democracy, if you will, was emerging in Russia on the eve of the war. Some chapters suggest that had the war not occurred Russia would have gradually developed balance between representative institutions and the government. Others imply that certain political and national groups were too alienated to preserve the old order. What is clear is that during the war, although the government still had sufficient financial resources, fractiousness on the part of representative institutions and antagonism on the part of their leaders toward the government intensified.

Several chapters make references to other European states. Indeed, additional comparisons with politics and political institutions in Europe would give context to late tsarist political institutions and politics.[49] Some chapters address the "bottom line," that is, finances and funding in the Russian government and representative institutions—zemstvos and the Duma. Further inquiry along these lines would more fully document the capability and viability of both governmental and representative institutions in the late imperial period. And, as stated, much more research is needed on the crucial period of Worl War I.

The intent of this collection is to enhance our knowledge of how government and representative institutions in late Imperial Russia actually worked. Nevertheless, these chapters may also contain a larger message for post-Soviet Russia and those dealing with the new Russia. On the one hand, once set in motion changes in the political system are difficult to stop. The participatory, representative institutions that developed in late Imperial Russia could be eradicated only by the most stringent measures during the Soviet period. On the other hand, changes in the political system need time to take root and bear fruit. Further, they must fit into the historical framework of a political entity. It appeared that Imperial Russia was just becoming comfortable with alterations in the political structure, that a balance was beginning to be struck between the government and representative, participatory institutions when the war and 1917 mutated the process. Thus post-Soviet Russians will need time to restore authentically democratic institutions. Foreign political transplants will be rejected unless they coincide sufficiently with Russia's historical evolution. Post-Soviet Russians must balance representative institutions with strong government in line with Russia's historical development and to ensure effective operation for present social and economic needs.

NOTES

1. For a survey on the fate of history writing in Soviet Russia, see Anatole G. Mazour, *The Writing of History in the Soviet Union* (Stanford, CA: Hoover Institution Press, 1975).

2. For details, see Geoffrey Swain, *The Origins of the Russian Civil War* (London, New York: Longmans, 1996), pp. 48–83; Oliver Radkey, *Russia Goes to the Polls: The Election to the All-Russian Constituent Assembly, 1917* (Ithaca, NY: Cornell University Press, 1990), pp. 62–63 and passim. On protests against Bolshevik-orchestrated elections in the first years of the regime, see Paul Avrich, *Kronstadt 1921* (New York: W. W. Norton, 1974), esp. pp. 73–74.

3. For control in the early Soviet period, see Peter Kenez, *The birth of the propaganda state: Soviet methods of mass mobilization, 1917–1929* (New York: Cambridge University Press, 1985).

4. Stalin's excesses are amply documented. For Lenin's harsh policies, see Richard Pipes, *The Unknown Lenin* (New Haven and London: Yale University Press, 1996), and A. L. Litvin, *Krasnyi i belyi terror v Rossii, 1918–1922 gg.* (Tatarskoe, gazetno-zhurnal'noe izdatel'stvo Kazan, 1995). Stephen Wheatcroft, among other historians, argues that the number of people repressed during the Stalin era was smaller than heretofore asserted. Nevertheless, repressive measures were severe and capriciously applied. See his "The Scale and Nature of German and Soviet Repression and Mass Killings, 1930–1945," *Europe-Asia Studies*, vol. 48, no. 8, 1996, pp. 1330–1353.

5. Non-Bolshevik socialists began seizing private enterprises immediately after October. Lenin's government soon stopped this grass-roots "municipalization" and began nationalizing private property and enterprises and those belonging to the former government and local communities. On early nationalization decrees, see M. P. Iroshnikov et al., eds., *Dekrety Sovetskoi vlasti o Petrograde: 25 oktiabria (7 noiabria) 1917 g.-29 dekabria 1918 g.* (Leningrad, Lenizdat 1986) and Mary Schaeffer Conroy, *In Health and In Sickness: Pharmacy, Pharmacists and the Pharmaceutical Industry in Late Imperial, Early Soviet Russia* (Boulder: East European Monographs; distributed by Columbia University Press, 1994), passim, esp. pp. 394–420. Lenin viewed nationalization as more rational than municipalization. Thomas F. Remington, *Building Socialism in Bolshevik Russia: Ideology and Industrial Organization, 1917–1921* (Pittsburgh: University of Pittsburgh Press, 1984). Mary McAuley sees nationalization as fulfilling the Bolsheviks' contract with the underprivileged. *Bread and Justice: State and Society in Petrograd, 1917–1922* (Oxford: Clarendon Press, 1991), pp. 70–86. On instances of frank economic debate but the precariousness of private production, trade, and debate during the NEP, see Alan Ball, *Russia's Last Capitalists: The NEPmen, 1921–29* (Berkeley: University of California Press, 1987), pp. 78–82 and passim; Vincent Barnett, "A Long Wave Goodbye: Kondrat'ev and the Conjuncture Institute, 1920–28," *Europe-Asia Studies*, vol. 47, no. 3 (1995), pp. 413–431, and Yuri Goland, "Currency Regulation in the NEP Period," *Europe Asia Studies*, vol. 46, no. 8 (1994), pp. 1266, 1278–1280, 1282–1292.

6. Nationalization of course choked the autonomy of former owners. See Conroy, *In Health and In Sickness*, pp. 394–420, and Charles A. Ruud, *Russian Entrepreneur: Publisher Ivan Sytin of Moscow, 1851–1934* (Montreal & Kingston: McGill-Queen's University Press, 1990), passim. Workers were made subordinate to the state in 1918. Gennady Shkliarevsky, *Labor in the Russian Revolution: Factory Committees and Trade Unions, 1917–1918* (New York: St. Martin's Press, 1993). See also, McAuley, *Bread and Justice*, pp. 87–258. For subordination of pharmacy employees see Conroy, ibid., pp. 392–393, 407–409. The Bolshevik government's first assault on the peasantry occurred during the civil war. Alec Nove, *An Economic History of the USSR, 1917–1991* (New York: Penguin Books, 1992), pp. 52–57. Collectivization of agriculture in the late 1920s and 1930s was pernicious for peasants and also for agriculture and the economy as a whole. See Robert Conquest, *The Harvest of Sorrow* (New York: Oxford University Press, 1986); Nove, *An Economic History*, pp. 159–188, 303–311; and Paul A. Gregory, *Before Command* (Princeton, NJ: Princeton University Press, 1994).

7. For collective farmers' adaptation, see Sheila Fitzpatrick, *Stalin's Peasants: Resistance and Survival in the Russian Village After Collectivization* (New York: Oxford University Press, 1994). Robert W. Thurston argues that Soviet workers enjoyed considerable autonomy and scope for creativity in the 1930s. *Life and Terror in Stalin's Russia, 1934–1941* (New Haven: Yale University Press, 1996), pp. 164–198. Valentin V. Peschanskii asserts that Soviet trade unions were creatures of the government and, as such, inhibited civil society in the Soviet Union. "Trade Unions and the Making of Civil Society in Russia," unpublished ms, 1996, pp. 2–3.

8. For discussion on the continuity between Soviet ministries and personnel and tsarists see M(ikhail) P(avlovich) Iroshnikov, *Predsedatel' Soveta Narodnikh Komissarov: Vl. Ul'ianov Lenin: Ocherki gosudarstvennoi deiatel'nosti v 1917–1918 gg.* (Leningrad: Nauka,

1974), pp. 341–396 and passim. Many of the former tsarist governmental personnel were, of course, coerced into working in the Bolshevik government.

9. See for example, W. Bruce Lincoln, *The Great Reforms: Autocracy, Bureaucracy, and the Politics of Change in Imperial Russia* (DeKalb: Northern Illinois University Press, 1990), pp. 21–22, 106, 111, 159–63, 171, 174, 188–89, 197–203; and Thomas C. Owen, *The Corporation Under Russian Law, 1800–1917: A Study in Tsarist Economic Policy* (New York: Cambridge University Press, 1991), chapter 5 and passim.

10. For details see Tsuyoshi Hasegawa, *The February Revolution: Petrograd, 1917* (Seattle and London: University of Washington Press, 1981). The term "soviet" originally had no political connotation; it meant council. In 1905 and 1917 the term "soviet" was applied to grass-roots radical political organizations. The present work translates *uezd*, provincial subdivisions, as "county" rather than "district" and uses the English rather than the Russian plural for *zemstvo* and *duma*. It also must be noted that at this time the Russian calendar was thirteen days behind the Western calendar. Before 1918 dates of events in Russia cited in Western reports were noted by the initials "OS" or "NS," or by two dates divided by a slash.

11. See Richard G. Robbins, Jr., *The Tsar's Viceroys: Russian Provincial Governors in the Last Years of the Empire* (Ithaca, NY: Cornell University Press, 1987), pp. 234–239, and Donald J. Raleigh, *Revolution on the Volga: 1917 in Saratov* (Ithaca, NY: Cornell University Press, 1986). Nationalist leaders in Finland, the Baltic States, the Ukraine and the Caucasus—Poland having been under German domination since 1915—clamored for the independence of their border regions. Economic productivity was affected by a rash of strikes, meetings, and congresses, and workers' interference in management. Conroy, *In Health and In Sickness*, pp. 379–391. See Allan K. Wildman, *The End of the Russian Imperial Army: The Old Army and the Soldiers' Revolt (March-April 1917)* (Princeton, NJ: Princeton University Press, 1980) for a breakdown of authority in the army.

12. For more on chaos in the provinces in 1917 and the impractical economic theories held by socialists, see Michael C. Hickey, "Local Government and State Authority in the Provinces: Smolensk, February-June 1917," *Slavic Review*, vol. 55, no. 4. 1996, pp. 863–881. The article includes valuable citations to other works.

13. Swain, *The Origins of the Russian Civil War*, p. 14.

14. For a full listing of works, see Dittmar Dahlmann, *Die Provinz wählt: Rußlands Konstitutionell-Demokratische Partei und die Dumawahlen 1906–1912* (Cologne: Böhlau Verlag GmbH & Cie, 1996), pp. 1–20 and passim.

15. Alfred Levin, *The Second Duma: A Study of the Social Democratic Party and the Russian Constitutional Experiment*, second edition (Hamden, CT: Archon Books, 1966).

16. Alfred Levin, *The Third Duma: Election and Profile* (Hamden, CT: Archon Books, 1973).

17. Geoffrey A. Hosking, *The Russian Constitutional Experiment: Government and Duma 1907–1914* (Cambridge: Cambridge University Press, 1973). See also George Tokmakoff, *P. A. Stolypin and the Third Duma: An Appraisal of the Three Major Issues* (Lanham, MD: University Press of America, 1981) and Mary Schaeffer Conroy, *Peter Arkad'evich Stolypin: Practical Politics in Late Tsarist Russia* (Boulder, CO: Westview Press, 1976).

18. Howard D. Mehlinger and John M. Thompson, *Count Witte and the Tsarist Government in the 1905 Revolution* (Bloomington: Indiana University Press, 1972).

19. Peter A. Zaionchkovsky, *The Russian Autocracy Under Alexander III* (first published 1970; English translation David R. Jones, Gulf Breeze, FL: Academic International Press, 1976).

20. V. A. Nardova, *Gorodskoe samoupravlenie v Rossii v 60-x — nachale 90-x godov XIX v.* (Leningrad, Nauka 1984).

21. Marc Szeftel, *The Russian Constitution of April 23, 1906: Political Institutions of the Duma Monarchy* (Brussels: Les Éditions de la Librairie Encyclopédique Rue du Luxembourg, 1976), p. 15.

22. Donald J. Raleigh and A. A. Iskenderov, eds., *The Emperors and Empresses of Russia: Rediscovering the Romanovs* (Armonk, NY: M. E. Sharpe, 1986).

23. W. Bruce Lincoln, *In the Vanguard of Reform: Russia's Enlightened Bureaucrats 1825–1861* (DeKalb: Northern Illinois University Press, 1982).

24. Daniel T. Orlovsky, *The Limits of Reform: The Ministry of Internal Affairs in Imperial Russia, 1802–1881* (Cambridge: Harvard University Press, 1982).

25. Thomas S. Pearson, *Russian Officialdom in Crisis: Autocracy and Local Self-Government, 1861–1900* (Cambridge: Cambridge University Press, 1989); Francis William Wcislo, *Reforming Rural Russia: State, Local Society, and National Politics, 1855–1914* (Princeton, NJ: Princeton University Press, 1990).

26. David A. J. Macey, *Government and Peasant in Russia, 1861–1906: The Prehistory of the Stolypin Reforms* (DeKalb: Northern Illinois University Press, 1987), pp. 238–249, esp. 243, 245, and passim.

27. Thomas C. Owen, *The Corporation Under Russian Law, 1800–1917: A Study in Tsarist Economic Policy* (New York: Cambridge University Press, 1991). The Russian government thwarted corporations because it feared stock swindles like those that occurred in France and America.

28. Jo Ann Ruckman, *The Moscow Business Elite: A Social and Cultural Portrait of Two Generations, 1840–1905* (DeKalb: Northern Illinois University Press, 1984); Ruud, *Russian Entrepreneur: Publisher Ivan Sytin*; Paul Gregory, *Before Command* (Princeton, NJ: Princeton University Press, 1994). Peter Gatrell, *Government, industry and rearmament in Russia, 1900–1914: the last argument of tsarism* (Cambridge: Cambridge University Press, 1994). Gatrell also shows how inefficient government arms and shipbuilding enterprises were in contrast to private enterprises. See also Conroy, *In Health and In Sickness*, pp. 9–25, 39–56, 219–228; P. A. Primachenko, *Russkii torgovo-promyshlennyi mir* (Moscow: Planeta, 1993); O. Platonov, *1000 let russkogo predprinimatel'stva* (Moscow: Sovremennik, 1995); and A. A. Bakhtiarov, *Briuko Peterburga: Ocherki stolichnoi zhizni* (Sankt-Peterburg: Fert, 1994).

29. Theodore H. von Laue, *Sergei Witte and the Industrialization of Russia* (New York: Columbia University Press, 1963).

30. See for example, Gatrell, *Government, industry and rearmament in Russia*, pp. 79, 111, 148, 166–167, 169, 212–213.

31. See Robert B. McKean, *St. Petersburg Between the Revolutions: Workers & Revolutionaries, June 1907–February 1917* (New Haven, CT: Yale University Press, 1990), p. 397 and passim; Don C. Rawson, *Russian Rightists and the Revolution of 1905*

(Cambridge: Cambridge University Press, 1995), pp. 101, 185, 190, and passim; Gatrell, *Government*, pp. 78–79, 87–88; Conroy, *In Health and In Sickness*, pp. 274–293, 380–387.

32. Anna Geifman, *Thou Shalt Kill: Revolutionary Terrorism in Russia, 1894–1917* (Princeton, NJ: Princeton University Press, 1993).

33. See especially Robbins, *The Tsar's Viceroys*. Robbins's earlier work, *Famine in Russia, 1891–1892* (New York: Columbia University Press, 1975), highlighted the tsarist government's operation in a crisis situation.

34. Walter Hanchett, "Tsarist Statutory Regulation of Municipal Government in the Nineteenth Century," in Michael F. Hamm, ed., *The City in Russian History* (Lexington: The University Press of Kentucky, 1976), pp. 91–114; Patricia Herlihey, *Odessa: A History, 1794–1914* (Cambridge: Harvard University Press, 1986); Daniel R. Brower, *The Russian City between Tradition and Modernity, 1850–1900* (Berkeley: University of California Press, 1990), pp. 92–124 and passim; Joseph Bradley, *Muzhik and Muscovite: Urbanization in Late Imperial Russia* (Berkeley: University of California Press, 1985).

35. Charles Timberlake, "The Zemstvo and the Development of a Russian Middle Class," in Edith W. Clowes, Samuel D. Kassow, and James L. West, eds., *Between Tsar and People: Education, Society and the Quest for Public Identity in Late Imperial Russia* (Princeton, NJ: Princeton University Press, 1981), pp. 164–179.

36. Robert Edelman, *Gentry Politics on the Eve of the Russian Revolution: The Nationalist Party, 1907–1917* (New Brunswick, NJ: Rutgers University Press, 1980.

37. William Gleason, *Alexander Guchkov and the End of the Russian Empire* (Philadelphia: American Philosophical Society, 1983).

38. For workers, see Theodore H. Friedgut, *Iuzovka and Revolution: Life and Work in Russia's Donbass, 1869–1924* (Princeton, NJ: Princeton University Press, 1989), pp. 101, 125–126 and passim; Barbara Alpern Engel, *Between the Fields and the City: Women, Work, & Family in Russia, 1861–1914* (Cambridge: Cambridge University Press, 1994). For peasants, see Esther Kingston Mann, "Peasant Communes and Economic Innovation: A Preliminary Inquiry," in Esther Kingston-Mann and Timothy Mixter, eds., *Peasant Economy, Culture, and Politics of European Russia, 1800–1921* (Princeton, NJ: Princeton University Press, 1991), pp. 23–51; and Elvira M. Wilbur, "Peasant Poverty in Theory and Practice: A View From Russia's 'Impoverished Center' at the End of the Nineteenth Century," ibid., pp. 101–127. Joseph Bradley describes manifestations of civil society in voluntary associations, "Voluntary Associations, Civic Culture, and *Obshchestvennost'* in Moscow," in Clowes et al., *Between Tsar and People*, pp. 131–148. See also Thomas Porter, *The Zemstvo and the Emergence of Civil Society in Late Imperial Russia, 1864–1917* (San Francisco: Mellen Research University Press, 1991).

39. Gatrell, *Government*, pp. 80–81, 113, 165–166, 185.

40. See Edward Acton, *Rethinking the Russian Revolution* (London: Hodder and Stoughton, 1990).

41. See especially Thomas C. Owen, "Impediments to a Bourgeois Consciousness in Russia, 1880–1905; the Estate Structure, Ethnic Diversity, and Economic Regionalism," in Clowes et al., *Between Tsar and People*, pp. 75–89; Joseph Bradley, ibid., p. 148; William Wagner, "Ideology, Identity, and the Emergence of a Middle Class," ibid., pp. 148–163, esp. pp. 162–63; Harley Balzer, "The Problem of Professions in Imperial Russia," ibid.,

pp. 183–198, especially p. 197. For a more pessimistic assessment of Russia's prospects for achieving democracy before 1917, see Jonathan Frankel, "1917: The Problem of Alternatives," in Edith Rogovin Frankel, Jonathan Frankel, and Baruch Knei-Paz, eds., *Revolution in Russia: Reassessments of 1917* (Cambridge: Cambridge University Press, 1992), especially pp. 8–9. In *Russia's Missing Middle Class: The Professions in Russian History* (Armonk, NY: M. E. Sharpe, 1996), Harley D. Balzer, the editor, blames both government and society for the failure of democracy to flourish in late Imperial Russia. Yet in general he and his fellow contributors present an encouraging picture of civic participation in late Imperial Russia. See Balzer, "Introduction," pp. 23–24, and "The Engineering Profession in Tsarist Russia," pp. 55–88; and John F. Hutchinson, "Politics and Medical Professionalization after 1905," pp. 89–116.

42. George L. Yaney, *The Systematization of Russian Government: Social Evolution in the Domestic Administration of Imperial Russia, 1711–1905* (Urbana: University of Illinois Press, 1973).

43. The Progressists represented liberal entrepreneurs in contrast to the Kadets who represented the liberal professions.

44. See Gatrell, *Government,* pp. 81, 84, 166–167, 185, 189, 192–193.

45. Both crises were very complicated. Alexandra Korros adumbrates the Naval General Staff Crisis of 1909 in note 20 of chapter 7, citing her work on this subject. The "Western Zemstvo Crisis" of 1911 occurred when a faction in the State Council opposed a bill Stolypin particularly supported to implement zemstvos in the six southwestern provinces of the empire with safeguards for electing "Russians" in sufficient numbers to offset Poles. Stolypin believed that his enemies in the upper chamber were using this bill to attack him. He convinced the Tsar to prorogue the Duma, which had passed the bill, as well as the State Council, thus artificially creating a situation whereby he could use Article 87 of the Fundamental Laws. This article allowed ministerial bills to be implemented when the legislature was not in session, provided these bills were submitted to the chambers at a later date. For further discussion of the two crises, see Conroy, *Peter Arkad'evich Stolypin,* pp. 163–178, and Hosking, *The Russian Constitutional Experiment,* pp. 74–149.

46. See Antti Kujala, "March Separately—Strike Together," and "The Letters of Colonel Akashi and His Aide Major Nagao Preserved in Finland and Sweden," in Olavi K. Falt and Antti Kujala, eds., *Akashi Motojiro, Rakka ryusui: Colonel Akashi's Report on His Secret Cooperation with the Russian Revolutionary Parties during the Russo-Japanese War* (Helsinki, Finnish Historical Society, 1988), pp. 85–177.

47. For example, the government subsidized zemstvo production of medicines and medical supplies during World War I. See Conroy, *In Health and In Sickness,* pp. 320–348. This would tend to lessen the independence of the zemstvos.

48. See, especially Hasegawa, *The February Revolution,* pp. 569–586.

48. In note 54 of her chapter 7, Alexandra Korros mentions that British observers invariably compared political factions in Russia to British parties. Indeed, further comparative studies on late Imperial Russia would be useful. They would show, for example, that debates on the place that local self-government ought to occupy in the governmental structure reverberated in Third Republic France as well as in late Imperial

Russia. Vivien A. Schmidt, *Democratizing France: The Political and administrative history of decentralization* (Cambridge: Cambridge University Press, 1990), pp. 43–65. They would also show that friction between government and legislature and the government's strong-arm measures to cow the legislature were not unique to Russia. For example, the measures Stolypin applied in his confrontation with the State Council in 1911 are reminiscent in spirit of those used by Asquith against the House of Lords at approximately the same time. Comparisons between Russia and latter-day states would show that power blocs jostling with each other are typical of legislatures, do not inhibit democracy, and are, in fact, integral to it.

The Tsarist Government's Preoccupation with the "Liberal Party" in Tver' Province, 1890–1905

Charles E. Timberlake
University of Missouri

At the end of the nineteenth and beginning of the twentieth centuries, a group of some forty liberals in Tver' Province[1] shared the belief that the best way to achieve a constitution for Russia was gradually to erode the foundation on which autocracy rested and replace it with institutions and a worldview that would create and defend representative government. They saw autocracy as both the cause and result of a backward and impoverished Russian population. Since the masses lived in the villages, the logical way to alter the foundation of Russian society was for a significant number of educated people to begin working in the villages to remove poverty and ignorance. They were convinced that the newly educated citizens would demand an end to autocracy and its replacement by a representative government. In short, they were classical liberals whose approach to reforming national political institutions was through changing people one at a time by education and practical experience. These liberals rejected the contention of the revolutionary terrorists that democratic reform could be implemented from above; that is, that a small group, acting in the name of the masses, could seize control of the institutions of the state and use them to build a democratic society with freedom of action and civil rights for citizens equal before the law.

Could liberals produce such local changes in Russia, and if so, would those local changes produce the national results the liberals anticipated? The collective experiences of these approximately forty liberals in Tver'

Province from approximately 1890 to 1905 serve as an excellent case study in our efforts to answer this question.

By 1890 a cluster of liberals had been forming in Tver' Province for at least two decades. The adhesives for the group were an attraction of kindred spirits that was reinforced by a web of marriages, friendships, and professional associations. The series of marriages formed a large extended family, at the core of which were three noble families in Novotorzhok County with links to various other families in Tver' Province. At the same time, this extended family was a political organization that incrementally extended its control over virtually all the major extragovernmental institutions of Novotorzhok County and some in adjoining counties.

The oldest of the three families at the core of this sociopolitical unit was the Bakunin family, living on its ancient *votchina* estate of Priamukhino (affectionately called "the tiny republic of Priamukhino" by members of the liberal clan in Tver') in the southwest corner of Novotorzhok County. The family comprised five brothers and several sisters. The eldest brother was the famous anarchist Mikhail, who from youth had been in Western Europe in pursuit of "The Revolution." The two brothers active in Novotorzhok political events were Pavel Aleksandrovich (a philosopher-poet) and Aleksandr Aleksandrovich. Before the 1890s, one of the Bakunin nieces (Ol'ga Bakunina, daughter of Pavel's younger brother Nikolai) had united the Bakunins with the nearby noble family of Povalo-Shveikovskii, whose estate was some ten miles northeast of Priamukhino at Shcherbovo. Pavel and Aleksandr Bakunin and a member of the Shveikovskii family dominated the Novotorzhok County zemstvo from the first year of its creation in 1866 in Tver' Province.[2]

In 1871 the Petrunkevich family became entwined through marriage with the Bakunin family. Mikhail Il'ich Petrunkevich, who in 1871 took the position as senior doctor of the Tver' Provincial Zemstvo Hospital in the city of Tver', married Liubov' Gavrilovna Vul'f, daughter of Pavel Bakunin's older sister, Aleksandra, during the winter of 1871–1872. Living in the city of Tver', Mikhail was repeatedly elected from the 1870s to approximately 1900 by the urban electoral congress as one of its deputies to the Tver' County Zemstvo Assembly. That county assembly, in turn, repeatedly reelected him to represent it as a deputy in the Tver' Provincial Zemstvo Assembly. Thus, in addition to his marital ties to the Bakunin family (where he visited often), Mikhail had a political relationship with the Bakunins in the zemstvos.[3]

Ivan Il'ich Petrunkevich, the elder brother of Mikhail by slightly more than one year, had become acquainted with Ol'ga Bakunina and her sister Varvara at the apartment of the painter N. N. Ge in Florence, Italy, in 1868. The young Petrunkevich had just completed St. Petersburg University and was on vacation before returning to his home estate in Chernigov Province to enter zemstvo work. Ivan Petrunkevich experienced "the friendly chaos" of life at Priamukhino when he visited the Bakunins in 1871 to meet his new sister-in-law, Mikhail's wife Liubov' Gavrilovna and her family.[4] In the 1890s the Bakunin-Petrunkevich web would become much thicker. Ivan Petrunkevich, having been exiled for life from Chernigov Province in 1885, bought and settled on the estate of "Mashuk," on the bank of the Tver'tsa River, in Ramen'e township (*volost'*) of Novotorzhok County some twelve miles north of the city of Torzhok. In 1891, when health forced Pavel Bakunin to retire from zemstvo work, I. I. Petrunkevich quickly purchased enough land in Tver' Province to be eligible for direct election to the Novotorzhok County Zemstvo Assembly, and he was subsequently elected to fill Pavel Bakunin's vacated seat.[5] Thus, he acquired a political relationship that rested, to a large degree, on the social relationship that already existed among the Bakunin-Shveikovskii-Petrunkevich families.

Ivan Petrunkevich's migration to Tver' Province increased the size of the core of the extended family, not only by his presence, but by the fact that his eldest son Mikhail married a Bakunin, and after Mikhail completed his university studies in Germany, he and his wife and children returned to Novotorzhok County where they settled on the Mashuk estate with Ivan and Ivan's second wife, Anastasia Sergeevna. Mikhail was soon elected Marshal of the Novotorzhok County nobility, which made him exofficio chairman of the sessions of the Novotorzhok County Zemstvo Assembly. His formal duties required him to enforce the rule that comments by his father, uncle, and other relatives in the assembly be limited to purely "local economic needs and wants" and that such deputies be restrained from making comments about topics "beyond the zemstvo's competence," that is, comments about actions by the tsarist government.[6]

This extended family relationship spread its influence through business and professional ties that, in turn, added to the political might of the core group. Some examples will suffice for illustrative purposes. First is the example of Sof'ia Panina, who was the daughter of Ivan Petrunkevich's second wife, Anastasia Sergeevna, from her marriage to Count Panin. (Anastasia Sergeevna herself was a member of the wealthy Maltsev family of merchants.) To manage the considerable fortune she inherited from her father, Sof'ia Panina hired as her financial manager a Mr. Arkhangel'skii, who with zemstvo doctor M. E. Zaitsev (a colleague of Dr. Mikhail Petrunkevich) by the year 1900 managed the affairs of the Rzhev County Zemstvo Board, which bordered Novotorzhok County on the southwest. Mr. Arkhangel'skii had an estate in northern Rzhev county, immediately south of Priamukhino.[7]

A second example is the medical network that existed in Tver' province. One of the Bakunin nephews became a doctor and worked with Mikhail Petrunkevich in the zemstvo hospital. Dr. Mikhail Petrunkevich was a very close friend of the famous psychiatrist M. P. Litvinov, director of the Tver' provincial zemstvo's facility for the mentally ill—called the Burashevo Colony for the Mentally Ill. As two of the founders of the Pirogov Medical Society in Moscow, these two doctors established an important link with doctors in Moscow who, in turn, rendered them a good deal of support through articles in the professional medical journal *Vrach* (*Doctor*) in the mid-1890s when a conflict in the Tver' provincial zemstvo between the liberals and the government-appointed provincial zemstvo executive board caused Dr. Litvinov and his immediate staff to resign their positions.[8]

Could such a sizeable group, anchored in a thick web of social support and controlling so many institutions in their respective counties, bring about socioeconomic change at the local level that would, if emulated in other counties of European Russia, ultimately form the necessary basis for national representative government? The objective of this chapter is to examine the conflict between this group of reformers and the central government from 1890 to 1905. From 1891 onward, the government very frequently referred to this group as "the liberal party," but it also used other attributives—such as "liberal group," "opposition party," "antigovernment party," and "the party of reds"—interchangeably with "liberal party." But none of these terms compared in frequency of appellation with the term "liberal party."[9]

This chapter first examines the government's perception of the problem the Tver' liberals posed. It then analyzes the measures Tsar Alexander III's legislation employed to try to control the liberal party, and, third, it assesses the degree of success those measures achieved from 1890 to approximately 1905.

THE GOVERNMENT'S PERCEPTION OF THE LIBERAL PROBLEM

Richard Robbins has stressed that a governor's tact and personality were crucial in the relationship between governors, who were government officials appointed by the Tsar and subordinate to the Ministry of Internal Affairs, and the new elective bodies, the zemstvos, which operated in thirty-four provinces after 1864. A. N. Somov, Governor of Tver' Province during the 1880s, appears to have been conscientious in carrying out his administrative duties, for example, ordering that hygiene in certain prisons be improved and, following a fire in the town of Kashin in the summer of 1883, taking immediate and constructive measures to succor the victims and rebuild the town. Somov also attempted to work with the provincial and county zemstvos in Tver' Province; his last annual report before leaving his post in 1888 was noticeably devoid of antizemstvo rhetoric.[10]

The annual reports of Somov's successor, P. D. Akhlestyshev, Governor of Tver' Province from 1888 to 1898, on the other hand, display his hostile attitude toward the zemstvos.[11] In his annual report for the year 1891, for example, Akhlestyshev described the troubles the liberals had caused him since he assumed the governorship in 1888. "When I first entered the administration of the province," he wrote,

> I found a dictatorship of a firmly united and well-organized liberal party. That party dominated completely in the zemstvo assembly and worked to isolate the zemstvo [from government control], to make it an institution not bound in its actions by the laws and decrees of the government. Furthermore, zemstvo funds were being spent to support that party. To strengthen that party, as I can prove, people who are politically suspect or compromised were especially invited into zemstvo service, and in order to evade control by the administration, these persons frequently were appointed secretly without soliciting—

as is required by law—the advance permission of the governor. In response to my question as to why the zemstvo board admitted such persons into service without advance permission, the board answered that it occurred through oversight. Such persons can be found in the statistical, insurance, and other agencies of the provincial zemstvo board. In addition, in 1891, several persons on the board were called to account for participating in state crimes.

[Tver'] zemstvo assemblies have devoted no small amount of time to high-flown phrases about freedom, about the worth of the individual, and the like; to inadmissible and sharp insinuations against the government; and they have considered petitions that had no connection with local needs—such as the petition that the zemstvo assembly considered in 1890 about the noninterference by officials of the Ministry of Public Education in the domestic life of high school students. They submitted a petition that the school officialdom stop observing the home life of the students and cease visiting students' rooms.

In its relations with the provincial administration [that is, the governor] the zemstvo has followed a system of opposition to all the administration's activities. The demands of the administration, which are based on a clear sense of the law, have met with opposition from the zemstvo.[12]

In subsequent reports covering the period until 1905, Governor Akhlestyshev and his successor, Prince N. D. Golitsyn, sought to identify the people of the "liberal party" and to explain the manner and degree to which they constituted a problem for the central government.[13] Governor Akhlestyshev and Prince N. D. Golitsyn used the devices of the governor's annual report and the new power of the audit, which the Zemstvo Statute of 1890 (the "zemstvo counterreform") extended to the governor, as the chief means of informing the central government of the evil deeds of the "liberal party" in Tver' and of seeking aid from the central government in the struggle against them. The general audit of five counties conducted in autumn 1903 produced an extensive report that defined the "liberal party" most precisely: the 187-page secret document, "A Review of the Zemstvo Institutions of Tver' Province."[14] This audit produced the most drastic action taken by the central government to that date. Collectively, the governors' annual reports and the secret report of the audit sketched the history, identified the members, and characterized the activities of the Tver' "liberal party" through the year 1903.

The government considered the core of the liberal party to be the Bakunin family, which had earlier linked with A. M. Unkovskii to criticize the tsarist government during the period of the emancipation of the serfs. Then, in the 1860s and 1870s the brothers Pavel and Aleksandr Bakunin and a circle of their friends "dominated both the Novotorzhok County zemstvo and Tver' provincial zemstvo."[15] More recently, this family had been joined by the Povalo-Shveikovskii and Petrunkevich families to form three "nests" hatching out other liberals in Novotorzhok County. The secret report from the audit in 1903 explained most, but not all, of the links by marriages and it noted that a Mr. Arkhangel'skii, who was a member of the Rzhev County Zemstvo Board, was linked to this extended family through Sof'ia Panina, whose estate he managed. Then, in 1891 Ivan Petrunkevich joined his brother Mikhail to complete the third family "nest."[16]

In Novotorzhok County, in addition to the members of this extended family, the government was concerned about V. N. Lind, who had a long history of work in Novotorzhok County (zemstvo institutions) and Tver' provincial zemstvo institutions. The government cited his "completely unacceptable" activities in the 1870s as one of the major reasons it closed the Tver' zemstvo's technical school in Rzhev.[17] Outside Novotorzhok County the government was most concerned about Fedor Rodichev of Ves'egonsk County, son of one of the largest landlords of Tver' Province, and K. D. Kvashnin-Samarin, marshal of the county nobility of Rzhev County.[18]

In summary, the government's perception of the problem it faced from the 1890s to 1905 in Tver' Province was that a small group of well-organized, intelligent liberals had seized control of the zemstvo institutions and was using, as it had for twenty-five years, zemstvo funds to build support for its party by providing sympathizers (people the government considered "politically unreliable") with employment and shelter in the zemstvo's bureaus as hired professionals. Within the latter category were persons exiled administratively from other provinces who chose, in part because of the national reputation Tver' had acquired as a haven for government critics, to settle in Tver' until the period of their exile ended. Thus a firm antigovernment alliance between zemstvo deputies and the zemstvo's hired specialists (the "Third Element") had come into existence.[19]

LEGISLATION AFFECTING THE ZEMSTVO

The tsarist government's abolition of the offices of the justices of the peace in 1889 reduced the zemstvos' sphere of influence and thereby the role of liberals in zemstvo activities. The zemstvos elected the justices of the peace, paid their salaries, built them jails, and paid for the staff in their offices. Many of the most active members of the group of reformers in Tver' Province had served as justices of the peace at some time during their careers. Examples of such liberals include various members of the Bakunin family, Fedor Rodichev, and Ivan Petrunkevich (in Chernigov before his exile in 1879).[20]

The zemstvo counterreform of the following year—June 12, 1890— was an even more direct effort to limit the activities of the zemstvos and to end what the central government considered the fiscal irresponsibility of big-spending liberals. Through this reform the government sought, first, to alter the composition of all the zemstvo assemblies of Russia in favor of the conservative noblemen and at the expense of the emerging liberal bourgeoisie, and second, to control the activities of those assemblies by granting the governor more arbitrary powers over them than he had been given by the Zemstvo Statute of January 1, 1864. The means the government employed to try to increase the number of noble deputies was to *decrease* the property qualification necessary for nobles to participate in the landowners' electoral congress so that a larger number of nobles could attend the congress and vote directly for their representatives in the county zemstvo assembly. The norm was reduced by approximately one-half to an average of 164 to 219 hectares (405 to 540 acres). At the same time, the government *increased* substantially the property qualification necessary for urban landowners to participate in the landowners' electoral congress that elected county zemstvo deputies. The norm was raised to real property valued at no less than 15,000 rubles.[21]

The government also restricted representation from peasant landowners elected by the peasant electoral congress. The percentage of the county zemstvo assembly's deputies elected by the peasantry was reduced from an average of 48 percent to an average of 30 percent, and the peasantry's electoral congress chose merely their deputies to the county zemstvo assembly. The governor acquired the right, by virtue of the new zemstvo statute, to appoint the peasantry's deputies from the list of candidates nominated.[22]

The new zemstvo statute increased the government's control over zemstvo activities by increasing the governor's arbitrary powers in still other areas. First, the statute retained the governor's right to confirm the election of chairmen of the county zemstvo boards, and it added the right to confirm the election of "members" of the provincial and county zemstvo boards. (The statute retained for the Minister of Internal Affairs the right to confirm the election of the chairmen of the provincial zemstvo boards.) Secondly, in cases where the candidates that the zemstvos elected to the board were repeatedly unacceptable to the government, the Minister of Internal Affairs acquired the right to appoint a chairman of the board. Third, and most important, the governor received the right to halt implementation of any zemstvo resolution that was illegal or that he felt "undesirable." Previously, he could halt implementation only if a resolution was "illegal."

The governor initiated the process by lodging a formal objection within thirty days after the resolution was passed, and the resolution then went to a new body, created by the new zemstvo statute, which had the right to veto the resolution under question. The new body, the Provincial Office of Zemstvo and City Affairs, was composed of the governor (who was its chairman), the vice-governor, the provincial marshal of the nobility, the government-appointed director of the fiscal chamber, the government-appointed prosecutor of the district court, the chairman of the provincial zemstvo board, and one representative the provincial zemstvo assembly elected from its members (or members of its board).[23] The zemstvos were, therefore, always outvoted five to two (or four to three even on those rare occasions when the marshal might support them) by bureaucrats appointed to the body by the central government.

EFFECTS OF THE ZEMSTVO REFORM IN TVER' PROVINCE

To what degree did the changes instituted by the zemstvo statute aid the government in controlling the liberal menace? Let us consider the first objective of the reform: to increase the role of the conservative nobility in the zemstvo assemblies. B. B. Veselovskii's research on the zemstvos of Russia as a whole shows an average increase for the nobility of some 8 percent in the provincial assembles (from 81.6 percent in 1883–1885 to 89.5 percent for 1897.)[24] In Tver' the election of a new assembly in

1891—the first conducted under the provisions of the 1890 statute—resulted in the election of fifteen new deputies in an assembly of sixty-two deputies.[25] In the county assemblies of Russia the average percentage of noblemen-deputies rose from 42.4 percent to 55.2 percent for the same years.[26] In the twelve counties of Tver' Province the election of 1891 produced only minor changes in the composition of the majority of the assemblies. For instance, Ves'egonsk had nine new deputies out of a total of thirty-six; Vyshnyi Volochek had a significant change of nearly half, with fifteen new deputies out of a total of thirty-two. Ostashkov had the largest change with twenty-two new deputies out of a total of thirty-eight.[27] These changes of deputies did not alter significantly representation among the three estates (nobility, urban, peasantry) in Russia, for the landowning nobility had a plurality of deputies and dominated the activities of the zemstvos of Russia from beginning to end.

The conservative elements made some gains in the election of 1891 in Tver' and, in alliance with the governor, played an important role during their first three-year term. However, they could not consolidate that position during the remainder of the decade to replace the "liberal party" that was, itself, composed primarily of landowning noblemen. Year after year during the period under study, the governors of Tver' Province reported that a strong conservative party was in the process of formation and was on the verge of paralyzing the liberals, but the governors had just as constantly to rely on the second device written into the 1890 statute to control the liberals: that of utilizing the extended arbitrary powers the statute gave the governors.

The election of 1891 increased the numbers of the conservative element in the provincial zemstvo assembly; however, at the same time among the fifteen new deputies elected to the provincial assembly were several of the most ardent champions of reform in the 1890s and afterward: Ivan Petrunkevich (one liberal replacing another in that he assumed the seat vacated by the ill Pavel Bakunin, who moved to the Crimea), A. A. Golovachev, L. A. Miasnikov, V. D. von-Derviz, and N. K. Miliukov. Although the liberals were unable during the period to control the membership of the provincial zemstvo board, thanks to the intervention of the governor and Minister of Internal Affairs, they continued in the 1890s to win even the most controversial debates by a margin of seven to thirteen votes (for instance, 30 to 23; 32 to 19), depending upon the issue and the number of deputies present.[28] Furthermore, the reform of 1890 forced the liberal group to become more intimate and more structured in their efforts to implement their program.

During the fifteen-year period of our study, 1890 to the end of 1904, the recurrent issue that most prolonged and intensified the struggle between the liberal party in the Tver' Provincial Zemstvo Assembly and the tsarist central government was the election every third year of a new chair and members of the provincial zemstvo board. The second most divisive issue was, in the last half of the 1890s, the governor's efforts to remove several of the hired "Third Element" professionals from their positions in zemstvo service.

In the 1891 session of the provincial zemstvo assembly—the first under the provisions of the zemstvo counterreform of 1890—the liberal and conservative groups aligned themselves for the battle to elect the chair and members of the provincial zemstvo board. By a majority of only one vote, the liberal group elected Fedor Rodichev as chair; but the central government refused to confirm his election or the election of B. B. Kostylev as "member" of the board. In a special session called in February 1892 to try to resolve the deadlock, both sides mentioned B. V. Shtiurmer as a possibility. When the actual vote was taken, he was defeated and no other candidate received a majority. Having reached no result, the special session was adjourned. The Minister of Internal Affairs then appointed B. V. Shtiurmer chair of the board, and E. A. Shellekhov, rather than the assembly's elected candidate N. F. Zmiev, as member of the board. The central administration named two other deputies from the liberal group—N. I. Kharlamov and A. A. Dem'ianov—members of the board.[29] Shtiurmer, also referred to as Stürmer, later was appointed governor of Yaroslavl' Province, east of Tver', and in 1916, during World War I, was appointed Chair of the Council of Ministers and Minister of Internal Affairs.[30]

In his report for 1891, Governor Akhlestyshev noted the change that had occurred in the provincial zemstvo assembly after the election of 1891. In the 1891 session, he said,

> for the first time in twenty-five years, a conservative party appeared and began a struggle with the liberals. Although the liberals were able to elect the chairman of the provincial zemstvo board—Deputy

Rodichev, who is clearly compromised and politically suspect—that occurred only thanks to several special measures taken by the liberal party, as for example, delaying the discussion of questions until several conservative deputies had gone.[31]

The governor had to admit later in the report, however, that "the authority of [the liberal party] is strong, and one can only hope that the Minister of Internal Affairs' naming Shtiurmer as chairman of the board and the not confirming Rodichev will straighten out the zemstvo's economy and cleanse the board's 'serving personnel' [the Third Element] of the suspect elements."[32] In the end, the government's power to withhold confirmation and to appoint a chairman of the board restrained the liberals; the "conservative party" did not.

What change occurred in the direction of the zemstvo's affairs during the three-year term of 1891 to 1894 while the zemstvo board was chaired by Shtiurmer, a conservative government-appointee? This query has additional significance since Shtiurmer's later performance was very controversial. Most historians consider him a reactionary; he claimed, however, that he was a liberal. Ivan Petrunkevich related in his memoirs that Shtiurmer "did not have the slightest understanding of the business that he was making his career. From the very first day of his appearance at the zemstvo board, he sensed his helpless condition and the necessity of finding assistance." Probably for that reason, Shtiurmer came to the liberal zemstvo group for advice, since that group directed almost all of the zemstvo's projects.[33]

During the period of Shtiurmer's chairmanship of the board, Governor Akhlestyshev's vigorous use of the powers the 1890 counterreform had given him took on such a strong flavor of "meddling" and of personal attacks against individual deputies that he destroyed the new "center" group that had begun to form in 1892 around new board chair Shtiurmer. By the end of the year, no more speeches in the assembly mentioned the possibility of forming a "center" party that could have become supportive of the government. Akhlestyshev filed significantly more formal protests against zemstvo resolutions than in the past.[34]

He also used the governor's new power to conduct audits. In the three-year period from 1891 through 1893, he ordered audits of various counties and a separate audit of the provincial zemstvo's Burashevo

Colony for the Mentally Ill. He also increased censorship of the published version of the provincial and county zemstvos' budgets (*otchety*) and their journals (*zhurnaly*), which contained the secretary's minutes of what was said in the county and provincial zemstvo assemblies and accounts of actions taken by them. Also, at the governor's insistence, chairmen of the zemstvo assemblies (marshals of the county and provincial nobility who served ex officio) began to remove various topics that had been listed on the assemblies' agendas for discussion and action. Collectively, these actions brought dissension into the provincial assembly and strengthened the liberal party as the government's opposition in the zemstvo assemblies.[35]

One example of Akhlestyshev's attacks on particular people was his response to the zemstvo's creation (in response to Fedor Rodichev's proposal) in the 1893 regular session of several student stipends in honor of A. M. Unkovskii who died December 20 of that year.[36] The governor stated his dislike for the zemstvo's stipends in his report to the Minister of Internal Affairs for 1893 and called Unkovskii "the main leader of the liberal inclination in 1859."[37] In his public protest, he tried to mask his real reason behind the formal language of the 1890 zemstvo counterreform. The governor explained that, because the zemstvo had "created stipends with a permanent title" for 6,000 rubles "without having received permission from the proper authority" by "submitting the required petition in the required form," he found the zemstvo's action "illegal" (*nezakonnym*).[38] He submitted his protest to the zemstvo assembly regular session for 1894. When the assembly voted against the governor's protest, the governor sent the resolution to the Provincial Office of Zemstvo and City Affairs.[39] All parties knew, of course, that in 1859 the Tver' noblemen's assembly had tweaked the central government's nose by creating stipends in Unkovskii's name at the University of Moscow and having Unkovskii (whom the government had just dismissed from his office as marshal of the Tver' provincial nobility and exiled for presenting the Tsar a radical proposal for emancipating the serfs) choose the recipients from his place of exile.[40]

The process that strengthened the liberal elements, destroyed the middle party, and isolated the conservative group developed still further in the next three-year term of 1894 to 1897. The second election of zemstvo deputies in Tver' Province under the conditions of the 1890 statute was in 1894. Did this election bring a conservative majority to the assembly? The governor again thought it had. In his report for 1895 he wrote:

> A completely opposite trend [in zemstvo elections] has emerged for the first time only during the new elections in the fall of this past year of 1894. Tired by the liberal regime, the population apparently ceased relating passively to the existing order of things. In many counties the leaders of the liberal party were defeated. In most cases persons elected to office were members from the party of order. The former situation was preserved only in Novotorzhok and Ves'egonsk counties. . . .
>
> For the first time a party has appeared in the assembly that has presented a completely opposite program of action, one based firmly on solving practical tasks, attending to purely local needs, and believing in thrift in the zemstvo economy.[41]

The hope, and even the phrases, contained in the report for 1895 are strikingly similar to those of the report for 1891. The conservative party that appeared "for the first time" as a result of the elections of 1894 had already appeared "for the first time in twenty-five years" as a result of the election of 1891, the governor had reported in 1891. One wonders whether the governor had forgotten the content of his report four years earlier. In the report for 1891 he had also noted that the liberal party had elected its candidate chairman of the board only by "special measures" that the governor obviously considered unfair. In the report for 1895, he cited the same dirty tricks by the liberals that again prevented election of the conservative candidate. In the report for 1891 the governor had praised the Minister of Internal Affairs for not confirming Rodichev chairman of the zemstvo board and for naming Shtiurmer instead. But in the report for 1895, the governor referred to the board chaired by Shtiurmer as "the liberal board" and chastised it for its fiscal policy.[42] Furthermore, the main base for the liberals had been Novotorzhok and Rzhev counties in 1891 (and one might note that Rodichev was from Ves'egonsk County), and in the report for 1895 the governor reported that "the former situation" had not changed in Novotorzhok and Ves'egonsk Counties. He need not have excluded Rzhev County, as will later be shown.

In the three-year period from 1894 through 1897 when, according to the governor's report the "conservative party," the "party of order," controlled the Tver' provincial zemstvo, the liberals elected three of the four candidates for the zemstvo board, including as board chairman S. D. Kvashnin-Samarin, of Rzhev County, by a vote of thirty-five to thirty-one. The Minister of Internal Affairs and the governor refused to confirm the election of any of the three, the fourth person then re-signed, and the government named, for the second time in a row, a member of the conservative group (this time A. S. Paskin) as chairman of the zemstvo board. And, once again, the government appointed *all* the members of the board as well.[43]

In December 1894, during the regular session of the assembly for that year, the liberal majority of the Tver' provincial zemstvo assembly adopted an address to Nicholas II, who had just ascended to the throne, that had been drafted by a group of zemstvo activists in St. Petersburg (among them Tver' deputies P. A. Korsakov, F. I. Rodichev, and others). The address stated the hope that Russia would "move forward along a path of peace and lawfulness with the development of all existing social forces. . . . in consultation with representatives from all estates of the Russian people."[44] Nicholas II made this address famous by his response of "senseless dreams."

The conservative minority among the provincial zemstvo deputies, protesting that the zemstvo was entering the forbidden political arena, refused to sign the address. After the local telegraph official refused to send the address to the Tsar as a telegram, the zemstvo board decided on December 10 to send it through the regular channel of the Minister of Internal Affairs. The governor added a handwritten note to the resolution: "I am extremely amazed and discontented by this inappropriate behavior of thirty-five deputies of the provincial zemstvo assembly." Having learned about the attached note, the assembly on January 23, 1895, unanimously resolved to add to the address its "most humble feel-ings of unlimited devotion and loyalty to the monarch and its complete willingness to serve His Majesty."[45]

The tsarist government responded by refusing to invite two of the three deputies the Tver' provincial zemstvo chose to attend the coro-nation of Nicholas II in St. Petersburg. Instead of inviting A. A. Golo-vachev and F. I. Rodichev of the liberal group, it invited S. P. Utkin from the conservatives. Subsequently, the central government deprived Rodichev of the right to participate in public activity and forced P. A. Korsakov to resign his position as manager of the St. Petersburg Legal Chamber.[46]

The conflict within the assembly continued in the regular session of 1895. Conservative party member Prince N. S. Putiatin proposed that the assembly send a telegram to the imperial family expressing the zemstvo's happiness on the occasion of the birth of Grand Princess Ol'ga into the imperial family. Calling the text of the telegram ungrammatical, the assembly voted to send it to the editorial committee, of which Ivan Petrunkevich was chairman. He and the committee added to the edited text of the telegram the statement: "And to mark such a happy event, the assembly has resolved to open twelve public reading rooms and to maintain them out of the provincial zemstvo's budget." Petrunkevich said the committee was motivated in its action "by the knowledge of the Emperor's love for public education." In fact, of course, founding public reading rooms had been a favorite activity of the populists and zemstvo reformers since the 1860s. The assembly adopted the resolution unanimously and voted 4,800 rubles to construct the reading rooms and an annual appropriation of 1,200 rubles to maintain them.[47] Thus, the liberals continued their role as big spenders for public welfare under the guise of joy derived from the Tsar's family life.

In addition to struggles every third year over election of the provincial zemstvo board, the second most contentious issue between the government-appointed board and the liberal majority that controlled the assembly was the governor's and board's decision in 1895 to begin a campaign to remove some of the suspect "Third Element" professionals about whom the governor had so often complained in his reports. Most notorious of these conflicts was "the Burashevo incident." After the special audit that the governor ordered in 1893 of the Tver' Provincial Zemstvo Hospital and the Burashevo Colony for the Mentally Ill, the board in 1895 criticized the colony's internationally known director, Dr. M. P. Litvinov, and proposed a reduction in the colony's budget. In response, Dr. Litvinov and the entire staff of doctors resigned. Mikhail Petrunkevich also resigned his position as senior doctor (director) of the Tver' Provincial Zemstvo Hospital. In January 1896 the liberal faction came to Dr. Litvinov's defense, and laid blame for his resignation at the feet of the provincial zemstvo board. An assembly-appointed commission, domi-nated by members of the liberal faction, reported to the assembly that the real issue in "the Burashevo incident" was that the board instituted a ma-jor change in policy and staff in the colony "without authorization by the assembly." The commission described the regime adopted by the new director, Dr. S. N. Sovetov, as "severe," placing "in oblivion" the inter-ests of the ill; the punishments introduced for the ill it called "depriva-tion of their freedom by incarceration." The commission reproached the board for trying to reduce the budget for Burashevo colony to the detri-ment of service.[48]

After a stormy debate, the assembly voted (thirty-one to twenty-one) to express to M. P. Litvinov its deep disappointment about his res-ignation and its gratitude for his fifteen years of useful service. It also re-solved to hang his portrait in one of the buildings of the colony. However, fifteen deputies submitted a "special opinion" in which they stated "the full correctness of the board in the fact of the resignation of the doctors" and the impossibility of their agreeing to express gratitude to Litvinov and disappointment on his resignation.[49]

In a special session in February 1897, the assembly once again re-turned to the question of Burashevo and (with twenty-three deputies abstaining) voted to ask the board to dismiss Dr. Sovetov. The Provin-cial Board on Zemstvo Affairs overturned this resolution.[50]

Election of the provincial zemstvo board for the new three-year term of 1897 to 1900 produced the traditional conflict between the zemstvo assembly and the central administration and the usual result that had oc-curred since 1890.[51] Results of the vote to elect the chair and members show that the general zemstvo elections of 1897 did not significantly change the party groupings within the Tver' Provincial Zemstvo Assem-bly. In the vote for chair of the board, the candidates of both parties (A. S. Paskin for the conservatives and S. D. Kvashnin-Samarin for the lib-erals) received thrity-five votes. To prevent the central government from naming the board for still another three-year term, representatives of both groups reached an agreement that resulted in election of a board composed of conservatives Vasili Nikolaevich Trubnikov as chair and F. N. Esaulov as member and, from the liberals, L. A. Miasnikov and A. P. Apostolov as members. However, the central administration refused to confirm the two representatives from the liberal camp and named in their place M. V. Islavin and Baron D. N. Del'vig. The administration also refused to confirm S. P. Maksimovich as member of the Committee on Provincial and Urban Affairs.[52]

The continuation of hostilities between the central administration and the liberals in the zemstvo assembly in 1898, after Prince N. D. Golitsyn replaced Governor Akhlestyshev, shows that the conflict was more fundamental than a disagreement with only one governor. During Golitsyn's governorship, the struggle became even more intense; he made greater use of the arbitrary powers the governor received in the zemstvo counterreform of 1890, and he proposed more drastic actions than his predecessor to destroy the liberal party. He began to refuse to confirm the election of several chairs of the county zemstvo boards; the number of protests he filed increased sharply, and the zemstvo turned even more often to the Senate to defend itself against the local administration.[53]

After enduring prolonged criticism of his activities by the Tver' provincial assembly, Dr. Sovetov resigned his position as director of the Burashevo Colony for the Mentally Ill in October 1898. V. N. Ergol'skii, manager of the psychiatric hospital of Kaluga zemstvo, replaced him. Upon the recommendation of the assembly, the board drafted an "Instruction for Burashevo Colony" that significantly clarified the senior doctor's responsibilities inside the colony and in his relationship with the provincial zemstvo board. This clarification removed many of the former conflicts between the colony's director and the provincial zemstvo assembly.[54]

On January 1899 the new governor, Prince N. D. Golitsyn, gave his first opening speech to the Tver' provincial zemstvo. He complained that the zemstvo's "ever-increasing taxation" was "exhausting the population."[55] At the end of that year, he correctly observed that the only way for the government to manage the Tver' zemstvo assembly was to prevent the election of a large number of specific persons then serving in it.[56] But how was the government to prevent their election? That was one of the major objectives of the zemstvo counterreform of 1890.

Unable to prevent such elections, Governor Golitsyn could only rely on the arbitrary powers he had been granted in the 1890 statute. In 1899 he protested all increases in county zemstvo taxation—a total of 166 separate items. By majority vote, the provincial zemstvo assembly rejected these protests, and the governor referred his protests to the Committee of Ministers. As a result, the Committee of Ministers on June 25, 1899, subjected the provincial zemstvo budget to a reduction of 67,200 rubles and ten of the county zemstvo budgets to a reduction of 41,900 rubles. In 1900 eight of the county zemstvos were, in the same way, subjected to reductions of 43,400 rubles.

Furthermore, Prince Golitsyn ended the long tradition of unrestricted public attendance at zemstvo assembly sessions. He closed the session to the public during the reports by the assembly-elected auditing and editorial commissions. These two committees had long been controlled by the liberal faction in the assembly. The zemstvo assembly appealed the governor's protests, but the Senate did not support the assembly's suit against the governor's closure of the session.[57]

Still seeking a means of weakening the liberal faction, the governor decided in 1899 to subject the Tver' provincial zemstvo to a general audit. Discussion of the details of this audit was the central issue of the 1899 session. The governor argued, in his notification to the assembly, that "the zemstvo should conduct a detailed and broad-scaled study of ways to economize more effectively in its expenditures and should create a plan whereby the zemstvo lives within the means available to it."[58]

The assembly considered the data in the governor's note and found that the note "contained many factual errors"; additionally the note "inaccurately condemned the entire state of zemstvo management." The assembly sent a report to the central government that contained what the assembly considered "a more accurate" account of its work.[59]

In addition to his general condemnation of the Tver' provincial assembly, the governor attacked the liberal stronghold of the Novotorzhok County zemstvo directly. Citing clauses from the Zemstvo Statute of 1890 regarding zemstvo budgets, the governor objected to a series of expenditures the Novotorzhok County Zemstvo Assembly voted to fund through various forms of credit. In 1901 the central government removed the entire Novotorzhok zemstvo board (A. P. Balavenskii, D. D. Romanov, and A. I. Bakunin). All the Novotorzhok zemstvo assembly could do was unanimously pass a resolution thanking the former board and expressing its hope that it "would soon see the board again in power."[60]

The election in 1900 of zemstvo deputies for the next three-year term strengthened the liberal party throughout Tver' Province. With the conservative faction seriously weakened, the conflict during the three-year term of 1900 to 1903 was more clearly between the zemstvo and the central government, rather than a conflict between conservative and liberal factions in the assembly, with the central government merely siding with the conservatives. The liberals' majority in the assembly was so strong that the opposition did not bother to try for a sharing of positions on the board as they had in 1897. The assembly elected V. D. von-Derviz as board chairman and Baron I. S. Vrevskii, N. K. Miliukov, and A. Il'ich Bakunin as members. Governor Golitsyn proposed to Minister of Internal Affairs D. S. Sipiagin that the entire slate be rejected. Sipiagin, however, approved everyone except A. I. Bakunin.[61] The new board then dismissed, during the three-year period of 1900 to 1903, 132 of the 238 employees the government-appointed boards had hired and replaced them with new people, or with rehired former employees, including seven of the ten heads of bureaus within the board.[62]

In 1902 and early 1903 the county and provincial zemstvo institutions in Tver' Province were primarily engaged in formulating responses requested by Minister of Finance Sergei Witte's local committees on the needs of agriculture. The governor, who was ex officio chair of the provincial committee that accumulated reports from county committees, attempted to hide from public view the detailed descriptions of peasant life revealed in the county committees' reports. His major tactic for obfuscation was to order, by use of his arbitrary powers, that the provincial committee would consider only summaries, rather than the full detailed reports, of the county committees. He also stated that the provincial committee would exclude from its considerations the report submitted by the Novotorzhok County committee. He then used his power of censorship to prevent the Novotorzhok committee's report from being printed as part of the official materials accumulated by the Tver' provincial committee. In protest against the governor's action, fourteen deputies (including the entire provincial zemstvo board and six chairs of county zemstvo boards) refused to participate in the provincial committee's work and petitioned the Minister of Internal Affairs to transfer the question of the needs of local agriculture to the zemstvos and to create a "central institution" to which they would send their proposals.

Among the members of this central body should be two representatives from Tver' Province, who would be elected by the Tver' Provincial Zemstvo Assembly, and who would "have rights equal to all other members and a guarantee of personal inviolability."[63] Surely, the Tver' zemstvo had in mind the process used to create the Great Reforms.

The election of 1903 strengthened the liberal party still further in the counties as well as in the provincial assembly. Only in Tver' Province did the zemstvo pass into the hands of the conservatives. Absenteeism among the conservatives in the provincial assembly made control of daily matters even easier for the liberal faction. Attempting to resist the liberals' dominance by using his arbitrary powers to the maximum, the governor conducted, from October 23 to November 19, 1903, the audit he had decided upon in 1899. After the three-person auditing team filed its secret report, and after the regular session of the provincial zemstvo assembly closed on December 15, 1903, the Minister of Internal Affairs implemented (on January 8, 1904) the "extraordinary measures related to the Tver' provincial and Novotorzhok zemstvos" that he had drafted.

By 1903, according to the conclusions the three-person team of auditors wrote in their final, secret report, the liberal faction in Tver' Province constituted an even more serious problem for the central government than they had in 1891 when Akhlestyshev outlined the problem in his lengthy report. The extended family around the three "nests" of the Bakunin, Petrunkevich, and Shveikovskii families was more in control of Novotorzhok County than it had ever been.[64] The first generation of the "old constitutionalists," having built the institutions, no longer controlled them. The second generation, the children of the old constitutionalists, now managed these institutions, and were using them to spread liberal ideas among the local, non-noble population in the villages. Additionally, the core group in Novotorzhok County had grafted onto itself various liberals across the county boundary in Rzhev County. The leading figure of the Rzhev liberals was S. D. Kvashnin-Samarin, who was marshal of the Rzhev County nobility and who, with assistance from two other people, ran the affairs of the Rzhev County Zemstvo Board. The others were Dr. M. E. Zaitsev, a colleague of Dr. Mikhail Petrunkevich, and Deputy Arkhangel'skii, the manager of the estate of Countess Sof'ia Panina, Ivan Petrunkevich's devoted stepdaughter. The conservative chairman of the Rzhev board, Potemkin, the secret report lamented, was "illiterate, stupid."[65]

Still worse, the bond between zemstvo deputies and members of the Third Element had grown stronger than in 1891. The authors of the secret report presented the scenario as follows:

> The old constitutionalists find fault with everything in the zemstvo assembly . . . using the articles of the Zemstvo Statute to find still newer and newer ways to escape the watch of the administration. . . . Their children organize peasant banks, consumer cooperatives, volunteer fire departments . . . always because such organizations give them the possibility of uniting closer with the *narod.* . . . These sons then find helpers among the narod itself, and these helpers become their pupils.[66]

The Ministry of Internal Affairs thus devised the following extraordinary measures to curb the Tver' liberals: (1) appointing the members of the Tver' provincial and Novotorzhok county zemstvo boards for the three-year term from 1903 to 1906; (2) preserving the budget of 1903 for the year 1904 as well; and (3) prohibiting "the presence, within the confines of the province or its local divisions, of people who have an evil influence on the course of zemstvo administration." It gave the Tver' governor complete authority in adopting measures related to "the Third Element."[67]

As a means of implementing the third of these three extraordinary measures—excluding from the confines of the province people with an "evil influence" on the zemstvos—the government, in January 1904, exiled Novotorzhok zemstvo deputies I. I. Petrunkevich, A. I. Bakunin, and M. P. Litvinov from Tver' Province. Ivan Petrunkevich's wife, Anastasia Sergeevna, explained in a letter to her stepson, Aleksandr Ivanovich, that on January 21, while the Petrunkevich family was having lunch, an assistant of the county manager (*ispravnik*) presented Ivan Il'ich with an order from the Minister of Internal Affairs exiling him from Tver' Province because the minister "considered his actions an evil influence on the course of zemstvo matters in the province." She painted a picture of paralysis left in Novotorzhok County after the governor's order exiling, or firing, large numbers of zemstvo Third Element specialists in Novotorzhok County "annihilated" the zemstvo. She said that all the eleven doctors, many teachers, and feldshers who were fired from their positions "will leave Torzhok and the Tver' provincial zemstvo. You can imagine what life will be like, considering how the county was given life by the zemstvo's cultural institutions."[68] In April the Minister of Internal Affairs exiled V. D. von-Derviz, N. K. Miliukov, and B. N. Tits, who had been elected chair and members, respectively, of the provincial zemstvo board.[69]

To implement the first point of the extraordinary measures, the government in January 1904 appointed a provincial zemstvo board composed of D. S. Zasiadko, as chair, and V. F. von Gasler, N. A. Ponomarev, and V. N. Trubnikov as members. The governor appointed to the Novotorzhok county board D. N. Dubasov as chair, and V. P. Kislovskii and Prince A. V. Obolenskii as members. Dubasov served simultaneously as chair of the board in Kashin County.[70]

The government later partially explained its actions by saying that in Tver' Province a strengthening of "undesirable people, in a political sense, especially among students," was underway "to transform school teaching into a weapon of propaganda not only against the existing state and social order, but even against religion."[71]

Near the end of 1904, in response to widespread social unrest, Minister of Internal Affairs Prince Sviatopolk-Mirskii allowed all the deputies exiled from Tver' Province to return to zemstvo service, and he restored the civil rights of F. I. Rodichev. He also allowed the Tver' and Novotorzhok zemstvo assemblies to replace their appointed boards with people they elected themselves. The government also replaced Governor Golitsyn with Prince S. D. Urusov.

Utilizing their new freedoms, many of the previously exiled deputies from the liberal faction of the Tver' zemstvo participated in the public congress of zemstvo activists November 6–9, 1904, in St. Petersburg. Among the representatives from the Tver' provincial zemstvo were V. D. von-Derviz, V. D. Kuzmin-Karavaev, M. I. and I. I. Petrunkevich, N. K. Miliukov, F. I. Rodichev, and P. A. Korsakov. This assembly adopted a resolution calling upon the Tsar to grant popular representation through a special elected institution, subjection of administration to rule by law, and other rights to citizens.[72]

In January 1905 the regular session of the provincial zemstvo assembly elected a board composed almost exclusively of its former exiled deputies: V. D. von-Derviz as chair, and as members N. K.

Miliukov, B. N. Tits, D. N. Kvashnin-Samarin, and A. S. Medvedev. On January 30 the provincial zemstvo assembly adopted a resolution (by a vote of thirty-four to nine) with virtually the same wording as the resolution adopted by the congress of zemstvo activists in St. Petersburg in November 1904.[73]

In an extraordinary session in January 1905, the Novotorzhok County Zemstvo Assembly elected a board composed almost exclusively of its formerly exiled deputies: M. P. Litvinov as chair, and D. D. Romanov and I. N. Tyrg as members. On September 29, 1905, the tsarist government removed all restrictions not already removed from Tver' zemstvo institutions.

Conclusions

In the period from 1890 to 1905, the liberals in the Tver' zemstvo assembly managed to elect and have their candidate for board chairman confirmed only in 1900 and 1903. From 1890 to 1897, the tsarist government had some assistance from a conservative party in the Tver' provincial zemstvo assembly. However, the conservatives could never stop, much less reverse, the direction of zemstvo affairs without the central government's utilization of its arbitrary powers in support of the conservatives. This intervention occurred in the person of the provincial governor, the Minister of Internal Affairs, and the members of the Provincial Office of Zemstvo and City Affairs. The more frequently the government used its arbitrary power, the more it strengthened the resolve of the liberals to overthrow autocracy. In 1904 and 1905 the government was forced by violence and organized nonviolent opposition to adopt some of the measures the liberal faction in Tver' had advised for fifteen years. At the same time, the government revoked the punishment it had inflicted on the Tver' zemstvo assembly generally and several of its deputies particularly.

Despite government interferences and internal battles, the provincial and county zemstvos in Tver' Province increased the sphere of their activities enormously from 1890 to 1905. The size of their employed staff increased from some 941 specialists in 1891 to approximately 3,000 by 1910.[74] They made major strides towards the introduction of universal elementary education in the province, and they upgraded the quality of medical care by replacing feldshers with fully qualified doctors. In the provincial zemstvo board, which had ten bureaus by 1900, the assembly had created a separate educational reference bureau and a school commission that aided the introduction of universal elementary education through funding construction of elementary schools and financing other educational activities. In the mid-1890s the zemstvo created a system for out-of-school education and organized conferences and courses for teachers. The provincial and county zemstvos also began to organize savings associations, created a new scheme for managing the roads in the province, and improved storage for agricultural products and supplies.[75]

Through taxation and expenditure of tax revenues to provide medical, educational, and other social services—such as a network of roads, postal operations, and public welfare—the zemstvos were, in fact, doing precisely what local self-governing agencies do. Their problem arose from the fact that they did their jobs too well. Zemstvo self-government became so active in so many areas that the zemstvos, rather than agencies of the autocracy, had become the initiators of action, controllers of events, in the provinces. They had become wielders of power, in that they controlled institutions, and participants in politics, in that they made decisions affecting all aspects of life in the counties of their respective provinces. While the governor and provincial zemstvo were not in disagreement 100 percent of the time, we see in the conflict between governor (as the local agent of autocracy) and the zemstvos (as the agencies of self-government, if not totally democratic), the struggle between two forms of government, two ideologies. Many scholars—East and West—have spent much time and space lamenting the domination of the zemstvos by members of the nobility and urban middle class, but in how many nations of the world do we find, in the period from 1890 to 1905 (or 1995 for that matter), local self-government functioning more effectively and with less domination by a local socioeconomic elite?

NOTES

1. Tver' Province is north of Moscow on the Volga River. See Maps 9–1 and 9–2.

2. I. I. Petrunkevich, *Iz zapisok obshchestvennago deiatelia*, in *Arkhiv russkoi revoliutsii*, vol. 21 (Berlin, 1934), pp. 173–174; "Obozrenie zemskikh uchrezhdenii tverskoi gubernii," pp. 43–67. The "Obozrenie" is the report of a three-person committee that conducted an audit of the Tver' provincial zemstvo October-November 1903. The report is extant in two versions. The first is a typescript copy, which until 1971 was located in the *fondy* of the former Free Economic Society in the Fontanka Filial of the Saltykov-Shchedrin

Library in St. Petersburg. A second version is in the Tsentral'nyi Gosudarstvennyi Istoricheskii Arkhiv (Central State Historical Archive in St. Petersburg [hereafter TsGIA]), fond 1289, opis' 2, delo 1842 [hereafter f., op., d.]. The second version is a retyped copy of the first, except that section IV, "Organization and structure," of the original is not contained in the archival version. Pages 43 to 67 of the first version were devoted to Novotorzhok County, and pages 67 to 76 to Rzhev County.

In February 1971 I sent the typescript copy from the Fontanka Branch Library to the main building of the Saltykov-Shchedrin Library to be copied on microfilm, along with other materials I was ordering on microfilm. When the microfilm and books were returned to the Fontanka Library staff at the end of May, this book was neither filmed nor among those returned. A handwritten note on my original order explained that the library did not film unpublished materials. Despite a careful search and several phone calls on my behalf, Viktor Kel'ner and the late V. Filatova of the Fontanka staff were unable to learn the fate of the typescript copy. Later, I located the archival copy.

In the present article, my citations of "Obozrenie" are based on handwritten notes I made before sending the document to be filmed. References to the TsGIA copy are to the shorter archival version. Since I merely noted "pages 43–67" for my handwritten notes, I must use the vague reference to all the pages of this full section, rather than to individual pages.

A *votchina* landholding was a hereditary estate, in contrast to the *pomest'e*, a smaller estate originally granted in the fifteenth and early sixteenth centuries in return for military service. Gradually both types of landholding fused.

3. Charles Timberlake, "Petrunkevich, Alexander Ivanovich" and "Petrunkevich, Mikhail Il'ich," *Modern Encyclopedia of Russian and Soviet History*, vol. 28 (Gulf Breeze, FL: Academic International Press, 1982), pp. 43–47, 50–53.

4. Petrunkevich, *Iz zapisok*, pp. 172–174.

5. Ibid. p. 249.

6. See Kermit McKenzie, "Zemstvo Organization and Role within the Administrative Structure," in Terence Emmons and Wayne Vucinich, eds., *The Zemstvo in Russia: An Experiment in Local Self-Government* (Cambridge: Cambridge University Press, 1982), pp. 31–78, for an explanation of the role of the marshal of the county nobility as ex officio chairman of the county zemstvo assembly and for explanation of other aspects of zemstvo structure.

7. "Obozrenie," pp. 46–73.

8. See Charles Timberlake, "Petrunkevich, Mikhail Il'ich," pp. 50–53, and, by the same author, "Higher Learning, the State, and the Professions in Russia," in Konrad Jarausch, ed., *The Transformation of Higher Learning, 1860–1930* (Chicago: University of Chicago Press, 1983), pp. 321–345, for further details regarding Litvinov's resignation, the role of the editors of *Vrach*, and the role played by M. P. Litvinov and M. I. Petrunkevich in founding the Pirogov society.

9. See the Tver' Governor's reports for 1891, TsGIA, fond D. O. D., op., 223, d. 526; for 1895, TsGIA, f. 1284, op. 223, d. 129, pp. 10–14; for 1897, TsGIA, f. 1284, op. 223, d. 23b, p. 16.

10. Richard G. Robbins, Jr., *The Tsar's Last Viceroys: Russian Provincial Governors in the Last Years of the Empire* (Ithaca and London: Cornell University Press, 1987), pp. 56, 166, 172. As appointed officials, governors made annual reports to the Tsar and the Ministry of Internal Affairs.

11. Robbins notes that Akhlestyshev's first report was replete with antizemstvo rhetoric. Ibid., p. 166.

12. TsGIA, f. D.O.D., op. 223, d. 526, pp. 24–25.

13. TsGIA, f. 1284, op. 223, d. 129, pp. 10–14.

14. See note 1, above, for bibliographical information on this report.

15. TsGIA, f. 1282, op. 2, d. 1842, pp. 4–17.

16. "Obozrenie," pp. 43–67; I. I. Petrunkevich explained in *Iz zapisok* that he had a relaxed, frank discussion with the committee in which he told them of his ideas and hopes for the future of Russia. He was shocked when he learned the way the committee had used this information in its report.

17. Charles Timberlake, "The Tver Zemstvo's Technical School in Rzhev: A Case Study in the Dissemination of Revolutionary and Secular Ideas," in Charles E. Timberlake, ed., *Religious and Secular Forces in Late Tsarist Russia* (Seattle: University of Washington Press, 1992), pp. 128–44.

18. "Obozrenie," pp. 67–76.

19. Professionals hired by the zemstvos were called "the Third Element" to distinguish them from government officials, known as "the First Element," and elected zemstvo deputies, known as "the Second Element."

20. Petrunkevich's description of the interrelationship between the zemstvos and the justices of the peace is typical of the group's view. The justices were "an inseparable part of local self-government, its special organ fulfilling a legal and educational function," *Iz zapisok*, pp. 63–64.

21. *Polnoe sobranie zakonov Rossiiskoi Imperii*, Tret'e sobranie, vol. 10 (1890), Pt. I, p. 498.

22. Ibid., p. 501 (article 51).

23. Ibid., p. 496 (articles 8–11).

24. B. B. Veselovskii, *Istoriia zemstva za sorok let*, 4 vols. (St. Petersburg, 1909–1911), vol. 3, p. 681.

25. B. B. Veselovskii, *Istoricheskii ocherk deiatel'nosti zemskikh uchrezhdenii Tverskoi gubernii, 1864–1913 gg.* [hereafter *Istoricheskii ocherk*] (Tver', 1914), pp. 41–42.

26. Veselovskii, *Istoriia zemstva za sorok let*, vol. 3, p. 680.

27. Veselovskii, *Istoricheskii ocherk*, p. 42.

28. Ibid. The votes given here refer to the vote to dismiss Dr. Sovetov from his duties as Director of Burashevo Colony for the Mentally Ill. See *Protokoly zasedanii Tverskogo ocherednago gubernskago zemskago sobraniia 6–15 fevralia i 5–9 marta 1897 g. i prilozheniia k nim* (Tver', 1897), p. 74 and other votes related to the Burashevo colony during the stormy session of 1897.

29. Veselovskii, *Istoricheskii ocherk*, pp. 569–570.

30. Shtiurmer is often called Stürmer in English-language histories dealing with World War I. His wartime activity is discussed in Antti Kujala's chapter 6 and in Kimitaka Matsuzato's chapter 9.

31. Governor Akhlestyshev's report for 1891, TsGIA, f. D.O.D., op. 223, d. 526, pp. 26–27.

32. Ibid., p. 27.

33. Petrunkevich, *Iz zapisok*, p. 270.

34. Veselovskii, *Istoricheskii ocherk*, pp. 570–571.

35. Ibid. p. 571. The editorial commission of the Tver' provincial zemstvo filed a protest against the governor's censorship.

36. *Protokoly zasedanii Tverskogo ocherednago gubernskago zemskago sobraniia 8–13 dekabria 1893 g. i 10–16 ianvaria 1894 g.* (Tver', 1894), p. 35.

37. TsGIA, f. 1284, op. 223, d. 163, pp. 83–84.

38. *Protokoly zasedanii Tverskogo ocherednago gubernskago zemskago sobraniia 8–17 dekabria 1894 g. i 23–29 ianvaria 1895 g.* (Tver', 1895), Appendices, p. 1; the governor's letter of July 7, 1894, is the first page after p. 129.

39. Ibid, p. 3, for the vote against the governor's protest.

40. This event is treated in a variety of places. See, for instance, Terence Emmons, *The Russian Landed Gentry and the Peasant Emancipation of 1861* (Cambridge: Cambridge University Press, 1968), p. 269.

41. TsGIA, f. 1284, op. 223, d. 129, p. 12.

42. Ibid., p. 11.

43. *Protokoly . . . 8–17 dekabria 1894 g. i 23–29 ianvaria 1895 g.*, p. 85, is the governor's formal statement of refusal to confirm Dem'ianov and Kostylev and asking for a new election on January 23, 1895. Veselovskii treats this event in two places: *Istoriia zemstva za sorok let,* vol. 4, p. 557, and *Istoricheskii ocherk*, pp. 572–573.

44. Veselovskii, *Istoricheskii ocherk*, pp. 557–558. Among other places, this document can be found in I. P. Belokonskii, *Zemskoe dvizhenie; Zemstvo i konstitutsiia* (2ND. edition, Moscow, 1910), pp. 40–41.

45. Veselovskii, *Istoricheskii ocherk*, p. 572.

46. Ibid., pp. 572–573.

47. *Protokoly zasedanii Tverskogo ocherednago gubernskago zemskago sobraniia 8–17 dekabria 1895 g. i 22–29 ianvaria 1896 g.* (Tver', 1896), pp. 3–6.

48. Veselovskii, *Istoricheskii ocherk*, pp. 573–574; Timberlake, "Petrunkevich, Mikhail Il'ich."

49. I have discussed this event in "Petrunkevich, Mikhail Il'ich." All the documents on this event are included, along with others on the history of the Burashevo colony, in *Materialy dlia istorii Tverskogo Gubernskago Zemstva, 1886–1908 gg.* (vols 6–10; Tver', 1909–1913), vol. 10, vypuski 1 and 2.

50. Veselovskii, *Istoricheskii ocherk*, p. 320.

51. *Protokoly zasedanii Tverskogo ocherednago gubernskago zemskago sobraniia 8–21 ianvaria i 19–27 fevralia i ekstrennogo 20 maia 1898 g. i prilozheniia k nim* (Tver'1898), p. 90.

52. Veselovskii, *Istoricheskii ocherk*, p. 574.

53. Ibid., p. 575.

54. Ibid., p. 321.

55. Ibid., p. 575.

56. TsGIA, f. 1282, op. 3, d. 420, pp. 11–12.

57. Veselovskii, *Istoricheskii ocherk*, p. 576.

58. Ibid., p. 576.

59. Ibid., p. 576.

60. Ibid., p. 577.

61. Ibid., p. 577.

62. Veselovskii, *Istoriia zemstva za sorok let*, vol. 4, p. 563; TsGIA, f. 1282, op. 2, d. 1842, p. 44.

63. Veselovskii, *Istoricheskii ocherk*, p. 580.

64. "Obozrenie," pp. 43–67.

65. Ibid., pp. 67–76. The authors of the secret report said that Rzhev's recent history "serves as a characteristic example of the internal process by which occurs the transformation of a zemstvo board from an organ for the economic life of the county into an organ laying claim to a political role." TsGIA, f. 1282, op. 2, d. 1842, pp. 2–3.

66. "Obozrenie," pp. 43–67.

67. Veselovskii, *Istoricheskii ocherk*, p. 581.

68. Anastasia Sergeevna Petrunkevich to Alexander Ivanovich Petrunkevich, January 30, Old Style/February 12, New Style 1904. Box 1, Alexander Petrunkevich Collection, Yale University Library. The Russians used the Julian calendar before 1918. This calendar was thirteen days behind the Western Gregorian calendar. Therefore, dates of events in Russia are often cited in the West with designations OS and NS or simply an earlier and later date, separated by a slash.

69. Veselovskii, *Istoricheskii ocherk*, p. 582.

70. Ibid., p. 582.

71. *Pravitel'stvennyi vestnik*, 1904, no. 12.

72. Veselovskii, *Istoricheskii ocherk*, pp. 582–583.

73. Ibid., p. 582.

74. I have analyzed in some detail the development of the service staff in Tver' Province in "The Zemstvo and the Development of a Russian Middle Class," in Edith W. Clowes, Samuel D. Kassow, and James L. West, eds., *Between Tsar and People: Educated*

Society and the Quest for Public Identity in Late Imperial Russia (Princeton, NJ: Princeton University Press, 1991), pp. 164–179.

75. Veselovskii, *Istoricheskii ocherk*, 577–578. The Tver' Provincial Zemstvo Board authorized publication in 1904 (by an author who identified himself only as "V. L.") of a short sketch explaining its increased activities in various areas of zemstvo affairs: *Ocherk deiatel'nosti Tverskogo gubernskago zemstva po sodeistviiu razvitiiu ekonomicheskago blagosostoianiia naseleniia 1866–1903 g.* (Moscow: I. N. Kushnerev, 1904). Approximately the last half of this 97-page book is devoted to the period from 1890 to 1903.

3

The Zemstvo and the Transformation of Russian Society

Thomas Porter
North Carolina Agricultural and Technical State University

William Gleason
Doane College

Until recently there were relatively few scholarly accounts devoted to
the upsurge of public activity in late Imperial Russia from the turn of
the century through to the collapse of the Romanov dynasty.[1] The
omission was curious since these years saw some significant developments in Russia's brief history of public participation in governance.
Whereas formerly doubts concerning the possibility of Russia's peaceful evolution, such as those evinced by professors Leopold Haimson and
Theodore H. Von Laue, had seemingly carried the day, recent research
suggests that the surge of reform that swept through both town and
countryside during the period under review led to a clear commitment
on the part of Russia's "middle" groups to civic activity and the regen-
eration of Russian social and political life.[2]

   This chapter adds to that now steadily growing body of works devoted to the study of the development of the professions brought about by
an increase in the public activity of Russia's educated elites, as well as to
an investigation of the search for an identity apart from the traditional *soslovie* system undertaken by nascent middle groups in Russian society—
the liberal *zemtsy* (elected zemstvo representatives) in the countryside
and especially their hired employees. These endeavors ultimately ended
the tsarist regime's paternal rule over both town and countryside and led

to the development of a public sphere. This remarkable transformation of Russia's sociopolitical order was made possible by the beginnings of a civil society.

The concept of civil society has surfaced as a useful analytical device for investigating the dynamics of modernization.[3] Notwithstanding the fact that the term "civil society" has been used in a variety of ways, there are certain definitional constants, among them a society with an abundance of voluntary associations and one in which professional elements have acquired autonomous structures vis-à-vis the state. In his treatise *Democracy in America*, Alexis de Tocqueville noted that both voluntary associations and independent institutions of local self-government serve to promote the development of an open, or civil, society. Voluntary associations exemplify the ideals of public service and philanthropy, while independent organs of local self-government provide for citizen participation in governance; they are both essential preconditions for the development of a public sphere. Tocqueville also noted the close ties between them: "Civil associations pave the way for political ones, but on the other hand, the art of political association singularly develops and improves this technique for civil purpose."[4]

These elements, voluntary associations and autonomously situated professional classes, exist within a larger nexus of political institutions, labor groups, business groups, and so forth that are fundamental in constituting the nuclei for political pluralism. An important step toward this end was society's attempt to limit the bureaucratic tsarist state's interference in both the economic and social realms. Of course, the fragmentation and isolation of the nascent middle class, composed both of non-noble professionals and those zemtsy who actively sought to integrate the peasantry into Russia's incipient civil society through the evisceration of its society of orders, served to thwart the emergence of middle-class identity.

In addition, the bourgeoisie's dependence upon the government as the principal agent of economic expansion and the zemstvos' reliance upon not only the largesse of the government but also on its monopoly on executive authority weakened still further those patterns of coherency and cooperation that did manage to manifest themselves. Thus, the middle class retained a "Janus-like" relationship with the regime; that is, it accepted the legitimacy of the state as the motor force of development while simultaneously seeking to free itself from the government's over-weening nature. At best then, the state-society link, symbolized by the professions, was one of "reciprocal ambivalency," and as a result Russia remained an immature and incomplete civil society.[5]

However, the middle class and the more liberal element of Russia's privileged elite ultimately succeeded in forcing the regime to cede much of its authority to society; historians are now searching for meaningful parallels between the social and political changes in contemporary Russia on the one hand, and on the other, the revolution of modernization that reached its peak in the first decade of the twentieth century, but was finally aborted in 1917. Was a civil society emerging in the last years of Russia's ancien regime, one which might reassert itself more fully in to-day's Russia? If so, we need to reexamine the past in order to suggest that the contemporary manifestations of public identity have deep roots that survived three quarters of a century of communism.

Recent scholarship along these lines has largely discredited the paradigm that made invidious comparisons between a "backward" Russia with its inert society and an idealized "West" which had tapped into the initiative and dynamism of its entrepreneurial classes.[6] The history of Imperial Russia should not be viewed as being sui generis, but instead as being within the context of European history. Thus, we should continue to look for evidence of a civil society and the development of a public sphere as Russia moved away, however slowly, from a service state with its society of orders toward a modern polity.[7]

This argument, first advanced by Marc Raeff, holds that the differ-ent concepts of natural law posited by the French Enlightenment ulti-mately led to friction between, on the one hand, an increasingly independent nobility and nascent middle class, and on the other, a state that still held to an ethos grounded in the German *Aufklärung*. The con-flict arose over the role that should be allotted to society in the govern-ment's quest for the cooperation of the public in order to resolve the social problems that inevitably arise in modernizing societies.[8] In the well-ordered police states of the German lands citizens received rights according to the duties that they performed for the polity; however, the savants of the French Enlightenment held that men had inalienable rights independent of their duty to the government.

This clash of ideas was instrumental in laying the groundwork for the conflict between elements of the bureaucracy (in particular the Ministry of Internal Affairs) and the emerging public sphere, as the last two Tsars remained wedded to the concept of an *état bien police* and never accepted the political consequences of modernization, while educated society moved away from *Rechtstaat* liberalism to constitutional liberalism.[9]

Ironically, the regime would continue to espouse outdated ideals and extol the virtues of autocracy while pursuing a modernization process that would fundamentally alter Russian society. Peter the Great's efforts to modernize Russia had borne much the same fruit; his efforts to graft Western technology onto a fundamentally different system of governance had sown the seeds of social and political pluralism by exposing the elite to the dynamic models of Western polities. Just as Peter the Great had virtually created a Westernized elite that began to demand a larger role in the governance of Russia and an extension of its privileges, the last Tsars' programs of modernization called into existence a middle class that would demand an end to the restrictions imposed upon it by the state.

In both cases, however, a schism ensued between the elites and Russia's peasant masses. So one must begin by acknowledging the obvious: the demographic reality of an overwhelmingly agrarian order overlaid with a small middle class and an even smaller gentry class, the latter bereft of its social underpinnings since the Great Reforms of the 1860s. At the same time, however, there were crosscurrents. By the turn of the century, for example, cities in European Russia were experiencing soaring rates of growth and social diversification, which implied the possibility of public identities more nearly in line with Western models. Thus, in 1912 the Moscow city directory listed about 600 independent associations and private groups devoted to civic improvement. Writing about the proliferation of voluntary associations in Moscow on the eve of World War I, Joseph Bradley concludes that these civic-minded, independent associations "contributed significantly to the formation of sensibilities commonly thought of as middle-class in Western Europe and North America."[10]

The educated men and women who participated in these associations took great pride in their professional qualifications and they demanded that responsibility for the common weal be shared between the government and its citizens. In addition, zemstsy—activists in the organs of local self-government—were calling for an increase in these organs' sphere of competence and the right to form an independent national association to coordinate public activity. The nexus between these two societal groups were the non-noble technical specialists employed by the zemstvos—the so-called Third Element.

By the turn of the century zemstvos employed over 70,000 of these specialists—statisticians, agronomists, veterinarians, teachers, doctors, etc.—who considered themselves to be engaged in public service as opposed to those who were in the tsarist civil service.[11] In addition, these professional men and women, whatever their social origins, did not think of themselves as being members of the soslovie system because the preemancipation system of social orders and their traditional assemblies no longer fit a rapidly modernizing Russia with its emerging middle class and the myriad voluntary and professional associations in cultural, social, and economic spheres.[12] Civil society provides for just such an interlocking network of nonpolitical relations among various groups that carry out economic and social functions independently of the state.

And since the nobility was no longer tied to the autocracy through the former symbiotic relationship that characterized the old regime, many noblemen would continue to press for an extension of their right to participate in the governance of the nation. When the zemstvos were introduced into the provinces and counties of European Russia in 1864, the government had hoped that a single, integrated bureaucratic apparatus had been formed that would enable the regime to provide for the welfare of its subjects. The zemstvos were to administer particular state functions because it was believed that they would simply be more efficient; there would be no independent activity by the organs of local self-government. There would be merely a deconcentration of power wherein the bureaucracy would retain control but assign specific functions to the zemstvos.[13] Many zemtsy, however, drew distinctions between state affairs and society's interests; they would demand a devolution of governing authority and the removal of the prohibition on interzemstvo contacts.

The chief architect of the Zemstvo Statute of January 1, 1862, was Minister of Internal Affairs P. A. Valuev. Although not opposed to the idea of public participation in governance, his principal concerns were to maintain the primacy of the bureaucracy (and in particular that of his own ministry) and to stifle the requests made by society for more autonomy and jurisdiction in local affairs. Valuev wanted to ensure that the role allotted to society would be minimal. He considered the zemstvo to be

> only a special organ of one and the same state power and from it [that state power] receives its rights and authority; the zemstvo institutions, having their place in the state organism, are not able to exist outside of it and, equally with other institutions, are subject to those general conditions and to that general guidance which are established by the state authority.[14]

Zemstvos were established in thirty-four of the provinces of European Russia and their counties. These institutions consisted of an assembly (which was to have decision-making powers) elected for a three-year term and an executive board to implement policies. The statute defined the duties of zemstvos as the management of "local economic welfare and needs" with fourteen different areas of jurisdiction.[15] Article 3 of both the 1864 and 1890 zemstvo statutes forbade activity beyond the borders of the particular county or province concerned (although provincial zemstvos were allowed to coordinate intercounty endeavors such as road building). This provision was designed to ensure that zemstvos would have no lateral contacts and would therefore be only a link in the administrative chain stretching from St. Petersburg to the countryside. In addition, zemstvos were reliant upon local tsarist officials to enforce those laws which were implemented.

The zemtsy, however, understood that the massive problems that beset Russia could not be addressed without the active and coordinated participation of the educated public. The statutes' nebulous language was in part responsible for the friction that developed between state and society. Some responsibilities were transferred in their entirety to zemstvos for management with zemstvos acting as the government's agents. Zemstvos were given the authority "to look after" the development of trade and industry, but allowed only the opportunity "to cooperate" with the government in preventing cattle diseases and preserving crops from destruction by insects. They were also granted the right "to participate . . . mainly in economic terms" in the management of public health and education. This vague language left the zemtsy to wonder what the limits of participation and cooperation were. Valuev's intention to utilize zemstvos merely as an extension of the bureaucratic apparatus is made evident by the statute's requirement that they assist "in the fulfillment of demands which might be placed upon them by the civil and military administration."[16]

More important, however, was the fact that the elective principle was inaugurated. In keeping with the emancipation's intention of making the peasants "free rural inhabitants," elections for zemstvos were based on the type of property held and not on the estate to which the voter formerly belonged. All males over the age of twenty-five who held (1) private rural property, (2) private urban property, or (3) allotment land (land entrusted to peasant communes in order to keep the peasantry from falling into peonage) were eligible to vote in one of these three curiae. Peasants who held private rural property were allowed to vote in the first curia. This gave further legal sanction to the peasants' new status in society; Russia was emerging from its society of orders to a nation composed of socioeconomic classes with all of its citizens equal before the law.

In addition, many zemtsy called for "the crowning of the edifice" with an all-Russian zemstvo. This political body would be the equivalent of a national representative assembly. No wonder, then, that a deadly struggle ensued between state and society over the next four decades. In 1866 the Senate reaffirmed the prohibition contained in the statute on interzemstvo contacts.[16] In December of the same year provincial governors were given the right to refuse to confirm in office persons elected by the assemblies but considered "unreliable" by the authorities.[17] Clashes also occurred over the issue of taxation powers. The statute had granted only limited tax powers to zemstvos, the result of Valuev's intention to hold down their revenues and thus force them to be dependent on government largesse.

Another decree promulgated on June 13, 1867, was designed to bring zemstvos more fully under state control. The law gave the chairmen of zemstvo assemblies sweeping new powers. These included the right to exclude topics from the agenda that were considered to be outside of zemstvo competence.[18] The chairmen, who were usually conservative noblemen serving in that capacity ex officio due to their having been elected as marshals of the now theoretically anachronistic provincial corporate bodies of the nobility, would henceforth be held responsible for the conduct of the delegates and the content of their proposals. This law in effect made the chairmen governmental representatives, thus realizing the bureaucracy's longstanding goal of manifesting its presence on the local level.

The government did, however, occasionally allow regional congresses to convene in order to deal with pressing problems. During the Russo-Turkish War of 1877 the regime permitted several provincial zemstvos to act jointly in order to succor the wounded. In December 1880 a congess met in Khar'kov to discuss measures to be taken to combat a diphtheria outbreak; in February 1881 another congress was allowed to meet in Odessa because of the need to take steps to alleviate damage caused by an infestation of crop-damaging beetles.[19] These problems were of such magnitude that they knew no boundaries and it was conceded that interregional cooperation was necessary to ensure the maximum efficiency of operations.

The government wanted to ensure that it retained its control over zemstvos and sought to integrate them more fully into the bureaucratic apparatus. The assassination of Alexander II in 1881 had brought his deeply conservative son to the throne. A new zemstvo statute was issued on June 12, 1890. The imperial decree that accompanied the introduction of the statute underscored the regime's intention merely to deconcentrate governing powers; it explained that the 1864 statute had been modified so that zemstvos "in proper unity with other governmental institutions could carry out with greater success the important state business entrusted to them."[20]

The revised statute underscored this point. Article 1 of the 1864 statute had defined the duties of zemstvos to be "the management of local economic welfare and needs." The corresponding article in the 1890 statute read simply "local welfare and needs." The word "economic" was dropped because proponents of zemstvo independence had argued that economic interests did not come under the purview of the state and that interzemstvo contacts were necessary to address effectively Russia's economic needs (this, despite the fact that economic development in Russian history had always been state sponsored and directed toward specific state ends).

Article 118 stipulated that all members of zemstvo executive boards at both the county and provincial levels had to be confirmed in office; all members of the executive boards and county executive board chairmen had to be approved by the governor of the province; the chairmen of the provincial executive boards had to be confirmed by the Minister of Internal Affairs. Article 119 of the statute provided for the appointment of chairmen by the minister himself if those men who had been chosen by the assemblies were not confirmed in office a second time. Finally, the government's intention to force zemstvos to be simply organs of state administration was shown by the requirement of Article 124, which declared that all members of executive boards were to be considered in the state's service.[21]

Even more significant was the fact that the 1890 statute abolished the "nonclass" character of the zemstvo and curtailed the elective principle insofar as the peasantry was concerned. The new law was designed to once again make the nobility into a bulwark for the regime and to freeze the sociopolitical evolution. However, at the same time economic and educational progress were making Russian society increasingly fluid.

As modernization accelerated, the archaic division of Russian society into estates simply ceased to have meaning; many noblemen took up professions and sought either employment with or election to zemstvos as they came to represent autonomous society and the idea of public service as opposed to civil service. Many younger members of the nobility were joined by other technical specialists, doctors, veterinarians, agronomists, and statisticians in forming an ethos of independent public initiative.

After Nicholas II came to the throne in 1894 yet another wave of agitation for the creation of a national representative body and more authority for zemstvos swept over Russia. It was led by Dmitrii Shipov, chairman of the Moscow provincial zemstvo board, who knew that some type of national organization was necessary for the successful defense of the public's sphere of action and the independence of local self-government.[22] Shipov was determined to emancipate the zemstvo from state tutelage. He presided over a series of conferences ("Shipov congresses") attended by likeminded zemtsy who called for the end of governmental supervision over their activities, the extension of zemstvo jurisdiction to all local needs, and most important, "the right to contact one another as well as to hold all-zemstvo congresses of representatives."[23]

However, Minister of Internal Affairs Viacheslav Pleve thought that his ministry should coordinate public activity and that "neither the Russian people in general nor the educated circles in particular were sufficiently well-trained to be allowed to govern their country or even to take an extensive part in the government . . . the most efficient way to ensure the future peaceful and systematic development of Russia would be to perfect the state machinery."[24]

Tsar Nicholas sent a reprimand to the participants, warning that "one more attempt on their part to bring about unity of action by the zemstvo institutions . . . and especially further attempts to incite the zemstvo assemblies to discuss all-Russian affairs would lead to their being barred from activity in public institutions."[25]

The regime still hoped to force zemstvos to act within the framework of the zemstvo statute. In effect, this would result in zemstvos' acting as the local representatives of the tsarist government.

Pleve then attempted to co-opt Shipov and other moderate zemtsy such as Prince Georgii E. L'vov into the governmental apparatus by suasion. He invited Shipov to visit him at his dacha on July 2, 1902. Pleve began the meeting by stressing his interest in cooperating with educated society. He noted that "no state structure is imaginable without the participation of society in local self-government."[26] Pleve promised to begin a series of meetings with Shipov and other leading public figures that apparently had the dual purpose of encouraging local activity while increasing the supervisory functions of the central government over this activity. Pleve hoped that this would bring zemstvos to work exclusively for state interests and forestall any further attempts at forming an independent national organization since the Ministry of Internal Affairs itself would function as one. In a revealing statement to Shipov in April 1903, Pleve said that "our conferences in the ministry on the basis of practical matters draw you together with representatives of the ministry, facilitate common work and mutual interaction." He added that this was "far better than those secret meetings."[27]

Pleve's attempt to subordinate the "zemstvo idea" to the needs of the state met with massive opposition. Pleve fought back by dealing harshly with anyone he thought might try to politicize the zemstvos. Administrative exile and deprivation of political rights, including the right to participate in public affairs, were the main weapons that he employed.

Another tactic the government frequently resorted to was the refusal to confirm elected zemstvo officials; between 1900 and 1905, twenty-two elected officials were denied confirmation.[28] By 1903 Shipov had concluded that Pleve was "a man without conscience and a sense of honor . . . who believes it possible to deal with everyone through lies and hypocrisy."[29] Pleve remained firmly convinced that his absorption of the zemstvo would lead to the perfection of the state apparatus. But the outbreak of war with Japan in January 1904 would force the government to allow the zemtsy more latitude.

Shipov and the other zemtsy immediately offered their services to the government. They met in Moscow to form a united zemstvo union in order to render assistance to the troops. Representatives from eleven provinces attended.

Pleve, however, thought that this was little more than a conspiracy against the throne. He immediately issued a circular to his officials in which he ordered them to block any meetings that took place without prior written permission.[30] He also refused to confirm Shipov's recent reelection as chairman of the Moscow provincial zemstvo board. This was a direct response to Shipov's continuing efforts to defend the independence of local self-government and to form an interregional zemstvo union. Pleve admitted in an interview with Shipov:

> I consider your activity harmful . . . in the political sense. When one speaks about political harmfulness, . . . one usually has in mind political unreliability, conspirative revolutionary activity, etc. In your case, however, this does not even arise. I consider your activity harmful in the political sense because you consistently strive for the widening of the competence and sphere of activity of the public institutions and for the establishment of an organization which would bring about the unification of the activities of zemstvo institutions in various provinces.[31]

The zemtsy were shocked when its well-intentioned relief efforts were thwarted by the bureaucracy. Paul Miliukov, the famous liberal leader, recounts hearing a military officer complain: "Is not every spontaneous action doomed? Is there any room left for conscious patriotism? Has not even the humble attempt of the self-governing assemblies to unite in helping the sick and wounded been denounced as criminal, and forbidden by Pleve?"[32]

At this point the zemtsy decided "to turn personally and directly to the Tsar."[33] Prince Georgii E. L'vov, then chair of the Tula provincial zemstvo executive board and future prime minister of the Provisional Government after the collapse of the monarchy, met with Nicholas II and received permission to form a national association, the General Zemstvo Organization (*Obshchezemskaia Organizatsiia*), which would draw its personnel and funds from participating zemstvos. Since joint zemstvo activity was still proscribed by law, it was "resolved that each provincial zemstvo would organize its own medical detachments completely independent of each other, equipping them with all the necessary supplies, and inviting the assistance of local persons."[34]

Fourteen provincial zemstvos agreed to post representatives in Moscow to draw up relief plans and "to facilitate the organization of doctors' conferences for the preliminary discussion of questions of a technical nature."[35] The organization's executive commission set to work compiling a list of the necessary equipment for each medical detachment. This list was then scrutinized by the commission's doctors to ensure that essential medicines and other vital supplies were made available. The Tula, Orel, and Moscow provincial detachments were ready to go within three weeks. But the majority of the provincial zemstvos required two months of feverish activity to prepare their units for departure. One reason for the delay was the fact that decisions taken by the association's executive commission had to be transmitted to the other provincial zemstvo boards for confirmation. This administrative procedure complicated affairs; it also undermined the raison d'être for the association—the coordination of independent zemstvo relief efforts.

Of course, the very existence of an association such as the General Zemstvo Organization was a significant step toward that end, but the zemtsy evidently hoped that this procedure would serve to diffuse the animosity with which they were viewed by many bureaucrats in St. Petersburg. By sending the resolutions of the executive commission back to the provincial zemstvo boards for final approval, the zemtsy were working within the parameters established by the zemstvo statute. The zemtsy, however, had decided to maintain complete fiscal independence so as to operate without government supervision.

The various provincial zemstvos therefore had to vote funds for their detachments. Khar'kov and Penza combined for an initial outlay of 281,000 rubles; the Moscow zemstvo combined with that of Tambov to earmark 250,000 rubles for their detachments; Kursk and Voronezh voted 100,000 rubles, Chernigov contributed 80,000 rubles; Tula voted 75,000 rubles, and Yaroslavl', Orel, and Kostroma all voted 50,000 rubles for their respective medical detachments. The total amount raised by society was a remarkable 1,036,000 rubles.[36] In addition, many private firms and businesses donated items to the organization. For example, tents were provided by the company of Gurevich, Pikhlau, and Brandt; pharmaceuticals were donated by Byl'ev and Vinogradov; and pots and pans were supplied by Miuller and Fugelzang. Nestlé . . . supplied milk, and Rattsel sent canned meats.

The General Zemstvo Organization equipped twenty-one medical units with 1,050 available beds. Included among the organization's 360 personnel were 10 commissioners (8 of whom volunteered to work gratis), 43 doctors, 9 accountants, 42 medical assistants, 100 nurses, 24 cooks, 92 orderlies, and 40 laundresses.[37] On average, the detachments' 7,400 verst journey (approximately 5,180 miles) to Harbin by rail took a little over a month. The trip was marked by oppressive heat, poor sanitary conditions, a monotonous diet, and inactivity. When the various units finally arrived in the Far East between May 15 and June 22, 1904, their personnel were usually "in quite a depressed mood."[38]

Upon arrival, the detachments were quickly stationed at twenty-mile intervals along the roads and railroads leading from the front. Two fully equipped zemstvo hospitals were established in Harbin. The zemtsy also provided four medical trains to aid in the transport of the wounded from Harbin to Irkutsk. The medical units began immediately to receive the Tsar's wounded soldiers. Sisters of Mercy washed, fed, and changed their dressings. The secretary took down their names and other vital information such as hometown, next of kin, etc. They were then placed in one of the wards. This routine took less than two hours per trainload. Early the following morning the wounded would be fed and washed again. Medicines that had been prepared overnight in the pharmacy were distributed. The soldiers were then reloaded onto the trains for the next stage of their journey northward to the hospitals and evacuation points in Harbin.

From Harbin the more seriously wounded were sent to Vladivostok in order to board Red Cross medical ships for the long voyage home, but most of the men boarded zemstvo medical trains for the trip home via the Chinese Eastern and Trans-Siberian Railways. This made necessary close cooperation between the Red Cross, the army's medical-sanitation corps, and the zemtsy.

From the start the zemtsy enjoyed a good working relationship with the army; General Kuropatkin, commander of the Russian armies in the field, soon became a staunch supporter of the zemstvo units and even contributed 50,000 rubles to the organization when Prince L'vov complained about a cash flow problem.[39]

Kuropatkin also sent a telegram to the Minister of Internal Affairs in which he testified to the useful and selfless activity of the zemstvo units. The text of the telegram was reprinted in *Pravitel'stvennyi vestnik* (*The Government Messenger*). Kuropatkin even expressed a desire for an increase in the number of these units. By this time there were portents of change in Russia's political weather; a terrorist bomb had killed Pleve in July 1904. His replacement was Prince P. D. Sviatopolk-Mirskii. He recognized the need for cooperation between state and society and in an interview with a French newspaper declared that the government would give zemstvos the broadest possible freedoms.

Sviatopolk-Mirskii soon gave official sanction to the General Zemstvo Organization. In one of his first speeches he said that the government "in light of the increased need for the relief of sick and wounded troops . . . does not want to act as an obstacle to the implementation of the relief efforts which are arising as a result of the united effort on the part of the zemstvos."[40]

This spirit of compromise was like a breath of fresh air to the zemtsy. The Tsar had finally appointed a minister who was not hostile to the "zemstvo idea." Prince L'vov was asked to visit Sviatopolk-Mirskii to request formally that all restrictions on the association be removed. A few weeks later the following announcement was published in *Pravitel'stvennyi vestnik*:

> By order of His Imperial Majesty, the Minister of Internal Affairs in circular no. 26, dated October 6, has notified the provincial governors that in view of the need to increase relief measures for the sick and wounded troops the circular which forbade joint zemstvo activity is to be disregarded. All future efforts by the zemstvos are to be encouraged, including contributions for the further development of

those activities being conducted by the zemstvo medical-sanitation units, and the formation of new ones.[41]

Not only did Sviatopolk-Mirskii welcome zemstvos' initiatives concerning joint relief efforts, he was not adverse to their holding national congresses to coordinate their independent activities. The regularity of these meetings throughout 1904 (June, July, September, October, and November) testifies to the government's acceptance of the need for interregional zemstvo contacts. However, Sviatapolk-Mirskii only approved of congresses that were devoted to a discussion of "technical zemstvo affairs."[42]

As is well known, the famous zemstvo congress that was held in Petersburg November 6–9, 1904, did not restrict itself to such mundane matters. Both resolutions passed at the congress (the majority resolution called for the establishment of a representative assembly, the minority resolution demanded only that a consultative representative body be granted by the Tsar) noted the abnormal deficiencies that had arisen as a result of the gulf between state and society. The zemtsy complained that they had been excluded "from participating in the administration of the state" because the regime had been seeking to centralize all aspects of political life and had done so in an arbitrary manner. The zemtsy demanded that they "be put in a position where they can successfully fulfill the responsibilities appropriate for properly and broadly organized organs of local self-government."[43]

The zemtsy also unanimously adopted a resolution that was sent to their colleagues in the Far East. It read: "The conference of 104 zemstvo activists sends to all personnel of the zemstvo detachments its hearty greetings and deep gratitude for your selfless work which underscores the strength and importance of unity."[44]

Prince L'vov then delivered a report on the organization's activities; it was resolved to have the report printed and distributed to all zemstvo executive boards. As a result, several executive board chairmen expressed the desire to affiliate their provinces with the new national zemstvo association. Accordingly, new detachments were to be formed from various provincial assemblies' personnel, bringing the total number of medical-sanitation units to twenty-seven. It was anticipated that another 1,350,000 rubles would be necessary for operations in

1905; 730,000 rubles were contributed by the original fourteen provincial zemstvos; the remaining funds were allocated by the newly affiliated provinces. The congress then adjourned sine die.

A delegation of four moderates (Shipov, L'vov, M. V. Rodzianko, and P. A. Geiden) and one radical (I. I. Petrunkevich) had been elected to discuss the congress' resolution with Sviatopolk-Mirskii. But Mirskii felt that he could not meet with such a delegation because that would be tantamount to giving the congress his official sanction. Therefore, he met privately with Shipov and gave him his assurances that he would bring their resolution to the Tsar's attention.

Mirskii also submitted a reform proposal from the moderates to the Tsar. Written by Sergei Trubetskoi, the rector of Moscow University, it noted that a civil society was emerging due to the reforms enacted by Nicholas' grandfather, Alexander II. They had "marked the end of the old patrimonial order and, along with it, of the personalized notions of rulership. Russia ceased to be the personal property and fiefdom of its ruler. . . .[The concepts of] 'public interest' and 'public opinion' suggested the emergence of the impersonal state . . . with its own body politic, separate from the person of the ruler."[45]

These hopeful signs encouraged the zemtsy and the rest of educated Russia. They began a "banquet campaign" modeled on the famous Paris banquets of 1847–1848. Various cultural and professional societies held meetings at which additional resolutions were passed calling for reform. The government was forced to respond to this groundswell of public opinion; Nicholas convened a council of high officials in December 1904 to consider reforms. However, the Tsar adamantly refused to admit society into a partnership with the government. He did promise to extend the sphere of competence of the zemstvo but also warned that "zemstvo and municipal assemblies and all types of organizations and societies must not exceed their prescribed limitations."[46]

Despite these pronouncements, the Tsar had been forced to permit the zemtsy to operate independently of state control. The zemtsy in the organization undoubtedly hoped that alterations would be made in Russia's political structure, but the movement for the establishment of a national zemstvo union had been pursued in order to be better able to fulfill the demands made upon local self-government by the zemstvo statutes; of course, this would ultimately entail far-reaching political change as well. The two related movements that sprang from the establishment of the zemstvo organizations in 1864—the desire to "crown the edifice" with some sort of national assembly and the need for a zemstvo union to facilitate interregional cooperation between provinces—had come together in November 1904. After the zemstvo congress the tie between the philanthropic activity of the liberal zemtsy and the political work of the zemstvo activists and their middle-class confreres was broken.

Tikhon Polner, the secretary of the General Zemstvo Organization, wrote that "the philanthropic organization went its own way . . . its history developed independently."[47] The government's subsequent cooperation with the organization may well have been the result of that association's seemingly apolitical stance. For an entire decade one of the seemingly irreconcilable differences that separated state and society would prove to be only a minor impediment once the government recognized the benefits of allowing independent zemstvo activity. The old argument about the nature of the zemstvo institutions was at least temporarily resolved; the government realized its goal of manifesting a presence in the countryside and the zemtsy were allowed to pursue their endeavors in the social and economic realm without let or hindrance. However, in the final analysis such activity could not but take on a political coloration as the zemtsy continued to assert that state and society were indeed separate entities and that they needed each other in order to secure the brightest possible future for the Russian people.

Nevertheless, the zemtsy continued to do their utmost to succor the Tsar's soldiers during the turbulent year of 1905. During the period from May 27, 1904, to September 1, 1905, they accepted for treatment 50,385 sick and wounded soldiers. They had also rendered medical assistance to another 25,698 men for minor ailments and evacuated yet another 9,068 soldiers on zemstvo trains. The canteens set up by the organization provided hot meals for 389,579 soldiers and distributed snacks of tea and bread to an additional 71,493 men. In the last month of the relief campaign they had also supplied boiled water for 107,193 men. The total number of individuals who had received some form of assistance from the organization was 652,164. In order to pay for these endeavors, the union had disbursed the stupendous sum of 2,080,894 rubles.[48]

On August 30, 1905, another national zemstvo congress was held in Moscow where thirty-two delegates representing seventeen provinces adopted a resolution that called for the continuation of united zemstvo work. It read:

> The unification of the zemstvos has been achieved at great cost and only after considerable struggle with the administration. At the present time unification is an accomplished fact and the General Zemstvo Organization has earned a deserved reputation and represents a considerable force; it would be an egregious mistake not to make use of this. Until the present time the administration has always interpreted the zemstvo statute in such a narrow fashion as to prevent the various provincial zemstvos from exceeding the sphere of local welfare and needs. The war forced the government to accept unification and joint activity, and even with the cessation of hostilities, there are still circumstances which dictate the need for the continuation of the joint work of "Russian zemstvos."[49]

Such a circumstance was the specter of famine once again threatening Russia. A serious crop failure had stricken twenty-three provinces of European Russia. The association's executive board recommended that its efforts be turned to famine relief; the board urged that the government not lose any time in endorsing this proposal. The zemtsy thereupon voted unanimously "to organize assistance for those who are suffering from the famine."[50] In effect, the zemtsy had voted to make the General Zemstvo Organization a permanent feature of Russia's political scene.

The tsarist government was well aware of its own limitations in this regard, and, as it had in 1891 and 1892, welcomed society's initiative. Prince L'vov was invited to St. Petersburg to coordinate government and zemstvo relief efforts.[51] He agreed to undertake the famine relief campaign only if the organization was given complete operational independence. The new Minister of Internal Affairs, P. N. Durnovo, ordered provincial governors "to render all possible assistance to the zemstvo union."[52] The decrees of June 12, 1900, which had made it illegal for zemstvos to plan for famine relief or even to maintain storehouses of grain, were suspended and the governmental bodies that had been established to administer such programs were ordered to work with the association.

In effect, a compromise had been struck between state and society. During the last years of the tsarist regime certain state functions would be deconcentrated in the statist tradition, but zemstvos would be allowed to coordinate their activities and carry out their operations independent of governmental control. The government disbursed funds that eventually were transferred to the association's coffers.[53] In 1905 and 1906 the government allocated 208 million rubles for zemstvo relief operations; fully 60 percent of these monies were spent on the purchase of foodstuffs prepared by volunteers for distribution to the peasantry.[54] Zemstvos organized an impressive number of 9,711 soup kitchens and bakeries in sixteen different provinces; these facilities provided almost 120 million meals.[55]

Upon completion of the 1905–1906 famine relief campaign, thirty-eight representatives from twenty-one provinces assembled in Moscow to review their accomplishments and to plan for the future. They adopted a resolution that stated:

> Given the existing statutes and the present conditions of governmental activity, any type of participation by the General Zemstvo Organization or the various zemstvos in alimentary or domestic operations is permissible. With the change in the structure of the higher central and the local administrations as a result of the realization of a state responsible before a legally convoked body of the people's representatives, conditions are ripe for further change by which zemstvos and the General Zemstvo Organization will be able to embark on other endeavors in the alimentary or domestic areas as a result of private agreements with the government's organs until such time as revisions of the existing statute can be made.[56]

In other words, the zemtsy had accepted the compromise wherein society would be permitted to engage in independent activity on a nationwide scale in order to fulfill not only the obligations laid upon them by the zemstvo statute but also those endeavors that they themselves chose to pursue. They also recognized that this was but a first step and that ultimately a devolution of governing powers to zemstvos instead of merely the deconcentration of specific tasks would be necessary to reflect Russia's new political conditions.

Peter Stolypin, Russia's last great statesman, would largely share these sentiments and the General Zemstvo Organization therefore continued to play an important role during the years preceding the outbreak of the Great War. However, Stolypin's concept of local self-government, like the still-prevailing view that political rights depended upon the type of service rendered to the state, was also rooted in Germanic practice. In the "free community" (*freie Gemeinde*), state and society were indeed separate entities, but autonomous organs of local self-government should not expand their horizons to include any questions of a national political character.

Stolypin did, however, seek to cooperate with society until such time as his project for zemstvo reform could be realized. He presided over a governmental commission "which unanimously recognized the benefits of the further development of the activity of the General Zemstvo Organization."[57] As a result, the zemtsy drew up a new charter that underscored the significant expansion of the association's role since its inception as a voluntary medical-relief organization. The new raison d'être of the association was to provide for

> the conduct of measures in the struggle with national calamities and the rendering of assistance to the needy population including those suffering from famine, to settlers, etc. Accordingly, the General Zemstvo Organization will take action when it is apparent that separate zemstvos are unable to cope or when the nature of the activities demands unified operations.[58]

Stolypin encouraged this independent activity despite the fact that interzemstvo contacts were still proscribed by law, and he strove mightily not only to reinvigorate the organs of local self-government, but also to increase their sphere of competence.

He curtailed government supervision over zemstvos and removed the restrictions on their powers of taxation.[59] But most of his projects, such as granting enforcement powers to zemstvos and the expansion of zemstvo jurisdiction over education, the rural economy, public health, and communications, were never implemented. Some contemporary observers believed that Stolypin envisioned the creation of a federal state, but that is highly unlikely.[60]

Stolypin undoubtedly understood that educated Russian society had evolved and the time had come to allow for public opinion and participation in governance. One of his principal assistants in the Ministry of Internal Affairs, V. I. Gurko, thought that Stolypin's plans for reform, which were loosely modeled after Prussian and French administrative procedures, were too radical because he "failed to take into consideration that the French government was the outcome of public tendencies, and that it worked under the constant and vigilant supervision of an organized and well-developed public opinion."[61] More likely, Stolypin had recognized the development of a society independent of the state and, like Pleve before him, sought to co-opt part of society in order to broaden the regime's support and to make possible effective administration in the countryside. This required some compromise and Stolypin was willing to accede to many of the demands of the zemtsy.

During the "Stolypin era" (1906–1911) and the years immediately before the outbreak of the Great War, government subsidies to zemstvo agricultural enterprises increased from 3.9 million rubles to 29.2 million rubles. By 1912 the overall budget of the thirty-four zemstvo provinces was 220 million rubles, a sum more than triple their combined budget in 1895. By 1914 the total budget of forty-three provinces was 347.5 million rubles. Fully three-quarters of these funds went to health, education, and welfare; only 12 per cent went to administrative overhead.[62] The expansion of zemstvo services in turn made necessary the hiring of tens of thousands of specialists, commonly called the Third Element, to distinguish them from provincial officials and elected members of the zemstvos. For example, the number of agronomists on zemstvo payrolls rose from 422 in 1905 to 2,363 in 1909.

These members of the Third Element were certainly very different from their noble supervisors, but like the moderate zemtsy these men and women saw themselves as being public servants, as opposed to being in government service (*gosudarstvennaia sluzhba*).[63] Like the zemstvo deputies, these highly educated professionals saw themselves as being outside of the government and yet not a part of the peasant masses; accordingly, as Charles Timberlake has noted, they constituted a middle group. And this group's expertise was crucial if the government was determined to resolve the social and economic problems brought about by modernization.

One need only look at the zemstvo schools to understand how crucial the Third Element was in Russia's prewar development. In 1879, 22,767 rural schools in the provinces of European Russia employed 24,389 teachers. Thirty-two years later 62,913 teachers filled the classrooms before a new generation of learners. As Jeffrey Brooks has indicated, of all the areas of zemstvo activity, primary education showed the most impressive growth between 1880 and 1914.[64]

Stolypin surely was aware that once autonomy was granted in the matter of public participation in governance, political consequences would inevitably ensue. And yet throughout his tenure as Chair of the Council of Ministers and Minister of Internal Affairs, Stolypin allowed the General Zemstvo Organization to play a crucial role not only in famine relief and related philanthropic endeavors, but in the facilitation of peasant resettlement in Siberia as well. Stolypin's attempt to break up the commune and to create a prosperous and satisfied peasantry by giving the head of household title to his plots, which were then to be consolidated into a contiguous farmstead, has received quite a bit of attention. Of equal importance was his effort to ease the alleged "land shortage" by resettling peasants east of the Urals. Like his plan to break up the commune, Stolypin did not devise the project himself, but he was the one who instituted it most energetically.

The government's migration budget doubled from 2.5 million rubles to 5 million rubles between 1905 and 1906, and was doubled again to 11 million rubles in 1908.[65] In 1908 the Third Duma approved the allocation of 13 million rubles for this enterprise.[66] Stolypin's study of internal migration in North America had convinced him that two preconditions were necessary to address effectively the needs of settlers.[67] The first, as might be expected, was sufficient capital. The second precondition was the existence of well-organized agencies to assist the settlers during their arduous journey east. As the government's resources were stretched to the limit, the General Zemstvo Organization's offer of assistance was quickly accepted by Stolypin and Prince Vasil'chikov (the head of the Chief Administration of Land Settlement and Agriculture, the latest incarnation of the oft-reorganized Ministry of Agriculture).

Thus, in 1908 zemtsy called yet another conference in Moscow that was attended by thirty-two representatives from sixteen provinces.[68] The executive board presented Vasil'chikov's reply to the organization's offer of aid. In it Vasil'chikov requested that zemtsy organize assistance for the settlers in eastern Siberia and the Far East. The zemtsy had already heard horrifying rumors from those regions (especially the Maritime Province) and prepared to mobilize for yet another herculean effort. Their plan called for the union to reestablish its medical-alimentary stations next to the Trans-Siberian Railroad from Irkutsk to the Far East, as well as along the Amur River. They were also to send teams of doctors into newly established settlements to treat peasants for typhus and cholera.

By the end of March 1908 the organization had dispatched 160 personnel to the Far East.[69] Along the way zemtsy "dispensed medicines, fed, and in general attempted to render every possible assistance" to the settlers.[70] Eighteen detachments were scattered along the railway; however, only 75,929 meals were doled out in May and the zemtsy felt underutilized. Prince L'vov met with a General Unterberger and requested that the association be permitted to establish medical-alimentary points along the roads leading into the Priamur, the region hardest hit by disease and hunger. At first the general refused, noting that the organization had been given permission to set up their aid stations "along the railroad line, not dirt roads." L'vov pointed out that they had received permission to set up stations "throughout the settlers' ways of migration." Unterberger relented and eight more aid stations were established in the Maritime region.[71]

The 1908 resettlement campaign, which had been launched amid fanfare after quite a bit of publicity, saw 758,812 migrants cross the Urals.[72] However, only 22,607 of these made the arduous journey to Irkutsk, and only 18,475 would remain in the Far East. The zemtsy remained on station from mid-April to the end of August. They distributed 276,210 rations of food and also "decided to open medical-alimentary stations in the settlements already established in the midst of the swamplands in order to distribute flour meal, combat epidemics, and end the malnutrition which afflicted the settlers as the result of their poor diet."[73]

They also undertook to investigate the potential resources and opportunities for the agricultural and industrial development of the region. The result of this effort was a 1,000-page report by L'vov entitled *Priamur'e, fakty, tsifry, nabliudeniia* (*Along the Amur, Facts, Figures, Observations*).

He also wrote an article in *Russkie vedomosti* (*Russian News*) in which he called upon society to recognize its responsibility "and take upon itself the necessary first steps for the colonization of the region."[74]

The zemtsy continued their famine relief efforts as well, spending about 1 million rubles per year. After the death of Stolypin in 1911, however, V. N. Kokovtsov, the new Chair of the Council of Ministers, informed L'vov that he would "not allow any kind of organization to act independently of the government. . . . The role of society is to contribute funds. . . . The General Zemstvo Organization will not be permitted to participate in the struggle with famine . . . and no new endeavors will be permitted. This because the union always overreaches the limits set by the government."[75]

Kokovtsov was forced to back down when the magnitude of the famine became known. As a consequence the General Zemstvo Organization continued to operate without government sanction down to the outbreak of the First World War; society was simply too powerful to be muzzled.

During the decade of its existence (1904–1914) the General Zemstvo Organization spent over 2 million rubles on assistance to the sick and wounded soldiers of the Russo-Japanese War, another 11 million rubles on famine relief campaigns, and 1 million for the alleviation of the plight of the settlers in the Far East. The zemtsy rightly noted that the significance of their efforts could not be found in these figures, but instead lay in the fact that society had demanded and won a role in governance and that henceforth "the center (the government) would be compelled to accept societal forces in all these affairs."[76]

The expansion of the Third Element during this period had one inevitable result: its radicalization. Particularly outspoken throughout the prewar decade was the Pirogov Society of Russian Doctors, which sought to elevate the doctors' role in public health administration. Meeting in 1910, in the midst of a cholera epidemic that ultimately claimed 100,000 lives throughout the country, the Pirogov Society called for the introduction of universal suffrage, arguing that the "success of public health hinges on the unhindered activities of citizens under strong local leadership."[77] Two years later, at a conference of epidemiologists sponsored by the Pirogov Society, A. A. Chertov, a Moscow sanitary physician, castigated tsarist officials for their handling of the antiepidemic measures. He demanded the creation of a uniform system of municipal and zemstvo sanitary councils, to be composed of medical representatives "empowered to enforce sanitary laws." The ultimate remedy was a political one in the form of the enfranchisement of the Third Element if Russia was to avoid disaster in the future.[78] Little did Chertov realize how prophetic that prediction was to become a few years later.

NOTES

1. A much condensed version of this chapter and its companion in chapter 8, "The Democratization of the Zemstvo During the First World War," without the broader set of interpretive claims contained herein, first appeared in *Russian History*, vol. 21, no. 4, pp. 419–437, 1994, under the title "The Zemstvo and Public Initiative in Late Imperial Russia."

2. Leopold Haimson's famous article "The Problem of Social Stability in Urban Russia, 1905–1917," which appeared in the field's flagship journal *Slavic Review* in December 1964 and March 1965, first posited the thesis that society was so afraid of revolution that it was unwilling to force social and political reforms from the regime lest such an effort spark the conflagration; Theodore H. Von Laue's classic *Why Lenin? Why Stalin?* (New York: Lippincott) which also appeared in 1964, echoed Haimson's argument by concluding that there was no chance whatsoever for Russia's peaceful evolution due to the rapid pace of industrialization that had separated the educated elites from the people. Recent research, such as that of Adele Lindenmeyer in her *Poverty Is Not A Vice: Charity, Society and the State in Imperial Russia* ([Princeton, NJ: Princeton University Press, 1996) and the work of Michael Hamm (*Kiev: A Portrait, 1800–1917* (Princeton, NJ: Princeton University press, 1993)], and "Kharkov's Progressive Duma, 1910–1914: A Study in Russian Municipal Reform," which also appeared in the *Slavic Review* in the spring of 1981), suggests that educated society was in fact becoming increasingly active and reformist and that a civil society was in the making.

3. For a thorough treatment of the concept of a "civil society," see John Keane, ed., *Civil Society and the State: New European Perspectives* (New York: Verso, 1988).

4. Alexis de Tocqueville, *Democracy in America*, ed. Phillips Bradley (New York: Vintage Press, 1945), vol. 2, pp. 114–123.

5. The phrase "reciprocal ambivalency" comes from an insightful essay by Harley Balzer on the conditions of Russia's professions in the early 1900s. See "The Problem of Professions in Imperial Russia," in Edith W. Clowes, Samuel D. Kassow, and James L. West, eds., *Between Tsar and People: Educated Society and the Quest for Public Identity in Late Imperial Russia* (Princeton, NJ: Princeton University Press, 1991), pp. 183–199.

6. See the discussion centered around this interpretation published as a conference report by Jane Burbank entitled "Revisioning Imperial Russia" in *Slavic Review*, vol. 52, no. 3 (1993), pp. 555–567.

7. For an inquiry into the nature of this historical phenomenon one needs only to consult Jurgen Habermas' *The Structural Transformation of the Public Sphere* (Cambridge, MA: MIT Press, 1989).

8. Marc Raeff, *Imperial Russia, 1682–1825: The Coming of Age of Modern Russia* (New York: Knopf, 1971), pp. 140–141.

9. Terence Emmons, *The Russian Landed Gentry and the Peasant Emancipation of 1861* (Cambridge: Cambridge University Press, 1968), pp. 417–418.

10. Joseph Bradley, "Voluntary Associations, Civil Culture and *Obshchestvennost'* in Moscow," in Clowes, Kassow, and West, eds., *Between Tsar and People*, p. 146.

11. B. B. Veselovskii, *Istoriia zemstva za sorok let*, 4 vols. (St. Petersburg, 1911), vol. 3, p. 465.

12. Charles Timberlake makes this point in his "The *Zemstvo* and the Development of a Russian Middle Class," in Clowes, Kassow and West, eds., *Between Tsar and People*, pp. 164–179.

13. The arguments over state control versus local initiative are discussed in S. Frederick Starr, *Decentralization and Self-Government in Russia, 1830–1870* (Princeton, NJ: Princeton University Press, 1972), pp. 69–70, 71, 75, 83–88; W. Bruce Lincoln, *In the Vanguard of Reform: Russia's Enlightened Bureaucrats 1825–1861* (DeKalb: Northern Illinois University Press, 1972), pp. 172, 177, 183–186; and Thomas S. Pearson, *Russian Officialdom in Crisis: Autocracy and Local Self-Government, 1861–1900* (Cambridge: Cambridge University Press, 1989), pp. 10–13, 39–59, passim.

14. Quoted in V. V. Garmiza, *Podgotovka zemskoi reformy, 1864 g.* (Moscow, 1957), p. 203.

15. *Polnoe sobranie zakonov Rossiiskoi Imperii* [hereafter *PSZ*], Sobranie vtoroc (St. Petersburg, 1876), vol. 39, no. 40457, January 1, 1864.

16. Ibid.

17. Veselovskii, *Istoriia zemstva za sorok let*, vol. 3, pp. 126–127.

18. Garmiza, *Podgotovka*, p. 251.

19. *PSZ*, Vtoroe, vol. 42, no. 44690, June 13, 1867.

20. Veselovskii, *Istoriia zemstva za sorok let*, vol. 3, p. 248.

21. *PSZ*, Sobranie tret'e, (St. Petersburg, 1890), vol. 10, no. 6922, June 12, 1890.

22. Ibid., no. 6927.

23. D. N. Shipov, *Vospominaniia i dumy o perezhitom* (Moscow: S. P. Iakovlev, 1918), pp. 52–58.

24. Ibid.

25. V. I. Gurko, *Features and Figures of the Past* (Stanford: Stanford University Press, 1939), p. 109.

26. Shipov, *Vospominaniia*, p. 169.

27. Quoted in Shipov, *Vospominaniia*, pp. 174–175.

28. Ibid., p. 220.

29. Veselovskii, *Istoriia zemstva za sorok let*, vol. 3, pp. 347, 357–358.

30. Shipov, *Vospominaniia*, p. 227.

31. Veselovskii, *Istoriia*, vol. 3, p. 592.

32. Shipov, *Vospominaniia*, p. 234.

33. P. N. Miliukov, *Russia and its Crisis* (New York: Collier Books, 1906), p. 221.

34. T. I. Polner, *Zhiznennyi put' Kniazia G. E. L'vova* (Paris, 1932), p. 66.

35. *Desiatiletiye obshchezemskoi organizatsii blagotvoritel'noi pomoshchi naseleniia, 1904–1914 gg.* (Moscow: Tipografiia Russkogo Tovarishchestva, 1914), p. 4.

36. *Obshchezemskaia organizatsiia na dal'nem vostoke* (Moscow: Tipografiia Russkogo Tovarishchestva, 1908), vol. 1, p. 19.

37. Ibid., p. 51.

38. Ibid., p. 59.

39. Ibid., p. 79.

40. Polner, *Zhiznennyi put'*, p. 79.

41. Veselovskii, *Istoriia zemstva za sorok let*, vol. 3, p. 592.

42. *Obshchezemskaia*, vol. 2, p. 55.

43. George Fischer, *Russian Liberalism* (Cambridge: Harvard University Press, 1958), p. 178.

44. I. P. Belokonskii, *Zemskoe dvizhenie* (Moscow, 1911), pp. 139–140.

45. *Obshchezemskaia*, vol. 2, p.65.

46. Andrew Verner, "Nicholas II and the Role of the Autocrat During the First Russian Revolution, 1904–1907" (Ph.D Dissertation, Columbia University, 1968), pp. 193–194.

47. S. S. Oldenburg, *Last Tsar! Nicholas II, His Reign and His Russia* (Gulf Breeze, FL: Academic International Press), vol. 2, p. 100.

48. Polner, *Zhiznennyi put'*, p. 131.

49. *Obshchezemskaia*, vol. 2, p. 451.

50. Ibid., pp. 398–340.

51. Ibid., p. 400.

52. Polner, *Zhiznennyi put'*, p. 132.

53. Ibid., p. 134.

54. *Izvestiia obshchezemskoi organizatsii*, vol. 1, October 14, 1905, p. 22.

55. *Otchet upravleniia delami obshchezemskoi organizatsii po okazaniiu prodovol'stvenno-blagotvoritel'noi pomoshchi naseleniia mestnostei, porazhennykh ot neurozhaia v 1905 g.* (Moscow: Tipografiia Russkogo Tovarishchestva, 1909), p. 25.

56. Ibid., p. 7.

57. *Izvestiia*, vol. 7, June 1–July 1, 1906, p. xii.

58. *Desiatiletiye*, p. 15.

59. Ibid., p. 23.

60. Mary Schaeffer Conroy, "Stolypin's Attitude Toward Local Self-Government," *Slavonic and East European Review*, vol. 46, no. 107 (1968) pp. 451–452.

61. A. V. Zenkovsky, *Stolypin: Russia's Last Great Reformer* (Princeton, NJ: Kingston Press, 1986).

62. Neil Weisman, *Reform in Tsarist Russia: The State Bureaucrcay and Local Government* (New Brunswick, NJ: Rutgers University Press, 1981), p. 146.

63. S. G. Pushkarev, *Self-Government and Freedom in Russia* (Boulder: Westview Press, 1988) p. 58.

64. Timberlake, "The *Zemstvo* and the Development of a Russian Middle Class," p. 178.

65. Jeffrey Brooks, "The *Zemstvo* and the Education of the People," in Terrence Emmons and Wayne Vucinich, eds., *The Zemstvo in Russia* (New York: Cambridge University Press, 1982), p. 255.

66. Donald W. Treadgold, *The Great Siberian Migration* (Princeton, NJ: Princeton University Press, 1957), p. 192.

67. Idem.

68. P. Stolypin and A. Krivoshein, *Poezdka v Sibir' i po volzhe* (St. Petersburg, 1911).

69. *Desiatiletiye*, p. 22.

70. *Ocherk deiatel'nosti zemskoi obshchestvenno-blagotvoritel'noi organizatsii pomoshchi pereselentsam v pereselencheskuiu kampaniiu 1908 goda* (Moscow, 1908), p. 2.

71. Polner, *Zhiznennyi*, p. 141.

72. Ibid., p. 142.

73. Treadgold, *Great Siberian*, p. 34.

74. *Desiatiletiye*, p. 26.

75. Idem.

76. Polner, *Zhiznennyi*, p. 164.

77. *Desiatiletiye*, p. 36.

78. The resolution was published in an article on the meeting in *Izvestiia Moskovskoi gorodskoi dumy*, vol. 6–7, 1910, pp. 38–48.

79. The full text of Chertov's speech in 1912 can be found in *Obshchestvennyi vrach*, no. 6, 1913, pp. 673–679.

Liberals in the Provinces:
The Kadets and the Duma Elections in
Saratov, 1906–1912

Dittmar Dahlmann
Rheinische Friedrich-Wilhelms-Universität Bonn

Saratov Province on the lower Volga is a part of that region of Russia that has received a relatively large amount of attention in recent Western historical writings.[1] One of the most important reasons for this is surely the fact that, because of the area's agrarian structure, it belonged to one of the most troubled regions of the country. During the Revolution of 1905–1906, Governor Peter A. Stolypin became notorious in the province and achieved national prominence. He succeeded in keeping the number of revolts quite low. The energy he demonstrated there established his reputation as a capable politician and brought him first the post of Minister of Internal Affairs and then that of Prime Minister.[2]

From the end of the nineteenth century Saratov Province was also one of the strongholds of the zemstvo movement. From this movement there gradually emerged the seeds of political parties after 1904: on the one hand the Constitutional Democrats or Kadet Party and on the other the Octobrist Party. Here we will deal with the Kadets, their local organization and their election campaigns for the four empire-wide elections for the Duma, the Russian parliament. Regional studies of Imperial Russia have been rare up to now, particularly with regard to the activity of political parties.[3] A glimpse into the province allows us, however, to make a productive analysis of the government's politics and the basis of its power.

During the census of 1897 in the Russian Empire, about 2.4 million residents were counted in Saratov Province. They lived predominantly in the countryside. The provincial capital, of the same name, had around 140,000 inhabitants; the next largest city in the province, Tsaritsyn, had not even half as many—barely 56,000 people.[4]

Along with a predominantly Great Russian population, comprising approximately 75 per cent of the total, there were also several national minorities in Saratov. Among these were Ukrainians, with more than 6 percent of the population; Mordvinians and Chuvashs, 7 percent; Germans, 7 percent; and Tatars, barely 5 percent.[5] The non-Slavic minorities lived in ethnically closed settlements. They were essentially, as Eric R. Wolf formulated, "closed corporate communities."[6]

The textile industry and grain milling were the determining factors in the province's industrial development. Both sectors had quite a high percentage of German enterprises, founded by the descendants of the colonists who had arrived in the eighteenth century, during the reign of Catherine II.[7] Farming predominated, however; the cultivation of cereals was the main activity. The pattern of land occupation was very uneven. While large-scale landholding by the nobility still predominated in the northern and western districts of the province, it played no role in Kamyshin County, where the colonists had been settled.[8]

Conservative forces predominated in the provincial and county zemstvos until well into the middle of the 1890s. Only then did a gradual shift to liberal groups make itself apparent. This changeover first took place in Balashov County, where liberal zemstvo members such as Nikolai N. L'vov, S. A. Unkovskii, and M. N. Orlov won more and more influence.[9] The decisive moment for the liberals occurred in 1899, when N. N. L'vov was elected to the post of chairman of the provincial zemstvo *uprava,* or executive council. Now the zemstvo in this province became almost a stronghold of the liberal movement. Next to L'vov, S. A. Kotliarevskii and A. M. Maslennikov stood at the helm of the reformist forces.[10]

Yet this did not mean that the conservatives had entirely lost their influence. Count A. A. Uvarov, Count D. A. Olsuf'ev, K. N. Grimm, and P. S. Ikonnikov were all among their leading figures. The liberals, however, attained a decisive influence upon the journal published by the zemstvo, *Saratovskaia zemskaia nedelia.*[11] It then became an organ of

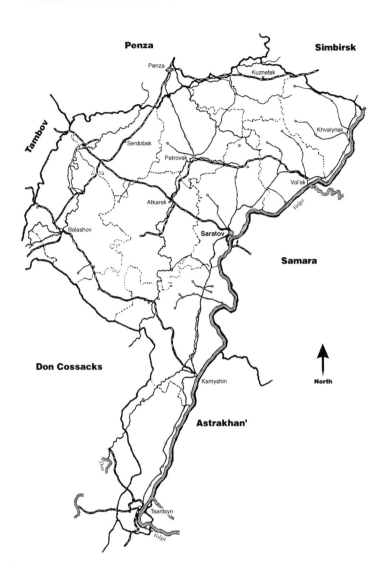

Penza

Simbirsk

Penza

Kuznetsk

Tambov

Khvalynsk

Serdobsk

Petrovsk

Vol'sk

Atkarsk

Volga

Balashov

Saratov

Samara

Don Cossacks

Kamyshin

North

Astrakhan'

Don

Tsaritsyn

Volga

MAP 4-1   Saratov Province

the liberal zemtsvo activists from other areas of Russia as well. The paper published many contributions about social and economic problems. It was also important that the so-called Third Element, the paid employees of the zemstvo, were sponsored, and their political work supported, by the circle around L'vov.[12]

Nikolai N. L'vov and several of his political friends were involved with most of the liberal zemstvo organizations and activities. These included participating in the discussion circle "Beseda" and zemstvo congresses, as well as collaboration in the Union of Zemstvo Constitutionalists (*Soiuz Zemtsev-Konstitutsionalistov*) and the Union of Liberation (*Soiuz Osvobozhdeniia*).[13] L'vov, who came from an old noble family and who, as a large landholder, possessed approximately 30,000 dessiatines in Balashov County, embodied, as it were, the entire scope of Russian liberalism between the turn of the century and the outbreak of the First World War. His political career led him from the Constitutional Democrats through the Party of Peaceful Renewal to the Progressists.[14]

Saratov was one of the strongholds of the Union of Liberation. Eight groups, with 150 members altogether, existed in the province. But there is little indication of significant activity on the part of this liberal faction up to the start of the banquet campaign in late autumn 1904.[15] L'vov, Kotliarevskii, Unkovskii, A. M. Maslennikov, and A. D. Iumatov were leading members and also were active in the Union of Zemstvo Constitutionalists. All of them, except for Unkovskii, who was educated in the Page Corps, had completed their university education.

Kotliarevskii taught public law at Moscow University. He, as well as L'vov and Maslennikov, was among the founding members of the Constitutional Democrats. L'vov—up to his withdrawal from the party in 1906—and Kotliarevskii belonged to the Central Committee of the Kadets. Both men thus held leading positions in all the liberal organizations.

Kotliarevskii lived, like many other Russian liberals during this time, in two different worlds at the same time. On the one hand he was a member of the zemstvo, and on the other he belonged, as a university professor, to the liberal professions. Like him, L'vov, Unkovskii, and Orlov also came from Balashov County, the regional center of the province's liberal movement, the core of which obviously developed on the basis of personal relationships.[16]

The formative phase for the liberal parties began in late autumn and winter 1904–1905, when a series of ceremonial banquets was held throughout the empire. The occasion for this campaign was the fortieth-anniversary celebration of the judicial reform of 1864.[17] The province of Saratov proved to be one of the centers for these countrywide banquets. In the capital of the province alone, four banquets took place; they were organized by the Union of Liberation or professional groups on November 5 and 20, and December 17, 1904, and on January 8, 1905.[18] Other social organizations also held banquets in the city. Moreover, there was another such event in the city of Balashov in the middle of December 1904.[19]

The province occupied a special place in the political ferment of 1904 and 1905. Not only liberals but also Social Democrats and Socialist Revolutionaries appeared in Saratov as coorganizers. In fact a united front of opposition organizations of leftists and liberals developed within Saratov. This coalescence of a united front, which was seldom achieved elsewhere, was one of the goals of the banquet campaign.[20]

This campaign alliance of liberals and socialists held together through the year 1906. Not only representatives of the intelligentsia and the academic professions, but also almost all social strata, including workers, took part in the banquets.[21] Moreover, internal doctrinal quarrels receded within both socialist parties and made room for a more pragmatic kind of politics.

Almost immediately after the events of January 9, 1905, the revolutionary wave engulfed Saratov as well. The province became a center of agrarian unrest and mass strikes by the workers. Only a few days after the bloody massacre on the square in front of the Winter Palace in St. Petersburg, the workers in Saratov also began to stage walkouts. On January 14 almost the total workforce in the city was on strike. At the head of the movement stood the workers and employees of the railroad line. By their action, Saratov was effectively cut off from the outside world during this period. However, the strike was primarily economically and not politically motivated. It ended with a victory for the strikers, whose demands were largely fulfilled.[22]

The unrest spread into the countryside as well.[23] Revolutionary parties, radical *zemtsy* (elected zemstvo representatives), and zemstvo employees often acted together. The first actions by the peasants had already begun in the middle of January 1905. They reached their first peak in February of that year, when peasants' petitions were drawn up on a massive scale. These actions finally culminated in the agrarian revolt of the autumn and winter of 1905–1906. The leadership role clearly lay in the hands of the Socialist Revolutionary Party.[24] Saratov remained one of the most turbulent provinces in Russia well into the following winter, despite all the efforts and small successes on the part of Governor Stolypin.[25]

In contrast to many other provincial governors, Stolypin demonstrated a decisive attitude and great personal courage while combatting the revolts during this period. This, as well as his reports to Tsar Nicholas II regarding the situation in Saratov and the suggestions he sent to the Ministry of Internal Affairs on how to fight the revolution, made him a perfect candidate for a post in the government. Finally he was called in April 1906 into Goremykin's cabinet as Minister of Internal Affairs and shortly thereafter, in July 1906, he was named Chairman of the Council of Ministers.[26]

Not only liberal and socialist parties and associations were active in Saratov, however; the political right also gained attention. In July 1905 a mob in the city of Balashov, incited by local priests and the police, attacked the local zemstvo doctors, claiming that they were collaborating with the Japanese enemy. The Saratov Archbishop Germogen, who was known as a reactionary, acted in the background.[27] On October 17, 1905, immediately before the release of the October Manifesto, clashes took place in the provincial capital itself between workers on the one hand and Cossacks and police on the other. The unrest escalated after the manifesto became widely known. Demonstrators in support of the Tsar, led by Archbishop Germogen, clashed with counterdemonstrators on Saratov's theater square. Shortly thereafter rightists attacked liberals and Jews. The havoc ended after Stolypin ordered troops to be sent in.[28]

During the general strike, the Constitutional Democratic Party (*Konstitutsionno-demokraticheskaia Partiia*) was founded in a convention in Moscow that lasted from October 12 to 18, 1905. S. A. Kotliarevskii and S. V. Anikin took part as delegates from Saratov.[29] The establishment of the party was preceded by internal discussions within the Union of Zemstvo-Constitutionalists and the Union of Liberation in the course of 1905 and between the two organizations. Each of the two elected a foundation committee, which in the first case consisted of twenty, in the second of forty, members. In this effort the groups partially overlapped, since fifteen of the twenty members of the Zemstvo-Constitutionalists' committee were also members of the Union of Liberation's group of forty. The program of the Union of Liberation from March 1905 served as the basis of the new party program. The program was only slightly modified during the party congresses of October 1905 and January 1906 and stayed in effect, with only minor modifications, until 1917.[30]

The party's third root, in addition to these two organizations, was the Union of Unions (*Soiuz Soiuzov*). The Kadets and their party leadership later quite frequently denied this strand in their tradition or tried to attach a rather minor meaning to it.[31] The initiative for the formation of the Union of Unions clearly lay with the Union of Liberation, which proposed the creation of professional organizations in the autumn of 1904.[32] The associations of academics, journalists, lawyers, agronomists, statisticians, and numerous other professions joined together in an umbrella organization at the head of which stood Paul Miliukov. The Union of Unions saw itself as a link between the intelligentsia on the one hand and the workers and employees on the other. Essentially however, the radical intelligentsia belonged to it, and more specifically, middle- and lower-level employees. Workers, with the exception of members of the railroad unions, were hardly represented.[33]

The Union of Unions was able to build a network of local groups with extraordinary speed. Thus in Saratov there were six member groups. These included the Association of Medical Personnel, the Association of Engineers and Technicians, and the Association of Lawyers.[34] What purposes all these associations and groups should serve was formulated by one of the most distinguished founders of the Kadets, Prince Peter Dolgorukov, in July 1905: "We must now create the connection between ourselves and the population and so prepare them for conscious and active participation in the present liberal movement. For this connection we must find, because of our small number, mediators or, one could say, translators."[35]

This role of mediator could be played by the professional organizations only during a few months in the summer and autumn of 1905. Afterwards, all further attempts in this direction came to nothing. The party could not create the bond to the masses that the liberals wished for. The radicalization of broad parts of the population after October 1905 led to growing alienation among the different social strata.

Mostly on the initiative of the Central Committee of the newly founded Constitutional Democrats, local party groups began to form.[36] However, the majority of the local groups had not come into existence by January 1906, as Evgenii Chermenskii and Terence Emmons believe they have shown, but rather they emerged during the course of the election campaign for the First Duma, between mid-January and April 1906.[37] The election campaign was decisive for the foundation of the local party committees. These committees had, for this reason, more the character of election organizations than party groups.

The development of the local party organization in Saratov began in November 1905 with a first group in the provincial capital. Not until February 1906 did another group emerge, in Tsaritsyn. Neither of these groups was shaped by the zemstvo but rather by the urban intelligentsia. At the head of these groups were lawyers, doctors, and managers.[38] The intelligentsia also shaped the Kadets' local party organization in the following years. Some veterans of the zemstvo and liberation movement, such as Nikolai N. L'vov, soon abandoned the party, and mainly for that reason the liberal professional element predominated.

In Saratov the two urban committees dominated until well into the summer of 1906. In the countryside, the foundation of further local groups was hardly possible apparently because of continuing unrest. Certainly there is no case in which the groups mentioned by Shelokhaev in Atkarsk, Vol'sk, and Kuznetsk showed any signs of activity before May 1906.[39] One must keep in mind that the Russian Empire was still being shaken by unrest during this entire period. All these new political organizations were born in this heated, turbulent atmosphere, in which it was nearly impossible to translate a political concept into action with a cool head and unemotional analysis.

Saratov was now, as has already been mentioned, one of the largest trouble spots in the country. Since the middle of November 1905, additional military units had been sent into the province to restore order and quiet once again. They only partly succeeded. However, the revolutionaries were not able to achieve the success they wanted with the rural population or the province. The peasants followed their own ideas.

Things were completely different in the provincial capital. By the end of the year a kind of alliance developed there between the Kadets and revolutionary, socialist parties to their left—the two wings of the Russian Social Democratic Labor Party, the Mensheviks and Bolsheviks, and the Socialist Revolutionary Party. The liberals were received well among the ranks of the workers. They were even more popular among the office and retail employees.[40] The most important voter group, though, was the peasants. They were the focus of the Kadets' attention.

For the election to the Duma, the lower chamber of Parliament, the regulations of the electoral law of December 11, 1905, were in effect.[41] The franchise was indirect and based on a curia voting system. The electorate was separated into four curiae: landholders, peasants living in communes, city-dwellers, and workers. A special franchise existed for the twenty largest cities in the country, each of which elected a representative to the State Duma. Moscow, which elected four representatives, and St. Petersburg, which elected six, were exceptions. There were special regulations for several national minorities and for the Russian minority in several border regions, such as the Polish provinces.[42]

In its essentials, the franchise was based upon the election ordinances for the zemstvos and the city dumas. Each curia in each province elected a certain number of delegates for the provincial electoral assembly. This body met in the provincial capital and elected from its members the required number of provincial representatives to the Duma. Yet the franchise was not only indirect, but multistage.

This voting system was especially clear in the peasants' curia. First, peasants in their village assemblies elected their representatives for the next level, the *volost'* or township assembly. This step could be bypassed, however. The law allowed for the possibility that the normal village representatives to the volost' could represent the village in this electoral volost' assembly without the need for a new election, and indeed this variant was not uncommon. In the volost' assembly, two representatives to the county assembly of the peasants' curia were now elected. This body then elected the single peasants' representative to the provincial assembly. That was where the representatives of all the curiae finally came together to determine who the members of the State Duma would be.

In all the votes, that is, at all levels of the election process, the principle in effect was that the delegates chose someone from their own category. Thus only people who actually belonged to the voting body could be elected. Peasants and Cossacks were, moreover, entitled to a special franchise. Their delegates could first choose a member of parliament from their own number at the provincial electoral assembly. Only then would they join with the delegates from the other curiae to elect the rest of the Duma deputies. In the cities the election process was far simpler. Here the citizens in each precinct with the right to vote—about 10 percent of the male population of the city[43]—elected their representatives. These then elected one or more urban Duma members from their own number.

The decisive body was thus the provincial electoral assembly, which actually elected the members of the Duma. Each party that wanted to send its representatives to the Duma in St. Petersburg had to take care that it could control a majority in this body or, at least, that it could place enough delegates there so that their votes could be the decisive factor in the election. Only in the urban centers, in which a two-stage vote existed, were the election and the campaign comparable to those in other European countries.[44]

In Saratov the provincial electoral assembly consisted of 150 delegates. Of these, sixty-four belonged to the peasants' curia, fifty-one to the landholders' curia, and thirty-five to the urban curia.[45] Because the franchise was weighted, landholders, and above all large landholders, were disproportionately represented. This group found itself, though, in the minority when faced with a coalition of peasants and city-dwellers. Thus these two groups were offered the chance to make arrangements and to operate together in the provincial electoral assembly.

The final decision of the Constitutional Democrats to take part in the election for the Duma was made at the Second Party Congress in the beginning of January 1906.[46] Like most of the other parties—with the exception of all the socialist parties, which boycotted the election— the Kadets had to organize a campaign while simultaneously building up a countrywide party organization. At the congress it was agreed that the central direction of the election campaign should be concentrated in the hands of the party's Central Committee.[47] However, there remained enough leeway for local party organizations to adapt to circumstances in their own territories.[48]

At the Party Congress, Vladimir Gessen explained the Kadets' guidelines as far as agitation and propaganda were concerned. One of the most important tasks was to recruit as many new members as possible while simultaneously making the party program known throughout the country. The party literature had to be distributed and trained party speakers had to give lectures. The provincial committees had to organize election campaign tours in their areas. Moreover, it was necessary to establish a party press, both at the central and local levels.[49]

There was in Saratov, in contrast to most of the other provinces, a smoothly functioning party press. In the capital of the province *Saratovskii listok* was published as the party organ; in Tsaritsyn the party newspaper was the *Tsaritsynskii vestnik*.[50] Both papers were published continuously between 1906 and 1917 without experiencing great difficulties with the censor.[51] In the middling and smaller locales, though, there was hardly any local press of any party orientation whatsoever.

In February 1906 the only two Kadet party organizations in Saratov Province existed in the province's two main urban centers, the cities of Saratov and Tsaritsyn.[52] Shelokhaev has come to the conclusion, based on his comprehensive archival research, that there were approximately 700 party members in the province at the time of the first election: about 300 in the capital and 400 in the cities of Tsaritsyn, Atkarsk, Vol'sk, Kuznetsk, and Kamyshin.[53] The majority of party members came from the educated bourgeoisie that was gradually developing in tsarist Russia. They were professors, lawyers, doctors, journalists, secondary school teachers, and engineers. The party also attracted merchants, office and retail employees, manufacturers, craftsmen, civil servants, zemstvo employees, and noble landholders; but there were only a few peasants and workers in the party ranks.[54] In the large cities and the university towns there were distinct groups within the party for office and retail employees as well as for students.[55]

Women were completely underrepresented in the party, in contrast to the socialist parties. The Kadets did in fact support the extension of the franchise to women—after some internal quarrels—but there seems to have been no attempt to increase the involvement of women in the party. The party members themselves quite often discussed this circumstance and found it "regrettable and deplorable."[56] In this respect, the Kadets remained wedded, on the whole, to the bourgeois-liberal thought patterns of the nineteenth century, which meant that political reforms came first and formal equality between men and women would only be addressed later.

Both in the centers of St. Petersburg and Moscow and in the local party groups, the leadership rested in the hands of the liberal professions and the liberal nobility. Local dignitaries constituted the most important leadership stratum. It is difficult to verify how many members the Kadets actually had. Missing membership lists are the most important reason for this gap in our knowledge; only a few local groups kept such lists.[57] The party itself maintained that it had between 70,000 and 100,000 members in the spring and summer of 1906. The police estimated more than 100,000.[58] Shelokhaev presented a very well-founded estimate to the effect that the party had between 50,000 and 55,000 members in the spring and summer of 1906.[59]

As the campaign for the First Duma election began in January 1906, the Constitutional Democrats were not an officially registered party. Their election meetings and party events were therefore allowed or forbidden on a purely arbitrary basis. The government apparently had no unified opinion in this matter. Much was left to the discretion of the local authorities. Moreover, from the middle of January 1906 civil servants were forbidden to join parties whose activities were directed against the government. The Kadets belonged to this group.[60]

The first election campaign in Saratov Province, and especially in its capital, was an extremely intensive affair. In the city a separate Duma representative was elected, in accordance with the election law. Almost all the political parties and social strata of the population took part in the electoral campaign, even those who had no right to vote at all. Despite several disturbances in the countryside, the political agitation associated with the campaign went off without serious incidents. An election campaign was even possible in the smaller locales, but it was really concentrated in the two largest cities, Saratov and Tsaritsyn, as well as in several county seats.

The authorities held themselves back to a remarkable degree during the campaign. There were only occasional arrests of political activists, among whom were some members of the Kadets. Serious attacks ceased, however.[61] The Kadets conducted their political agitation in nearly all cities and counties in close collaboration with the Union of

Workers (*Soiuz trudiashchikhsia*) against an alliance of rightist parties with the Octobrists at their head.

At the same time, however, there were constant disputes at political gatherings between the Constitutional Democrats and the leftist parties, such as the Social Democrats, over the question of a campaign boycott. The election meetings, which took place in almost all the towns in Saratov Province, commonly lasted until late into the night. The Kadets also sponsored, in addition to those meetings, gatherings for certain target groups, such as merchants or employees. The speakers' topics were the tasks of the future Duma, questions of economics and finance, autonomy for Poland, the party's agrarian program, and—again and again—the election boycott.[62]

The atmosphere in the provincial capital and the province as a whole was highly politicized. Different viewpoints were uncompromisingly exchanged between political opponents. The Octobrists and rightist Union of Russian People seldom appeared at events sponsored by the Kadets and their political allies. This dispute was carried forward, as it were, in absentia, while leftist groups agitated constantly at the Constitutional Democrats' gatherings.[63]

Kadet election campaign events were also held for peasant communities in county seats and in villages. Here the agrarian question was at center stage, as one would expect. For all the radicalism of the liberal agrarian program espoused by the Kadets, it nevertheless did not go far enough for the majority of peasants. Moreover, the Kadets were regarded as the embodiment of urban Russia. Their speakers wore the frock coat (*siurtuk*), not the peasants' overalls.[64]

Members of the Kadet Party debated all these issues and distributed their fliers at numerous events. They posted their placards on the streets and squares.[65] A gathering in the city theater in Saratov on March 16, 1906, formed the high point of the campaign. Vasilii Maklakov and Sergei Kotliarevskii, both members of the Central Committee, presented lectures and in spite of high prices, the gathering was sold out. The two prominent party leaders talked for approximately four hours about all aspects of the Kadets' program, including the future tasks of a Constitutional-Democratic foreign policy. Following these remarks there was an intensive debate with the audience.[66] Interest in political questions as well as eagerness to play a part in decisions of all kinds was widespread in the ranks of the population.

The Kadets also achieved several successes among the German colonists who were concentrated in Kamyshin County. The lawyer Jakob Dietz led the party's election campaign there almost completely on his own.[67] He motivated the previously lethargic and unpolitical German settlers, to whom the leadership of the Constitutional Democrats finally conceded their own representative in the Duma. Alone, the German minority could not have gained a seat.[68]

In the city and province of Saratov the Kadets and their ally, the Union of Workers, won with an overwhelming majority. In the urban curia of Saratov, the election alliance attracted about 24,000 votes, as against approximately 6,000 for the coalition of Octobrists and the Right. With that, all eighty delegates who had to vote for the city's one Duma representative went to the election alliance. In the provincial capital the voter turnout was a good 48 percent.[69] Percentages in remaining areas cannot be established with any accuracy.

In the provincial electoral assembly none of the political groups could achieve a clear majority. The Kadets' domain was the cities. In Saratov fourteen rural delegates were elected, at any rate, from a total of sixty-four who were either party members or were sympathetic to the Kadets. This, however, was one of the best results in the country.[70]

Just before the assembly of the electoral body, the alliance of the Kadets with the non-party-affiliated Left fell apart. The Right was clearly in the minority. Before the delegates' assembly came together for the election of the Duma members, several gatherings took place at which suitable candidates were discussed. The negotiations turned out to be difficult. The agricultural delegates refused to be recruited by the Kadets because of the party's agrarian program.

Negotiations were still being carried out the evening before the vote, but they failed. In the end each of the two groups went into the first ballot with its own list of nine deputies that it wanted to support. At the end of the vote, which turned out to be extremely problematic, only two candidates fell to the Kadets against seven to the Trudoviks, as they were later called. In addition there was also that deputy for whom the peasants could vote to start with. He, too, belonged to the Trudovik faction in the First Duma.[71] In the city of Saratov the Kadets succeeded in achieving a relatively easy victory. Their leading member Aleksandr Tokarskii, was elected almost unanimously by the eighty urban delegates.[72]

The decisive body for the elections was the provincial assembly. Its composition is crucial for an analysis of the election results. The results of the delegate selection process play only a subordinate role here. Thus the Kadets in Saratov gained not even a third of the delegate seats—45 of 150 seats. Fifteen went to the Octobrists and the Right; the rest went to the Left or unaffiliated delegates.[73] The party thus received far more votes than its final number of seats in the Duma reflected. In other provinces, where the Kadets did not face a united leftist bloc, the picture was different. There they won more Duma seats than their proportionate share of delegates in the provincial electoral assembly. For the whole of European Russia the party's share in the provincial assembly was about one-third of the seats. This was the party's core of voters and it only changed very slightly in the next three elections.[74]

The Kadets' victory in the first elections was not based upon a majority in the population, but upon the fact that they succeeded in taking advantage of the country's mood and particularly the attitude of the large group of opposition-minded, non-party-affiliated rural delegates. The Kadets were able to convince them that only a Kadet victory would help them to achieve their demands, hopes, and wishes. The Constitutional Democratic Party members offered themselves as the correct ally, one that would successfully represent rural interests in the Duma. It should not be forgotten that at the same time the core of the party's voters clearly lay in the cities, and the exceptions, such as Kostroma and Tver', only prove this rule.[75]

The three following elections in the province of Saratov ran along a similar pattern. In the second election in the winter of 1906–1907 all the Duma deputy seats fell to leftist parties. The Social Democrats and the Socialist Revolutionaries, which took part only in this second election, received four delegates each; the Trudoviks were reduced from eight to one seat, and the People's Socialists received the remaining two places.[76] Again, this did not correspond to the percentage of delegates the Kadets had won in the provincial assembly. Against sixty-six seats on the left, delegates from the Constitutional Democrats and those described as "progressive" together won thirty-one seats. But in order to keep the Octobrists and the rightist Union of Russian People, which together had forty-seven seats in the delegate assembly at their disposal, from gaining ground, the Kadets, whether they liked it or not, had to support the leftist candidates.[77]

After the so-called coup of June 3, 1907, when Prime Minister Stolypin changed the franchise unilaterally,[78] rightist parties—the Octobrists, the Group of the Moderate Right (*Gruppa umerenno-pravykh*), and the Group of the Rightists (*Gruppa pravykh*)—won the election to the Third Duma in this province. The Orthodox Church, landowners, and the local administration now entered into a peculiar alliance.[79] Eight of the eleven seats fell to the Octobrists and the Right, one seat each to the Kadets, the Trudoviks and the Party of Peaceful Renewal.[80] In the provincial electoral assembly, the liberals' share remained nearly the same. Kadets and Progressists received 27 of the 127 delegate seats that now remained (in the previous elections there had been 150 delegates), 31 fell to the left, and 64 seats to the Octobrists and the right.[81]

Five years later, in the autumn of 1912, when the circumstances had returned to normal to a certain extent, a sort of balance arose between the middle-Left and the middle-Right. Kadets, Progressists, and Trudoviks gained six delegates altogether; the Octobrists, the Group of the Moderate Right, and the Group of the Rightists together gained five.[82] In the provincial assembly the Kadets and the Progressists together won thirty-nine seats, twelve fell to the Left, and fifty-seven to the Right. Eight delegates were considered moderate, three as unaffiliated, and the political orientation of eight was unknown.[83]

On the whole, the proportion of delegates in the provincial assembly from the Kadets and the Progressists remained roughly the same in all four Duma elections. With small variations the Kadets' delegates fluctuated between 20 percent and 30 percent of the delegate seats. The parties' shares of seats in the Duma changed each time, but solely because the need to get particular candidates into office forced the parties to form coalitions. The provincial electoral assembly opened the way for party haggling and also for distortion of the voters' will. In any case, it is important to emphasize that, in measuring the degree to which the parties were anchored in the population, the number of seats in the provincial assembly, not the number of parliament members, is the important issue. From that it is clear that the Kadets' share remained relatively constant over the course of the four elections. As a party, though, the

Constitutional Democrats only existed on a rudimentary level in most provinces. Shelokhaev, on the basis of extensive archival research, reports that there were never more than thirty active members in the party's Saratov provincial committee in the period from 1908–1909 to 1913–1914.[84]

Moreover, the last two election results, from the years 1907 and 1912, clearly show to what a great extent workers and peasants were marginalized by the government. In the late tsarist empire there was no adequate institution in the political system that could—or was allowed to—represent their interests.[85] This demonstrates the high degree of alienation that existed between the various social strata in Russia. A discourse in whatever form simply did not exist.

Until 1914 the Kadets, who in the Russian provinces could only gain a foothold in the larger cities, saw themselves at least partially as a sort of mediator between the government and the different social strata. However, the majority of the socialist parties, as well as the mass of workers and peasants, expressed little or no interest in this arrangement. The Kadets' social liberalism found little interest and hardly any agreement outside their own camp. Attitudes were too entrenched to allow this and the tension too great. Certainly the Kadets can be considered a possible political alternative. But realistically, when one examines the election results and the Kadets' reception among the predominantly rural population, they were not in a powerful position.

A look at the provinces, at the circumstances on the periphery, demonstrates to what a large extent the political center, that is, the government, had lost its influence there after 1906. After disbanding the First Duma, the tsarist government could do nothing but tolerate the actions of the local authorities and protect them against an ever stronger public. The government, as became crystal clear during the election campaign, formulated no guidelines, but rather decided upon an unconditional defense of the status quo. It produced no more ideas or concepts, but depended upon nothing more than administrative measures.[86] In none of the four election campaigns did the tsarist government put forth any kind of political or other program.

The dream of the Russian liberals—to bring into being an alliance between the liberal, urban citizenry and the Social Democratic workers' movement—had already failed in October 1905, in the course of the revolution. Also, the connection with the peasants never got beyond the initial stages. The Kadets looked for the magic solution. They wanted to set Russia on the path to Western-style democracy, through a program and a strategy that would encompass all classes and strata. They never succeeded, however, in reconciling divergent sociopolitical ideas. This clearly demonstrates the explosive force of the social conflicts in Russia that culminated in revolution and civil war between 1917 and 1921.

Notes

1. Rex A. Wade, Scott Seregny, eds., *Politics and Society in Provincial Russia: Saratov, 1590–1917* (Columbus: Ohio State University Press, 1989); Donald J. Raleigh, *Revolution on the Volga: 1917 in Saratov* (Ithaca, London: Cornell University Press, 1986); Timothy R. Mixter, "Of Grandfather-Beaters and Fat Heeled Pacifists: Perceptions of Agricultural Labor and Hiring Market Disturbances in Saratov, 1872–1905," *Russian History*, vol. 7, no. 1–2 (1980) pp. 139–168; Jonathan Sanders, "Lessons from the Periphery: Saratov, January 1905," *Slavic Review*, vol. 46, no. 2 (1987) pp. 229–244; W. E. Mosse, "Revolution in Saratov: Revolution in Saratov: October-November 1917," *Slavonic and East European Review*, vol. 49, no. 117 (1971) pp. 586–602; Klaus Heller, Herbert Jelitte, eds., "Das mittlere Wolgagebiet,": *Geschichte und Gegenwart* (Frankfurt/ M. 1994).

2. Thomas Fallows, "Governor Stolypin and the Revolution of 1905 in Saratov," in Wade, Seregny, eds., *Politics*, pp. 160–190.

3. The following works should be mentioned: Rex Rexheuser, *Dumawahlen und lokale Gesellschaft. Studien zur Sozialgeschichte der russischen Rechten vor 1917* (Cologne, Vienna, 1980); Rexheuser, "Kirche und Politik im späten Zarenreich: Der Fall Volhynien," in K.-H. Ruffmann, A. Rexheuser, eds., *Festschrift für Fairy von Lilienfeld zum 65. Geburtstag* (Erlangen, 1982), pp. 251–284; Rexheuser, "Die lokale Gesellschaft im späten Zarenreich als Forschungsproblem," *Jahrbücher für Geschichte Osteuropas* N. F. 30, 1982, pp. 212–226; V. I. Sedugin, *Bol'sheviki povolzh'ia protiv Kadetov (1905-fevral' 1917)* (Saratov, 1990); Don C. Rawson, "Rightist Politics in the Revolution of 1905: The Case of Tula Province," *Slavic Review*, vol. 51, no. 1 (1992) pp. 99–116; Igor' V. Narskii, *Obrazovanie i organizatsionnaia deiatel'nost' kadetov Urala v gody pervoi rossiiskoi revoliutsii* (Cheliabinsk, 1986 [typed manuscript]); Igor' V. Narskii, *Kadety na Urale (1905–1907)* (Sverdlovsk, 1991); Leopold H. Haimson, ed., *The Politics of Rural Russia, 1905–1914* (Bloomington, London: Indiana University Press, 1979).

4. Henning Bauer, Andreas Kappeler, Brigitte Roth, eds., *Die Nationalitäten des Russischen Reiches in der Volkzählung von 1897*, 2 vols. (Stuttgart, 1991), vol. B, p. 56; *Vsia Rossiia* (St. Petersburg, 1899), col. 875 ff. The map of Saratov Province in the present chapter is from Dittmar Dahlmann, *Die Provinz wählt. Rußlands Konstitutionell-Demokratische Partei und die Dumawahlen 1906–1912* (Cologne, Weimar, Vienna: Böhlau Verlag, Gmoh & Cie, 1996), p. 443.

5. Raleigh, *Revolution*, p. 28.

6. Eric R. Wolf, "Closed Corporate Peasant Communities in Mesoamerica and Central Java," in Jack M. Potter, May N. Diaz, George M. Foster, eds., *Peasant Society: A Reader* (Boston: Little, Brown, 1967), pp. 230–246, here p. 231; cf. Wolf, *Peasants* (Englewood Cliffs, NJ, 1968); Teodor Shanin, "Peasantry as a Political Factor," in Teodor Shanin, ed., *Peasants and Peasant Societies* (Harmondsworth: Penguin, 1971), pp. 238–263.

7. James Long, *From Privileged to Dispossessed: The Volga Germans, 1860–1917* (Lincoln, London: University of Nebraska Press, 1988), p. 140 ff.

8. Ibid., p. 162 f.

9. Boris B. Veselovskii, *Istoriia zemstva za sorok let*, 4 vols. (St. Peterburg, 1909–1911), vol. 4, p. 384.

10. Ibid.

11. Ibid., p. 384 ff.

12. Dahlmann, *Provinz*, p. 78.

13. N. M. Pirumova, *Zemskoe liberal'noe dvizhenie. Sotsial'nye korni i evoliutsiia do nachala XX veka* (Moscow, 1977) p. 258 f.; K. F. Shatsillo, *Russkii liberalizm nakanune revoliutsii 1905–1907 gg. Organizatsiia, programmy, taktika* (Moscow, 1985), p. 117 ff.; cf. also Shmuel Galai, *The Liberation Movement in Russia, 1900–1905* (Cambridge: Cambridge University Press, 1973).

14. Shatsillo, *Russkii liberalizm*, p. 203; Dahlmann, *Provinz*, p. 85. A dessiatine equals about two and two-thirds acres. The Party of Peaceful Renewal included both former Kadets and former Octobrists. The party was established in the summer of 1906 by disaffected Kadets N. N. L'vov and M. A. Stakhovich. Octobrists such as D. N. Shipov and others, who disagreed with Stolypin's courts martial and with A. I. Guchkov and the Octobrist Party Central Committee who supported Stolypin in this matter, also joined the Party of Peaceful Renewal at this time. The Progressists represented liberal entrepreneurs. From 1909 the Progressists became a haven for Moscow industrialists who chaffed at government regulation of corporations and businesses. In the Fourth Duma, which began in 1912, the Progressists had an extremely liberal political agenda. By 1914 they advocated combining with revolutionary parties—Social Democratic and Socialist Revolutionaries—in opposition to the government and even offered financial help to the Bolsheviks for convocation of a party congress. On the Progressists see Lawrence W. Lerner, "The Progressists in the Russian State Duma, 1907–1915," Ph. D. Diss., University of Washington, 1976; V. N. Seletskii, "Obrazovanie partii progressistov. K voprosu o politicheskoi konsolidatsii russkoi burzhuazii," *Vestvik MGU*, series 9, no. 5, 1970, pp. 32–48; James L. West, "The Riabushinsky Circle: *Burzhuaziia* and *Obshchestvennost'* in Late Imperial Russia," in Edith W. Clowes, Samuel D. Kassow, and James L. West, eds., *Between Tsar and People: Educated Society and the Quest for Public Identity in Late Imperial Russia* (Princeton, NJ: Princeton University Press, 1991), pp. 41–56.

15. Shatsillo, *Russkii liberalizm*, p. 205.

16. Dahlmann, *Provinz*, p. 87.

17. Terence Emmons, "Russia's Banquet Campaign", *California Slavic Studies*, vol. 10 (1977) pp. 45–86; Heinz-Dietrich Löwe, "Die Rolle der russischen Intelligenz in der

Revolution von 1905," *Forschungen zur Osteuropäischen Geschichte*, vol. 32 (1983) pp. 229–255; Shatsillo, *Russkii liberalizm*, p. 293 ff.

18. Emmons, "Russia's Banquet Campaign," pp. 55 f., 65, 84 f.; L–ii (I. M. Liachovetskii), "Banketnaia kampaniia v Saratove 1904–1905 gg.," *Minuvshie gody*, no. 12, (1908) pp. 29–62; Fallows, "Governor Stolypin," p. 163 ff.

19. Emmons, "Russia's Banquet Campaign," pp. 84–86.

20. Ibid., p. 62; Liachovetskii, "Banketnaia kampaniia," p. 44.

21. Fallows, "Governor Stolypin," p. 164 f.

22. Sanders, "Lessons," pp. 229–244.

23. See Abraham Ascher, *The Revolution of 1905*, vol. 1, *Russia in Disarray* (Stanford: Stanford University Press, 1988); vol. 2, *Authority Restored* (Stanford: Stanford University Press, 1992).

24. Manfred Hildermeier, *Die Sozialrevolutionäre Partei Rußlands. Agrarsozialismus und Modernisierung im Zarenreich 1900–1914* (Cologne, Vienna, 1978), p. 216 ff; Michael Melancon, "Athens or Babylon? The Birth of the Socialist and Social Democratic Parties in Saratov, 1890–1905," in Wade, Seregny, eds., *Politics*, pp. 73–112, here: p. 73 ff.; I. Rakitnikov, *Revoliutsionnaia rabota v krest'ianstve v Saratovskoi gubernii v 1902–1906 gg.* (Moscow, 1928).

25. Timothy R. Mixter, "Peasant Collective Action in Saratov Province, 1902–1906," in Wade, Seregny, eds., *Politics*, pp. 191–232.

26. Mary S. Conroy, *Peter A. Stolypin: Practical Politics in Late Tsarist Russia* (Boulder, CO: Westview Press, 1976), p. 17; Francis William Wcislo, *Reforming Rural Russia: State, Local Society, and National Politics, 1855–1914* (Princeton, NJ: Princeton University Press, 1990), p. 197 ff.; Fallows, "Governor Stolypin," p. 187; Ascher, *Revolution of 1905*, vol. 2: *Authority Restored*, pp. 75 f., 216 ff.

27. Fallows, "Governor Stolypin," p. 170 ff.

28. Ibid., p. 179 f.; Raleigh, *Revolution*, p. 55 f. In the city of Vol'sk, clashes between high school students and the Black Hundreds occurred. P. G. Kutyrev, A. G. Chulkov, "Sobytiia pervoi rossiiskoi revoliutsii v Vol'ske," *Voprosy istorii*, vol. 55, no. 6 (1981) pp. 184–187.

29. *Otchet tsentral'nogo komiteta konstitutsionno-demokraticheskoi partii (Partii narodnoi svobody) za dva goda s 18 oktiabria 1905 g. po oktiabr' 1907 g.* (St. Petersburg, 1907), p. 18. Anikin became one of the leaders of the Trudovik Party in the spring of 1906. On the emergence of the Constitutional Democratic Party, see Dahlmann, *Provinz*, p. 98 ff.

30. Dahlmann, *Provinz*, p. 99 f.; Valentin V. Shelokhaev, *Kadety—glavnaia partiia liberal'noi burzhuazii v bor'be s revoliutsiei 1905–1907 gg.* (Moscow, 1983), p. 52 f; Terence Emmons, *The Formation of Political Parties and the First National Elections in Russia* (Cambridge, MA: Harvard University Press, 1983), p. 39; Judith E. Zimmerman, "Between Revolution and Reaction: the Russian Constitutional Democratic Party, October 1905 to June 1907," Ph.D. Diss., Columbia University 1967, p. 42.

31. Löwe, *Die Rolle der russischen Intelligenz*, p. 246; see also Paul Miliukov, *Political Memoirs 1907–1917* (Ann Arbor: University of Michigan Press, 1967), p. 28 ff. On the

participation of the liberal movement in the national congresses of various professional groups and in philanthropic and other organizations see Zimmerman, "Between Revolution," pp. 16–24.

32. Dmitrii I. Shakhovskoi, "Soiuz Osvobozhdeniia," *Zarnitsy*, vol. 2, no. 2 (1909) pp. 81–171, here p. 131 f.

33. Jonathan E. Sanders, "Union of Unions: Political, Economic, Civil, and Human Rights Organizations in the 1905 Russian Revolution," Ph. D. Diss., Columbia University, New York, 1985; Galai, *The Liberation Movement in Russia*, pp. 245 ff. and 258 ff.; Shmuel Galai, "The Role of the Union of Unions in the Revolution of 1905," *Jahrbücher für Geschichte Osteuropas* N. F. 24 (1976), pp. 512–525; Löwe, *Die Rolle der russischen Intelligenz*, p. 243 ff.; S. I. Dmitriev, "Soiuz Soiuzov v gody pervoi rossiiskoi revoliutsii," *Istoriia SSSR*, vol. 33, no. 1 (1990) pp. 40–57.

34. Dmitriev, "Soiuz Soiuzov," p. 45 f.; S. D. K. (S. D. Kirpichnikov), *Soiuz Soiuzov* (St. Petersburg, 1906), p. 21 ff.

35. *Osvobozhdeniia, Prilozhenie k No. 78/79*, 1905, p. 9.

36. Dahlmann, *Provinz*, p. 115 f.

37. Evgenii D. Chermenskii, *Burzhuaziia i tsarizm v pervoi russkoi revoliutsii*, second edition (Moscow, 1970), p. 162; Emmons, *The Formation of Political Parties*, p. 160 f. See, in opposition, Shelokhaev, *Kadety*, pp. 299–309, with whose conclusions I mostly agree.

38. Gosudarstvennii arkhiv Rossiiskoi Federatsii [hereafter GARF], Moscow, fond 523, opis' 1, delo 362, list 14 [hereafter f., op., d., l.] and d. 363, l. 12.

39. Ibid., d. 362, l. 43; Shelokhaev, *Kadety*, p. 306.

40. *Saratovskii listok*, no. 39, February 19, 1906, p. 2 and no. 45, February 26, 1906, p. 2.

41. Emmons, *The Formation of Political Parties*, p. 10 ff.; F. I. Kalinychev, ed., *Gosudarstvennaia Duma v Rossii v dokumentakh i materialakh* (Moscow, 1957), pp. 94–102. The first electoral law, worked out under Minister of Internal Affairs Bulygin, was published on August 6, 1905. Further electoral regulations followed in September, October, and December, 1905, as well as in February and March, 1906. See ibid., pp. 30–54, 102–104. In this essay I will not deal with the question of the character of the Russian Empire, that is to what extent it may be seen as a half-parliamentary, a pseudo-constitutional or a semi-constitutional system. On this problem see Wolfgang J. Mommsen, and Dittmar Dahlmann, eds., *Max Weber. Zur Russischen Revolution von 1905. Schriften und Reden 1905–1912* (Tübingen 1989), p. 46 ff.

42. Kalinychev, *Gosudarstvennaia Duma*, pp. 123–132; Mommsen, and Dahlmann, eds., *Max Weber.* p. 448 f.

43. Women were excluded from participation in the election. However, if a woman was qualified for the vote on the basis of the property census, she could transfer her vote to her husband or her son. See §9 of the law of August 6, 1905.

44. On the Duma and the elections see especially the studies by *Alfred Levin: The Second Duma: A Study of the Social Democratic-Party and the Russian Constitutional Experiment*, second edition (Hamden, CT: Archon Books, 1966); *The Third Duma: Election and Profile* (Hamden, CT: Archon Books, 1973); *The Reactionary Tradition in the*

Election Campaign to the Third Duma (Stillwater: Oklahoma State University Publications, 1962) "The Russian Voter in the Elections to the Third Duma," *Slavic Review* vol. 21, no. 4 (1962) pp. 660–677.

45. Kalinychev, *Gosudarstvennaia Duma*, p. 51.

46. Dahlmann, *Provinz*, p. 146 f; Emmons, *The Formation of Political Parties*, p. 158 ff.; Shelokhaev, *Kadety*, p. 175 ff. The minutes of the party congress were edited by Raymond Pearson, ed., *Vtoroi vserossiiskii s"ezd konstitutsionno-demokraticheskoi partii 5–11 ianvaria 1906 g.* (White Plains, NY: Kraus International 1986).

47. The provinces were underrepresented in the Party's Central Committee. Most members of the Central Committee came from St. Petersburg and Moscow. N. N. L'vov represented Moscow. Additionally, Prince D. I. Shakhovskoi represented Yaroslavl' and N. N. Chernenkov, Tver.' Pearson, ed., *Vtoroi vserossiiskii s"ezd*, p. 191.

48. Dahlmann, *Provinz*, p. 147 ff.

49. Pearson, ed., *Vtoroi vserossiiskii s"ezd*, pp. 21–27, 90–96; see the discussion on these matters in ibid., pp. 96–101, 221–245, 264 f.

50. Shelokhaev, *Kadety*, p. 306, with the incorrect detail that *Saratovskii dnevnik* was the organ of the Kadets in the provincial capital. See, in opposition, Dahlmann, *Provinz*, p. 154; GARF, f. 523, op. 1, d. 362, l. 14. L. N. Beliaeva, M. K. Zinov'eva, M. M. Nikiforov, eds., *Bibliografiia periodicheskikh izdanii Rossii 1901–1916*, 4 vols. (Leningrad, 1958–1961); vol. 2, p. 649, and vol. 3, pp. 119–121, 573 f.

51. Dahlmann, *Provinz*, p. 154.

52. *Alfavitnyi spisok adresov mestnykh grupp konstitutsionno-demokraticheskoi partii (partii narodnoi svobody)* (Place of publication unknown, February 23, 1906). A second register was published under the same title a short time later. It appeared in St. Petersburg.

53. Shelokhaev, *Kadety*, p. 306.

54. Ibid., p. 67 ff.

55. Dahlmann, *Provinz*, p. 161 f.

56. Pearson, ed., *Vtoroi vserossiiskii s"ezd*, pp. 196–199.

57. GARF, f. 523, op. 1, d. 177, l. 32 ff.

58. I. N. Kiselev, A. P. Korelin, V. V. Shelokhaev, "Politicheskie partii v Rossii v 1905–1907 gg.: Chislennost', sostav, razmeshchenie. Kolichestvennyi analiz," *Istoriia SSSR* vol. 33, no. 4 (1990) pp. 73 f.; Miliukov, *Political Memoirs*, p. 87.

59. Shelokhaev, *Kadety*, p. 64; Shelokhaev, "Chislennost' i sostav kadetskoi partii," in *Politicheskie partii Rossii v period revoliutsii 1905–1907 gg. Kolichestvennyi analiz. Sbornik statei* (Moscow, 1987), p. 96 ff.; Kiselev et al., "Politicheskie partii v Rossii," p. 73 ff.

60. Emmons, *The Formation of Political Parties*, p. 183 f.

61. *Vestnik partii narodnoi svobody*, no. 1, 1906, col. 57; GARF, f. 523, op. 1, d. 362, l. 4.

62. *Saratovskii listok*, no. 39, February 19, 1906, p. 2.

63. Ibid., no. 44, February 25, 1906, p. 2 f. The Octobrists or Party of October 17 was organized in the fall of 1905, following Nicholas's promulgation of the October

Manifesto, which promised an elective Duma and civil rights. The Octobrists have been categorized as moderate rightists. Politically, they were not completely democratic; they did not favor an equal electoral law and were nationalistic. On the other hand they were not anti-Semitic and, although they were more willing to compromise with the tsarist government than the Kadets, they were not subservient to the government, as chapters 5 and 7 show. Further, although their economic program for agriculture was capitalistic, they exhibited hostility toward business people, as chapter 5 details. A branch of the rightist Union of Russian People (*Soiuz russkogo naroda*) was formed in Saratov Pronvince in the fall of 1905. (Raleigh, *Revolution on the Volga*, p. 56. The Union was the main rightist organization in Saratov Province during the First and Second Duma periods. The main leftist groups in Saratov Province were the two wings of the Social Democrats, the Socialist Revolutionaries, and the Union of Workers, later called the Trudoviks, as discussed in the following pages.

64. *Tovarishch*, no. 186, February 8, 1907, p. 5; *Vestnik partii narodnoi svobody*, no. 4, 1907, col. 272.

65. GARF, f. 523, op. 1, d. 362, p. 25 f. and 33 f.

66. *Saratovskii listok*, no. 62, March 18, 1906, p. 2; and no. 64, March 21, 1906, p. 3.

67. Finally, however, Dietz left the party shortly before the gathering of the provincial electoral assembly and joined the newly created Trudovik Party. Long, *From Privileged to Dispossessed*, p. 209 f.

68. Ibid., p. 203 ff.

69. Emmons, *The Formation of Political Parties*, p. 278.

70. Dahlmann, *Provinz*, p. 219.

71. *Saratovskii listok*, no. 78, April 14, 1906 and no. 79, April 15, 1906; Emmons, *The Formation of Political Parties*, p. 321 f.; Dahlmann, *Provinz*, pp. 233–235. On the origins of the Trudovik Party, see Hannu Immonen, "Auf der Suche nach der ideologischen und organisatorischen Identität: Die Trudoviki von der Ersten Duma bis zu ihrem ersten Parteitag im Jahre 1906," in *Acta Societatis Historiae Finlandiae Septentrionalis X Faravid* (Jyväskylä, 1987) Oulun Yliopisto Historian Laitos, no.170, pp. 259–275.

72. *Saratovskii listok*, no. 81, April 18, 1906, p. 2; Dahlmann, *Provinz*, p. 236 f.

73. Dahlmann, *Provinz*, p. 218.

74. More exact proofs are in Dahlmann, *Provinz*, appendix of tables.

75. On the election results in these two provinces, see ibid., appendix of tables.

76. Ibid.

77. Ibid., p. 349 f.

78. Geoffrey Hosking, *The Russian Constitutional Experiment: Government and Duma, 1907–1914* (Cambridge: Cambridge University Press, 1973); Alfred Levin, "June 3, 1907: Action and Reaction," in Alan D. Ferguson, Alfred Levin, eds. *Essays in Russian History: A Collection of Articles Dedicated to George Vernadsky* (Hamden, CT: Archon Books, 1964), pp. 233–273.

79. Dahlmann, *Provinz*, p. 432 ff. The Group of Rightists and the Group of Moderate Rightists became part of the Nationalist faction in the Third Duma. The Nationalists were strong in the southwestern border provinces of the empire; as their name implies one of their cardinal tenets was Great Russian nationalism in this mixed ethnic area. They were progressive capitalists in their economic agenda. For more on the Nationalists, see Robert Edelman, *Gentry Politics on the Eve of the Russian Revolution: The Nationalist Party, 1907–1917* (New Brunswick, NJ: Rutgers University Press, 1980). The Union of Russian People actively participated in the elections to the Third Duma but got no seats in the legislature.

80. Dahlmann, *Provinz,* appendix of tables. The representative of the Party of Peaceful Renewal was N. N. L'vov.

81. Ibid., p. 421. Two seats fell to moderate and five to nonaffiliated candidates. On the Progressists see note 14 in this chapter.

82. Ibid., appendix of tables.

83. Ibid., p. 543. See also Eduard Vishnevskii, *Liberal'naia oppositsiia v Rossii nakanune pervoi mirovoi voiny* (Moscow, 1994) p. 98 f.

84. Valentin V. Shelokhaev, *Ideologiia i politicheskaia organizatsiia rossiiskoi liberal'noi burzhuazii 1907–1914 gg.* (Moscow, 1991), p. 202.

85. On the representation of the peasants in the Duma, see Joachim von Puttkamer, "Die Vertretung der Bauernschaft in der Dritten Duma und ihr Beitrag zur Debatte über die Stolypinschen Agrarreformen," in *Jahrbücher für Geschichte Osteuropas*, N. F. 41 (1993), pp. 44–80.

86. Dahlmann, *Provinz*, p. 505 ff, 585 ff.; Vishnevskii, *Liberal'naia oppositsiia*, p. 93 ff.

5

P. A. Stolypin, Marxists, and Liberals Versus Owners of Pharmacies and Pharmaceutical Firms in Late Imperial Russia

Mary Schaeffer Conroy
University of Colorado, Denver

Peter Arkad'evich Stolypin left an indelible impression on political, social, and economic developments in late Imperial Russia. From 1906 until his untimely death in 1911 Stolypin occupied the positions of Chairman of the Council of Ministers and Minister of Internal Affairs. The Ministry of Internal Affairs was a massive ministry that dealt with peasants, local government, non-Russian nationalities of the empire, the police, and medical and health matters. Thus, ipso facto, Stolypin was directly or indirectly involved with these matters.[1] Further, Stolypin tried to turn the post of Chair of the Council of Ministers into one more resembling that of Prime Minister. His forceful personality led to the enactment of a number of important reforms (some of which were drafted when he took office). In large part he determined the Russian government's stance toward the new parliament, which consisted after 1906 of a popularly elected lower chamber, the State Duma, and an upper chamber, the revised State Council. To contemporaries and historians Stolypin symbolized the tsarist government's opposition to radicals and revolutionaries. Indeed, both Stolypin's detractors and admirers have labelled his slightly more than five-year administration "The Stolypin Era."

Historians have looked at Stolypin through a variety of lenses— the agrarian reforms that bore his name; his treatment of Finland, Russian Poland, and nationalist groups in the Caucasus; his views on self-government and plans for extending it to the *volost'* or township level and to the western border provinces; his management of the police and maintenance of law and order; his relationship with Constitutional Democratic (Kadet) and Octobrist Party leaders; and his relationship with the Third Duma, which following Stolypin's summary revision of the electoral law, lasted its full five-year term from 1907 to 1912.[2]

The portrait of Stolypin emerging from these studies is that of an authoritarian and centralist-minded Russian official, not hamstrung by an excessively bureaucratic mentality and possessed of enough vision and decency to be called a statesman.

Stolypin's supervision over the Medical Council and Medical Department in the Ministry of Internal Affairs has been little examined. But this facet of his jurisdiction is noteworthy. His participation in issues handled by the Medical Council, particularly those dealing with pharmacy and the pharmaceutical industry, helps round out Stolypin, his political activity, and political and economic developments in Russia as a whole in the late nineteenth early twentieth centuries.

Pharmacists themselves were a microcosm of Russian society, although there were only approximately 10,000 in the Russian Empire on the eve of World War I out of a population close to 144 million Some pharmacists were employees; others were proprietors of pharmacies and pharmaceutical enterprises. Some were researchers who made major scientific breakthroughs. Pharmacists reflected the multinational character of the Russian Empire. About one-third of all *Provizors* or fully qualified pharmacists were Poles, another third were Jewish, some 13 percent were German. There were also women pharmacists at the turn of the century, comprising about 3 percent of the total. Mostly Poles and Jews, women pharmacists were as diverse as men.[3]

Pharmacists reflected the class disparities that existed in late Imperial Russia but also the social mobility available to citizens. Pharmacists' status and income were largely determined by educational level. Pharmacy apprentices and most Assistant Pharmacists, who amounted to two-thirds of all certified pharmacists, were at one end of the spectrum. Assistant Pharmacists' training consisted of incomplete secondary school education, apprenticeship, short preparatory courses, and an examination. For many, this level was terminal. Assistant pharmacists could not manage fully stocked "normal" pharmacies. Most, along with pharmacy students, were employed in pharmacies and pharmaceutical establishments. Assistant Pharmacists, however, could manage partially stocked village pharmacies. Further, they could *own* any type of pharmacy, and some 15 percent owned 18 to 20 percent of the pharmacies by World War I. Provizors, with two years of university education, constituted the other one-third of the pharmacists. Most were owners or managers of pharmacies. About 1 percent of all pharmacists had reached the apex of the profession, the level of *Magistr* or Master, by World War I. Masters had done advanced study and written a thesis in addition to completing the full university course. Two-thirds owned pharmacies or pharmaceutical enterprises. Others taught, did research, or held government positions.[4]

Pharmacists typified the "Janus-faced" relationship between the middle class and the government of late Imperial Russia discussed in Thomas Porter and William Gleason's chapter 3 of this volume. On the one hand, pharmacists testified to the autonomy and business acumen that percolated through Imperial Russia. The pharmaceutical corporation, or *soslovie* as members called it,[5] showed many signs of self-sufficiency, capably managing, throughout the nineteenth century, affairs pertaining to pharmacists. During the nineteenth century pharmacists' mutual assistance and pension funds sprouted in eight cities of the empire. The pharmaceutical corporation organized societies and conferences and published journals. That all these activities were approved by the government did not diminish the self-starting mechanism they indicated. Individual pharmacists showed initiative by relentlessly pressuring local authorities, the Medical Council of the Ministry of Internal Affairs, and the Governing Senate, to relax or waive the criteria that limited the number of normal or fully outfitted pharmacies—census figures, prescription turnover, and the consensus of those owning normal pharmacies in the area—and grant them permission to establish new normal pharmacies. Of course, owning and managing a village pharmacy was always an option, but many pharmacists who wished to stay in urban areas circumvented the strict limitations on normal pharmacies by establishing *aptekarskie magaziny* or drug stores, which sold sundries in addition to prepared, packaged medicines and were less regulated than pharmacies. By the early twentieth century these businesses were almost twice as numerous as pharmacies. A few pharmacists became wealthy and famous owners of pharmaceutical factories, using innovative production and marketing techniques to compete with foreign houses. Pharmacists demonstrated social responsibility by contributing to the "pure food and environment movement" in the late nineteenth and early twentieth centuries, essaying food and household products in their pharmacies or specially constituted laboratories.[6]

However, because the Medical Council and Medical Department in the Ministry of Internal Affairs assiduously regulated most aspects of Russian pharmacy and the pharmaceutical industry, its heavy hand was more often visible than not. Indeed, pharmacy and the pharmaceutical industry vividly illustrate the triangular nature of the prerevolutionary Russian economy: government paternalism and control, energized by lively entrepreneurship and market forces and tempered by socialist currents.[7] Government domination generated dependency among pharmacists. Even revolutionary pharmacists sometimes looked to the government to subsidize their socialist programs.

In the last years of the nineteenth century and first decade of the twentieth, pharmacy matters became politicized and enmeshed with debates about the economic system appropriate for Russia.

Revolutionary pharmacists, probably Marxists, organized "professional societies" from the mid-1890s. In Moscow radical pharmacists transformed the Mutual Assistance Fund, established in 1867, into the Marxist Russian Pharmacy Society in 1895. Petersburg Marxist pharmacists established their Northern Society in 1901. The Russian Pharmacy Society had its own journal.[8]

During 1905 radical pharmacists organized strikes. Some strikes were clearly warranted, others seemed forced. In any case, even when striking pharmacists' separate demands were justified, the entire package of their demands—shorter hours, double and triple shifts, higher pay, two weeks' to a month's vacation with pay—were not economically feasible for pharmacy owners. To pharmacy owners and managers, radical pharmacists' insistence that staff pharmacists approve hiring and firing appeared undue interference.[9]

The number of radical pharmacists is uncertain, although we know the names and histories of many, women as well as men. From 1906 through World War I, radical pharmacists zealously tried to organize unions and generate hostility on the part of rank-and-file pharmacists toward pharmacy owners. But they themselves admitted that rank-and-file pharmacists were little interested in the radical message. Employed pharmacists had to be enticed to join unions, attend meetings, and subscribe to radical journals. All sorts of blandishments were used. During this period radical pharmacists also honed their plans for municipalization or turning over private pharmacies to municipal dumas and zemstvos, through buyout schemes subsidized by the government.[10]

During Stolypin's administration, members of two newly established mainstream parties—the "liberal" Kadets and their slightly more conservative cousins the Octobrists—also became embroiled in pharmacy controversies.

Five main pharmacy issues erupted during Stolypin's administration: (1) resolution of the ongoing Pharmacy Pension Fund conflict; (2) proposals on pharmacy schools; (3) a program to enhance the Russian pharmaceutical industry; (4) the drafting of a new pharmacy statute; and (5) an Octobrist bill, introduced into the Third Duma, to increase the number of public pharmacies (zemstvo- and city-owned pharmacies, where socialized pharmacy often prevailed) to the detriment of private pharmacy owners.

Stolypin's policies and behavior in these matters reveal him as more flexible politically—more of a risk taker, more willing to look at all sides of controversial questions—than hitherto depicted. At the same time, the economic and fiscal principles to which Stolypin adhered, as reflected in these issues and other projects that he sponsored, mark him as a traditional Minister of Internal Affairs—fiscally lenient, committed to government paternalism, and contrasting sharply with fiscally conservative ministers of Finance, like his colleague Count Vladimir Kokovtsov. In the bargain Stolypin emerges as combative about foreign pharmaceutical houses' competition with domestic producers supervised by his ministry.

Three of the pharmacy issues—the Pension Fund conflict, the new Pharmacy Statute, and the Octobrist bill to expand public pharmacy—provide information on political parties that played important roles in Russia in the first two decades of the twentieth century. The Pension Fund conflict particularly highlights revolutionary pharmacists' (probably Bolshevik and Menshevik) modus operandi. Discussion surrounding the new Pharmacy Statute sheds light on the operation and mind-set of the "liberal" Kadets and their continued interaction with radical-left groups, which had begun in 1902 and 1903. The Octobrist proposal to expand public—zemstvo and municipal—pharmacies gives a new slant on their organization and mentality.

STOLYPIN AND THE NATIONAL PHARMACY PENSION FUND CONFLICT

The Marxist Russian Pharmacy Society in Moscow began a hostile takeover of the National Pharmacy Pension Fund in 1898. The design for the fund had emerged at the Second Pharmacy Congress of 1889. The fund, also headquartered in Moscow, began operating in 1894. Both pharmacy owners and pharmacists employed in pharmacies and pharmaceutical factories contributed to the fund. Monies were deposited in bank accounts and invested in stocks and bonds.[11]

Assisted by elected administrative and supervisory-audit boards, Vladimir Karlovich Ferrein, pharmaceutical tycoon, directed the National Pharmacy Pension Fund from its inception until 1905. Under his management the basic capital of the fund swelled to over 1 million rubles. Only a small amount was devoted to operating costs. Through "boring from within"—manipulating elections and causing chaos at general meetings—revolutionary Marxist pharmacists captured key fund offices between 1903 and 1907.[12]

Their takeover attempts reached a crescendo during Stolypin's administration. Since elections had increased their membership on the Fund's Administrative Board, radical pharmacists demanded that Vladimir Karlovich Ferrein, chairman of the board, turn over to them the assets, books, and the headquarters of fund. Ferrein and the remaining original members of the Administrative Board refused.

The fund statutes stipulated that the Ministry of Internal Affairs assume management of the fund in the event of disorders and irregularities. When Ferrein suggested this course to thwart the hostile takeover, the Marxist pharmacists opposed him. Instead, radical pharmacists turned to the courts and lobbied the Ministry of Internal Affairs. They sued in a Moscow Justice of the Peace Court, appealed to the jurisconsult of the Moscow State Bank, and in 1907 petitioned the

Insurance Department of the Ministry of Internal Affairs to rule in their favor.[13] Ministry officials were sympathetic to radical members of the new administration and censorious toward the old administration, although by 1909 Stolypin called for a general meeting to elect a new Administrative Board.[14]

Historians generally insist that Stolypin was uniformly and implacably hostile to revolutionary individuals and groups. They likewise often imply that this was an error on his part. The National Pharmacy Pension Fund controversy helps undermine these assertions. Given the extensive discussion of all aspects of the fund controversy in the pharmaceutical press, it is possible but unlikely that Stolypin and the Ministry of Internal Affairs were not familiar with the revolutionary Marxist orientation of the perpetrators of the conflict. Nevertheless, they appear to have been convinced that since the radicals had been elected to their administrative posts they were entitled to manage the National Pharmacy Pension Fund. Stolypin's treatment of the radical pharmacists in the fund conflict squares with the fairly wide latitude his ministry accorded their pharmacy journals after 1908, allowing them to broadcast a rather audacious political and social message to apathetic constituents.[15] In other words, if radicals were not engaged in political disobedience and outright social upheaval, Stolypin was likely to keep them under surveillance but not necessarily assault them.

With regard to revolutionary pharmacists themselves, the National Pharmacy Pension Fund controversy exhibits their willingness to sacrifice concrete and immediate benefits for their constituents in order to achieve a future utopia. One Marxist pharmacist, O. G. Gabrilovich, originator of a program to buy out private pharmacies, discussed below, was financially sophisticated. However, he was an exception among revolutionary pharmacists. His colleagues who took over the National Pharmacy Pension Fund lacked the financial acumen of the old administration. They spent lavishly on administration and overhead. Additionally, their wrangling over management of the fund depleted membership and contributions and stifled the fund's growth.

In any case, the intervention of the Ministry of Internal Affairs did not solve the conflict between the old and new administrations of the National Pharmacy Pension Fund. In 1910, Octobrist D. N. Shipov accepted chairmanship of a committee to resolve the differences. However, debates on the fate of the fund raged until the revolutions of 1917.[16]

Stolypin and Pharmacy Education Reform

The second pharmacy issue in which Stolypin became involved was pharmacy education. Russian pharmacy education for Provizors and Masters was quite good and compared favorably with that in other continental states in the nineteenth and early twentieth centuries. Foreign observers gave Russian pharmacy education high marks in the middle of the nineteenth century. In the ensuing decades a number of Provizors obtained their Master's degrees at foreign universities. They performed well, sometimes staying on to work in the laboratories of famous researchers. Their prolific publications were well received in the medical community.

In the closing decades of the century, however, Russian pharmacists regarded the prevailing admission requirements and early pharmacy training and education inadequate. Indeed, pharmacists in a number of other countries also viewed their pharmacy training in the same light. In Russia, a school-leaving certificate was not demanded of entrants to the profession. They were required to have completed only four years of the eight-year classical *gimnaziia* or an equivalent secondary school. Training for the Assistant Pharmacist title, the first rung of the profession, consisted largely of hands-on work in a normal or fully stocked pharmacy. Pharmacy apprentices mainly studied on their own for the Assistant Pharmacist examination, although there were a few organized courses to prepare them. Those who wished to become fully qualified pharmacists were forced to perform another three-year stint of service after passing the Assistant Pharmacist examination and before entering a university. There they were regarded as auditors rather than full-fledged students.

During the second half of the nineteenth century, progressive-minded pharmacists urged that entry requirements and lower-level specialized pharmaceutical education be upgraded. They especially desired pharmacy entrants to have a secondary school-leaving certificate. They also campaigned for higher-level pharmacy courses. The pharmacy corporation diverged, however, on how much apprenticeship should be retained and whether the courses should be housed in state universities or independent proprietary pharmacy schools.[17]

After decades of indecision on the part of the pharmacy corporation, the Ministry of Internal Affairs stepped in to reform pharmacy education.

Between 1904 and 1906 a number of proposals for improving higher- and lower-level pharmacy education emerged from the ministry. But the Russo-Japanese War of 1904–1905 and the revolutionary upheaval of those years had been costly for the state treasury.[18] Thus while ministerial proposals continued to include government supervision over pharmacy education, because the government was short of funds the proposals advocated proprietary pharmacy schools and institutes rather than state schools or pharmacy departments in universities. Both Stolypin and Chief Medical Inspector V. K. von Anrep signed the ministry's proposal of November 1906, intended for submission to the Second Duma. The November 1906 proposal only slightly raised educational qualifications for pharmacists and reiterated that "hope rested with private initiative" because "contemporary conditions did not permit the government or public institutions to establish pharmacy schools."[19]

One might have assumed that such policy statements would have spurred the pharmacy corporation into taking more control over professional education. But internal dissention within the corporation continued. Therefore, in 1909 the Medical Council subsumed the pharmacy education reform debate. The council advocated two tiers of pharmacists—technicians and educated pharmacists. Pharmacist technicians, in turn, would be comprised of two types, those with incomplete secondary education (increased, however, to six years instead of the previous four) who would apprentice in a pharmacy and receive the terminal title Assistant Pharmacist; and those with incomplete secondary education who would attend (probably private) pharmacy schools with two-year programs, take the examination for Assistant Pharmacist, and then audit university pharmacy courses where they would be eligible for the Provizor degree. They then would be able to manage a village or zemstvo pharmacy, drug store, or pharmacy warehouse. Full-fledged pharmacists, likewise, were to include two groups. The first would finish full secondary education and complete natural science courses at a university. These pharmacists would be eligible for the degree of Master or Doctor of Pharmacy and could manage a normal pharmacy or pharmaceutical factory producing galenical preparations. The second group would finish the full gimnaziia course, take a three-year pharmacy program at a university, apprentice in a pharmacy, receive the degree of Provizor, and be eligible for the Master's degree.[20]

Pharmacists' reactions to the proposals varied. Military and naval pharmacists accepted the proposals with modifications. The St. Petersburg Pharmacy Society, spokes-group for the pharmacy corporation, on the contrary, rejected the ministery's proposals, insisting that all pharmacists must finish secondary school. With a school-leaving certificate they could practice as Assistant Pharmacists or enter a university and acquire the higher degrees of Provizor, Candidate, and Master. The Petersburg Society further opposed the bifurcation of pharmacists into technicians and educated pharmacists, considering the post of pharmacist-technicians unprofessional, even demeaning.[21] The society also was annoyed that pharmacists had not been consulted about the government project.[22] Still, some pharmacists approved the ministry's proposals because they offered them the opportunity to become a Doctor of Pharmacy.[23]

The pharmacy education issue illustrated how lack of funds on the part of both the government and male pharmacists, combined with lack of decisiveness on the part of the latter stalemated pharmacy education reform in Russia and established codependency between male pharmacists and the tsarist government. Russian physicians and bureaucrats dominated and discounted pharmacists in the nineteenth and early twentieth centuries. Yet, strained finances forced the government to propose devolving expensive education projects onto the pharmacy community. There were a few proprietary pharmacy schools in Russia in the late nineteenth century. The Medical Council of the Ministry of Internal Affairs would never have completely relinquished supervision over pharmacy education since it impacted public health. In the United States, state-supported pharmacy schools were supplanting proprietary schools in the late nineteenth and early twentieth centuries. But, in any case, the Russian pharmacy corporation, in the main, rejected the opportunity to establish a network of its own schools.

On the other hand, an enterprising woman pharmacist, Antonina Lesnevskaia, established a pharmacy school for women, duly sanctioned by the government, attached to her "First Women's Pharmacy" in St. Petersburg in the early twentieth century. Supported by tuition, the school had some difficult moments, but in general the school and its more than 300 graduates were successful. The government recognized the transformation of Lesnevskaia's school into a higher pharmacy institute in 1916 during World War I.[24]

Stolypin and the Russian Pharmaceutical Industry

The Russian pharmaceutical industry was under the thumb of the Russian government. But in contrast to the torpor of the pharmacy community on the question of improving pharmaceutical education, pharmacists involved in the production of ready-made medicines and health supplies displayed initiative and dynamism. Indeed, they were among the entrepreneurs that drove industry and the Russian economy in the nineteenth and early twentieth centuries.

The Russian pharmaceutical industry in many ways mirrored Russian industry and industrialization in the late imperial period. In the early twentieth century there were almost a hundred pharmaceutical enterprises scattered throughout the European section of the empire. Seven were located in Warsaw, seven in the Baltic region, three in Kremenchug, Ukraine, seven in Tver', and two in Kazan', two in Kostroma Province, three in Nizhni-Novgorod, two in Khar'kov. One or more enterprises were located in Olonets, Dvinsk, the Caucasus, Kiev, Saratov, Minsk, Grodno, Kishinev, and Vil'na. Some twelve enterprises were located in St. Petersburg, but Moscow was definitely the hub of the pharmaceutical industry with some twenty enterprises. Owners included individuals, zemstvos, medical societies, closely knit associations or partnerships (*Tovarishchestva*), and publicly held joint-stock companies (*Aktsionernye obshchestva*). Medical societies and zemstvos in Poltava, Chernigov, Khar'kov, Kherson, Odessa, and Samara began to produce smallpox and antirabies vaccines and tuberculin in the 1880s.[25] In 1896 the government established a factory in St. Petersburg to produce medicines for the military. This factory and the Military Medical Academy in St. Petersburg produced over sixty kinds of tablets and other pharmaceuticals.[26]

Many of these nineteenth-, early twentieth-century pharmaceutical enterprises in Russia were small workshops. Some, however, including Pel' and Sons in St. Petersburg and R. R. Keler and V. K. Ferrein in Moscow, were large operations with hundreds of workers and sophisticated technology. The Ferrein firm employed chemists and had laboratories for testing and quality control. Ferrein, Keler, and Pel' used modern marketing techniques, selling medicines, bandages, soaps, cosmetics, cleaning powders, etc. to the hinterlands through wholesale warehouses, agents, and illustrated catalogues or *preis kuranty*. They produced their own packages and containers. These Russian firms competed with each other and with foreign pharmaceutical firms operating or selling medicines and supplies in Russia such as Merck, Shering, and Parke, Davis and Company. A few Russian pharmacists and pharmaceutical firms made internationally recognized discoveries. The quality of some goods produced by Russian firms was equal to that of foreign houses. When customers preferred foreign goods, large Russian firms lured them by offering favorable prices, credit, and delivery terms. In contrast to extravagant claims made by purveyors of American patent or proprietary medicines, Russian firms' advertising was sober and to the point.

The Russian pharmaceutical industry (supplemented by popular remedies) supplied about half the empire's medicines and medical needs before World War I. On the eve of World War I, Russian pharmaceutical enterprises produced some 7 million rubles' worth of wares; only 3 million rubles' worth were imported. Put another way, thirty-nine crucial medicines and disinfectants were produced in Russia and forty-eight were imported. Some zemstvos procured most or all their medicines and supplies from Russian firms.

But despite successes, several factors hampered the Russian pharmaceutical industry from competing on a level field with foreign pharmaceutical houses and lessening Russia's dependence on imports. Some problems, such as lack of key raw plants and chemicals and foreign houses' strangleholds on patents for crucial medicines, were difficult to surmount, although more intensive research and development might have helped close the gap to some extent. Similarly, preference for foreign medicines on the part of physicians and consumers and opposition to factory-produced medicines on the part of protectionist pharmacists themselves were difficult to combat.

But the chief obstacles to growth of the industry were government regulations and government tariff policies. Although the government had nurtured the pharmaceutical industry in the eighteenth and early nineteenth centuries, by Stolypin's administration government policies were pernicious to the industry. An overabundance of government regulations choked start-ups and innovation. High tariffs raised expenditures on imports of raw materials lacking in Russia but necessary for domestic production, whereas low tariffs on foreign packaged medicines increased competition for Russian firms.[27]

In 1911 Stolypin and his ministry made a rather clumsy attempt to bolster Russian pharmaceutical houses against their foreign competitors. A circular emanating from the Ministry of Internal Affairs, undoubtedly with Stolypin's sanction, authorized pharmacies and pharmaceutical factories to produce generic versions of foreign medicines. They were required only to put disclaimers on the label indicating Russian provenance. French pharmaceutical manufacturers were particularly outraged. The Russian Minister of Justice averred that the circular violated international trade agreements. In any case, the Russian government's attempt to boost the domestic pharmaceutical industry had little practical result because the government continued a tariff policy that imposed low duties on foreign-made medicaments and high duties on raw materials needed for Russian production, continued to meddle in Russian pharmaceutical production, and continued to show greater leniency to sales of foreign pharmaceuticals in Russia.[28]

Stolypin's policies for the pharmaceutical industry reflected an economic credo typical of many tsarist bureaucrats. The proposals appeared to be a belated and somewhat misguided effort to strengthen the industry against foreign competitors without relinquishing the ministerial controls that inhibited the industry's growth.

Nevertheless, the Russian pharmaceutical industry continued to expand. Between 1909 and 1911 Russian production of salicylic acid increased markedly, although it dipped between 1911 and 1912.[29] Although salicylic acid was inferior to the febrifuges produced in Germany, this development was promising. Similarly, a laboratory established in 1914 as a section of the Stock Company, "Russian Dye," a chemical firm, formed the basis for producing a Russian version of the new antivenereal Salvarsan.[30] However, the government would only unfetter the industry during World War I when the exigencies of the times demanded this course.

STOLYPIN'S PHARMACY STATUTE, KADET AND POPULAR DEBATES THEREON, AND THE OCTOBRIST BILL TO EXTEND "PUBLIC" PHARMACY

The new Pharmacy Statute produced by the Ministry of Internal Affairs; Kadet, Octobrist, and popular reaction to it; and the Octobrist M. K. Safonov's bill to extend "public," that is, zemstvo- and city-owned pharmacies, were perhaps the most interesting pharmacy issues to emerge during Stolypin's administration.

On the economic front, the Pharmacy Statute, debates swirling around the statute, and the bill to extend zemstvo- and city-owned pharmacies emphasize the strong, deep, widespread attraction to socialism that jockeyed against private enterprise in late Imperial Russia. The hostility that liberals in the Duma (and outside it) displayed toward private pharmacists parallelled liberal antipathy toward metallurgical industrialists[31] and supplemented—and ultimately supported—Russian revolutionaries' opposition to private enterprise.

In the political arena, the Pharmacy Statute, the Kadet caucus on it, and the Octobrist bill to expand zemstvo and municipal pharmacies reveal the Kadets as still cocky and the Octobrists as more aggressive than usually depicted, and suggest that had World War I not intervened the parliament might have become a more equal player with the government.

On June 3, 1907, following dissolution of the fractious Second Duma, Stolypin issued an electoral law for the Third Duma that weighted representation in favor of propertied or conservative elements as opposed to communal peasants, workers, and urban intelligentsia. This has often been called Stolypin's coup d'état, an "alliance with the gentry reaction." A specialist on Russian medical history once claimed that the "June 3 system" represented Stolypin's repudiation of liberalism on the national level as well as on the local level, in the zemstvos.[32] His new work on the Third Duma period is more nuanced.[33]

Stolypin did mistrust the Kadets in 1906 because of their radical economic agenda and alignment with leftist parties in their formative period. He also considered zemstvos ancillary to the government and undoubtedly wanted to control them as other government agencies.[34] However, the Pharmacy Statute, along with other evidence, underscores the fact that Stolypin by no means repudiated zemstvos or moderate zemstvo liberals wholesale. Similarly, the Kadet caucus on the Pharmacy Statute and the Octobrist bill to expand public pharmacies go far toward proving that the "propertied elements" who dominated the Third Duma after the June 3 Law were not uniformly reactionary and, further, that the Third Duma was not submissive.

As for Stolypin's relationship with the zemstvos, Gleason and Porter have recounted that Stolypin appreciated zemstvo help in famine relief and resettling peasants in Siberia. The Pharmacy Statute that Stolypin tendered constituted a modest attempt to strengthen zemstvo pharmacy. This effort synchronized with Stolypin's attempts to co-opt "public figures" into the Council of Ministers during 1906, his good relationship with zemstvo figures while Minister of Internal Affairs, his abolishing limitations on zemstvos' policy making and tax levying, his proposals to extend zemstvos to the volost' level,[35] his approval in 1908 of a proposal brought by thirty-three Duma members to increase zemstvos in Astrakhan' Province,[36] and his periodic requests for treasury assistance to zemstvos and cities.

Indeed, the government subsidized zemstvos' grants to citizens suffering from poor harvests and assisted local self-government in other ways. The zemstvos were supposed to pay back government loans but financial setbacks frequently made them request extensions.[37] Stolypin's assistance toward the zemstvos was not diminished by the fact that he (and other ministers) generously doled out money to individuals and groups for all sorts of reasons and underwrote projects of every variety.[38]

Tsarist gold reserves amounted to over 1 billion rubles in 1908.[39] Nevertheless, Russia's financial position was still shaky from losses incurred during the Russo-Japanese War of 1904–1905 and the costs of putting down unrest in those and following years.[40] The lion's share of government spending was devoted to large-ticket items—rearmament, shipbuilding, railroad maintenance, and administration.[41] However, government assistance to zemstvos and multiple petty causes contributed to the drain on the state treasury. Minister of Finance Count Kokovtsov was sufficiently disturbed to frequently caution his colleagues that the state budget was in straitened circumstances[42] and to attempt to curb their largesse. He consistently stressed the benefits of privately operated services (such as telephone lines)[43] and chipped away at Stolypin's budget allocation requests to increase provincial staff salaries,[44] augment city police forces,[45] hold a national census,[46] modernize the Moscow postal department,[47] and fund other projects, both serious and trivial.[48] Kokovtsov further insisted that Stolypin and other ministers request allocations through the State Duma,[49] presumably to prune ministerial budgets.

As for the allegation that the June 3 Law resulted in a swell of reaction during the Third Duma period, zemstvo activists and Duma members who campaigned to expand public pharmacies during this time came largely from professional and nonpropertied backgrounds. Moreover, in matters pertaining to pharmacy the influence of professionals and ideologues increased in the Third Duma whereas the interests of private pharmacy owners were weakened.

Further, the Octobrist bill to extend public pharmacy manifested self-confidence on the part of zemstvo activists and Duma representatives, despite Stolypin's cavalier treatment of the latter in 1909 and again in 1911. There are many examples of Stolypin's willingness to work with and strengthen the Third Duma.[50] However, he sacrificed the Duma in 1909 during the so-called Naval General Staff Crisis and again in the spring of 1911 during the so-called Zemstvo Crisis in order to save his own position and program.[51] The procedures the Octobrists used to submit their bill on zemstvo pharmacy and the Duma's subsequent passage of it signalled the parliament's comeback after the Naval General Staff and Zemstvo Crises, stubborn refusal on the part of the parliament to submit to Stolypin or the government, and an attempt to make the government accept the Duma as more than a junior partner in policy making. This augured well for the viability of representative institutions in Russia's future.

On the other hand, the debates surrounding the Pharmacy Statute and the Octobrist bill to expand public pharmacies also sounded a disquieting note, for secure property rights, economic autonomy, and ample scope for private enterprise are key ingredients for a healthy civil society and effective representative political system.[52] Yet zemstvo activists and Duma representatives sought to strengthen the prerogatives of public zemstvo and municipal pharmacies at the expense of owners of private pharmacies.

The Russian pharmacy system combined government supervision and privately owned pharmacies, with some free trade and socialized dispensing. The Ministry of Internal Affairs, through the Medical Council and provincial medical inspectors, zealously regulated both the establishment and the operation of all Russian pharmacies. As noted, the establishment of normal or fully stocked pharmacies, both privately owned and those belonging to zemstvos and cities, depended on population quotas, prescriptions, approval of existing pharmacy owners in the vicinity, and the sanction of local and central authorities. A plethora of statutes spelled out every detail of pharmacy operation, including prices that could be charged for drugs. Village pharmacies were established on a geographical basis. Regulations decreed that only pharmacies were allowed to dispense medicines made up on site. This regimen was dubbed the "Pharmacy Monopoly."[53]

Aptekarskie magaziny, drug stores or drug emporia, were permitted to purvey ready-made medicines as well as sundries if they adhered to certain guidelines. Actually, the drug stores operated under more lenient rules than pharmacies. The fact that there were nearly twice as many drug stores as pharmacies by World War I testifies to the benefits of free trade. However, the protectionist mentality of the majority of pharmacists and the legalism of the Medical Council and Medical Department preserved the existing system, the "Pharmacy Monopoly," until the last decades of the old regime.[54]

The number of public pharmacies was minuscule. Of the approximately 4,800 pharmacies that existed in Russia on the eve of World War I, only some 200 were public pharmacies owned by zemstvos and municipal dumas. Zemstvo pharmacies were very unevenly distributed among the thirty-four provinces of European Russia in which zemstvos existed. For example, in 1909, Vladimir Province had 7 zemstvo pharmacies; Vologda, 9; Voronezh, 8; Viatka, 14; Kaluga, 12; Kostroma and Kursk each had 7; Nizhni-Novgorod, 9; Penza, 7; and Perm, 15. In other provinces the number of zemstvo pharmacies ranged from one to five; Yekaterinoslav and St. Petersburg had none at all. Of the 160 zemstvo pharmacies in existence in 1909, 141 were located in county seats and 18 in villages.[55]

Pharmacies owned by private individuals and groups discounted or dispensed medicine free to the poor.[56] Zemstvo pharmacies also gradually acquired the right to dispense medicine at a discount or free, in some cases to certified poor, in other cases to all zemstvo taxpayers. Private pharmacy owners in the vicinity of zemstvo pharmacies claimed this gave public pharmacies an unfair advantage because prices for medicines that private pharmacies dispensed to other than certified poor were set by law. On the other side of the ledger, prodigal spending on medicines and health care and liberal dispensing led a number of zemstvos into financial straits by the first decade of the twentieth century. Pharmacy expenditures for district zemstvos in Riazan' and Simbirsk Provinces far exceeded their budgets. During the 1890s and the first decade of the twentieth century, several county zemstvos in Tver' Province ordered medicines and supplies haphazardly, stored them carelessly, and dispensed them too liberally, wreaking havoc with their budgets and causing them to fall into arrears in payments to the Tver' provincial zemstvo pharmacy warehouse for these supplies; the provincial zemstvo itself suffered financial problems during part of this time as a result of poor accounting procedures. In 1908 radical Marxist B. N. Saltykov came under fire from socialist comrades for mismanaging the Moscow provincial zemstvo pharmacy warehouse and dissipating its budget.[57]

The well-publicized plight of impecunious zemstvos should have raised flags about socialized dispensing. On the contrary, support for public pharmacy and disapproval of private pharmacy swelled during the late nineteenth century. Advocates for public pharmacy included many physicians, elected zemstvo activists, professionals hired by the zemstvos (the so-called Third Element), radical-left pharmacists (Mensheviks and Bolsheviks, most of whom did not own pharmacies or even practice pharmacy), nonpharmacist Kadets and Octobrists, Duma and State Council representatives, governors, and officials in the Medical Council of the Ministry of Internal Affairs. Their promotion of public pharmacy gained increasing adherents among citizens at large by 1910.

It was laudable that advocates for public pharmacy desired more and better medicine in the hinterlands. However, the methods they proposed were not the most efficient, cost-effective, or beneficial for the public. In fact rural pharmacies were growing at a faster pace than normal pharmacies. Dearth of pharmacies in rural areas was partly due to government restrictions on establishing pharmacies. Additionally, pharmacists were reluctant to live in remote areas. Still, the pharmacy monopoly limited the supply of pharmacies and made those available expensive. Thus, many pharmacists, unable to purchase pharmacies, eagerly established pharmacies in Siberian and Central Asian towns.[58] American and British observers in late Imperial Russia, familiar with a laissez-faire pharmacy system, opined that the best way to increase the number of pharmacies for both pharmacists and the public would be to abolish the restrictive pharmacy monopoly and institute a system that permitted free establishment of pharmacies.[59]

Nevertheless, suggestions about the benefits that would accrue from free trade met with widespread rejection in late Imperial Russia. On the one hand, many pharmacists desired to preserve the status quo. On the other, many physicians, bureaucrats, politicians, and journalists (the last two categories included radical pharmacists who were not pharmacy owners) attacked owners of private pharmacies and advocated that the government boost public pharmacies to counter them. Some radicals proposed transferring all pharmacies to zemstvos and municipal dumas.

Many reasons were adduced for curbing private pharmacy owners. Some were more altruistic than others. From the mid-nineteenth century, social-reform-minded physicians railed against the "pharmacy monopoly" because it allegedly allowed private pharmacy owners to reap fantastic profits at the expense of "the people."[60] These assertions were largely unfounded.

During the 1880s and first half of the 1890s, social-minded zemstvo activists fulminated against "rapacious" owners of private pharmacies. They established zemstvo pharmacies in part to fulfill the zemstvo mandate to protect the public against epidemics and in part to curtail owners of private pharmacies. Zemstvos also agressively purchased private pharmacies. By 1904, in thirteen provinces, zemstvos owned the majority of pharmacies in the capital city or in the county seats of the province. Naturally this behavior fueled apprehension on the part of private pharmacy owners who repeatedly lobbied against free or discounted zemstvo dispensing.[61] But buying up private pharmacies did not increase the total number of pharmacies available to the public nor, as most zemstvo pharmacies were located in the capital city of the province or in its county seats, did this increase pharmacies in villages where the need was greatest. Indeed, in 1909, some private pharmacy owners claimed that zemstvo activists themselves were motivated by the profit motive rather than concern for the common weal. They assumed zemstvo pharmacies could be as profitable as private pharmacies and thus increase zemstvo revenue. Nevertheless, in the opinion of the private owners, most zemstvo representatives realized that zemstvo pharmacies were money-losing ventures.[62]

From the late 1890s, radical pharmacists (apparently Marxist Social Democrats), mainly journalists and labor organizers, lambasted private pharmacy owners because they allegedly exploited staff pharmacists as well as the general populace and also because the pharmacy monopoly thwarted growth of the Russian pharmaceutical industry, mass production of medicaments being more progressive in the Marxist worldview than small-scale compounding in the pharmacy. However, these radical pharmacists did not yet suggest expropriating private pharmacies. Rather, from 1904 they propounded buyout schemes to transfer private pharmacies to zemstvos and cities.[63] They also fomented strikes against pharmacy owners from 1905, partly to improve the lot of staff pharmacists but also to cause private owners economic hardship, thus hastening their demise.[64]

Preference for zemstvo pharmacy over private pharmacy was not confined to idealistic physicians, zemstvo activists, or Marxist radicals. At times, in the late nineteenth and early twentieth centuries the Ministry of Internal Affairs appeared to be on the verge of abolishing the pharmacy monopoly and supplanting it with a system that would permit free establishment of pharmacies—the so-called *iavochnyi poriadok*. More often, the ministry supported a policy of strengthening zemstvo pharmacy while maintaining restrictions that limited the establishment of private pharmacies, as well as their dispensing. The ministry took this stance as early as 1887.[65] The ministry's draft revision of the Pharmacy Statute in 1898 and the draft formulated under V. K. von Pleve between 1902 and 1904 proposed greater latitude for municipal dumas and zemstvos to establish pharmacies while retaining restrictions on private pharmacies. Progressive Octobrist physician V. K. von Anrep, Chief Medical Inspector during Pleve's, Durnovo's, and the early part of Stolypin's administration (until 1907), was committed to extending zemstvo pharmacy.[66] Yet P. N. Durnovo himself apparently was not terribly sympathetic toward public pharmacy. During the first years of Stolypin's administration it was rumored that the draft of the Pharmacy Statute being prepared in the Medical Council aimed to abolish the pharmacy monopoly in favor of free establishment of all pharmacies.[67] But the pendulum soon swung back to promoting public pharmacy. In 1906, Stolypin received a deputation from the radical All-Russian Pharmacy Union; he assured them that he would look into the Swedish pharmacy system, which included a fund to buy out private pharmacies and turn them over to management of the whole pharmacy corporation.[68] The draft Pharmacy Statute issued under Stolypin's aegis in 1908 gave preference to public bodies over private individuals in establishing pharmacies, but only in areas where no private pharmacies existed.[69] Thus Stolypin's stand on zemstvo pharmacy versus private was more moderate than that of socialist-oriented physicians, pharmacists, zemstvo activists, and Duma representatives. This was only to be expected from a minister who vociferously advocated that communal peasants become private property owners.

Octobrists in the Third Duma supported Stolypin's program for encouraging communal peasants to establish private farmsteads. At the same time, they and the Kadets unequivocally disapproved of the "pharmacy monopoly" enjoyed by owners of private pharmacies. In 1909, the Kadet Cossack and physician Matvei Petrovich Bakin[70] chaired a commission formed in the Third Duma to review the Pharmacy Statute developed by the Medical Council in Stolypin's Ministry of Internal Affairs. Bakin held a series of meetings in the apartment of Left-Kadet Prince Peter D. Dolgorukov.[71] Representatives from far-left organizations, Kadets, Octobrists, and pharmacy owners attended to thrash out differing views on the "pharmacy monopoly."[72] Bakin had served as a physician in a zemstvo hospital and with the Red Cross during the Russo-Japanese War.[73] His sympathies did not lie with private pharmacy owners and prevailing opinion at the meetings in Dolgorukov's apartment opposed private pharmacy.[74]

Meanwhile, in 1908, thirty-four Octobrist Duma members under the leadership of M. K. Safonov introduced a bill in the first session of the Third Duma that proposed scrapping the pharmacy monopoly and allowing both private individuals and public institutions to freely establish pharmacies.[75] By May 1911 the Safonov bill had metamorphosed into one allowing *only public institutions* to freely establish pharmacies.[76]

The thirty-four Octobrists who sponsored the bill mirrored the heterogeneity of the Octobrist Party. They came from a wide spectrum of backgrounds, including three peasants, a teacher who had become a landowner, a professor, a physician, a merchant, a businessman, three hereditary honored citizens, three hereditary nobles, one "landowner," and six Orthodox priests. Their only common links were their affiliation with zemstvos or municipal dumas, on the one hand, and on the other, the fact that while they were altering the fate of private pharmacy, none were pharmacists or pharmacy owners.[77] Mikhail Kos'mich Safonov himself was a comfortably well-off "Homeowner" and "Hereditary Honored Citizen." Although he derived his income from trade, he had served thirty-seven years as municipal secretary and member of the city *uprava* (steering committee) in the Zaraisk municipal duma, Kazan' Province. He also served on the county education council and was trustee of various schools as well as trade deputy and secretary of the orphan's court.[78]

The Safonov bill unleashed a torrent of criticism against private pharmacy owners in the popular press.[79] Increasing competition to combat private pharmacy owners was not considered a viable alternative. Rather, publicly owned pharmacies and socialized dispensing were touted as antidotes to high prices and undue profits allegedly resulting from the pharmacy monopoly. Journalists enthused that increasing the rights of zemstvos and city dumas over private individuals in the matter of establishing pharmacies was the first step toward "municipalization," that is, transferring all private pharmacies into public hands.[80] The St. Petersburg Pharmacy Society lobbied hard against giving public pharmacies privileges denied to pharmacists and private individuals, but to no avail.[81]

The Duma passed the Safonov bill May 23, 1911.[82] A commission in the State Council, the upper chamber of the parliament, reviewed the bill. The State Council amended the bill November, 1911, to prevent zemstvos and municipalities from selling their pharmacies.[83] It then passed the bill in December 1911.[84] Hostility toward private enterprise was very much in evidence in the State Council, where supporters of the bill equated freeing citizenry from private pharmacy owners with emancipating the serfs in 1861![85] The Safonov bill was signed into law February 12, 1912.

Stolypin was assassinated in 1911. His successors in the Ministry of Internal Affairs attempted to mitigate the negative impact of the Law of February 12, 1912, on private pharmacy owners through explanatory circulars. Local authorities, however, immediately began implementing the law, even to the obvious detriment of private pharmacy owners who desperately petitioned the Senate to issue a ruling that would protect their property rights and income.[86]

In conclusion, pharmacy issues add to our picture of Stolypin and spotlight important political and economic trends in late Imperial Russia. The Bakin Commission and the Safonov bill are particularly significant. In the political realm, the commission and the bill refute the notion that lack of cohesiveness and variegated political outlooks signified weakness in the civil society of late Imperial Russia or retarded the development of democracy.[87] The Bakin Commission's meetings in Prince Dolgorukov's apartment and the St. Petersburg Pharmacy Society's lobbying represented very different mind-sets but showed political astuteness on the part of both groups. Such instances, combined with the political savvy of the Nationalist Party so aptly described by Robert Edelman,[88] document the fact that by 1910 the representative political system established in 1905 was maturing. The Kadet caucus on the Pharmacy Statute and the Octobrist bill promoting public pharmacy in the Third Duma display these opposition parties as self-assured and aggressive. Owners of private pharmacies resented Kadet and Octobrist machinations but, in fact, vested interest groups are integral to democratic systems and legislatures.

The Safonov bill confirms Geoffrey Hosking's analysis that the Octobrists were ambivalent about cooperating with the government and Stolypin in particular.[89] The Safonov bill portrayed a strong, independent-minded Third Duma, on the rebound from the Naval General Staff Crisis of 1909 and the Zemstvo Crisis of 1911. Stolypin had treated the Octobrist-dominated Duma as expendable in these crises. The Safonov bill showed that body was still a force to be reckoned with. The bill violated Duma statutes, which stipulated that Duma bills be submitted in tandem with ministerial bills. According to eminent historian Mark Szeftel, the Duma had long tried to surmount its limitations in this arena. For example, the Duma considered discussion about the desirability of a measure tantamount to discussing an actual bill.[90] But the revised 1911 "socialist" version of the Safonov bill particularly moved beyond the strictures placed on Duma legislative initiative, as commentators noted at that time. Ready before the Ministry of Internal Affairs

Pharmacy Statute, the Safonov bill was submitted independently of the government.[91] Further, the government did not receive back its own version of the project from the Duma.[92] The State Council's passage of the Safonov bill also supported legislative autonomy.

Unfortunately, the Safonov bill emphasizes that while contemporary commentators and latter-day historians have disparaged the *proizvol* of the tsarist government, representative legislatures also can be guilty of arbitrariness. In the interests of their vision of the public good, Duma and State Council delegates who passed the Safonov bill cavalierly dismissed the rights of private pharmacy owners.[93]

The Bakin Commission, the Safonov bill, and the Law of February 12, 1912, confirm a strong attraction to socialism, well before the Bolshevik Revolution, not only on the part of revolutionaries who comprised a minority of the population but on the part of tsarist administrators and politicians such as Kadets who are considered "mainstream liberal" and Octobrists whose political credo has been categorized as "moderately rightist."[94] This attraction to socialism escalated during World War I and neutralized the lively entrepreneurship exhibited by many pharmacists, particularly those who founded pharmaceutical firms. This entrepreneurship, in turn, had leavened the government-dominated economy and had allowed democracy to grow in late Imperial Russia.

NOTES

1. For a description of the Ministry of Internal Affairs prior to Stolypin's administration, see Daniel T. Orlovsky, *The Limits of Reform: The Ministry of Internal Affairs in Imperial Russia, 1802–1881* (Cambridge, MA: Harvard University Press, 1981). For an analysis of the relationship between the ministry and local self-government (zemstvos) prior to Stolypin's administration, see Thomas S. Pearson, *Russian Officialdom in Crisis: Autocracy and Local Self Government, 1861–1900* (New York: Cambridge University Press, 1989).

2. See, for example, Geoffrey A. Hosking, *The Russian Constitutional Experiment: Government and Duma, 1907–1914* (Cambridge: Cambridge University Press, 1973); Mary Schaeffer Conroy, *P. A. Stolypin: Practical Politics in Late Tsarist Russia* (Boulder, CO: Westview Press, 1976); George Tokmakoff, *P. A. Stolypin and the Third Duma: An Appraisal of the Three Major Issues* (Lanham, MD: University Press of America, 1981). In the present compendium William Gleason and Thomas Porter examine Stolypin's interaction with the zemstvos, Antti Kujala's reviews Stolypin's Finnish policy, and Alexandra Korros looks at Stolypin, the Nationalist Party, and the State Council.

3. Detailed discussion of these issues, based on primary sources, is contained in Mary Schaeffer Conroy, *In Health and In Sickness: Pharmacy, Pharmacists and the Pharmaceutical Industry in Late Imperial, Early Soviet Russia* (Boulder, CO: East European Monographs; Distributed by Columbia University Press, New York, 1994). See especially chapters 2, 6, 7, pp. 26–39, 100–137; chapter 8, pp. 141–142.

4. Ibid., chapter 2.

5. The term *soslovie* technically referred to social estates recognized for centuries by the Russian government. Pharmacists, however, used this term to denote their professional corporation.

6. Conroy, *In Health and In Sickness*, chapters 3, 4, 5, 8, 10, 12, pp. 39–100, 137–162, 175–200, 219–228. The population figures that allowed the establishment of a new normal pharmacy varied according to the status of the city or town. Village pharmacies were determined by the radius of the area they served.

7. Ibid., chapter 1, pp. 9–26; chapter 9, pp. 162–175.

8. Ibid., chapter 13, pp. 229–232. For more on revolutionary pharmacists, see chapter 14, pp. 257–293.

9. Ibid., chapter 14, pp. 259–268.

10. Ibid., pp. 257–259; 268–293.

11. Ibid., pp. 232–236.

12. Ibid., pp. 237–246.

13. Ibid., chapter pp. 238–252.

14. "Ob uporiadochenii del Rossiiskoi pensionno—vspomogatel'noi kassy farmatsevtov v g. Moskve," *Osobye zhurnaly Soveta Ministrov* [hereafter OZhSM] (Vysochaishe razsmotrennym i utverzhdennym osobym zhurnalam) [hereafter (VRiU)], no. 116, August 4, 1909, pp. 1–5. "Khronika," *Farmatsevticheskii zhurnal* [hereafter F. Zh.], no. 25, vol. 48 (1909) p. 280.

15. Conroy, *In Health and In Sickness*, pp. 278–292.

16. Ibid., pp. 229–256.

17. Ibid., pp. 26–38.

18. Peter Gatrell, *Government, industry and rearmament in Russia, 1900–1914: the last argument of tsarism* (Cambridge: Cambridge University Press, 1994), pp. 93–94.

19. Conroy, *In Health and In Sickness*, p. 313.

20. "Farmatsevty razlichnykh rangov," *F. Zh.*, vol. 48, no. 20 (1909) pp. 219–220.

21. "Ot pravleniia Peterburgskago Farmatsevticheskago Obshchestva," *F. Zh.*, vol. 48, no. 23 (1909) pp. 251–252.

22. "Farmatsevty razlichnykh rangov," pp. 219–220.

23. "K voprosu o reforme farmatsevticheskago obrazovaniia," *F. Zh.*, vol. 48, no. 21 (1909) pp. 230–231.

24. Conroy, *In Health and In Sickness*, pp. 37–38, 312–319, 124–125, 129–134.

25. Ibid., pp. 142–143, 144–147.

26. Ibid., p. 145, and *Istoriia farmatsevticheskogo dela v Peterburge—Petrograde—Leningrade* (Leningrad, 1960), p. 160.

27. Conroy, *In Health and In Sickness*, pp. 137–174.

28. Ibid., pp. 308–312.

29. F. Ferrein, "Tamozhennye tarify i ikh znachenie dlia khimiko-farmatsevticheskoi promyshlennosti," *Khimiko-farmatsevticheskii zhurnal* [hereafter *Kh-f Zh*], no. 7 (1924) p. 10. In 1924 Ferrein, a wartime critic of Imperial tariffs, still attributed fall in production to poorly designed tariffs.

30. V. A. Izmail'skii, "O stovarsole i sal'varsanovykh preparatakh," *Kh-f Zh.*, no. 2 (5) (1924) p. 14.

31. Peter Gatrell has noted the hostility of zemstvo and Duma members, particularly liberals (Kadets and also Octobrists), toward private entrepreneurs producing arms and ships but also agricultural machinery and consumer items. See his *Government, industry and rearmament*, pp. 83–84, 165, 189.

32. Such, for example, is the claim propounded by John F. Hutchinson, *Politics and Public Health in Revolutionary Russia, 1890–1918* (Baltimore and London: Johns Hopkins University Press, 1990), pp. 53–54.

33. John Hutchinson, "Politics and Medical Professionalization after 1905," in Harley D. Balzer, ed., *Russia's Missing Middle Class: The Professions in Russian History* (Armonk, NY: M. E. Sharpe, 1996), p. 97.

34. Stolypin's desire to dominate government bodies is reflected in such proposals as that to establish a government statistical committee subordinate to no one ministry but under the authority of the Chairman of the Council of Ministers (himself), "Po vnesennomu Ministerstvom Vnutrennikh Del proektu polozheniia ob ustroistve statisticheskoi chasti," *OZhSM* (VRiU), no. 169, September 26, 1908. For Stolypin's views on local self-government, see Conroy, *P. A. Stolypin*, pp. 62–64. For Stolypin's management of the central government and Professor A. V. Zenkovsky's belief that Stolypin wished to make the post of Chairman of the Council of Ministers more like that of Prime Minister, see Conroy, *P. A. Stolypin*, p. 75, and passim.

35. See Conroy, *P. A. Stolypin*, pp. 34, 156, 59–69, 69–70.

36. "Po zaiavleniiu 33 Chlenov Gosudarstvennoi Dumy o rasprostranenii na Astrakhanskuiu guberniiu Polozheniia o Zemskikh Uchrezhdeniiakh," *OZhSM* (Osobykh Soveshchanii pri Soveta Ministrov) [hereafter OSSM], no. 289, October 7, 1908. However, Stolypin and the Council of Ministers did not approve a simultaneous proposal brought by fifty-four Duma representatives to introduce zemstvos to Arkhangel'sk because of the small population, large extent of the province, and dearth of private landowners there. "Po zaiavleniiu 54 Chlenov Gosudarstvennoi Dumy o vvedenii v Arkhangel'skoi gubernii zemskago samoupravleniia," ibid., no. 288, October 7, 1908.

37. For example, "O pokrytii dolgov chisliashchikhsia na uezdnykh upravleniiakh vos'mi gubernii Tsarstva Pol'skago, *OZhSM*, (OSSM), no. 201, September 11, 1907; "Ob assignovanii kredita v 23,299 r. 2 k. iz zapasnoi summy zemskikh povinnostei

Arkhangel'skoi gubernii na pokrytie defitsita po vedomstvu mestnago prikaza obshchestvennago prizreniia," ibid., no. 212, September 18, 1907. (Admittedly, the Boards of Welfare in Arkhangel'sk Province were pre-zemstvo-era bodies, dating from the eighteenth century. Nevertheless, they fulfilled a public welfare function.)

In "O vydache ssud zemstvam postradavshikh ot neurozhaia gubernii dlia organizatsii prodazha nuzhdaiushchemusia naseleniiu khleba po zagotovitel'noi tsene," *OZhSM*, (VRiU), no. 177, October 7, 1908, it was stated that zemstvos were to begin paying back the central government by September 1, 1908. Unable to do so they asked for an extension to begin paying back their loans from October 1, 1909. "O razsrochke uplaty Ostrovskim uezdnym zemstvom, Pskovskoi gubernii, dolga obshchemu po Imperii prodovol'stvennomu kapitalu, v summe 150,000 r., po ssude, vydannoi nazvannomu zemstvu v 1905 godu na organizatsiiu prodazhi mestnomu naseleniiu semennogo khleba," ibid., no. 179, October 7, 1908, recounted that the central government had loaned the Ostrov district zemstvo, Pskov Province, 150,000 rubles from the provisioning fund to enable it to sell seeds of oats and flax to local peasants on credit. Meanwhile the flax turned out to be useless and the zemstvo was saddled with suits from disgruntled purchasers. Court costs amounted to 70,000 rubles, preventing the zemstvo from paying back the loan. The zemstvo asked the central government to spread out the loan for twenty years. The Council of Ministers complied. See also "O vozmeshchenii zemstvam i sel'skokhozaistvennym organizatsiiam chasti raskhodov po zheleznodorozhnym perevozkam zagotovliaemykh imi khleba i kormov," ibid., no. 215, December 9, 1908.

38. For example, the government assisted a First Guild Merchant whose property had been confiscated by the Japanese. "Po vsepoddanneishemy khodataistvu Khabarovskago 1-i gil'di kuptsa Tifontaia o vozmeshchenii emu iz sredstv kazny stoimosti ego imushchestva, konfiskovannago iapontsami," *OZhSM* (VRiU), no. 91, April 20, 1908 (no specific amount was mentioned). In "O naznachenii zemlevladelitse Tifliskoi gubernii Sagarda-Paserbskoi ssudy na vostanovlenie khozaistva," ibid., no. 163, September 23, 1908, Stolypin asked for 6,312 rubles to be given to a landowner on the basis of a 1906 law assisting landowners who suffered from agrarian disorders. In "Po predstavleniiu Ministerstva Vnutrennikh Del. . . ." Stolypin asked for additional credits of 59,058 rubles to cover expenditures for medical matters, *OZhSM* (OSSM) no. 134, June 5, 1907. In "Po predstavleniiu Ministerstva Vnutrennikh Del. . . ." he requested 12,266 rubles, 85 kopeks to clean up a river in Kaluga, ibid., no. 157, July 31, 1907. In 1908 Stolypin requested loans to landowners suffering from agrarian disorders amounting to over 21,000 rubles in Smolensk Province, 7,000 rubles for Nizhni Novgorod, and over 7,000 rubles for Simbirsk Province. "O naznachenii ssud nekotorym zemlevladel'tsam Simbirskoi, Smolenskoi i Nizhegorodskoi gubernii, postradavshim ot agrarnykh bezporiadkov," *OZhSM* (OSSM), no. 215, August 5, 1908.

39. J. D. Smele, "White Gold: The Imperial Russian Gold Reserve in the Anti-Bolshevik East, 1918-? (An Unconcluded Chapter in the History of the Russian Civil War)," *Europe-Asia Studies*, vol. 46, no. 8 (1994) p. 1318.

40. Gatrell, *Government, industry and rearmament in Russia*, pp. 125, 143–149.

41. Ibid. See also Paul R. Gregory, *Before Command: An Economic History of Russia from Emancipation to the First Five-Year Plan* (Princeton, NJ: Princeton University Press, 1994),

p. 34. Gregory notes that through the 1880s government spending was primarily devoted to the military and administration, rather than health care and education. Although he does not specify spending targets for the period before World War I, presumably they were the same.

42. "O proizvodstve v 1910 g. vtoroi vsenarodnoi perepisi naseleniia Rossiiskoi Imperii," *OZhSM* (OSSM), no. 136, April 17, 1908. (The new census was to cost 7 million rubles.)

43. "O poriadke dal'neishei eksploitatsii Tifliskoi telefonnoi seti," OZhSM (OSSM), no. 182, June 17, 1908.

44. "Po proektu shtata gubernskago upravleniia," *OZhSM* (VRiU), no. 51, March 4, 1908, pp. 1–13. See also Kokovtsov's disapproval of Stolypin's request for 1 milion rubles to strengthen the chancelleries of governors and provincial boards in fifty provinces, in "Po predstavleniiu Ministerstva Vnutrennikh Del, ot 20 Oktiabria 1908 g., za No. 21881 (po Dep. Obshch. Del.), ob usilenii sredstv kantseliarii gubernatorov i gubernskikh pravlenii v 50 guberniiakh, upravliaemykh po obshchemu uchrezhdeniiu," ibid. (OSSM), no. 329, October 28, 1908, p. 3. The request was to go before the Duma. Stolypin defended the proposal on the grounds that the situation for *sluzhashchie* or staffs in provincial administration was "extremely difficult," *loc. cit.*

45. In "Po predstavleniiu Ministerstva Vnutrennikh Del, ot 4 Oktiabria 1908 goda, za No. 36218 (po Dep. Pol.), ob usilenii Ufimskoi gorodskoi politsii," *OZhSM* (OSSM), no. 308, October 21, 1908, pp. 1–2, Kokovtsov censured Stolypin's request for 100,800 rubles for increases in the Ufa police—double the allocations for 1907 and four times the allocations for 1903—on the grounds that this request "aggravated the present difficult financial situation of the state treasury." In "Po predstavleniiu Ministerstva Vnutrennikh Del, ot 4 Oktiabria 1908 goda, za No. 36225 (po Dep. Pol.), ob usilenii politsii v gg. Kieve i Samare," ibid., no. 309, pp. 1–2, Kokovtsov voiced no objection to increasing the police force in Samara, as long as the city and not the central treasury paid for the augmentation. In "Po predstavleniiu Ministerstva Vnutrennikh Del, ot 10 Oktiabria 1908 g., za No. 36341 (po Dep. Pol.), ob uvelichenii shtata Chitinskoi gorodskoi politsii," ibid., no. 310, pp. 1–2, Kokovtsov criticized Stolypin's request for 57,760 rubles, "three times the allocation for 1901," but agreed "not to oppose the measure if the city of Chita fully bore the monetary burden" and compensated the treasury. In "Po predstavleniiu Ministerstva Vnutrennikh Del, ot 10 Oktiabria 1908 goda, za No. 36371 (po Dep. Pol.), ob uvelichenii chisla uriadnikov uezdnoi politseiskoi strazhi v Moskovskom uezde," ibid., no. 311, pp. 1–2, Kokovtsov favored limiting police in Moscow *uezd* (county) to one per volost', as stipulated by a 1903 regulation. In view of increased crime, the Council of Ministers approved Stolypin's request for increased staff. In "Po predstavleniiu Ministerstva Vnutrennikh Del, ot 4 Oktiabria 1908 goda, za No. 36220 (po Dep. Pol.), ob obrazovanii v gg. Liubline i Sosnovitsakh otdel'nykh politseiskikh upravlenii," ibid., no. 312, pp. 1–2, Kokovtsov withdrew his earlier objection to enlarging mounted police salaries in Liublin and Sosnovitsakh because these cities were to cooperate with the Ministry of Internal Affairs in paying for the measure. In "Po predstavleniiu Stats-Sekretaria Nol'de, ot 18 Oktiabria 1908 goda, ob usilenii shtata Tifliskoi gorodskoi politsii," ibid., no. 313, pp. 1–2, Kokovtsov slashed salaries for police in Tiflis "in order to save Treasury funds."

46. "Po predstavleniiu Ministra Vnutrennikh Del, ot 19 Marta 1908 goda, za No. 440 (po Tsentr. Stat. Kom.), o proizvodstve v 1910 godu vtoroi vsenarodnoi perepisi naseleniia Rossiiskoi Imperii," *OZhSM* (OSSM), no. 136, August 17, 1908, pp. 1–2.

47. "Po predstavleniiu Ministerstva Vnutrennikh Del, ot 24 Sentiabria 1908 g., za No. 1247 (po Glavn. Upr. Pocht i Tel.), o pereustroistve i rasshirenii pomeshchenii Moskovskago pochtamta," *OZhSM*, (OSSM), no. 305,October 14, 1908, pp. 1–2.

48. See "O naznachenii sluzhivshei po vol'nomu naimu v Kantseliarii Irkutskago General-Gubernatora dvorianike Babkovoi edinovremennago posobiia iz kazny, v razmere 300 r.," *OZhSM* (OSSM), no. 164, May 6, 1908; "Ob obrazovanii v Nikol'skom uezde, Vologodskoi gubernii, odnogo novago stana," ibid., no. 216, August 5, 1908; "O prisvoenii chinam Kaluzhskoi gorodskoi politsii raz"ezdnykh deneg," ibid., no. 217, August 12, 1908. In "O voznikshikh v mezhduvedomstvennom soveshchanii po razsmotreniiu proekta smety Ministerstva Vnutrennikh Del (po Obshchei chasti) na 1909 goda raznoglasiiakh," ibid., no. 234, August 19, 1908, Stolypin's request for over 2 million rubles was cut to less than half. In "Ob ustanovlenii razmerov voznagrazhdeniia predsedatelia i chlenov likvidatsionnoi komissii po delam S.-Peterburgskoi kompanii 'Nadezhda'," ibid., no. 282, September 30, 1908, Kokovtsov cut Stolypin's requests for remuneration for the chair of the liquidation commission for the company "Nadezhda" from 6,000 rubles to 4,000 and requests for each member from 2,500 to 2,000 rubles. The Council of Ministers approved the lower request for the chair but raised the members' remuneration back to 2,500 rubles.

49. See, *OZhSM* (OSSM), nos. 216 and 217.

50. See, for example, Conroy, *P. A. Stolypin*, pp. 163–165, 170–171, 172.

51. Ibid., pp. 166–170, 174–178.

52. The connection between individual freedom and private property is emphasized by Professor Litvin of Kazan' University in a recent work detailing the Bolshevik government's repressive policies following its takeover of Russia in October 1917. On page 12 of *Krasnyi i belyi terror v Rossii, 1918–1922 gg.* (Kazan', Tatanskoe gazetno-zhurnalnoe Izdatel'stvo, 1995), Professor Litvin argues that the Bolsheviks' seizure of private property, prohibitions on free trade, and the government's "bread monopoly" destroyed Russian citizens' autonomy and their ability to counter a government that had no popular sanction.

53. Conroy, *In Health and In Sickness*, pp. 9–25, 39–56.

54. Ibid., pp. 57–63.

55. "Novyia pravila otkrytiia aptek," *F. Zh.*, vol. 48, no. 26, 1909, pp. 282–83.

56. Conroy, *In Health and In Sickness*, pp. 52–54.

57. Ibid., pp. 63–76. See also "Korrespondentsii" (Kazan'), *F. Zh.*, vol. 48, no. 15 (1909) p. 170, and "Novyia pravila otkrytiia aptek," ibid., no. 26, p. 281.

58. Conroy, *In Health and In Sickness*, pp. 39–56.

59. Ibid., pp. 94–96.

60. Ibid., p. 80.

61. Ibid., pp. 69–70.

62. "Novyia pravila otkrytiia aptek," *F. Zh.*, vol. 48, no. 26 (1909) pp. 282–283.

63. Conroy, *In Health and In Sickness*, pp. 258–59, 270–72, 282. One of the most innovative schemes was propounded by O. G. Gabrilovich in 1906. His plan is discussed ibid., pp. 270–272.

64. Ibid., pp. 259–268; 274–292.

65. "Novyia pravila otkrytiia aptek," *F. Zh.*, vol. 48, no. 25 (1909) pp. 272–273.

66. Conroy, *In Health and In Sickness*, p. 296. For other examples of Pleve's outreach toward the zemstvos, see Conroy, *P. A. Stolypin*, pp. 61–62.

67. Conroy, *In Health and In Sickness*, pp. 296–97; "Otdel deputatov pri Meditsinskom Sovete," *F. Zh.*, vol. 48, no. 8 (1909) pp. 89–93.

68. Conroy, *In Health and In Sickness*, pp. 269–73.

69. "Otdel Deputatov pri Meditsinskom Sovete," *F. Zh.*, vol. 48, no. 8 (1909) pp. 89–93; Conroy, *In Health and In Sickness*, pp. 297–302.

70. Bakin received his preliminary education in the Orenburg Seminary and the Kazan' Orthodox Academy. He graduated from the Kazan' University medical faculty (School of Medicine) in 1900. In 1903, after surgical training, he served a city zemstvo hospital in Viatka Province. During the Russo-Japanese War he served with the Red Cross in Mukden, Manchuria. "Biuro konstitutsionno-demokraticheskoi fraktsii," *Tretii Sozyv Gosudarstvennoi Dumy: Portrety, Biografii, Avtografii,* N. N. Ol'shanskii, ed., (St. Petersburg, n.d.; Ann Arbor Microfilms reprint), p. 43.

71. For Dolgorukov's political affiliation see references to him in Olavi K. Falt and Antti Kujala, eds., *Akashi Motojiro, Rakka ryusui: Colonel Akashi's Report on His Secret Cooperation with the Russian Revolutionary Parties during the Russo-Japanese War* (Helsinki, Finnish Historical Society, 1988), pp. 25, 30, 105.

72. Untitled, *F. Zh.*, vol. 48, no. 8 (1909) pp. 88–89.

73. "Biuro konstitutsionno-demokraticheskoi fraktsii," *Tretii Sozyv*, p. 43.

74. "Komissiia," *F. Zh.*, vol. 48, no. 1 (1909) p. 11; "Aptechnyi vopros v komissii parlamentskoi fraktsii narodnoi svobody," ibid., no. 4, pp. 43–45. Also, "Aptechnyi vopros komissii parlamentskoi fraktsii narodnoi svobody," ibid., no. 5, p. 52; ibid., no. 6, pp. 65–66; untitled, ibid., no. 8, pp. 88–89.

75. No. 111, "Ob izmenenii zakona ob otkrytii aptek," and "Ob"iasnitel'naia zapiska," *Prilozheniia k stenograficheskim otchetam Gosudarstvennoi Dumy*, Tretii sozyv, Sessiia I, 1907–1908, vol. 2 (St. Petersburg, 1908), pp. 478–483; No. 89, "Doklad po peredannomu na osnovanii § 64 Nakaza Gosudarstvennoi Dumy zakonodatel'nomu zaiavleniiu ob izmenenii zakona ob otkrytii aptek" (Dokladchik M. K. Safonov) and "Ob izmenenii zakona otkrytii aptek," *Prilozheniia k stenograficheskim otchetam Gosudarstvennoi Dumy*, Tretii sozyv, Sessiia tret'ia, 1909–1910 g.g., vol. 1 (St. Petersburg, 1910), pp. 1–5.

76. No. 360, "Doklad po zakonodatel'nomu predlozheniiu ob izmenenii zakona ob otkrytii aptek" (Dokladchik M. K. Safonov) *Prilozheniia k stenograficheskim otchetam Gosudarstvennoi Dumy*, Tretii sozyv, Sessiia chetvertaia, 1910–1911 g.g., vol. 4 (St. Petersburg, 1911), pp. 1–3, esp. p. 3.

77. "Biuro fraktsii 'Soiuza 17-go oktiabria'," *Tretii Sozyv Gosudarstvennoi Dumy: Portrety Biografii, Avtografii*, pp. 20–33. The Kadet Party in the Third Duma was less varied. Duma representatives from this "fraction" included a preponderance of Cossacks and hereditary nobles. "Biuro konstitutsionno-demokraticheskoi fraktsii," ibid., pp. 42–47.

78. "Biuro fraktsii 'Soiuza 17-go oktiabria'," p. 31.

79. Conroy, *In Health and In Sickness*, pp. 298–302. See also "Otdel Deputatov pri Meditsinskom Sovete," *F. Zh.*, vol. 48, no. 8 (1909) p. 90.

80. "K voprosu o poriadke otkrytiia aptek," *F. Zh.*, vol. 48, no. 5 (1909) p. 55.

81. See, for example, the untitled report in *F. Zh.*, vol. 48, no. 8 (1909) pp. 88–89.

82. "Materialy k voprosu o proekt pravil ob otkrytii munitsipal'nykh aptek," *F. Zh.*, vol. 51, no. 10 (1912) p. 109.

83. Ibid., no. 10 (1912) pp. 108–109.

84. "20-go ianvaria sostoialos' zasedanie soglasitel'noi komissii," *F. Zh.*, vol. 51, no. 4, 1912, p. 48.

85. *Prilozhenie k stenograficheskim otchetam Gosudarstvennago Soveta*, Sessiia VII, 1911–1912 g.g. (St. Petersburg, 1913), pp. 2222–2226.

86. Conroy, *In Health and In Sickness*, pp. 302–308.

87. For a sample of this viewpoint, see Edith W. Clowes, Samuel D. Kassow, and James L. West, eds., *Between Tsar and People: Educated Society and the Quest for Public Identity in Late Imperial Russia* (Princeton: Princeton University Press, 1991), particularly Joseph Bradley, "*Obshchestvennost'* in Moscow," p. 148, and William G. Wagner, "Ideology, Identity, and the Emergence of a Middle Class," pp. 162–163.

88. Robert Edelman, *Gentry Politics on the Eve of the Russian Revolution: The Nationalist Party, 1907–1917* (New Brunswick, NJ: Rutgers University Press, 1980), passim.

89. Hosking, *The Russian Constitutional Experiment*, pp. 39–40.

90. Mark Szeftel, *The Russian Constitution of April 23, 1906: Political Institutions of the Duma Monarchy* (Brussels: Les Éditions de la Encyclopédique, 1976), pp. 307–309.

91. A. Shingarev (Kadet physician), "Novyi zakon o zemskikh i gorodskikh aptekakh, *F. Zh.*, vol. 51, no. 8 (1912) p. 84.

92. "Kak nasazhdaetsia iavochnyi poriadok inym zakonoproektom," *F. Zh.*, vol. 51, no. 2 (1912) p. 13.

93. This was noted in the "Materialy k voprosu o proekte pravil ob otkrytii munitsipal'nykh aptek," *F. Zh.*, vol. 51, no. 9 (1912) pp. 97–99,

94. See, for example, Dittmar Dahlmann's chapter 4.

THE POLICY OF THE RUSSIAN GOVERNMENT TOWARD FINLAND, 1905–1917: A CASE STUDY OF THE NATIONALITIES QUESTION IN THE LAST YEARS OF THE RUSSIAN EMPIRE

ANTTI KUJALA
University of Helsinki

THE FINNISH CONSTITUTION

A new idea took root in Finland during the course of the nineteenth century suggesting that the country had its own constitution based on the Form of Government of 1772 and the Act of Union and Security of 1789, both dating from the reign of Gustav III when Finland was still part of Sweden. According to this, the Russian Tsars, in vowing to observe Finland's fundamental laws inherited from the period of Swedish rule, shared legislative power with the Finnish Diet, thereby making the Tsar (referred to as the Emperor in Finnish usage) a constitutional ruler in Finland, although an autocrat in Russia. This idea was based on modern parliamentary thinking and in reality had no place in a situation where Finland had been annexed by force of arms to the Russian Empire in 1809. The Finnish interpretation helped Finland develop as a separate state and one that became increasingly separate from Russia.

In fact, the Gustavian Form of Government and Act of Union and Security could only be in force mutatis mutandis, with necessary alterations, in post-1809 Finland. However, not a single Russian emperor between 1809 and 1917 gave a final answer to the question of what parts of the Swedish Fundamental Laws they considered as being in force. A definition of the Fundamental Laws would have required the updating and partial rewriting of old legislation. Because of the divergence between Finnish and Russian interpretations, however, all efforts to codify these Fundamental Laws failed. The result was that Finland lacked an agreed-upon and precise constitution.

In practice, the Emperors, particularly Alexander II and Alexander III, observed the decrees of the Gustavian Form of Government and the Act of Union and Security as far as possible. The new Diet Act of 1869 brought an important addition to Finland's administration, but so did the institutions created by executive measures instituted by the Emperor, such as the Senate, which acted as Finland's domestic government, and the system for presenting Finnish affairs in St. Petersburg headed by the Minister Secretary of State for Finland. The members of the Senate and the Minister Secretary of State were the emperor's official Finnish advisors, and in general their influence in the administration of the country was more significant than that of the Diet.[1]

Finland's political system was defined de facto by the system for balancing Finnish and Russian interests formed by the institutions of both countries in handling Finnish affairs. The establishment of this practice gave rise to the idea, encouraged in Finland, that Finland had her own constitution.

The Russian Emperors voluntarily accepted the established political system in Finland as long as the benefits of doing so—above all, the preservation of the country as a peaceful corner of the empire—outweighed the disadvantages. They even encouraged the development of Finnish, the language of the majority of the population, and Finnish-language culture, toward equality with Swedish. The Emperors believed that the rise of Finnish nationalism would eliminate the basis for any political separatism aimed at reuniting the country with Sweden. Separatist activity indeed remained a mere curiosity in Finland throughout the nineteenth century.[2]

Administrative Integration, 1899–1905

With the February Manifesto of 1899, Nicholas II reduced the Finnish Diet to the status of an advisory body for the enactment of imperial legislation, laws that were to be implemented in both Finland and Russia, or just in Finland but which touched on imperial interests. Up to this point, the Diet had had the right to alter and reject legislative proposals that it deemed unacceptable and determine the final content of legislation. The Emperor only had the power to either pass a law or leave it unratified. The February Manifesto eliminated the Diet's say in imperial affairs. From then on, the Diet had the right to submit statements on proposals for imperial legislation, but these statements did not in any way bind the Emperor or the Russian State Council.

Most Finns considered the February Manifesto a gross violation of Finland's Fundamental Laws, and as being equivalent to a virtual coup d'état. From the imperial viewpoint, however, the Emperor had merely enacted a new system of legislation, as he was entitled to do in his own opinion.[3]

The Russian government primarily needed the February Manifesto to put an end to Finland's own army and introduce Russian-style conscription. The manifesto was issued to induce the reluctant Finnish Diet to accept the reform. If it would not submit, it would simply be passed over. This confrontation demonstrated that the system for balancing mutual interests that had operated up until then no longer functioned. This was due both to the modernization of Russia's administration and to the rise of popular political activity in both Finland and Russia, which prevented officials from finding solutions agreeable to both countries as they had before.

The February Manifesto gave rise to peaceful opposition in Finland which Governor-General N. I. Bobrikov (1898–1904) began to heavy-handedly repress. At the same time, he began to integrate Finland's administration into that of the empire.

From the Russian government's standpoint, these moves meant the suppression of a rebellious Finnish separatist movement. Bobrikov was blind to the fact that the majority of Finns had been completely loyal to the Emperor and the Russian Empire up until then. As Sergei Witte observed in his memoirs, Bobrikov imagined that he had been sent to Finland to put down a revolt, but in reality he provoked one.[4] The Russian government's policy on Finland can be seen as a self-fulfilling prophecy.

The Finnish Constitutionalists (comprising the Swedish Party and the Young Finns) called on young men of conscription age to boycott the draft that was to be implemented under the new conscription legislation.

The boycott was the most noteworthy form of the passive resistance that developed across the country in response to Russian moves.

In spite of the many actions initiated by Bobrikov, the fact remains that his integration policy failed to progress more than halfway. When he was felled by an assassin's bullet on June 16, 1904 (New Style [NS], June 3 Old Style [OS]),[5] Finland was still far from having the status and conditions of a Russian *guberniia* or province.[6]

THE REVOLUTION OF 1905 AND
PLANS FOR MILITARY ACTION AGAINST FINLAND

As a result of the General Strike in Russia and Finland, the Emperor issued what has come to be known as the November Manifesto on October 22/November 4, 1905.[7] This rescinded the laws and decrees considered by the Finns as illegal and terminated the implementation of the February Manifesto until further notice.[8] The Constitutionalists now became the governing party in Finland. Finland regained her former autonomy and the Senate and the Diet began preparing for thorough parliamentary reform.

The new Diet Act of 1906 replaced Finland's Diet of four estates with a unicameral parliament elected through universal and equal suffrage. Women also received the right to vote, the first to do so in Europe. This reform was implemented as a result of the successful pressure put on the Diet by the Social Democrats through mass action, and because the General Strike in the autumn of 1905 had persuaded the Constitutionalists of the necessity of change.[9] Without the uncertainty surrounding the situation in Russia itself, however, the reform would not have been possible. By consenting to reform, the Tsar tried to preserve peace in at least one corner of his restless empire. The Diet Act did not, in any case, reduce his political powers in favor of the Finnish assembly.[10]

The freedoms of association, assembly, and the press were established constitutionally. Only the possibility to practice the freedom of assembly was made concrete by law. Nicholas II consented to all reforms that had some form of Russian equivalent. He had no wish to go any further, however. With state-of-emergency regulations in force in Russia, civil and political rights were to a large degree restricted. In Finland, however, political freedom increased considerably.[11]

The Sveaborg mutiny of Russian revolutionary soldiers at the beginning of August 1906 NS remained the only bid for revolution seen on Finnish soil between 1905 and 1907. The mutiny was crushed after less than three days.[12]

THE EMPIRE STRIKES BACK

According to Osmo Jussila's interpretation, the Russian government's policy on Finland after 1907 was primarily aimed at preventing any repetition of the General Strike of 1905.[13] The government sincerely believed that Finland represented a threat to Russia's social system and government, as well as to the city of St. Petersburg. This threat can be divided into three components:

(1) The Russian revolutionaries that had made their base in Finland and on the Karelian Isthmus in particular. Taking advantage of the indifference or sympathy of local officials, they organized revolutionary activity among the Russian troops stationed in Finland and staged assassinations in nearby St. Petersburg;

(2) The Finnish quasi-military organizations, such as the Activists' *Voimaliitto* (Power Union) and the Red Guard, whom the government saw as intent not only on revolutionary goals but separatist ones as well; and

(3) The possibility that a foreign power might use Finnish opposition movements as a jumping-off point for an attack against St. Petersburg.[14] This latter fear became most evident only from 1909 and 1910 onwards, when international tension heightened and Russia began to emerge from the inward-looking mentality that had set in following her defeat in the Russo-Japanese War (1904–1905).

As the foregoing indicates, military "pacification" of Finland nearly took place during the 1905 General Strike. The highest echelons of the Russian military, particularly the Commander-in-Chief of the St. Petersburg military district, Grand Duke Nikolai Nikolaevich, believed that action of this sort, or at least preparation for such action, was appropriate the following year as well. The Russian navy initiated action to prevent the smuggling of arms into Finland and from there into Russia; although this was a problem in 1906, it was not as serious as the government assumed.[15] A good example of the suspicion felt by the military command toward Finland was the proposal by the Chief of the General Staff, F. F. Palitsyn, in 1906 to forbid citizens of the Grand Duchy from serving as officers.[16]

The St. Petersburg military district drew up its first battle plan to counter the Finnish opposition movement at the end of 1906 and the beginning of 1907.[17] A special interagency conference chaired by Tsar Nicholas II considered declaring a state of war in Finland on February 1, 1907 OS. The Chairman of the Council of Ministers, or Prime Minister, P. A. Stolypin, believed, however, that the "boil" could not yet be lanced as any unnecessary resort to force would be inadvisable when the Second State Duma was due soon to convene. Minister of War A. F. Rediger and Nikolai Nikolaevich, the commander of future military action, considered military operations virtually impossible during the winter in any case. As a result, the plan was temporarily shelved. It is worth noting that the government incorrectly believed that the Finnish "rebel army" had machine guns and artillery.[18]

On October 18, 1907 OS, the Tsar established a Committee on Finnish Affairs (*Osoboe soveshchanie po delam Velikogo kniazhestva Finliandskogo*) to assist the Prime Minister and the Council of Ministers. In this, Stolypin, a number of other ministers, and a group of senior Russian officials who had been or were involved in Finnish affairs considered ways of restoring order in Finland and integrating it more closely with the rest of the empire.[19] The aim of the committee was to provide expertise for decision making by the Council of Ministers and to speed up the handling of matters by the council.[20]

Finland's Russian Governor-General, N. N. Gerard, was not included as a member of this committee. According to Stolypin, Gerard intentionally diverted attention away from the true nature of Finnish separatism and from the disinterested attitude taken toward it by the country's authorities and the latter's secret support for separatism. Stolypin relied on the police sources of his own Ministry of Internal Affairs; some of the information passed on by these sources was completely unfounded, but some of it was, in fact, more accurate than that supplied by the Finnish authorities to Gerard and forwarded to Stolypin. In particular, Stolypin pointed to the congress held by the Socialist Revolutionaries in Tampere in February 1907.[21] Deputy Minister of Internal

Affairs A. A. Makarov had told Gerard to ban the congress, which he had done. The local Finnish authorities, however, had argued that the congress was a harmless meeting of "neutral, progressively minded people." Gerard had passed on this assessment to the Russian Ministry of Internal Affairs, although he himself had suspected that this description was far from the truth.[22]

On November 3, 1907 OS, the Committee on Finnish Affairs decided to recommend to the Tsar that a state of war be declared in the province of Vyborg (Viipuri) to allow the headquarters and bases of the Russian revolutionary parties located there to be eliminated and party leaders and terrorists to be imprisoned. It was proposed that the army take over the province, temporarily separating it from Finland, and that the commander of the Twenty-Second Corps based in Finland, V. A. Bekman (Boeckman), be appointed its governor-general. Stolypin devised a detailed plan under which Gerard, who was considered too sympathetic to the Finns, was to step to one side and be replaced as Governor-General of Finland by Bekman. Gerard was to be forced to resign by the appointment of F. A. Zein (Seyn) as his assistant without consulting him. Zein had served as chief secretary to Bobrikov and belonged to what were known as the Old Bobrikovites, a small chauvinist group influential in shaping Finnish affairs. Zein was to serve as acting governor-general in Helsinki until Bekman had successfully restored order in the province of Vyborg.

Rumors of the military preparations that had started in St. Petersburg rapidly reached the ears of the Russian revolutionaries, however, causing something approaching panic in their ranks. Stolypin's open threats to August Langhoff, the Minister Secretary of State for Finland, convinced the latter that something serious was afoot and he urged the Finnish Senate to try to keep the initiative in its own hands. The Finnish police finally decided to take energetic action; they imprisoned and handed over to the Russian authorities those revolutionaries and terrorists who did not flee abroad like Lenin and many others. Stolypin initially recommended to the Tsar that a declaration of a state of war be postponed to give the revolutionaries the illusion that things had calmed down so that they would walk into the trap. The action taken by Finnish officials served to put the cat among the pigeons, however, and nothing ultimately came of the plan to declare a state of war. The only part of Stolypin's plan to be put into practice was the appointment of Bekman as Governor-General of Finland and Zein as his assistant.[23]

It was surprising that Stolypin urged Langhoff so strongly to eliminate the problem posed by the Russian revolutionaries on Finnish territory as Langhoff quickly understood that, unless the Finnish Senate acted, the Russian authorities would take the situation into their own hands.[24] If Stolypin had really wanted a state of war declared in the province of Vyborg, he would not have warned Langhoff as he did. Stolypin appears to have feared that declaring a state of war would have created difficulties abroad and above all with left-wing and middle-of-the-road politicians in the Duma. In the final analysis, it would seem that Stolypin himself averted the declaration of a state of war being and the complications that would have ensued from such an operation for both Finland and Russia.

The government did not, however, stop preparations for declaring a state of war in Finland in the event of rebellion breaking out in the Grand Duchy. In the spring of 1908, the Council of Ministers and the Tsar approved a plan for appointing a special commander in chief in such a situation with command over the Baltic Fleet, the customs authorities, and the border guards. The thinking behind this was to give the Commander in Chief of the St. Petersburg military district, Grand Duke Nikolai Nikolaevich, control over all military and paramilitary forces in the region. Such a special commander in chief would also be entitled to introduce imperial criminal legislation and military courts. A little later, the grand duke issued a separate customs standing order designed to prevent imports of all military material into Finland during a state of war.[25]

Finnish contemporaries and historians have presented a number of interpretations as to who was ultimately responsible for the Russian government's policy on Finland: Nicholas II, Stolypin, or their Bobrikov-inspired advisers who were committed supporters of integrating Finland more closely into the empire. Stolypin had only a cursory knowledge of Finnish affairs and was very much dependent on the information he received from his advisers. V. F. Deitrikh (Deutrich), in particular, has been considered as the power behind the scenes and mainly responsible for Stolypin's hard line.[26] Deitrikh served as assistant to the Finnish Governor-General between 1902 and 1905, and after 1905 was a member of the Russian State Council, becoming its vice chairman on January 1, 1917 OS. The Tsar appointed him a member of the Committee of Finnish Affairs in 1907.[27] Like many of his Bobrikov-inspired contemporaries, Deitrikh belonged to the Russian nationalist Right.[28] During the First World War, he and another member of the Committee on Finnish Affairs, M. M. Borodkin, were members of a group led by the reactionary B. V. Stürmer that opposed granting any concessions to either the Poles or the Finns.[29]

Based on the documentary evidence, it is clear that throughout his period as Chairman of the Council of Ministers (1906–1911), Stolypin was *in practice* responsible for heading the government's policy on Finland. He presented virtually complete action proposals to the Tsar, who generally gave them his approval. Zein worked for Stolypin, rather than the other way around. It would be truly surprising if Deitrikh played a larger role. In those few meetings of the Committee on Finnish Affairs at which he attempted to carve out an independent role for himself, he was unable to win any or very little support for his opinions.[30]

Stolypin sincerely believed in the Russian nationalist objectives of his policy, but he also deliberately employed Russian nationalism and centralist borderland policies to bolster his government and its cooperation with the majority parties in the Duma and State Council, on which he was very much dependent. As Russia could not channel nationalism into an assertive foreign policy after being defeated in the Russo-Japanese War, nationalism had to be diverted to strengthening the central government at the expense of self-government in the empire's borderlands. As a result, the Finnish question shifted from being one of borderlands politics to becoming part of wider domestic politics within Russia. Nationalism was a substitute for Stolypin for his failed political and social reforms.[31]

In fact, Stolypin did not only have to take the majority parties in the Duma into account but also the Tsar, on whom his continuance in office ultimately hinged. Strong and competent prime ministers (Witte, Stolypin, and Kokovtsov) were a problem for Nicholas II. He was unable to function without them and left the practical aspects of government up to them, but at the same time he conspired with others behind their backs, thereby preventing a number of what they saw as important plans from materializing, something that only served to weaken the position of the prime ministers concerned and their governments. Nicholas used this approach to try to prevent any of his prime ministers from developing into any kind of threat to his position as Russia's autocratic ruler.[32]

Nicholas II had felt bitter toward the Finns since 1899 when they had accused him of breaking his word and had started an international campaign against the government, passive resistance, and openly rebellious action.[33] Nicholas revealed his anti-Finnish feelings to the German envoy at the beginning of 1907, averring that the Finns were at an even lower level than the Russians "especially with regard to morality, and nothing good is to be expected from them."[34]

The St. Petersburg military district had its own intelligence network that monitored the situation in Finland, and information generated by this network went straight to the Tsar's desk.[35] It has generally been believed that the tough policy on Finland adopted by the Tsarist government was the result of distorted information supplied by the Russian secret police, the *Okhrana* and the gendamerie, but in fact the information provided by military intelligence had the most impact during 1906 and 1907. The St. Petersburg military district was commanded by the Tsar's uncle, Nikolai Nikolaevich. Some of the most determined opponents of Finnish "separatism" in the Russian establishment were to be found in this area. As indicated before, Nikolai Nikolaevich was inclined during 1905 and 1906 to solve the Finnish question by military means and he had influence over the Tsar and unrestricted access to the latter. It seems clear that the Tsar was truly concerned about the turn developments seemed to have taken and that he had a significant role in the actions that resulted in the start of plans for military measures against Finland in the winter of 1906 and 1907.[36]

In many respects, the Tsar proved willing to go further in limiting Finland's autonomy than Stolypin. In September and October 1909, for example, Nicholas supported the temporary abolition of the Finnish Senate and the transfer of its powers to the governor-general. The Council of Ministers headed by Stolypin, in contrast, resolved the crisis by allowing the Tsar to appoint a group of Finns who had served long periods in Russia and had become largely Russified and who owed allegiance to the Russian government rather than Finnish parties to replace the Finnish politicians who wanted to resign from the Senate. This was a completely legal solution, at least formally, and was intended to prevent a repetition of the wave of passive resistance that had been seen between 1899 and 1905. Stolypin believed Bekman, who argued that every possible effort should be made to rule Finland through Finnish institutions and officials, and above all, using legal means, as coercive measures would lead to the same kind of dead end experienced during Bobrikov's time.

The appointment of Russified Finns to the Senate was Stolypin's idea, and one that he had argued for back in the spring of 1908. Nicholas had also believed at that time that an end had to be put to the Senate's dependence on political parties. For his part, Bekman believed, at least up until the autumn of 1909, that senators free of party political allegiances would lack sufficient authority and that, as a result, the country should be governed through senators enjoying the trust of the Finnish parties. The governor-general expressed a conflicting view on this and various other issues, and became in the process an encumbrance for Stolypin and his nationalist policy. Bekman was therefore replaced in autumn 1909 by Zein—to punish the Finns, as Stolypin put it the previous spring.

The Tsar agreed reluctantly to the solution proposed by Stolypin in autumn 1909 to the problem of the Finnish Senate, but he did not believe it would succeed.[37] Stolypin proved, however, to have read the situation correctly. No passive resistance of the type that had emerged during Bobrikov's time developed. Stolypin was somewhat more composed than the Tsar since, in his role as the true head of the empire's affairs, he also had to consider which measures were practical and which would produce the best result. Although the creation of the "Admirals' Senate" represented a totally unacceptable oppressive measure on the part of the imperial authorities in Finnish eyes,[38] the total abolition of the Senate supported by the Tsar would have been an even worse alternative.

During the early stages of the crisis in the autumn of 1909, Stolypin believed that the Finnish situation would in time deteriorate and degenerate into virtual revolt; therefore he suggested to the Tsar that troop reinforcements be transferred to Finland. The Tsar agreed and gave permission for preparations to begin.[39] Stolypin discussed the question with Minister of War V. A. Sukhomlinov and the assistant to the Commander in Chief of the St. Petersburg military district, M. A.

Gazenkampf, who were of the opinion that sufficient forces were already stationed in Finland and saw no military or political reasons for reinforcements. Such transfers, they argued, would only unnecessarily exacerbate the situation. Stolypin basically agreed but, as the Tsar had already shown his distrust by questioning the wisdom of Stolypin's proposed solution to the problem of the Senate, the Prime Minister could not change his position. By way of compromise, Stolypin, Sukhomlinov, and Gazenkampf decided to propose transferring one new regiment of Cossacks to Finland.

This was insufficient in the Tsar's eyes and he was not convinced by the additional arguments advanced on behalf of this approach by Sukhomlinov. In the end, however, the Tsar became tired and scribbled "Do what you think best" in the margin of one of the documents on the matter. He stated that the transfer of one regiment within the military district did not require his permission and that the military district commander could decide himself. To communicate his dissatisfaction and his concern, Nicholas made Stolypin and Sukhomlinov personally responsible for the preservation of law and order in Finland.

Following from this decision by the Tsar, Stolypin organized a conference with senior military officials on October 5 OS, at which he was forced, to protect his exposed position, to demand increasing Russia's military presence in Finland in advance of the possible outbreak of a revolt or general strike. The conference would not agree to this, however, and instead only initiated preparations for troop transfers and declaring a state of war in Finland in the event that a general strike or revolt should take place in Finland. It is clear that the question of whether and when to declare a state of war remained on the agenda because of the Tsar's specific concerns on the matter. The military establishment, for its part, saw no particular reason in 1909 to concern itself overmuch with developments in what was only a minor corner of the empire.

The preparations set in motion ultimately resulted not only in the drawing up of war plans (troop transfers and operations) but also the production of a declaration of a state of war signed by the Commander in Chief of the St. Petersburg military district in which citizens resorting to armed resistance were threatened with the death penalty. The military plans drawn up to counter a general strike and rebellion included bringing in personnel from Russia to keep rail traffic open and setting up two Finnish prisons to hold political prisoners. There also was a provision to replace police and similar officials in Finland with personnel from Russia. The navy would seal and patrol Finland's maritime borders. At the Tsar's insistence, the plans also included a requirement that Finland's state funds and those of the Bank of Finland were to be confiscated when a state of war was declared and the monies made available to the imperial authorities. The Finns were to be made to pay for the "disciplinary action" taken against them. The intention was to give Grand Duke Nikolai Nikolaevich overall responsibility for the entire operation.

These various indications underline the fact that the grand duke considered the situation in Finland as giving grave cause for alarm; the widespread smuggling of weapons that was believed to be going on, although none was, was advanced as just one worrying development. Minister of Finance V. N. Kokovtsov, some professional military men, and even Stolypin, in contrast, attempted to take the sting out of some aspects of the plans. The threat posed by Finland was not as acute as all that, they believed, but their political sense told them that openly opposing the Tsar and his uncle on this would not be wise.[40] It is difficult to say whether these conflicting views had anything to do with the fact that the influence of Nikolai Nikolaevich over the Tsar had begun to decline by this stage.[41]

Some high-ranking officials attempted to provoke the Finns into rebellion, thereby facilitating a military solution to the Finnish question. A memorandum to the Tsar on the annexation of the province of Vyborg to Russia proper, and which was probably written somewhere around 1910, stated that the time was favorable for such an annexation as there were no external threats and unrest in Russia had subsided, all of which would allow a Finnish rebellion to be crushed easily.[42]

Stolypin was not quite as much of a narrow-minded nationalist as some Finnish scholars in particular have painted him to be. He did not, for example, dismiss the arguments of the opponents of his policy out of hand and spent time looking into them. While this was partly a purely practical consideration, it shows that he did not simply shut his ears to criticism. He read extensive reviews of the Finnish question by Professor E. N. Berendts, although the latter was critical toward the policies pursued by both Bobrikov and Stolypin himself. Berendts dismissed, for example, the Russian government's official doctrine that the imperial legislative procedure introduced in 1910 was a direct and natural outcome of the Fundamental State Laws of 1906.[43]

On the other hand, Stolypin did promote the careers of Bobrikov-inspired extremists—not only Zein's, but also that of Borodkin, a member of the Committee of Finnish Affairs, who was appointed on Stolypin's initiative to Russia's Ruling Senate in 1911.[44]

Stolypin resorted to the Finnish card for the last time on his deathbed after he had been fatally wounded by an assassin in September 1911 in Kiev. His wife, Ol'ga, informed the Tsar that twenty minutes before he died her husband had said: "What's most important is that the word 'Finland' should be heard."[45] Resolving the Finnish question in a way acceptable to the empire was undoubtedly an important matter for Stolypin, but it was hardly as central as this.[46] He used Finnish affairs to acquire and retain the trust of the Tsar. In this respect, he followed in the footsteps of V. K. Pleve, who allowed himself to be appointed Finland's Minister Secretary of State in 1899 to further his own career.[47] By September 1911, it was only a matter of time before Nicholas would have taken the chairmanship of the Council of Ministers away from Stolypin.[48] By referring to Finland, Stolypin wanted to win back some of the latter's confidence.

If one had to pick out one figure from the historical continuum of the period who could have been said to have been *ultimately* responsible for the government's policy on Finland, it would have to be the Tsar himself. It was he who persistently kept first Bobrikov and then Zein as governor-general, despite the fact that their misjudged measures only served to alienate the Finns without generating any real benefit for Russia. It would certainly be unfair nevertheless to label Nicholas as an ogre when it comes to Finland. It would be more accurate to describe him as seriously unaware of the realities of his empire, something which his constant focus on declarations of a state of war indicates only too well. In any case, a determined and consistent ruler would have had plenty of time to bring a small and powerless country like Finland to heel, instead of which the Russian government and its many shifts of mind wasted valuable time in endless discussions and conferences.

Dove and Hawk Approaches to Finland

A minority view somewhat in opposition to Stolypin's main policy also made itself felt within the Council of Ministers and the Committee of Finnish Affairs between 1908 and 1910. While in principle supporting the policy on integration, it also argued for solutions more amenable to the Finns that were acceptable to the majority of the members of the Council of Ministers.[49]

This body of opinion was born out of the moves taken by Minister of Finance Kokovtsov, at the beginning of 1908, to oppose the proposal by the Stolypin-led Committee on Finnish Affairs for requiring that presentations by the Finnish Minister Secretary of State to the Tsar should be examined in advance by the Council of Ministers to determine whether the matters they touched upon concerned issues of overall imperial interest.[50]

Governor-General Bekman emerged as a second dissident. Through his work, he became convinced that the government's policy was too uncompromising and that by unnecessarily exacerbating conflicts made the administration of Finland more difficult. Although he believed that "the Emperor had the right to change the laws governing Finland, he could not as an honorable soldier interpret and execute the laws of Petersburg to suit the convenience of Petersburg." In other words, Bekman believed that Stolypin's policy on Finland was excessively based on domestic political maneuvering that had nothing to do with the Finnish question. Bekman put a lot of trust in the Old Finns and tried to keep its members in the Senate, unlike Stolypin, who argued that those members representing Finnish political parties should be replaced by Russified senators free of party political allegiances unless they were willing to bow to the wishes of the imperial government.[51]

Foreign Minister A. P. Izvol'skii was concerned about the foreign policy problems caused by a worsening of the situation in Finland. Kokovtsov, from his position as Minister of Finance, argued that unnecessarily increasing troop strengths and the Okhrana was a waste of imperial funds.[52] It is clear, however, that Kokovtsov was not only swayed by purely financial considerations, but that his liberal attitude on the nationalities question and probably also his competitive instincts with regard to Stolypin shaped his position. The opposition (Kokovtsov, Izvol'skii, and Minister of Justice I. G. Shcheglovitov) presented its less radical alternative in the Council of Ministers' meeting of February 22, 1910 OS, during debate on imperial legislative procedure;[53] Kokovtsov alone did so at the Council of Ministers' meeting of August 3, 1910 OS, during debate on the matter of equality of rights.[54] Kokovtsov, Bekman, and Deputy Minister of Internal Affairs S. E. Kryzhanovskii voiced their opposition in the Committee of Finnish Affairs on December 29, 1908 OS, during discussion of imperial legislative procedure[55] and Bekman did so on May 23, 1909 OS, during the committee's discussion on equality of rights.[56] These attempts by the opposition within the government to introduce a less uncompromising line failed, however, with the refusal by Stolypin and the majority behind him to countenance such a change.

In the autumn of 1911, in the wake of the death of Stolypin, Governor-General Zein attempted to push through a declaration of a state of war in Finland or, at a minimum, an official government statement to the effect that one would be declared in the event of a political assassination. Only one political assassination had taken place in Finland, and that not by any conspiracy or organization, but Zein argued that a campaign against high-ranking Russian officials in Finland was being planned. His intention was to use a state of war to gain the same powers as governor-generals in Russia enjoyed.

The idea of resorting to a declaration of a state of war was not Zein's own; it had been put forward by Grand Duke Nikolai Nikolaevich at the beginning of 1910 as a means of countering terror and gun-running. By dusting off the grand duke's original idea, Zein clearly identified himself with the most conservative wing of Russian political life. He certainly also knew that the Tsar had told Langhoff in December 1909 that he would severely punish Finland if there was any attempt to assassinate his recently appointed governor-general (Zein). The idea can therefore be traced to the "highest sources." Zein's proposal formed part of an attempt by the right wing and extreme right wing in Russia after the death of Stolypin to push the government further to the right. These political groups wanted to put pressure on the new prime minister, Kokovtsov, who was considered too conciliatory to the Finns; the calls for a tougher approach to policy on Finland, Poland, and the Jewish question and, in the case of Finland, the threat of a declaration of a state of war, were useful ways of applying such pressure.

The political nature of Zein's proposal, as well as its place in attempts to exert political control over the Council of Ministers, can be clearly seen. As a result, Zein's proposal was rejected by the Council of Ministers at its meeting on October 14, 1911 OS. Ministers expressed their doubts about the reliability of the intelligence supplied to Zein. Conditions in Finland were simply too peaceful to warrant a declaration of a state of war. Even during the turbulent times between 1904 and 1906 no such declaration had been needed. A state of war was not deemed suitable as a mode of government, least of all for an extended period, and would tend to increase rather than reduce the level of revolutionary activity, it was argued. A threat to declare a state of war would also undermine the government's (more specifically the Tsar's) authority. Nevertheless, the Council of Ministers did recommend granting additional powers to the Finnish governor-general.[57]

The St. Petersburg military district virtually ignored the Council of Ministers' decision. Its Chief of Staff, Lieutenant General A. Brinken, organized a consultative meeting on November 11–12 OS to prepare for a state of war being declared in Finland because of an armed uprising or general strike. This meeting also prepared the ground for implementing such a declaration as a preventative measure or as a response to an act of terrorism, even if social calm remained undisturbed. Although this was not a public threat of the possible declaration of a state of war, the general tone of the meeting was broadly similar to that promoted by Zein at the meeting of the Council of Ministers. T. Starkov, representing the Governor-General at the meeting, went so far as to broach the possibility of "Finland's total incorporation" into the empire, i.e., the elimination of autonomy, as a consequence of putting down a rebellion. Nobody at the meeting made reference to the recent decision taken by the Council of Ministers.[58] This only highlighted the very different nature of Kokovtsov's hold on the reins of power compared to Stolypin's.

The leadership of the St. Petersburg military district ordered the commanders of the Twenty-Second Army Corps to act in putting down unrest "in the most determined way possible, fearing to be held responsible not for exceeding their authority but only for inaction or weakness." The commanders of the corps units were instructed to give the order to take up arms without waiting for permission to do so from the civilian authorities.[59]

Although the St. Petersburg military district continued its preparations for a possible declaration of a state of war, the General Staff, Minister of War Sukhomlinov, and the Military Council led by him were much more cautious about the need for such radical action and what might follow, and tried in 1913 to block funds for such preparations.[60]

For the majority of Russia's ministers, Finnish affairs were of peripheral interest and they felt little enthusiasm about them. In addition to the pressures caused by the internal political struggle in Russia itself, the ministers' lack of interest was also shaped by the growing suspicion that the situation in Finland was not as serious as the Russian secret police had suggested for a number of years.

The socialists' Red Guards and the Activists' Voimaliitto, which had emerged in Finland in 1905, undeniably represented dangerous quasi-military revolutionary organizations from the Russian government's point of view. The Voima could also be considered a separatist movement, although it was not to the extent it was perceived as such by the Russian government. By the beginning of 1908 at the latest, however, the activities of both organizations had ended.[61] The headquarters and outposts of the Russian revolutionary parties on the Karelian Isthmus emptied at around the same time.[62] After this, no underground revolutionary organizations existed in Finland, with the exception of small groups active among Russian soldiers and workers.[63] Declaring a state of war would have been completely out of proportion to the insignificance of the forces it was meant to counter.

Although the imperial authorities did have cause to be concerned about Finland being used as a base for revolutionaries in 1906 and 1907, the plans made in 1909 and 1911 for declaring a state of war were based on a fundamentally inaccurate reading of the situation. The Finnish parties remained firmly committed to parliamentary procedures and other legal methods. The most the authorities had to fear was a campaign of passive resistance, and even this did not develop as a result of the government's caution and fractious disputes between the Finnish parties.

The intelligence officers of the St. Petersburg military district, the Russian gendarmerie in Finland, Governor-General Zein, and the imperial

Ministry of Internal Affairs continued to report, however, that there was a movement in Finland planning armed rebellion and harboring plans for independence with the help of foreign powers, and that it was only waiting for the right moment to rise up against Russia. It was reported that an organization known as *Vapausliitto* (Union of Liberation) had been set up to continue the work of the Voima, but this did not exist outside the imaginings of the Russian secret police. The Japanese colonel Akashi, who had financed Russian revolutionary movements during the 1904–1905 Russo-Japanese War, was reported by police sources as being in Finland at the beginning of 1910 fomenting rebellion, although in reality he was on Japanese government business in Korea.[64] In addition to artillery and machine guns, the Finns also had some 160,000 rifles, it was claimed, of which more than 100,000 were fully serviceable.[65] This figure probably referred to hunting weapons. The claim alleging Finland's heavy level of armaments was never really undermined, despite the fact that not even one machine-gun or artillery piece was ever produced as evidence.

It is clear that those in the Russian government and Ministry of Internal Affairs did not believe a fair proportion of the reports they received, but they did suspect that something untoward was taking place in Finland. Such fears could, in any case, easily be appealed to when justifying government policy. Some comments made by Stolypin indicate that he did not take all the accounts literally, but nevertheless he very rarely revealed his doubts. The Russian gendarmerie in Finland had little time for the niceties of honest reporting and supplied St. Petersburg with the type of information that it knew the Ministry of Internal Affairs expected.[66]

As the gap between the peaceful state of affairs in Finland and the lurid picture painted in police reports coming from there began to grow, the Police Department of the Russian Ministry of Internal Affairs commissioned an investigation of the activities of the Russian gendarmerie in Finland at the beginning of 1909. The gendarmerie emerged from this largely unscathed,[67] but its true nature was revealed in a review of its activities carried out by Colonel N. I. Balabin of the gendarmerie in 1912.

Balabin discovered that the Vapausliitto, whose members were reported to include such prominent subversives as Minister Secretary of

State Langhoff and the Japanese emperor, did not exist and that nobody in Finland was planning a rebellion. Balabin went through all of the gendarmerie's secret agents in Finland, both Finnish and Russian, and came to the conclusion that the majority of them were no better than "blackmailers," "useless," or "feeble." He described how some agents clumsily forged circulars supposedly produced by subversive organizations in Finland and used the money they earned to buy liquor.[68]

Most Finns wanted nothing to do with the Russian gendarmerie and as a result it was forced to recruit the majority of its agents from among the drunks, petty criminals, and mentally disturbed elements of Finnish society. Agents quickly discovered the kind of information their superiors wanted and set about providing it.[69]

It is difficult to understand how a great power was able to operate such an ineffectual intelligence-gathering network, but ultimately it was not a question of whether any credence was given to the distorted picture of reality that it provided. True or not, its distortions served the goals of Russian politicians keen to make use of the Finnish question only too well.

The head of the gendarmerie in Finland, K. K. Utgof, was relieved of his duties and replaced in 1913 by A. M. Eremin. Following his appointment, the content of the gendarmerie's reports changed dramatically, and the exaggeration of previous years was replaced by a new sense of realism.[70] It is interesting to note, however, that one prime suspicion remained. Even Balabin in his 1912 investigation believed that the Finns were prepared for rebellion, although he argued that such a rebellion would only become reality if Russia were to encounter serious internal or external difficulties.

Following the Russian government's realization in 1912 and 1913 that its policy on Finland up until then had been based on a serious misreading of the situation, it could in theory have changed tack and begun to build bridges with the Finnish nonsocialist parties then in the majority in the Finnish Diet. The Finns stubbornly clung to the letter of their fundamental laws and showed relatively little understanding of even those of the government's imperial-driven initiatives aimed more at modernizing administration than subjugating Finland. In an administrative structure that was beginning to be rapidly modernized, Finnish autonomy represented an anachronistic relic, but with good will on both sides it could have had something to contribute. A new approach would undoubtedly have been difficult, but it would not have been impossible. No such attempt was made, however.[71]

It is difficult to say whether Stolypin would have had the courage and wisdom to take such a step if he had still been prime minister. Perhaps not, as he very much built his career on the basis of aggressive Russian nationalism. Stolypin's successor, Kokovtsov, in any case was no match for him and proved unable to control the government as Stolypin had done.[72] Governor-General Zein continued his divisive approach in Finland with the full consent and approval of the Emperor,[73] even though one would have been very justified in expecting that the behind-the-scenes scandal in the Finnish gendarmerie would have forced him to resign as well. This highlights how badly Russia was governed after Stolypin's death.

Despite his previous conciliatory approach, Prime Minister Kokovtsov proved a disappointment to the Finns. In a speech in the Duma on October 28, 1911 OS, covering the legislation on equality and the substitution of military service with an annual charge, he committed himself to the policies of his predecessor. Russian nationalists and the Right were very satisfied with the position he took, and even the Tsar congratulated him on the speech. As a politician, Kokovtsov had, of course, primarily to consider what the Russian population thought of him rather than a couple of million Finns. In a discussion with Minister Secretary of State Langhoff, Kokovtsov explained apologetically that he had no other option if he wanted to continue as prime minister. Russian nationalist opinion would not have accepted any change in government policy, nor would the Tsar, although Kokovtsov neglected to mention this to Langhoff.

On the indirect basis of Langhoff's memoirs, it can be concluded that Kokovtsov did not have a clear idea of the Tsar's views on Finland prior to discussing the Finnish question with the Tsar for the first time after being appointed prime minister. It seems that Kokovtsov had previously imagined that the Tsar was not particularly committed to Stolypin's policy and that a gradual and partial shift in course might be possible. Now he knew better, but hid this knowledge from Langhoff. Witte claims, with the benefit of hindsight, to have seen through Kokovtsov. He says that he knew the new prime minister would continue the nationalist policy of his predecessor, even though Kokovtsov did not have the same emotional attachment to this policy that Stolypin did.

In line with his promises, Kokovtsov succeeded in blocking some of Zein's most extreme proposals but, generally speaking, the policy of integration continued to progress as before.[74] Stolypin before him had also acted to prevent the governor-general from going too far. Kokovtsov was not the man to undermine Zein's position, however, let alone topple him from office. The number of critical comments on the Finnish question at meetings of the Council of Ministers fell during Kokovtsov's term as prime minister. As before during Stolypin's time, it was the Tsar who was ultimately responsible for the government's policy on Finland; on the practical level, however, control shifted from the prime minister to Governor-General Zein, if anyone.

Following the outbreak of World War I in the summer of 1914, a state of war was declared in Finland but without recourse to the sort of draconian measures included in the plans drawn up in preceding years.[75] The more than 800 leading members of various parties that were supposed to be imprisoned were, with a few exceptions, not taken into custody.[76] The state of war proved much more amenable than its peacetime counterpart. The Finnish governor-general and administration were subordinated to the Sixth Army and through this to the Northern Front and Headquarters. The governor-general was also required to take orders from the St. Petersburg military district and the Baltic Fleet. The state of war brought Zein the exceptional powers he had long hankered after.[77]

On November 19, 1914 OS, Governor-General Zein was sent a letter from the Russian Council of Ministers informing him that the local administration should avoid all measures that might strengthen Swedish antipathy toward Russia and encourage Sweden to ally herself with Germany. The banishment of the former speaker of the Diet, P. E. Svinhufvud, to Siberia was criticized as a serious mistake in this respect. Zein was requested to attend the next Council of Ministers meeting to discuss "the necessity of softening our policy on Finland."[78]

In the summer of 1915, Minister of Internal Affairs N. B. Shcherbatov and State Controller P. A. Kharitonov argued at the Council of

Ministers that Finland was benefiting from the war at the expense of the rest of the empire without contributing to the war effort. Foreign Minister S. D. Sazonov argued against encouraging Zein, however, and argued for the council leaving Finland alone, if only to discourage the Swedes from becoming nervous. Prime Minister I. L. Goremykin agreed. In the war "we wouldn't benefit much from a handful of Finnish buffoons, let them go to hell." The Committee of Finnish Affairs was in the process of preparing a number of important issues, but their time was yet to come.[79] A little later the same summer, Goremykin confirmed to the Council of Ministers that Zein had been instructed to relax imperial policy toward Finland. The so-called progressive bloc in the Duma put pressure on the government to sack Zein, but the Council of Ministers decided to leave things unchanged.[80]

When one looks at the Russian government's policy on Finland between 1914 and 1917,[81] one can see that the directions received by Zein at the end of 1914 remained unchanged until the fall of the autocracy. Finland was the only part of the empire where conscription or prescribed labor was not introduced. The softer Russian approach did not change even in 1915 when it was revealed that contingents of Finnish youths had been dispatched to Germany for military training with the intention of using them to form the backbone of a future army of liberation.[82]

After learning that plans were afoot for an uprising in Finland and that Germany was planning a landing to break the country away from Russia, the supreme commander of the armies on the Northern Front, General P. A. Pleve, proposed on January 7, 1916 OS, to Goremykin, then in his last weeks as prime minister, that exports of foodstuffs from Russia to Finland be halted completely. These foodstuffs would only benefit the rebels and the German invaders, he said, and food was not in short supply in Finland in any case.

Goremykin asked the opinion of Minister of the Navy I. K. Grigorevich, who in his reply a few days later described General Pleve's suggestion as not only unjustified but extremely dangerous. The threat of a German landing did not give major cause for concern, even if Sweden were to join in the operation, he suggested. The Russian navy had complete control of the Gulf of Bothnia and the Gulf of Finland, and there was no evidence of unrest that might call for such radical action. It would only help German agents in their efforts to foster an uprising.[83] Minister of War A. A. Polivanov's comments were similar. Punishing the Finns with hunger would not only create problems in Finland but also antagonize Sweden. The Tsar was informed of the situation in Finland on January 23 OS by Minister of Internal Affairs A. N. Khvostov. His report was objective and avoided excesses, leading one to suspect that his information came from Eremin.[84] Overall, it seems that the surprising calm shown by the government during the war years was partly the result of the lesson taught by the Utgof case and personal efforts on the part of Eremin. The contrast to earlier years is very significant.

The threat to Finnish food supplies did not completely disappear, however, as General Pleve sent a modified version of his earlier proposal on February 4 OS to the Chief of Staff of the Supreme Commander in Chief (the Tsar had assumed this position), General M. V. Alekseev. Pleve now proposed a whole batch of measures to strengthen border and police control, banning Finnish men between the ages of nineteen and thirty-five from leaving the country, and careful monitoring and rationing of food exports to Finland. Alekseev gave his approval to the proposal and forwarded it to the new prime minister, B. V. Stürmer (Shtiurmer).[85]

Based on the prime minister's presentation at Headquarters, on February 20 OS the Tsar ordered Adjutant Generals F. F. Trepov and A. N. Kuropatkin to investigate the stocks of food and animal feed in Finland that the enemy might be able to use. As a previous minister of war and an owner of a dacha on the Karelian Isthmus, Kuropatkin was familiar with Finnish affairs. He had recently replaced Pleve as commander of the Northern Front. Kuropatkin asked Trepov also to investigate Finnish recruitment into the German army and the possibility of a German landing. Trepov camouflaged his detective work as a mission to hand out medals to wounded soldiers. His report to the Tsar dated March 7, 1916 OS, was observant and reassuring. There was no evidence of preparations for an uprising to break Finland away from Russia, either alone or with German assistance. Some of the population would support the Germans if they invaded, he said, but many wanted Finland to remain out of the war. There were too few weapons in the country for a rebellion, and it appeared that none were being imported. Although German agents were nevertheless active, Trepov could find no evidence of foodstuffs or animal feed having been stockpiled for an enemy invasion. Trepov concluded with a proposal merely to step up monitoring and control, and added that Kuropatkin and Stürmer agreed with his views.[86]

Governor-General Zein also sent reassuring information to Headquarters. The crisis posed to Finnish food supplies finally therefore evaporated. The comments of ministers in January show that they did not completely accept the arguments put forward by Pleve; opinion at Headquarters followed a similar track.[87] The disciplinary action planned against Finland was opposed at a high level from the beginning. If it had been implemented, it would have been completely out of proportion to the situation in Finland and it would have probably been counterproductive for the government as a result of its impact on the whole population, not just the supporters of the *Jäger* movement. For all its realism, the government, in fact, underestimated the situation in Finland, which was more dangerous than at any point between 1908 and 1914. The exaggeration of earlier years now came home to roost in the shape of playing down real risks.

General Pleve's proposal reflected the dissatisfaction of certain nationalist circles with the insufficiency of Finland's contribution to the war effort and with what they saw as the favored treatment given to the empire's minority nationalities generally, particularly the Finns and Poles. During 1916, *Novoe vremia* repeatedly criticized the Russified Senate in Helsinki for neglecting the imperial war effort. Deitrikh and Borodkin argued within right-wing circles that Zein was being too lenient to the Finns and was too much controlled by the Finnish Senate and should be removed from his post as governor-general. Zein learned of this in time, however, and managed to rebuild his bridges with Deitrikh and Borodkin.[88]

An examination of the dilemma Russian authorities faced regarding whether and when to declare a state of war in Finland shows that, for Russian politicians, the Finnish question was primarily not one of maintaining the security of the empire's northwest frontier but rather a weapon they used in the empire's domestic politics. This is the only explanation for the strange fact that the issue of ensuring law and order in Finland only became a matter of importance in Russian politics when law and order was not a problem in Finland, while amid the threats posed by the war Finland was largely left to her own devices. During the war, the Finnish question lost its significance in Russian domestic politics and avoiding anything that might provoke Sweden to join forces with Germany became a more important priority.

Two approaches shaped Russian government attitudes to the Finnish question: one uncompromisingly saw Finland as a danger, whereas the other preferred to play things more by ear. The dominance enjoyed by the more uncompromising approach until the outbreak of World War I ultimately derived from the fact that it was the one supported by the Tsar.

The Essence of Russian Policy on Finland:
Administrative Integration, 1907–1917

On the subject of things Finnish, Stolypin first addressed the practice used for presenting Finnish issues to the Emperor. This was done through the Minister Secretary of State for Finland. Under a statute issued on August 1, 1891 NS, the Minister Secretary of State was responsible for deciding whether individual legislative matters affected general imperial interests. If they did, he was required to request the opinion of the relevant Russian minister, which was forwarded to the Emperor along with his own presentation.[89] In an internal circular issued on January 5, 1907 OS, Stolypin ordered ministers to send their statements on Finnish matters first to the prime minister rather than directly to the Minister Secretary of State as before, thereby allowing them to be discussed in the Council of Ministers if appropriate. The aim of the order was to coordinate government policy on Finland.[90]

Stolypin, the Committee on Finnish Affairs, and the Council of Ministers believed that Finnish ministers state secretary, most recently Langhoff, had misused the 1891 statute and gained the Tsar's approval for laws without consulting the Russian minister concerned on subjects that could be considered as having general imperial implications.[91] The Russian government's concept of what constituted "general imperial implications" was, of course, completely different and much broader than the Finns'. In the summer of 1907, Stolypin protested to Nicholas that Langhoff had bypassed the relevant Russian ministers when presenting a proposed law on trade practices to the Tsar.[92] It was difficult for a strong-willed man like Stolypin to accept matters being put before the Tsar without their first having passed his own desk and those of the members of his Council of Ministers.

Nicholas II ordered the introduction of a new procedure initiated by the Russian Council of Ministers for presenting Finnish matters to the Tsar on May 20/June 2, 1908. Under this, presentations by the Finnish Minister Secretary of State were subordinated to the Russian Council of Ministers. All legislative and administrative matters affecting Finland were to be forwarded to the Council of Ministers before going to the Emperor for the Council to decide whether they touched on imperial interests. In cases where the Council of Ministers and the Minister Secretary of State were unable to reach agreement on a matter for presentation, the prime minister or another Russian minister would act as the second presenting official alongside the minister state secretary. This new procedure was enacted under the Russian system and was never published in the Finnish statute book.[93] The Finns saw it as conflicting with the Finnish constitution and therefore illegal.

Stolypin was the father of this reform. The new arrangement was not only the first major change resulting from his policy on Finland but also reflected his aim of concentrating responsibility for the entirety of the highest echelon of the empire's government in the hands of the Council of Ministers headed by himself. He could not allow the Finnish Minister Secretary of State to present Finnish affairs to the Emperor bypassing the Council of Ministers. Although he was unable to bring the foreign, war, and naval ministries, who were jealously guarded by Nicholas, under the control of the Council of Ministers,[94] he did not have to tolerate independence from the Finnish Minister Secretary of State.[95]

The new presentation procedure was unwieldy and slow in its insistence that all Finnish matters had to be examined by the Council of Ministers. Kokovtsov drew attention to this when he defended Finland's right to separate administration. He would have been willing to leave the assessment of whether Finnish matters had general imperial implications up to the governor-general. Kokovtsov was successful in getting the Council of Ministers to slightly modify the Committee of Finnish Affairs' proposal, which perhaps indicates that various other ministers similarly did not stand unequivocally behind Stolypin's tough line.[96]

The new procedure reflects Stolypin's deep suspicions about the activities of the Finnish Senate and Minister Secretary of State. These suspicions and Stolypin's determined aim of introducing an imperial legislative procedure into Finnish affairs of the type proposed in the February Manifesto can be clearly seen in numerous official documents produced by the Council of Ministers. Nobody could have been left in any doubt that Stolypin wanted to halt Finland's development in the direction of becoming a state increasingly separate from Russia.

The new procedure also worked, however, indirectly against the autocracy in placing the Council of Ministers as a guard dog between the Tsar and his Minister Secretary of State. Whenever the Council of Ministers and the Committee of Finnish Affairs criticized the Minister Secretary of State for presenting matters in such a way as to ignore imperial interests,[97] they also implicitly criticized the autocracy and the system of personal presentation that it encouraged, and therefore Nicholas II himself, who was seen as unable to defend Russia's interests without the intervention or assistance of his ministers. If Nicholas had been a stronger ruler, he would perhaps have rebuffed the Council of Ministers' attempts to thus reduce his power and retained the previous system of presentation.

Regardless of the legal status of the new system, as such it was not a danger to Finnish autonomy. When the Tsar had acceded to pressure in 1905 and made the Council of Ministers the empire's government or cabinet, it was not unreasonable that it should be kept up to date on Finnish matters, although this could have been achieved in a more flexible way than that ultimately adopted. Problems for Finnish autonomy were created, however, by the way in which Stolypin began to make use of the new presentation procedure. It became the prime instrument of his policy of integration.[98] The new procedure gave the Council of Ministers the opportunity to defend imperial interests when legislation and decisions were still at the drafting stage. One major issue remained unresolved, however, and that was under which procedure imperial legislation affecting Finland should be enacted: the local Finnish system, the imperial or Russian one, or perhaps through a process of compromise between the Russian and Finnish authorities?

On June 17/30, 1910, the Tsar sanctioned a new law on imperial legislative procedure. This covered legislation to be introduced throughout the empire, Finland included, or only in Finland. In the case of the latter, the procedure embraced those laws and statutes that affected imperial interests. These had to enacted under the Russian procedure; in other words, the Council of Ministers and, when legislation was concerned the State Council and the Duma also, considered them, after which they were confirmed by the Tsar as laws or statutes. The Finnish Senate and Diet were only entitled to have an advisory voice in all matters of imperial legislation. This meant that the Diet lost the legislative authority that it had previously exercised together with the Emperor. The old legislative procedure was only retained for matters considered to be exclusively of a Finnish domestic nature.

The new law listed nineteen legislative areas that were defined as being of a general imperial nature. Laws and statutes in these areas as they were enacted would assume priority over local Finnish legislation. The scope of general imperial legislation was broadly drawn, but despite this Finnish legislation continued to reign supreme in Finland in a number of economic, social, and more minor administrative matters. The law required the Finnish Diet to select two representatives to sit on the State Council and four to sit in the Duma. The law poured further salt on the wound by requiring that these representatives be competent in Russian.[99]

The change eliminated the possibility of the Finnish Diet preventing reforms desired by the government from coming into force. In other words, the outcome was much the same as that aimed at by the February Manifesto issued during the Bobrikov period in 1899.

As *Novoe vremia* wrote in April 1910, the Russian government and its supporters believed that "as the competence of the Finnish Diet does not extend to questions of imperial concern, it cannot have the power of decision on these. Therefore decisions on questions of imperial concern are solely the responsibility of imperial legislative bodies."[100]

In other words, the legislation of only one part of the empire could not restrict or contradict legislation by the imperial government. The idea of a separate Finnish state had become incompatible with the modern institutions of the Russian Council of Ministers and the Duma.[101]

Article 2 of the Fundamental State Laws (April 23, 1906 OS) stated that "The Grand Duchy of Finland, while it constitutes an indivisible part of the Russian State, is governed in its domestic affairs by special institutions on the basis of a special legislation."[102]

At the time of the consideration by the Committee of Finnish Affairs on December 29, 1908 OS, of the appointment of a mixed Finnish-Russian commission to draft an enactment procedure for imperial legislation affecting Finland, Kokovtsov and Bekman argued that Russia's Fundamental State Laws of 1906 had in no way changed the legislative relationship between the empire and Finland. In his manifesto on the establishment of the Duma of August 6, 1905 OS, the Tsar had only stated that he would determine at a later date the nature of the Finnish representation in the Duma for consideration of matters common to Finland and the empire. An imperial manifesto on Finland of October 22/November 4, 1905, terminated implementation of the 1899 February Manifesto until further notice. A subsequent imperial manifesto of February 20, 1906 OS, on the reorganization of the State Council and the Duma, stated that the Tsar would issue regulations on the enactment of laws common to the empire and Finland at a later date.[103] Kokovtsov and Bekman argued that the question of defining the nature of this legislative procedure had therefore remained open. Together with Kryzhanovskii, they proposed that the Tsar should decide the issue once and for all with a binding decision on the subject. While Stolypin wanted to put the matter before the new legislative bodies of the Duma and the imperial council, his competitor Kokovtsov skillfully tried to undermine his position by putting forward solutions that would bolster the Tsar's traditional autocratic status.

Stolypin and the other members of the Committee of Finnish Affairs decided, however, that Article 2 of Russia's Fundamental State Laws meant that only Finland's internal matters were left outside the scope of these laws. The enactment procedure for imperial legislation affecting Finland came within the sphere of the requirements laid down by the Fundamental State Laws, it was argued, and had to be considered in line with Articles 7 and 86 of these laws; these stated that the Tsar exercised the legislative power in conjunction with the State Council and the Duma and that "no new law may be passed without the approval of the State Council and the State Duma and take force without the sanction of Our Sovereign the Emperor." The Council of Ministers had allowed the Tsar to sanction this interpretation back on August 19, 1907 OS. The committee's majority presented an adroit argument that, if the Tsar were to resolve the question of the enactment procedure for imperial legislation affecting Finland without consulting the Duma and the State Council, he could be accused of ignoring the Fundamental State Laws. The committee left the difference of opinion between the majority and the minority on how to proceed on this matter up to the Tsar to resolve, but expressed its hope that the Tsar would take his decision under general legislative procedure, without recourse to the Finnish Diet. The committee recommended the appointment of a mixed Finnish-Russian commission to consider the content of the proposed legislation.[104]

Such a commission was, in fact, appointed in 1909 (chaired by State Controller P. A. Kharitonov), and its Russian majority pushed through the principle of general imperial legislative procedure in line with Stolypin's solution, paying no attention to the counterarguments advanced by the commission's Finnish members.[105]

In a discussion of the conclusions of Kharitonov's commission by the Council of Ministers on February 22, 1910 OS, Minister of Education A. N. Shvarts called for the partial introduction of the general imperial education system into the Finnish school system. Russian language teaching should be increased in grammar schools, he argued, but with the lack of suitable teachers he accepted that it would as yet be impossible to extend Russian to primary schools. Finnish schoolbooks should also be subjected to government scrutiny, said Shvarts. Kokovtsov opposed the politicization and Russification of the Finnish school system, as he put it. It is rare to see mention of Russification in official government documents; the Russification that Shvarts and Kokovtsov had in mind was of an administrative rather than a cultural nature, following the classification proposed by Edward C. Thaden. The government's policy on Finland between 1899 and 1917 was based on administrative integration, or to follow Thaden, administrative Russification. As Finland was so different from Russia in all respects, ethnic and cultural Russification could not become such an issue as, for example, in Poland and the Ukraine.[106]

Speaking at the same meeting of the council, Kokovtsov argued that Kharitonov's commission had not taken sufficient account of Finland's autonomy. Kokovtsov proposed including Finnish representatives in imperial legislative bodies only when matters affecting Finland were discussed, reducing the scope of general imperial legislation, and increasing the number of Finnish representatives compared to that of all other imperial borderlands in order to emphasize Finland's special position in the empire. With the support of Minister of Justice Shcheglovitov, Kokovtsov proposed that the Emperor's broad administrative (exercised independently of the Diet) and legislative power based on constitutional law inherited from the Swedish period should be excluded from the sphere of general imperial legislative procedure; in other words, he again tried to defend the traditional autocracy against what he saw as the usurpist inclinations of the new governmental bodies in Russia.

The Council of Ministers ultimately decided to propose only minor modifications to the proposal put forward by Kharitonov's commission, however. It recommended putting the proposal before the Duma and State Council for consideration. The Finnish Diet was only to be requested to provide a statement of its opinion and not allowed to have any say on the final outcome. This approach received the Tsar's blessing[107] and on June 17/30, 1910, the Tsar approved the law that resulted from the debate within the Duma and the State Council on the subject.[108]

Criticizing the proposed legislation in May 1910, Professor Berendts had argued that Finnish legality was based on a stronger foundation than its Russian equivalent. As a result, extending the sphere of general imperial legislation to Finland could result in extending the sphere of illegality or, at best, weak legality. Berendts also doubted the government's promise to introduce the new legislative procedure on a phased basis and with due care. By way of reply to his question of who would guarantee this, Stolypin wrote in the margin of his memorandum: "By having laws pass through the State Duma."[109] He saw the Duma therefore as a form of check against excessive integration and repression. Time would soon tell whose view was the more accurate.

The Emperor convened the Diet in August 1910 for a sitting to begin on September 14 to draw up the basis for electing the Finnish representatives to be sent to the State Duma and State Council and to hold the necessary elections. In addition, the Diet was also requested to give its consultative opinions on two draft laws prepared by the Council of Ministers covering the payment of military-related funds and the granting of equivalent rights to Russian subjects as those accorded Finnish citizens in Finland. The Diet refused to discuss either law, arguing that they were illegal and irrelevant in light of the fact that the law enacted on June 17/30, 1910, was not in force in Finland and that, as a result, the Council of Ministers was not entitled to put draft laws before the Diet. The Tsar dissolved the Diet as a result and called new elections. Stolypin also asked Nicholas to order the Council of Ministers to forward the draft laws to the Duma for consideration.[110]

Back in March/April 1906, when the Finnish-Russian conference chaired by E. V. Frish was reviewing a proposal for a new Finnish Diet Act, its Russian members had drawn attention to the fact that the right to vote in Finland was restricted to Finnish citizens and did not extend to Russians living in Finland, who were treated as foreigners, despite being subjects of the same Tsar as the Finns.[111] Nicholas nevertheless approved this section of the act[112] but, following the counterarguments advanced against it, he ordered the Finnish Senate without delay to draw up a proposal for a procedure under which imperial subjects could gain Finnish citizenship.

Meeting on July 20, 1907 OS, the Council of Ministers condemned the Senate's proposal as discriminatory toward Russians and concluded that the matter should proceed under general imperial legislative procedure when the Minister of Internal Affairs considered it appropriate. Stolypin believed that 1907 was too early for such a move as, if Russians were able too easily to become Finnish citizens, this would encourage growing numbers of revolutionaries and terrorists to gravitate toward Finland. The Council of Ministers concluded that the question of citizenship rights was part of the wider question regarding the necessity of enabling Russians living in Finland to enjoy the same rights as Finns living in Russia, in other words that Russians should be granted equivalent rights to those held by Finns. The Tsar approved these principles on August 19, 1907 OS.[113]

The Russian Right and Russian Nationalists raised the question of equality of rights to the same level of importance as those of the need for general imperial legislative procedure and the annexation of the province of

Vyborg to Russia.[114] This strengthened Stolypin in his conviction that he was acting in the interests of a wide sector of patriotic opinion.[115]

Equality of rights came up for discussion on Stolypin's initiative at the Committee of Finnish Affairs on May 23, 1909 OS. Governor-General Bekman forwarded his proposal via Stolypin to the committee that equality of rights should be implemented with the exception of the right to vote in elections to the Diet, which Bekman wanted to reserve for Finns alone. Such a restriction was unacceptable to the committee, of course. Stolypin was authorized to ensure that the legislation was enacted under general legislative procedure.[116]

Approximately a year later, on August 3, 1910 OS, a proposal drafted by Governor-General Zein on granting equality of rights was discussed by the Council of Ministers. The proposal stipulated that "Russian subjects who are not Finnish citizens shall be granted equivalent rights to those enjoyed by local citizens in Finland." The proposal also granted equivalence to examinations and degrees passed in Russia to comparable Finnish qualifications and granted Russia's Christian subjects the right to teach history in Finnish schools. Finnish civil servants who deliberately opposed the implementation of such equality of rights would be arraigned under Russian law before a Russian court. While stressing that he completely agreed with the principle of the equality of rights, Minister of Finance Kokovtsov questioned whether such equality extended beyond civil rights to voting rights at the national and local level. The Council of Ministers approved Zein's proposal with only minor modifications.[117]

His proposal became law and was enacted under imperial procedure through the Duma in 1912. This granted Russian subjects the same rights in Finland as Finnish citizens. This effectively pulled the rug out from under the concept of separate Finnish citizenship, an important foundation of Finland's autonomy, and opened up access to Finnish civil service positions to Russians.[118] Court members who refused to abide by the law would be stripped of their position in a Russian court and required to serve their sentences in a Russian prison.[119]

Russian power in Finland ultimately rested on the points of the bayonets of the Russian troops stationed in the country. The reality of this state of affairs was only revealed at times of crisis, such as the General Strike of the autumn of 1905. In order to be able to put down the Finnish uprising that was expected to take place and to strengthen its position with regard to possible external threats, the government increased the level of the Russian military presence substantially after 1905. By the time World War I broke out, the number of Russian troops had grown from under 20,000 in 1905 to over 30,000. During the war, their number rose even further.[120]

In the years after 1905, Finland paid financial compensation to Russia, reluctantly it is true, in return for the exemption of Finnish males from required military service. This apparent flexibility on the part of the Russian authorities was not the result of any conciliatory approach on their part, but derived from the simple fact that they considered the Finns so unreliable that they had no wish to train an able-bodied reserve. The Finnish Senate would very much have liked to reestablish Finland's own army, but the Russian government blocked this. Following disagreements on the financial authority of the Diet, Nicholas II issued a manifesto in 1909 covering the payment of this compensation, bypassing the Diet entirely. The dispute this generated led to the resignation of the last Finnish politicians from the Senate and the appointment of what became known as the "Admirals' Senate" or "Sabre Senate," which duly paid the agreed-upon compensation. In 1912, the government enacted a law under imperial procedure through the Duma and the State Council resolving the compensation arrangement in a way acceptable to the government.[121]

Stolypin's policy was aimed at ensuring that Finland paid its share of the empire's "general imperial" costs.[122] This bore fruit in some areas such as the military question. Voices were heard in Russia from time to time asserting that Finland's prosperity was built at the expense of the empire and the Russian population in particular.[123] There is no doubt about the objectives of those who advanced such views. The imperial government failed, however, to win significantly larger funds from Finland, not even during the war years, as the country's Russified Senate relatively quickly learned the value of stable government and a solid state economy and social peace, and it resisted St. Petersburg's attempts to gain a bigger piece of the Finnish financial pie.[124] The imperial authorities remained dissatisfied, as evidenced by the complaints of Minister of Finance P. L. Bark to N. D. Golitsyn, the last prerevolutionary prime minister, as late as February 15, 1917 OS, on the benefits enjoyed by Finland.[125] Time had run out by then to correct the situation, however, since the February Revolution erupted in less than two weeks.

The imperial government had a rather narrow and unsophisticated view of Finnish society and Finnish political parties. The Swedish Party was typically seen as the party of the upper classes and as heading the opposition to Russian rule. Many official reports linked the party to the underground and terrorist-inspired Activist Party. It was not until Balabin's study of 1912 that these views were seriously undermined; he showed that the activities of the Activists had ceased years previously. It is nevertheless clear that the government did not completely accept this view of the Swedish Party since its representatives were allowed to sit in the Senate for many years. The other half of the Constitutionalists, the Young Finns, was seen as the obvious ally of the Swedish Party, and the Social Democrats were lumped together under the same heading. Little or no significance was attached by the Russians to the class-related issues dividing the Finnish parties. And it is true that on matters affecting Finland's status as a nation the socialists allied themselves with the Constitutionalists, albeit not formally. As a result of its views, the government perhaps did not act as forcefully as it could have to break up the Finnish opposition by courting the Social Democrats but, on the other hand, the potential of either the government or the socialists to draw closer to each other was relatively minimal.

During 1908 and 1909, Stolypin's, Bekman's, and Zein's plan was to try to rule Finland with the help of the conciliation-minded Old Finns, as Bobrikov had done before. The party had learned its lesson from Bobrikov, however, and refused to resume a role that had earned it the suspicion of many other Finns on matters patriotic. Stolypin therefore allowed the Old Finns to move to the ranks of the opposition. The Russians attached particular hopes to Ossian Wuorenheimo, who had been a member of the Senate during Bobrikov's time and who they considered the most amenable of the Old Finns, but he too let them down.[126]

Following the refusal of the Old Finns to implement his imperial reforms, Stolypin was forced to fill the empty seats in the Finnish Senate at short notice with Russified Finns assembled from all corners of the empire and others closer to home whose main ambition was power rather than political conviction. The result of this move in autumn 1909 did little to improve the government's position and tarnished Stolypin's image as a reformer of government. He simply pushed through his own solution with little regard for the consequences even over the short term, let alone the longer term. Rear Admiral A. A. Virenius, who found himself the deputy chairman of the Senate's Finance Department, the equivalent of Finland's prime minister, by dint of his seniority in years served tried, for example, to convince Governor-General Bckman that he be freed from this duty as his command of Finnish and Swedish, the languages of the Senate, was "completely inadequate," as he put it.[127]

Although Stolypin was motivated by a sincere desire to handle matters differently from Bobrikov and allow the Duma to act as a counterbalance to the most repressive-minded opinion, his at times uncompromising approach and good relations with those who advocated tough policies served to undermine his good intentions. In the final analysis, the government appeared to believe that even granting one concession would have been a fateful show of weakness.[128]

Yet a number of scholars believe with good reason that the government proceeded very slowly and cautiously in passing new imperial legislation.[129] There was no question of a complete elimination of Finnish autonomy or crude oppression. In its attempts to implement the interests of Russians at the expense of those of minority nationalities, the government made plain that not all the Emperor's subjects were equal. This did nothing to increase Finns' affection for the empire.[130]

Nevertheless, particularly blatant example of undue attention to Russian national interests that needlessly alienated the Finns were the recommendations by the Committee on Finnish Affairs for the annexation of two parishes in the province of Vyborg and subsequently the entire province to Russia on November 13, 1910 OS, and April 21, 1914 OS, respectively. The Tsar gave his blessing to the idea in principle and at the suggestion of the Council of Ministers on August 4, 1911 OS, he ordered a special commission to draft a law on the subject for enactment under imperial procedure. This work eventually led in 1914 to a project to annex the entire province. The province was defined on the basis of the borders of 1811 and included the town of Savonlinna (Nyslott) and its surroundings, which had been transferred to the province of Mikkeli (St. Michel) in 1816. The Tsar approved the recommendation of the Committee on Finnish Affairs for annexation on July 13, 1914 OS. This provisional decision was not implemented, however. The matter went to a commission for drafting and never reemerged. The entire project was mainly motivated by a desire to guarantee the security of St. Petersburg. The army was equally able to defend the empire from Finnish soil as from Russian territory, but this was downplayed by the Russians. Finland, or rather the Finnish authorities, were suspect, and that was sufficient reason to propose annexation.

Kokovtsov had promised Langhoff in the autumn of 1911 that preparing and implementing the process of annexation would take years. He did not, however, give any promise that he would stop it, nor is there any evidence that he worked to slow down the process. By way of protecting himself and avoiding tripping himself up over the Finnish question, Kokovtsov supported Zein's proposal for banning the celebrations planned for the centenary of the province's joining Finland proper. The Tsar naturally acceded to this proposal.

The annexation of the two parishes proved difficult from a legal standpoint. The Committee on Finnish Affairs came to the slightly surprising, but understandable, conclusion in 1914, therefore, that annexing the entire province would be simpler as part of Finnish legislation could be more easily left in force in an area of this size, compared to the case in a couple of border parishes. The rapid progress made by the question in the first part of 1914 could have resulted from Kokovtsov's replacement as prime minister by the extreme conservative I. L. Goremykin. The fact that Grand Duke Nikolai Nikolaevich had set annexation of the entire province as a goal back on March 28, 1913 OS, indicates, however, that the change of prime ministers was not the only factor at work. More specifically, it was a consequence of the gradual increase in international tension. The province would certainly have been annexed to Russia at some point if the war had not given the government more important food for thought.[131] If the border had been shifted westwards, the province's male population would have been conscripted.

Stolypin liked to promote his aims by packaging them into action programs that included an estimate of the potential for implementing the measures in question, tactical moves, and plans for the appointment of the appropriate people to key positions. In the spring of 1909, when planning the replacement of Bekman with Zein, he informed the Tsar that Zein should be given an action program. This should be based, he suggested, on the realization that the type of measures favored during Bobrikov's time were no longer appropriate and that instead Finnish legislation should be respected, thereby preventing the emergence of both passive and active resistance.[132] Stolypin undoubtedly thought that Zein was a sufficiently determined Russian patriot, but felt that his overzealous tendency to Bobrikov-like gestures had to be reined in.

Stolypin should be seen as the ultimate father of the "Russification Program" of 1914 that saw a number of Finns lose their last shreds of loyalty to the empire and begin to start moves to separate Finland from Russia.

After his appointment as governor-general, Zein began to bombard Stolypin with various proposals for legislative and other changes. The Committee on Finnish Affairs, chaired by the prime minister, reviewed these proposals in detail on May 28, 1911 OS, and concluded that some of them could be introduced under imperial legislative procedure through the Duma and the State Council. It was not considered worth pursuing the others through these bodies because of the political resistance they would encounter. The first group of issues included introducing imperial legislation on the press, enabling recalcitrant civil servants to be dealt with under Russian law in a Russian court, and adopting Russian as the main language of administration or at least enhancing its position. The second group of issues, which were politically impossible, included handling political crimes in imperial courts and under imperial law and granting the gendarmerie the same authority that it enjoyed in Bobrikov's time and continued to enjoy in Russia.

It seems relatively certain that this was Stolypin's personal view. While wanting to promote positive measures, he also probably wished to give a light rap on the knuckles to his overeager subordinate, who busied himself with drawing up proposal after proposal without due attention to whether they were actually feasible. On the other hand, it is clear that

Zein knew he could present his demands to the Council of Ministers because of the support he had from the Tsar. The Committee on Finnish Affairs passed the proposals for improving law and order in Finland and Finland's administrative integration with the rest of the empire to a separate preparatory commission headed by N. N. Korevo.

Immediately after the introduction of imperial legislative procedure, the Tsar, at Stolypin's suggestion, had ordered imperial institutions on July 18, 1910 OS, to prepare material on legislative questions that came within the sphere of the procedure. The Ministry of Internal Affairs forwarded its proposal to the Korevo Commission in 1912. The planned reforms contained in this would have meant a substantial increase in the power of the police. They were crowned by a proposal for reintroducing the gendarmerie statutes in force during Bobrikov's period in office. Stolypin had argued the previous year that bringing up matters of this type was counterproductive, as they would hamper the government's relations with the Duma and its image in society. No such problem was seen as existing by the ministry.

The Korevo Commission grouped the issues presented to it under three headings: law and order, defense, and political and economic integration. In itself, this left many areas of Finnish autonomy unaddressed. The commission nevertheless proposed that, when drafting new legislative proposals, imperial institutions should be required to always assess whether the legislation in question should be extended under imperial procedure to cover Finland as well. Over the long term, this provision would have considerably narrowed the extent of Finland's autonomy. It is a little difficult to believe that this had been Stolypin's intention, but he had unleashed forces that did not feel bound by the same constraints that he felt.

The leaking of the "Russification Program" approved by the Tsar that emerged as the result of this drafting work in the spring of 1914 and again in the autumn of the same year led to the birth of the Finnish independence movement.[133] The movement turned to Germany for support. The Council of Ministers ordered Zein to soften his policies in the autumn of 1914, but neither Zein nor the Russian government proved able to give a clearly positive signal to the Finns. Great Russian nationalism was intended to be a means for ruling the empire, but it divided more than it united. When the fortunes of war turned against Russia, the ultimate fruits of Russian nationalism were harvested by the opponents of imperial centralism.

CONCLUSION

In his memoirs, Minister Secretary of State Langhoff puts forward the belief that has subsequently been long held in Finland that Stolypin and his "Bobrikov-inspired" advisers were responsible for the government's policy on Finland during the Duma period. Although Langhoff was aware that Nicholas II was not well-disposed toward Finland, he never realized the central role played by the Tsar in the various military solutions that were proposed for Finland. He draws attention to the fact that Nicholas decided some matters on the advice of the Minister Secretary of State rather than Stolypin, but fails to see that this reflected the Tsar's general aim of defending his autocratic position against the prime minister and the Council of Ministers.[134] Ruling through trusted confidantes was typical of the Russian autocracy. Langhoff's occasional successes are explained by the good relations he established with Nicholas. Thanks to them, he kept his position for so long, until 1913. Langhoff saw Nicholas as Stolypin's unwitting puppet, without understanding that the prime minister was always dependent on the good will of the Tsar and could be replaced if the Tsar saw fit. Langhoff never understood the true dynamics of Russian society and the role of nationalism in gaining some measure of consensus. His worldview was that of the traditional monarchist, for whom bad decisions were the result of bad advisers.

Loyalty to Nicholas II in Finland went to the grave with Langhoff. Nevertheless, even the most recent Finnish research has failed to draw sufficient attention to the independent role played by Nicholas. Too often, he has been made the rubber stamp for other people's decisions.[135]

Geoffrey Hosking analyzed the various forms Russian nationalism took and identified a variant that he described as right-wing and internally repressive in terms of nationalities policy while cautious on foreign policy, and another that he characterized as more liberal internally while more expansionist externally.[136] Although the Tsar and his ministers cannot be considered party members in the true sense of the word, the research that has been done to date indicates clearly that Nicholas II belonged to the first of these categories, while Stolypin belonged more to the second. Up until 1914, the Finnish question was primarily part of an internal struggle within Russia on the direction of overall policy, which explains the weight given to Finnish matters that was out of all proportion to Finland's status as a minor border area of the empire.

The relatively moderate policy on Finland represented by Stolypin, in which the Duma acted as a brake on overly repressive measures, was replaced by a more uncompromising stance following his death. The Tsar no longer allowed Stolypin's successor, Kokovtsov, to bolster the position of the Council of Ministers with the help of the majority parties in the Duma. The empire's policy on Finland did not, however, become more offensive in nature as the Tsar did not permit anyone to assume the powers that would have been needed to do this, and he himself lacked the determination to use them. With the fragmentation of the Council of Ministers and the parties in the Duma[137], Bobrikov-inspired bureaucrats were given an increasingly free hand to push through their programs for reducing Finland's autonomy. We will never know how they would have succeeded in implementing their plans through the Duma and the State Council had the First World War and the fall of the autocracy not intervened.

★   ★   ★

I am grateful to the Academy of Finland, the Finnish Cultural Foundation, the Helsinki Institute for Russian and East European Studies, and the Japan Foundation for funding to support the research for this chapter. Many thanks to Peter Herring for translating the chapter and to D. B. Pavlov for his assistance in collecting archival materials.

NOTES

1. Finnish senators were not chosen by parliamentary means but were appointed by the Emperor; the Diet had no say in the matter. The Diet was divided into four estates until 1906, and members represented these estates. Suffrage was neither universal nor equal. The majority of the population did not have the right to vote.

2. See Robert Schweitzer, *Autonomie und Autokratie: Die Stellung des Grossfürstentums Finnland im russischen Reich in der zweiten Hälfte des 19. Jahrhunderts* (Giessen, 1978); Osmo Jussila, "The Russian Government and the Finnish Diet: A Study of the Evolution of Political Representation, 1863–1914," in Geoffrey Alderman, ed., *Governments, Ethnic Groups and Political Representation, Comparative Studies on Governments and Nondominant*

Ethnic Groups in Europe (1850–1940), vol. 4 (Dartmouth, Eng: Hants, Aldershot, European Science Foundation, 1993).

3. Osmo Jussila, "The Historical Background of the February Manifesto of 1899," *Journal of Baltic Studies* [hereafter *JBS*], vol. 15, no. 2/3, 1984, pp. 141–147. For a brief account of the years 1899–1917 in Finnish history, see David Kirby, *Finland in the Twentieth Century* (London: C. Hurst & Co., 1979) and Kirby, *The Baltic World, 1772–1993* (London: Longman, 1995).

4. Sidney Harcave, ed., *The Memoirs of Count Witte* (Armonk, M.E. Sharpe, 1990), p. 258.

5. The modern Gregorian calendar [New Style, hereafter NS] was used in Finland. The Julian [Old Style, hereafter OS] calendar still in use in Russia was only used by the Russian administration in Finland. Western reports about events in Russia cited dates either "OS" and "NS" or provided the Russian date, which was two weeks behind the Western, followed by the Western date, separating them with a slash.

6. On Bobrikov as governor-general, see Tuomo Polvinen, *Valtakunta ja rajamaa: N. I. Bobrikov Suomen kenraalikuvernöörinä 1898–1904* (Porvoo, 1984) [English translation: *Imperial Borderland* (London, 1995)].

7. The Finnish General Strike (October 30-November 6, 1905, NS) ended peacefully with concessions made by the Russian authorities. All the same, the country came close to seeing military intervention and bloodshed with all the fatal consequences that would have ensued for Finnish autonomy. Governor-General I. M. Obolenskii requested assistance in the shape of a naval detachment from Kronstadt on October 19/November 1. He planned to use this to bombard Helsinki if needed, but nothing came of this as Obolenskii and the commander of the Twenty-Second Army Corps stationed in Finland, A. E. Zal'tsa, were unable to agree on common tactics. In any case, after Obolenskii had reached agreement with the Finnish Constitutionalists, a military solution was no longer in his interests. Preparations for dispatching the detachment from Kronstadt nevertheless continued in St. Petersburg. The Tsar declared a state of war in the fortresses at Sveaborg and Vyborg on October 23/November 5, and the Commander in Chief of the St. Petersburg military district, Grand Duke Nikolai Nikolaevich, the Tsar's uncle, began preparations to send two infantry battalions and a machine-gun company to Helsinki by sea, and an infantry battalion to Vyborg. Although Obolenskii had been responsible for initiating the preparations for a military intervention, he now worked to prevent its taking place; he was also unhappy that he was not consulted on the issue. Together with the Finnish Constitutionalists in St. Petersburg, Obolenskii succeeded in convincing the Russian government that there was no need to send a punitive expedition to Finland. By placing himself at odds with the Tsar's uncle and indirectly with the Tsar as well, Obolenskii realized, however, that he had stepped on too many toes and handed in his resignation on October 24–25 OS. A week later, Nikolai Nikolaevich again interfered in matters that Obolenskii considered his own, which only further convinced Obolenskii of the need to resign as soon as possible. See Finnish National Archives [hereafter NA], Helsinki, Archive of the Chancellery of the Governor-General [hereafter ACGG], 1905, Section 1, delo [hereafter d.] 9[8], vol. 2, listy [hereafter l. or ll.] 11–19, 24–39, 41–3, 52, 130. (On the dispute between Obolenskii and Zal'tsa, see ACGG, Hd 80, passim.) Rossiiskii gosudarstvennyi

istoricheskii arkhiv [hereafter RGIA], St. Petersburg, fond [hereafter f.] 1538, I. M. Obolenskii, opis' [hereafter op.] 1, d. 5, Obolenskii to Nicholas II, 21–22, 22, 24, 25 and 26 Oct. 1905 OS; Rossiiskii gosudarstvennyi arkhiv Voenno-morskogo flota [hereafter RGA VMF], St. Petersburg, f. 417, Glavnyi morskoi shtab, op. 1, d. 3285, ll. 28, 35, 39, 57, 78; *Revoliutsiia 1905 goda i samoderzhavie* (Moscow, 1929), pp. 146, 159; E. J. Bing, ed., *The Letters of Tsar Nicholas and Empress Marie* (London: I. Nicholson and Watson, Limited, 1937), p. 192; Adolf Törngren, *Med ryska samhällsbyggare och statsmän åren 1904–1905* (Helsingfors: Macmillan, 1929), pp. 190–193.

8. For an English-language translation of the Manifesto, see D. G. Kirby, ed., *Finland and Russia 1808–1920: From Autonomy to Independence, A Selection of Documents* (London, 1975), pp. 115–116.

9. On Finnish parties, see Antti Kujala, "Finnish Radicals and the Russian Revolutionary Movement, 1899–1907," *Revolutionary Russia*, vol. 5 (1992) pp. 172–192.

10. This was the issue that the Russian government's representatives drew most attention to when the Finnish-Russian conference headed by E. V. Frish looked at the Grand Duchy's new Diet act project in March/April 1906. See Gosudarstvennyi arkhiv Rossiiskoi federatsii [hereafter GARF], Moscow, f. 543, Tsarskosel'skii dvorets, op. 1, d. 490, Zhurnal Osobogo soveshchaniia dlia rassmotreniia proekta Vysochaishego predlozheniia Zemskim chinam Finliandii o novom Seimovom ustave.

11. Osmo Apunen, "Rajamaasta tasavallaksi," *Suomen historia*, vol. 6, Espoo, 1987, pp. 201–204.

12. John Bushnell, *Mutiny amid Repression: Russian Soldiers in the Revolution of 1905–1906* (Bloomington: Indiana University Press, 1985), pp. 205–220; Antti Kujala, *Vallankumous ja kansallinen itsemääräämisoikeus: Venäjän sosialistiset puolueet ja suomalainen radikalismi vuosisadan alussa* (Helsinki, 1989), pp. 207–245.

13. Osmo Jussila, *Nationalismi ja vallankumous venäläis-suomalaisissa suhteissa 1899–1914* (Helsinki, 1979), p. 207 sq.

14. See, for example, Petr Arkad'evich Stolypin, *Nam nuzhna Velikaia Rossiia: Polnoe sobranie rechei v Gosudarstvennoi dume i Gosudarstvennom sovete 1906–1911* (Moscow, 1991), pp. 130–149 (Duma, May 5, 1908 OS); A. Rumiantsev (P. A. Nive), *Finliandiia vooruzhaetsia!: Soiuz "Sila" ("Voima")* (St. Petersburg, 1907); GARF, f. 586, Pleve, op. 1, d. 1491, Zapiska o revoliutsionnom dvizhenii v Finliandii, January 1907 OS, and d. 1508, Politicheskii obzor Finliandii za vremia s maia 1908 po aprel' 1910 goda, April 8, 1910 OS; RGIA, f. 1276, Sovet ministrov, op. 26, d. 40, *Zhurnal Osobogo soveshchaniia po delam Velikogo kniazhestva Finliandskogo* [hereafter ZhOSVKF], no. 40, April 21, 1914 OS, "Po voprosu o prisoedinenii Vyborgskoi gubernii k Imperii"; Rossiiskii gosudarstvennyi voenno-istoricheskii arkhiv [hereafter RGVIA], Moscow, f. 2000, Glavnoe upravlenie General'nogo shtaba, op. 1, d. 470, Zapiska o naibolee vrednom plane deistvii protiv Rossii shvedskoi armii sovmestno s germanskim desantnym otriadom, 1907.

15. RGA VMF, f. 417, op. 1, d. 3478, l. 7 and passim; RGIA, f. 1276, op. 18, d. 67, *Zhurnal Osobogo soveshchaniia po voprosu o vosprepiatstvovanii tainogo vvoza oruzhiia v Imperiiu*, May 15 and 18, 1906 OS; "Dnevnik G. O. Raukha," *Krasnyi arkhiv* [hereafter KA], no. 19 (1927), pp. 100–102; Pertti Luntinen, *F. A. Seyn: A Political Biography of a Tsarist*

Imperialist as Administrator of Finland (Helsinki, 1985), pp. 64–65; Luntinen, "Suomi Pietarin suojana ja uhkana venäläisten sotasuunnitelmissa 1854–1914," *Historiallinen Arkisto*, vol. 79 (Helsinki, 1983), pp. 90–91.

16. RGVIA, f. 2000, op. 1, t. II, d. 1495, Quartermaster-General N. V. Dubasov to the Main Staff, No. 3155, September 1906 OS (draft).

17. GARF, f. 601, Nikolai II, op. 1, d. 2362, Kratkii doklad okruzhnogo general-kvartirmeistera gen.-maiora Raukha po chastnoi mobilizatsii No. 1, December 20, 1906 OS.

18. GARF, f. 601, op. 1, d. 2366, *Zhurnal Osobogo soveshchaniia po nekotorym voprosam, kasaiushchimsia Finliandii*, February 1, 1907 OS.

19. A. Ia. Avrekh, *Stolypin i Tret'ia Duma* (Moscow, 1968), pp. 45–46; Luntinen, *F. A. Seyn*, p. 92.

20. The latter intention is highlighted in the minutes of the Council of Ministers of October 7 and December 23, 1908 OS. See *Osobye zhurnaly Soveta ministrov tsarskoi Rossii*, vol. 4, 1908 (reprinted Moscow, 1988), pp. 850–51; vol. 5, pp. 1140–53.

21. GARF, f. 102, Departament politsii, Osobyi otdel [hereafter OO], 1906, op. 236 (11), d. 833, ll. 64–77, Stolypin to Gerard, March 1907 OS (draft). According to this letter, which was never sent, Stolypin stated that he now considered keeping Gerard up to date on security matters only a formal requirement.

22. Antti Kujala, "Suomi vallankumouksen punaisena selustana 1905–1907," *Lenin ja Suomi*, vol. 1, (Helsinki, 1987), p. 194.

23. RGIA, f. 1276, op. 18, d. 57, ll. 156–68, "O merakh bor'by s kramoloi v Finliandii," *ZhOSVKF*, 2, November 3, 1907 OS; GARF, f. 601, op. 1, d. 2364, Dokladnye zapiski Stolypina Nikolaiu II, November 8, 10, 11, 1907 OS and January 6, 1908 OS and d. 2392, Pamiatnaia zapiska Nikolaia Nikolaevicha Nikolaiu II, 1909; f. 586, op. 1, d. 1490, Proekt ukaza Nikolaia II; "Perepiska N. A. Romanova i P. A. Stolypina," *KA*, no. 5 (1924), pp. 115–117; "Iz perepiski P. A. Stolypina s Nikolaem Romanovym," *KA*, no. 30 (1928), p. 81; Aug. Langhoff, *Sju år såsom Finlands representant inför tronen: Minnen och anteckningar åren 1906–1913*, vol. 1 (Helsingfors, 1922), pp. 256–257, vol. 3 (1923), pp. 84–103. On the actions taken by Finnish officials against Russian revolutionaries, see Kujala, "Suomi vallankumouksen punaisena selustana 1905–1907," pp. 207–217.

24. Langhoff, *Sju år såsom Finlands representant inför tronen*, vol. 1, pp. 256–7, vol. 3, pp. 84–7; "Iz perepiski P. A. Stolypina s Nikolaem Romanovym," p. 81; GARF, f. 601, op. 1, d. 2364, Dokladnaia zapiska Stolypina Nikolaiu II, November 10, 1907 OS.

25. NA, ACGG, 1910, I dept, d. 58[3]: "Po voprosu o merakh na sluchai besporiadkov v Finliandii," *Osobyi zhurnal Soveta ministrov* [hereafter OZhSM], December 1, 1909 OS; RGVIA, f. 2000, op. 1, d. 1802, Instruktsiia sudam voenno-tamozhennoi okhrany u beregov Finliandii, December 16, 1908 OS.

26. Edv. Hjelt, *Vaiherikkailta vuosilta: Muistelmia*, vol. 1 (Helsinki, 1920), p. 213; Luntinen, *F.A. Seyn*, pp. 93–4, 106–7. Luntinen's view is: "But it does not fit in with the picture we have of Stolypin that he should have let himself be led by his subordinates." Also see P. Esperov, "O starom i novom kurse v Finliandii," *Birzhevye vedomosti*, September 28, 1911 OS.

27. GARF, f. 1467, Chrezvychainaia sledstvennaia komissiia Vremennogo pravitel'stva, d. 642, Formuliarnyi spisok o sluzhbe Deitrikha.

28. Avrekh, *Stolypin i Tret'ia Duma*, pp. 23–24, 45–46.

29. *Padenie tsarskogo rezhima*, vol. 4 (Leningrad, 1925), pp. 382–386, 473–474 ("Pokazaniia S. P. Beletskogo").

30. RGIA, f. 1276, op. 26, d. 8; *ZhOSVKF*, No. 8, October 30, 1908 OS and d. 20, *ZhOSVKF*, No. 20, February 1, 1910 OS. An indication that Deitrikh had influence: "Perepiska N. A. Romanova i P. A. Stolypina," p. 116.

31. Dietrich Geyer, *Der russische Imperialismus: Studien über den Zusammenhang von innerer und auswärtiger Politik 1860–1914* (Göttingen, 1977), pp. 220–238; I. V. Bestuzhev, *Bor'ba v Rossii po voprosam vneshnei politiki, 1906–1910* (Moscow, 1961), p. 151. On Stolypin's mode of government, see Avrekh, *Stolypin i Tret'ia Duma*; Geoffrey A. Hosking, *The Russian Constitutional Experience: Government and Duma, 1907–1914* (Cambridge: Cambridge University Press, 1973); Mary Schaeffer Conroy, *Peter Arkad'evich Stolypin: Practical Politics in Late Tsarist Russia* (Boulder, CO: Westview Press, 1976). Stolypin used the Finnish question as a tool for retaining his support of the Tsar, the Duma, and the State Council for his political leadership. See Alexandra Shecket Korros, "The Landed Nobility, the State Council, and P. A. Stolypin," in Leopold Haimson, ed., *The Politics of Rural Russia, 1905–1914* (Bloomington: Indiana University Press, 1979), pp. 133–134; Peter Waldron, "Stolypin and Finland," *Slavonic and East European Review* [hereafter *SEER*], vol. 63, no. 1 (1985) pp. 41–42, 54–55; Hannu Immonen, "Pääministeri Stolypin ja vuoden 1909 maanvuokra-asetus," *Historiallinen Aikakauskirja* [hereafter *HAik*], 1988, pp. 200–205.

32. Hosking, *The Russian Constitutional Experiment*; Andrew M. Verner, *The Crisis of Russian Autocracy: Nicholas II and the 1905 Revolution* (Princeton: Princeton University Press, 1990).

33. Polvinen, *Valtakunta ja rajamaa*, pp. 113–114.

34. Abraham Ascher, *The Revolution of 1905: Authority Restored* (Stanford: Stanford University Press, 1992), p. 256. See also Hjelt, *Vaiherikkailta vuosilta*, vol. 1, pp. 212–213; Langhoff, *Sju år såsom Finlands representant inför tronen*, vol. 1, pp. 125–128. There was a great deal of similarity between Stolypin's and Nicholas II's attitudes towards the Jews and the position they adopted on the Finnish question. See Abraham Ascher, "Prime Minister P. A. Stolypin and His 'Jewish' Adviser," *Journal of Contemporary History*, vol. 30 (1995) pp. 513–532.

35. GARF, f. 601, op. 1, d. 2365, Svodki svedenii iz Finliandii, January 28, 1907 OS–July 23, 1908 OS. The same information from November 22, 1908 OS–December 25, 1909 OS is in the Council of Ministers' archive, RGIA, f. 1276, op. 18, d. 162 (on the funding of intelligence work, see Rediger to Stolypin, January 8, 1909 OS, l. 12). See the following as an example of the matters that the general staff of the military district considered appropriate to inform the highest-ranking authorities in the empire: "At every turn, the Finns try to underline the setbacks encountered by the Russian army and navy in the last war [Russo-Japanese War of 1904–1905]." Thus, when describing the case when Russian soldiers were caught fishing in an illegal area, the papers note ironically that this time the Russians "had not secured their withdrawal," despite the

fact that during the last war they showed themselves to be masters of "always withdrawing in exemplary fashion." (l. 60)

36. GARF, f. 601, op. 1, d. 2366, *Zhurnal Osobogo soveshchaniia po nekotorym voprosam, kasaiushchimsia Finliandii,* February 1, 1907 OS; Nicholas II to Stolypin, January 30, 1907 OS, "Perepiska N. A. Romanova i P. A. Stolypina," p. 107; *Dnevniki imperatora Nikolaia II* (Moscow, 1991), p. 352. The Tsar considered the conference held on February 1 important enough to warrant inclusion in his diary. While many significant events were not recorded in his diary, he considered it essential to inform posterity how many hares, pheasants, or crows he had shot. Also see A. V. Gerasimov, *Na lezvii s terroristami* (Paris, 1985), p. 96; Langhoff, *Sju år såsom representant inför tronen,* vol. 2 (1923), pp. 158–97. Matters related to the state of war form a large part of Nicholas II's papers on Finland dating from 1906 to 1914 (f. 601).

37. GARF, f. 601, op. 1, d. 2364, Dokladnaia zapiska Stolypina Nikolaiu II, September 26, 1909 OS; d. 2390, Stolypin to Court Minister Frederiks, September 25, 1909 OS and to Nicholas II, September 27, 1909 OS; Nicholas II to Stolypin, September 26, OS and Frederiks to Stolypin, September, 27, 1909 OS, d. 2385; f. 1467, op. 1, d. 787, Doklad Stolypina Nikolaiu II, March 12, 1909 OS; f. 586, op. 1, d. 1485 and d. 1495, Zapiska Bekmana Nikolaiu II, December 3, 1908 OS; RGIA, f. 1662, P. A. Stolypin, op. 1, d. 110, Stolypin to Frederiks, September 20, 1909 OS; f. 1276, op. 18, d. 97, ll. 8–11, Stolypin to Bekman, April 11, 1908 OS and Bekman's memorandum; NA, ACGG, 1909, section 3, d. 21 I, Stolypin to Bekman, February 18, 1909 OS, "Po zapiske general-gubernatora kasatel'no obnovleniia sostava Senata," *OZhSM,* September 23, 1909 OS and its draft, and the correspondence between Stolypin and Bekman covering the matters of the minutes, September 20–28, 1909 OS, Bekman to Langhoff, September 28/October 11, 1909; P. Esperov, "O starom i novom kurse v Finliandii," *Birzhevye vedomosti,* September 28, 1911 OS; Langhoff, *Sju år såsom Finlands representant inför tronen,* vol. 1, pp. 135–136, vol. 3, pp. 174–188. According to Langhoff's memoirs, the Emperor informed him in the Crimea on September 25/October 7 that Stolypin had written from St. Petersburg proposing the appointment of Russians to the Finnish Senate but no such letter or telegram from Stolypin appears to exist. It seems clear that Nicholas attempted to shift responsibility for measures unpopular with the Finns onto Stolypin's shoulders and succeeded, as Langhoff's memoirs make plain. If Stolypin behaved a little unloyally towards the Emperor in the autumn of 1907 on the issue of a declaration of a state of war, the Emperor behaved even more unloyally towards his subordinate in this matter.

38. On the appointment of the "Admirals' Senate," see also Taimi Torvinen, "Autonomian ajan senaatti," in *Valtioneuvoston historia 1917–1966,* vol. 1 (Helsinki, 1978), pp. 71–78.

39. GARF, f. 601, op. 1, d. 2390, Stolypin to Frederiks, September 25, 1909 OS and Nicholas II to Stolypin, September 26, 1909 OS and d. 2364, Dokladnaia zapiska Stolypina Nikolaiu II, September 26, 1909 OS.

40. GARF, f. 601, op. 1, d. 2391, Perepiska Sukhomlinova s Frederiksom, September 28-October 2, 1909 OS and d. 2392, Pamiatnaia zapiska Nikolaia Nikolaevicha, 1909; RGIA, f. 1276, op. 18, d. 51, ll. 14–16 (especially Stolypin's comment in the margin) and passim, d. 162, l. 67, 91–2, d. 230, ll. 66–77, Soveshchanie po voprosu o merakh na sluchai vozniknoveniia besporiadkov v Finliandii, October 5, 1909 OS, and ll. 150–154, d. 238, l.

3, 11, 12–13, Vozzvanie Nikolaia Nikolaevicha k zhiteliam Finliandii, d. 241, ll. 2–10; NA, ACGG, Hd 14 and 1910, dept 1, d. 58³: "Po voprosu o merakh na sluchai besporiadkov v Finliandii," *OZhSM*, December 1, 1909 OS; Manfred Hagen, "Nikolaj II. an Stolypin" (October 18, 1909 OS), *Jahrbücher für Geschichte Osteuropas*, vol. 26, 1978, p. 68; A. A. Polivanov, *Memuary* (Moscow, 1924), pp. 82–85, 88; Langhoff, *Sju år såsom Finlands representant inför tronen*, vol. 3, pp. 186–187; Luntinen, "Suomi Pietarin suojana ja uhkana venäläisten sotasuunnitelmissa 1854–1914," pp. 95–96; Jussila, *Nationalismi ja vallankumous suomalais-venäläisissä suhteissa 1899–1914*, pp. 214–222.

41. William C. Fuller, *Civil-Military Conflict in Imperial Russia, 1881–1914* (Princeton: Princeton University Press, 1985), pp. 231–232; Harcave, ed., *The Memoirs of Count Witte*, pp. 518–521, 728–730.

42. GARF, f. 601, op. 1, d. 2406, Zapiska o neobkhodimosti otdeleniia ot Finliandii Vyborgskoi gubernii.

43. GARF, f. 586, op. 1, d. 1494, Zapiski Berendtsa Stolypinu, 1907, 1910.

44. RGIA, f. 1276, op. 18, d. 329, Stolypin to Shcheglovitov, November 26, 1910 OS, Shcheglovitov to Stolypin, March 12, 1911 OS.

45. GARF, f. 601, op. 1, d. 1352, Ot Stolypina Nicholaiu II, September 9, 1911 OS.

46. Stolypin's personal papers in St. Petersburg (RGIA, f. 1662) do not contain very much on Finland, which indicates that he was ultimately not all that interested in the Finnish question.

47. Polvinen, *Valtakunta ja rajamaa*, p. 141. V. K. Pleve's son, Nicholas, was the Council of Ministers' manager between 1906 and 1914, in which capacity he acted as secretary of the Committee of Finnish Affairs and was one of the powers behind the scenes on the government's policy on Finland. He was a member of this committee during the First World War. Pleve's collection (GARF, f. 586) contains memoranda by high-ranking civil servants, police documents, background reports, plans, etc. that Nikolai V. Pleve allowed to be copied for the purpose of policy making on Finland. Pleve was considered as belonging on the extreme right wing and an anti-Semite, and for good reason. See Harcave, ed., *The Memoirs of Count Witte*, p. 493; Heinz-Dietrich Löwe, *Antisemitismus und reaktionäre Utopie: Russischer Konservatismus im Kampf gegen den Wandel von Staat und Gesellschaft, 1890–1917* (Hamburg, 1978), pp. 186–187.

48. Hosking, *The Russian Constitutional Experiment*, pp. 147–148.

49. Conroy, *Peter Arkad'evich Stolypin*, p. 126, 131–132, 142; Waldron, "Stolypin and Finland," pp. 50–51.

50. "O poriadke napravleniia finliandskikh del, kasaiushchikhsia interesov Imperii," *Osobye zhurnaly Soveta ministrov tsarskoi Rossii*, vol. 3, 1908, pp. 452–454.

51. For Bekman's assessment of the government's policy, see Harcave, ed., *The Memoirs of Count Witte*, pp. 683–684. Also see Luntinen, *F. A. Seyn*, pp. 109–111.

52. P. Esperov, "O starom i novom kurse v Finliandii", *Birzhevye vedomosti*, September 28, 1911 OS.

53. RGIA, f. 1276, op. 20, d. 42, *OZhSM*, February 22, 1910 OS; GARF, f. 586, op. 1, d. 1513, ll. 1–5.

54. RGIA, f. 1276, op. 20, d. 46, *OZhSM*, August 3, 1910 OS.

55. RGIA, f. 1276, op. 26, d. 14, *ZhOSVKF*, No. 14, December 29, 1908 OS.

56. RGIA, f. 1276, op. 26, d. 17, *ZhOSVKF*, No. 17, May 23, 1909 OS. Also see op. 20, d. 34, *OZhSM*, May 5, 1909 OS; op. 26, d. 7, *ZhOSVKF*, No. 7; GARF, f. 586, op. 1, d. 1495.

57. RGIA, f. 1276, op. 20, d. 54, "O merakh bor'by s politicheskim terrorom v Finliandii," *OZhSM*, October 14, 1911 OS; op. 18, d. 51, l. 64, d. 230, ll. 56–61, d. 393, ll. 1–5, Zein to Prime Minister Kokovtsov, September 27, 1911 OS, l. 12, d. 392, ll. 1–3, Dokladnaia zapiska Natsional'no-monarkhicheskikh organizatsii Kokovtsovu, September 20, 1911 OS, ll. 11–12, 84–85; GARF, f. 499, Kantseliariia Finliandskogo general-gubernatora, op. 1, d. 2, l. 48 sq.; Langhoff, *Sju år såsom Finlands representant inför tronen*, vol. 1, pp. 162–163, 167–168; P. Esperov, "O starom i novom kurse v Finliandii," *Birzhevye vedomosti*, September 28, 1911 OS; V. N. Kokovtsov, *Out of My Past* (Stanford: Stanford University Press, 1936), pp. 274–275, 278, 286–287; Luntinen, *F. A. Seyn*, pp. 170–172; Avrekh, *Stolypin i Tret'ia Duma*, pp. 83–86. For later criticism directed to Zein for getting overexcited by the Council of Ministers, see RGIA, f. 1276, op. 20, d. 62, "Po petitsii Seima," *OZhSM*, December 11, 1912 OS.

58. NA, ACGG, Hd 14, No. 6; RGIA, f. 1276, op. 18, d. 230, ll. 150–154. The memorandum in this dossier in the Council of Ministers' archive states quite bluntly that the conclusions of Brinken's consultative meeting on declaring a state of war as a preventative measure conflicted with the Council of Ministers' separate minutes of October 14, 1911 OS, that had been approved by the Tsar on December 25 OS.

59. RGVIA, f. 2000, op. 2, d. 954, ll. 24–34, Brinken to the Main Administration of the General Staff, December 19, 1911 OS.

60. RGVIA, f. 2000, op. 3, d. 320.

61. Kujala, *Vallankumous ja kansallinen itsemääräämisoikeus*.

62. Kujala, "Suomi vallankumouksen punaisena selustana 1905–1907," pp. 196–223.

63. Juhani Piilonen, "Yhteinen vihollinen yhdistää, 1908–1917," in *Lenin ja Suomi*, vol. 1, pp. 261–264 and passim.

64. GARF, f. 586, op. 1, d. 1508, Politicheskii obzor Finliandii za vremia s maia 1908 goda po aprel' 1910 goda, April 8, 1910 OS. On Akashi, see Akashi Motojiro, "Rakka ryusui," in O. Fält and A. Kujala, eds., *Rakka ryusui: Colonel Akashi's Report on His Secret Cooperation with the Russian Revolutionary Parties during the Russo-Japanese War* (Helsinki: Finnish Historical Society, 1988).

65. RGIA, f. 1276, op. 18, d. 51, l. 52, Zhurnal zasedaniia komissii Kurlova, February 17, 1910 OS, l. 146, memorandum June 8, 1911 OS.

66. L. Men'shchikov, *Russkii politicheskii sysk za granitsei*, vol. 1 (Paris, 1914), pp. 219–243; Adolf Törngren, *Från Finlands strid för rätt och frihet: Personliga upplevelser åren 1901–1914* (Helsingfors, 1942), pp. 285–289. For Stolypin's comments, see GARF, f. 601, op. 1, d. 2364, Dokladnaia zapiska Stolypina Nikolaiu II, January 7, 1907 OS; RGIA, f. 1276, op. 18, d. 51, l. 14, d. 241, l. 7, Stolypin to Zein, January 6, 1910 OS.

67. GARF, f. 102, OO, 1909, op. 239, d. 41.

68. GARF, f. 102, OO, 1912, op. 316, d. 315.

69. Osmo Jussila, "Suomen santarmihallituksen toiminnasta toisella sortokaudella," *HAik*, 1976, pp. 197–210.

70. Good examples of Eremin's desire for accuracy are his two reports to the Russian Deputy Minister of Internal Affairs in February and October 1916 OS. Eremin calmly analyzed the Finnish situation and avoided any exaggeration, even though it had been established that hundreds of Finns had engaged in treacherous activities with Germany. RGIA, f. 1282, Kantseliariia ministra vnutrennikh del, op. 2, d. 117.

71. The Finnish nonsocialist parties tried to sound out the potential for compromise with Kokovtsov's successor as prime minister, I. L. Goremykin, in February 1914, but the latter was unwilling to make any conciliatory move. See Yrjö Blomstedt, *K. J. Ståhlberg: Valtiomieselämäkerta* (Helsinki, 1969), pp. 296–297.

72. Hosking, *The Russian Constitutional Experiment*, p. 197 sq.

73. On Zein's actions, see Luntinen, *F. A. Seyn.*

74. *Gosudarstvennaia Duma, Stenograficheskie otchety* [hereafter *GDSO*], Tretii sozyv, Sessiia 5, ch. 1, cols 690–701; Langhoff, *Sju år såsom Finlands representant inför tronen*, vol. 1, pp. 165–168, 308–354; Kokovtsov, *Out of My Past*, pp. 274–275, 278, 286–287; Harcave, ed., *The Memoirs of Count Witte*, p. 742; Luntinen, *F. A. Seyn*, p. 142, 170–175, 178–179. The only difference between the policy on Finland pursued under Kokovtsov and that followed under his predecessor was that the new prime minister lacked the wherewithal to be master of this policy. On the other hand, Kokovtsov proved much more capable than Stolypin in maintaining a good relationship with Minister State Secretary Langhoff.

75. RGIA, f. 1276, op. 20, d. 72, "Po voprosu ob ob"iavlenii Velikogo kniazhestva Finliandskogo na voennom polozhenii," *OZhSM*, July 17, 1914 OS; op. 18, d. 530, l. 5, Ukaz tsaria Pravitel'stvuiushchemu senatu, July 17, 1914 OS.

76. GARF, f. 102, OO, 1912, op. 13, d. 41, l. 138 sq., Utgof to the Police Department, December 13, 1912 OS.

77. Oiva Turpeinen, "Jägarrörelsen och de ryska planerna på att inkalla finländare till militärtjänst år 1916," *Historisk Tidskrift för Finland* [hereafter *HTF*], 1979, p. 331; Torvinen, "Autonomian ajan senaatti," p. 104; GARF, f. 627, B. V. Stürmer, op. 1, d. 115, Doklad general-ad"iutanta Trepova Nikolaiu II, March 7, 1916 OS.

78. GARF, f. 499, op. 1, d. 2, ll. 3–4, Manager of the Council of Ministers I. Lodyzhenskii to Zein, November 19, 1914 OS.

79. A. N. Iakhontov, "Tiazhelye dni (Sekretnye zasedaniia Soveta Ministrov, 16 Iiulia–2 Sentiabria 1915 goda)," in *Arkhiv russkoi revoliutsii*, vol. 18 (Berlin, 1924), p. 35 (July 30, 1915 OS). On Sweden's relations to Russia and Germany, see W. M. Carlgren, *Neutralität oder Allianz: Deutschlands Beziehungen zu Schweden in den Anfangsjahren des ersten Weltkrieges* (Uppsala, 1962); Seikko Eskola, *Suomen kysymys ja Ruotsin mielipide: Ensimmäisen maailmansodan puhkeamisesta Venäjän maaliskuun vallankumoukseen* (Helsinki, 1965); Pertti Luntinen, "The Åland Question During the Last Years of the Russian Empire," *SEER*, vol. 54, no. 4 (1976) pp. 557–571.

80. Iakhontov, "Tiazhelye dni," p. 112 (August 26, 1915 OS), pp. 119–120 (August 28, 1915 OS). On the Russian political situation between 1914 and 1917, see V. S. Diakin, *Russkaia burzhuaziia i tsarizm v gody pervoi mirovoi voiny* (Leningrad, 1967); Raymond Pearson, *The Russian Moderates and the Crisis of Tsarism, 1914–1917* (Basingstoke: Macmillan, 1977); A. Ia. Avrekh, *Tsarizm nakanune sverzheniia* (Moscow, 1989).

81. See Luntinen, *F. A. Seyn*, pp. 235–263; Turpeinen, "Jägarrörelsen och de ryska planerna på att inkalla finländare till militärtjänst år 1916," pp. 329–340; Torvinen, "Autonomian ajan senaatti," pp. 104–118.

82. On the attitude of government representatives to the Jäger movement, see Oiva Turpeinen, "Keisarillisen Venäjän viranomaisten suhtautuminen jääkäriliikkeeseen," *Helsingin yliopiston historian laitoksen julkaisuja*, vol. 7 (Helsinki), 1980.

83. RGIA, f. 1276, op. 18, d. 530, l. 38, Pleve to Goremykin, January 7, 1916 OS, ll. 40–42, Grigorevich to Goremykin, January 13, 1916 OS.

84. RGIA, f. 1282, op. 2, d. 117, Polivanov to Goremykin, January 15, 1916 OS, Doklad Khvostova Nikolaiu II, January 23, 1916 OS.

85. RGIA, f. 1276, op. 18, d. 530, ll. 43–47, Alekseev to Stürmer, February 8, 1916 OS; Mikh. Lemke, *250 dnei v tsarskoi stavke (25 sent. 1915–2 iiulia 1916)* (St. Petersburg, 1920), p. 542. Stürmer's name is spelled in the transliteration of the Russian as "Shtiurmer" but in histories of Russia in World War I often is cited as Stürmer, as it is in this chapter. In chapter 2 Charles Timberlake describes Shtiurmer as chair of the Tver' provincial zemstvo board in the 1890s. In chapter 9 Kimitaka Matsuzato describes Shtiurmer as Minister of Internal Affairs, a post he also occupied in 1916.

86. GARF, f. 627, op. 1, d. 115, Doklad Trepova Nikolaiu II, March 7, 1916 OS.

87. Lemke, *250 dnei v tsarskoi stavke*, pp. 667–669, 683; Turpeinen, *Keisarillisen Venäjän viranomaisten suhtautuminen jääkäriliikkeeseen*, pp. 112–141; Luntinen, *F. A. Seyn*, pp. 255–257.

88. *Padenie tsarskogo rezhima*, vol. 4, pp. 382–386, 473–474 (pokazaniia Beletskogo); Taimi Torvinen, "Borovitinov-kahden kansan syntipukki," *HAik* (1976), pp. 226–231; Luntinen, *F. A. Seyn*, pp. 271–272.

89. *Suomen asetuskokoelma 1891*, No. 27.

90. Tuomo Polvinen, *Die finnischen Eisenbahnen in den militärischen und politischen Plänen Russlands vor dem ersten Weltkrieg* (Helsinki, 1962), pp. 125–126; Waldron, "Stolypin and Finland," p. 41.

91. RGIA, f. 1276, op. 26, d. 1, "O poriadke napravleniia finliandskikh del, kasaiushchikhsia interesov Imperii," *ZhOSVKF*, no. 1, October 19 and November 3, 1907 OS; *Osobye zhurnaly Soveta ministrov tsarskoi Rossii*, vol. 3, 1908, pp. 443–462.

92. GARF, f. 543, op. 1, d. 527, Stolypin to Nicholas II, June 24, 1907 OS.

93. *Osobye zhurnaly Soveta ministrov tsarskoi Rossii*, vol. 3, 1908, pp. 443–462; *Polnoe sobranie zakonov Rossiiskoi Imperii* [hereafter *PSZ*], Sobranie tret'e, vol. 28/I, No. 30379.

94. Hosking, *The Russian Constitutional Experiment*, p. 78. Cf. David MacLaren McDonald, *United Government and Foreign Policy in Russia, 1900–1914* (Cambridge, MA: Harvard University Press, 1992), p. 87 sq.

95. RGIA, f. 1662, op. 1, d. 101, Proekt zaprosa k Sovetu ministrov o podchinenii ministra stats-sekretaria i general-gubernatora Finliandii Sovetu ministrov, 1908. It is clear that in one way or another Stolypin engineered this interpellation by the Octobrists, which was presented in a slightly different form in the Duma. See *GDSO*, Tretii sozyv, Sessiia I, ch. 2, May 5, 1908 OS, cols 2913–18 and *GDSO*, Prilozheniia, Tretii sozyv, Sessiia I, vol. 1, cols 502–9; Avrekh, *Stolypin i Tret'ia Duma*, pp. 46–53. Tokmakoff argues, however, that the interpellations came as a complete surprise to Stolypin. See George Tokmakoff, *P. A. Stolypin and the Third Duma: An Appraisal of the Three Major Issues* (Lanham, New York–London: University Press of America, 1981), p. 74; Manfred Hagen, "Edinenie und obnovlenie: Traditionale und modernistische Züge in Stolypins Staatsnationalismus gegenüber Finnland," *JBS*, vol. 15, no. 2/3 (1984) pp. 151–153, 166–167.

96. *Osobye zhurnaly Soveta ministrov tsarskoi Rossii*, vol. 3 1908, pp. 443–462.

97. Ibid; RGIA, f. 1276, op. 26, d. 1, "O poriadke napravleniia finliandskikh del, kasaiushchikhsia interesov Imperii," *ZhOSVKF*, no. 1, October 19 and November 3, 1907 OS; d. 16, "Po proektu Vysochaishego predlozheniia Seimu kasatel'no zakona o soiuzakh i obshchestvakh," *ZhOSVKF*, no. 16, May 23, 1909 OS; GARF, f. 586, op. 1, d. 1497, Zapiska po povodu zakonoproekta o svobode organizatsii soiuzov i obshchestv v Finliandii, d. 1503, Spravka po voprosu ob izdanii i primenenii Vysochaishego poveleniia 20 maia 1908 goda.

98. GARF, f. 586, op. 1, d. 1503, Spravka po voprosu ob izdanii i primenenii Vysochaishego poveleniia 20 maia 1908 goda.

99. *PSZ*, Sobranie tret'e, vol. 30, No. 33795; Conroy, *Peter Arkad'evich Stolypin*, pp. 125–131. The Russian legal specialist and civil servant N. N. Korevo, who was closely involved in drafting this law, defined the matters remaining within the sphere of Finnish local legislation at a congress of the United Nobility in 1910. See N. N. Koréwo, *La question finlandaise: Rapport lu au Congrès de la Noblesse Unifiée de l'Empire Russe en la séance du 17/30 mars 1910* (Paris, 1912), p. 33; GARF, f. 586, op. 1, d. 1519.

100. "Zarubezhnaia agitatsiia," *Novoe vremia*, April 16, 1910 OS.

101. See Heikki Ylikangas, "Finlands administrativa ställning inom det ryska riket," *HTF* (1995), p. 308.

102. Translation: Marc Szeftel, *The Russian Constitution of April 23, 1906: Political Institutions of the Duma Monarchy* (Brussels: Les Éditions de la Librarie Encyclopédique, 1976), p. 84.

103. Osmo Jussila, "Finland and the Russian Duma," *JBS*, vol. 19, no. 3, 1988, pp. 242–248. This contains Jussila's description of the pattern of events that led to Finland's remaining outside of the Duma in 1905 and 1906. At the beginning of 1906, it was probably the result of the action of Prime Minister Witte. President of the State Council D. M. Sol'skii considered it essential to draw up regulations governing the participation of Finnish representatives in the Duma. N. S. Tagantsev, a member of the council, tried to include a section in the Fundamental State Laws of 1906 to the effect that "representatives of the Finnish Grand Duchy shall take part in the State Council and State Duma when they debate laws that are considered common to the empire and the Finnish Grand

Duchy, in accordance with regulations separately issued on this matter." See GARF, f. 499, op. 2, d. 9, E. Ershtrem (Oerstroem) to Gerard, December 24, 1905 OS; f. 586, op. 1, d. 1488, Materialy po proektu Osnovnykh zakonov Imperii, Zapiska Tagantseva.

104. RGIA, f. 1276, op. 26, d. 14, "Ob uchrezhdenii russko-finliandskoi komissii," ZhOSVKF, No. 14, December 29, 1908 OS; *Osobye zhurnaly Soveta ministrov tsarskoi Rossii*, vol. 2, part 2, 1907 (1985), pp. 343–353; Szeftel, *The Russian Constitution of April 23, 1906*, pp. 85, 99.

105. Langhoff, *Sju år såsom Finlands representant inför tronen*, vol. 1, pp. 268–282, 368–373; *Finland and Russia 1808–1920*, pp. 129–130; Avrekh, *Stolypin i Tret'ia Duma*, pp. 53–64.

106. RGIA, f. 1276, op. 20, d. 42, "Po proektu pravil o poriadke izdaniia kasaiushchikhsia Finliandii zakonov i postanovlenii obshchegosudarstvennogo znacheniia," *OZhSM*, February 22, 1910 OS, pp. 15–17, 38–40; "Introduction" in Edward C. Thaden, ed., *Russification in the Baltic Provinces and Finland, 1855–1914* (Princeton: Princeton University Press, 1981), pp. 7–9. The actions that the government focused on the Orthodox population in Finland cannot be considered an example of the cultural Russification of Finland as they did not cover the vast majority of the population. As to the existence of a single Russification policy covering all the border areas of the empire, the author can only concur with Hagen, who argues that the very variety of non-Russian peoples and areas made such a policy an impossibility. See Hagen, "Edinenie und obnovlenie," pp. 158–161. Also see Robert Schweitzer, "The Baltic Parallel," *JBS*, vol. 15, no. 2/3 (1984) pp. 195–215.

107. RGIA, f. 1276, op. 20, d. 42, "Po proektu pravil o poriadke izdaniia kasaiushchikhsia Finliandii zakonov i postanovlenii obshchegosudarstvennogo znacheniia," *OZhSM*, February 22, 1910 OS.

108. On the discussion on the subject by Russian legislative bodies, see Avrekh, *Stolypin i Tret'ia Duma*, pp. 64–78; Tokmakoff, *P. A. Stolypin and the Third Duma*, pp. 84–107; Hagen, "Edinenie und obnovlenie," pp. 156–157.

109. GARF, f. 586, op. 1, d. 1494, Zapiska Berendtsa Stolypinu, May 3, 1910 OS, l. 42.

110. GARF, f. 601, op. 1, d. 956, Telegrammy Stolypina i Sazonova Nikolaiu II i otvetnye telegrammy tsaria po povodu otkloneniia Seimom rassmotreniia zakonoproektov predlozhennykh emu Sovetom ministrov, July 16–September 22, 1910 OS; "Perepiska N. A. Romanova i P. A. Stolypina," p. 122; Uuno Tuominen, "Autonomian ajan yksikamarinen eduskunta 1907–1916," in *Suomen kansanedustuslaitoksen historia*, vol. 5 (Helsinki, 1958), pp. 208–209, 267.

111. GARF, f. 543, op. 1, d. 490, Zhurnal Osobogo soveshchaniia dlia rassmotreniia proekta Vysochaishego predlozheniia Zemskim chinam Finliandii o novom Seimovom ustave, pp. 5–11.

112. Langhoff, *Sju år såsom Finlands representant inför tronen*, vol. 2, pp. 80–81.

113. *Osobye zhurnaly Soveta ministrov tsarskoi Rossii*, vol. 2, part 2, 1907, pp. 343–353.

114. RGIA, f. 1276, op. 18, d. 20, ll. 11–12, M. Bubnov (Kievskii komitet Partii pravovogo poriadka) to Stolypin, January 28, 1908 OS; d. 159, l. 136, A. A. Bobrinskii (predsedatel' Postoiannogo soveta Ob"edinennykh dvorianskikh obshchestv) to Stolypin, May 18, 1910

OS; ll. 137–138, Spisok s postanovlenii s"ezda Ob"edinennykh dvorianskikh obshchestv po finliandskomu voprosu; Koréwo, *La question finlandaise*, pp. 3–30.

115. For a couple of private Russification programs for Finland, see GARF, f. 586, op. 1, d. 246 and 1485.

116. RGIA, f. 1276, op. 26, d. 17, "Ob uravnenii v Finliandii prav russikh urozhentsev s pravami mestnykh grazhdan," *ZhOSVKF*, No. 17, May 23, 1909 OS.

117. RGIA, f. 1276, op. 20, d. 46, "Po voprosu ob uravnenii v pravakh s finliandskimi grazhdanami drugikh russkikh poddannykh," *OZhSM*, August 3, 1910 OS.

118. Apunen, "Rajamaasta tasavallaksi," pp. 240–241; Avrekh, *Stolypin i Tret'ia Duma*, pp. 78–89.

119. Luntinen, *F. A. Seyn*, pp. 188–191.

120. Matti Närhi, "Venäläiset joukot Suomessa autonomian aikana," in *Venäläiset Suomessa 1809–1917* (Helsinki, 1984), pp. 161–180.

121. Pertti Luntinen, *Sotilasmiljoonat* (Helsinki, 1984). On the enactment of the law, see Avrekh, *Stolypin i Tret'ia Duma*, p. 81 sq.

122. RGIA, f. 1662, op. 1, d. 103, Proekt zaprosa o privlechenii Finliandii k neseniiu obshchegosudarstvennykh raskhodov, 1908.

123. GARF, f. 586, op. 1, d. 1509, Zapiska general-leitenanta Zolotareva o finansovom polozhenii Finliandii, April 30, 1910 OS.

124. Luntinen, *Sotilasmiljoonat*.

125. RGIA, f. 560, Ministerstvo finansov, op. 28, d. 1288, Bark to Golitsyn, February 15, 1917 OS (l. 27).

126. On Russian views of the Finnish parties, see GARF, f. 601, op. 1, d. 2385, Zapiska i spravka o zameshchenii senatorskikh vakansii, 1908; f. 102, OO, 1906, op. 236 (11), d. 833, ll. 64–77, Stolypin to Gerard, March 1907 OS (draft); f. 494, Finliandskoe zhandarmskoe upravlenie, op. 1, d. 89, Obzor o polozhenii v Finliandii v sviazi s voinoi, 1916; RGIA, f. 1276, op. 18, d. 97, ll. 8–11, Stolypin to Bekman, April 11, 1908 OS and Bekman's memorandum, d. 598, Zein to Stürmer, July 25, 1916 OS; f. 1282, op. 2, d. 117, Doklad Khvostova Nikolaiu II, January 23, 1916 OS; f. 1662, op. 1, d. 92, Zapiska Zeina Stolypinu, January 17, 1908 OS, d. 93, Zapiska Stolypina Nikolaiu II, March 25, 1908 OS; NA, ACGG, 1909, III section, d. 21 I, Stolypin to Bekman, 18 February 18, 1909 OS, Wuorenheimo to Bekman, September 17/30, 1909, Osoboe mnenie Bekmana, September 25/October 8, 1909. On the Old Finns, see Tuomo Polvinen et al., *J. K. Paasikivi: Valtiomiehen elämäntyö*, vol. 1 (Porvoo, 1989), pp. 178–182, 210–220.

127. NA, ACGG, 1909, III section, d. 21 I, Virenius to Bekman, October 22, 1909 NS; Torvinen, "Autonomian ajan senaatti," p. 78.

128. "Iz perepiski P. A. Stolypina s Nikolaem Romanovym," p. 82; *Osobye zhurnaly Soveta ministrov tsarskoi Rossii*, vol. 2, 1908, p. 302.

129. Conroy, *Peter Arkad'evich Stolypin*, p. 131–136; Edward C. Thaden, "The Russian Government," in Thaden, ed., *Russification in the Baltic Provinces and Finland*, (Princeton,

NJ: Princeton University Press, 1981) p. 86; Tokmakoff, *P. A. Stolypin and the Third Duma*, p. 109; Jussila, "The Historical Background of the February Manifesto of 1899," p. 145.

130. Zein's belief in 1914 was that, by refusing to accede to Russian wishes, the Finnish Diet harmed both Russian and Finnish interests. The big-brother tone of his comments reminds one of Soviet propaganda of the 1970s. Another good example of big-brother sentiments is Bobrikov's secret circular to governors from April 8/20, 1899, stating that "for the population of the Finnish Grand Duchy, Russians are not foreigners but rather their elder brothers in one joint and common all-Russian family of subjects under the Russian Tsar." See RGIA, f. 1276, op. 18, d. 562, ll. 132–4, Spravka k petitsii ocherednogo Seima 1914 goda o vosstanovlenii v krae zakonnogo poriadka; Hämeenlinnan maakunta-arkisto, Hämeen lääninhallitus, kanslia, saapuneet salaiset kirjeet 1899, No. 9.

131. RGIA, f. 1276, op. 26, d. 25, "Po voprosu o prisoedinenii dvukh prikhodov Vyborgskoi gubernii k sostavu S.-Peterburgskoi gubernii," *ZhOSVKF*, No. 25, 13 November 13, 1910 OS; d. 40, "Po voprosu o prisoedinenii Vyborgskoi gubernii k Imperii," *ZhOSVKF*, No. 40, April 21, 1914 OS; op. 20, d. 61, "Po petitsii Seima ob ostavlenii bez posledstvii proektiruemogo sokrashcheniia territorii Finlandii," *OZhSM*, November 16, 1912 OS; op. 18, d. 395, ll. 4–5, Doklad Kokovtsova Nikolaiu II, October 19, 1911 OS; GARF, f. 601, op. 1, d. 2406, Zapiska o neobkhodimosti otdeleniia ot Finliandii Vyborgskoi gubernii; NA, ACGG, 1913, I dept, d. 1[7], Nikolai Nikolaevich to Sukhomlinov, March 28, 1913 OS; Langhoff, *Sju år såsom Finlands representant inför tronen*, vol. 1, pp. 298–361; Vilho Hämäläinen, *Karjalan kannaksen venäläinen kesäasutus ja sen vaikutus Suomen ja Venäjän suhteiden kehitykseen autonomian ajan lopulla* (Tampere, 1974), pp. 171–204.

132. GARF, f. 1467, op. 1, d. 787, Doklad Stolypina Nikolaiu II, March 12, 1909 OS.

133. RGIA, f. 1276, op. 26, d. 26, "Po zapiske Finliandskogo general-gubernatora o nekotorykh zakonodatel'nykh merakh," *ZhOSVKF*, No. 26, May 28, 1911 OS and d. 41, "Po proektu programmy zakonodatel'nykh predpolozhenii i mer," *ZhOSVKF*, No. 41, April 21, 1914 OS; op. 20, d. 73, *OZhSM* under the same heading, August 29, 1914 OS; op. 18, d. 39, ll. 42–50, Ministry of the Interior to Korevo, 10 September 10, 1912 OS; d. 393, ll. 1–5, Zein to Kokovtsov, September 27, 1911 OS; Viljo Rasila, "Vuoden 1914 venäläistämisohjelman synty," *HAik*, 1966, pp. 1–16; Jussila, *Nationalismi ja vallankumous venäläis-suomalaisissa suhteissa 1899–1914*, pp. 241–244. For a slightly incomplete English version of the "Russification Program," see *Finland and Russia 1808–1920*, pp. 135–138.

134. See, for example, Langhoff, *Sju år såsom Finlands representant inför tronen*, vol. 1, pp. 157–162.

135. This is partly because Nicholas II's papers and the Council of Ministers' archive are known in Finland on the basis of a microfilm collection presented to the National Archives during the Soviet period. The selective nature of this Soviet collection was at least partially intentional. This censorship had a clear purpose. The Soviets were keen to hide the face of Russian imperialism for fear that its similarities with Soviet imperialism might be too obvious. In so doing, they effectively ended up protecting their arch-enemy, Tsar Nicholas II.

136. Hosking, *The Russian Constitutional Experiment*, pp. 215–242.

137. See ibid., passim.

7

NATIONALIST POLITICS IN THE RUSSIAN IMPERIAL STATE COUNCIL: FORMING A NEW MAJORITY, 1909–1910

ALEXANDRA S. KORROS
Xavier University, Cincinnati, Ohio

Peter A. Stolypin is remembered today as the politician of pre-1917 who might have been the savior of the Russian Empire. Among those regularly extolling his virtues are Great Russian nationalists who cite Stolypin's strong nationalist credentials as well as his reform agenda as the route by which Russia might have avoided revolution and communism. While Stolypin undoubtedly did favor Great Russian nationalist policies during the last two years of his life, it is important to examine the context and purpose of his turn to nationalism to better understand the complex motivations and permutations that such policies played in the politics of late Imperial Russia. Although Stolypin personally may have favored a nationalist agenda, it was when his other choices were either eliminated or greatly minimized that he turned to it as a means of mobilizing political power.

In his first three years as Chairman of the Council of Ministers (1906–1909), Stolypin had not been particularly associated with Russian nationalist policies. His policy directions were largely concerned with restoring order in the aftermath of 1905, inaugurating agricultural reform to create a prosperous conservative peasantry, and enacting new institutions of local government on the village level. Throughout his dealings with the legislative chambers, Stolypin depended on the Union of October 17 (the Octobrists) in the Duma and on the Center Group in the State Council to form a majority to pass his recommended legislation. Both factions were heterogeneous in their composition. Additionally, they were not particularly associated with nationalist movements.[1]

Stolypin's legislative allies were not entirely reliable. By the spring of 1909, it was apparent that the Center Group[2] was unable to guarantee a majority vote in the upper chamber and that Stolypin's enemies on the right were growing more and more anxious to discredit him and his policies. As we shall see, it is at this point that Stolypin began to advocate a series of nationalist measures in both the Duma and State Council. While his Duma majority had not been seriously imperiled, Stolypin's agenda still had to pass through the State Council in order to become law. It was through advocacy of nationalist policies that Stolypin saw the opportunity to reconfigure his majority in the upper chamber and transform some of his most obdurate opponents into reluctant colleagues.

This chapter examines the way Stolypin used nationalist legislation to form his new majority as well as how State Council factions responded to this new politics. We will see that conflicting pressures stemming from the push to the right forced the Center Group in the upper chamber to alter its policies to accommodate itself to the new political realities in order to retain its reason for existence.

Having survived a government crisis precipitated by the Naval General Staff bill, Stolypin now faced a new challenge from his opponents as they prepared another campaign to embarrass him.[3] This time, the issue would be a proposal to alter State Council election procedures in the nine western provinces to favor landowners of Russian nationality over Poles. Word of this new effort leaked out in late March 1909 when the bourse newspaper, *Birzhevye vedomosti*, condemned the new tactic in an editorial entitled "The Trial Stone."[4] While the proposal by State Council member D. I. Pikhno was not a new one, the Right Group was raising it as Stolypin's political strength seemed to be at an ebb. The editorial considered the proposal an open attack, based on political as well as national grounds, on the Poles in the State Council demanding that "[s]uch an anti–State attempt . . . be repelled in the most decisive manner."[5]

Property qualifications, length of ownership, and electoral rights in other provinces determined the right to elect representatives from the western provinces to the State Council. Just as the largest landowners in the nine western provinces were Poles, so too their State

Council delegation was composed entirely of Poles. Pikhno proposed introducing nationality qualifications into the electoral law so that elections would take place in separate assemblies of Russian and Polish landowners. The nine provinces would be divided into three regions. In each a Russian assembly would elect two members and the Polish assembly one. Henceforth the delegations from the region would comprise six Russians and three Poles.

The Pikhno proposal was a two-pronged attack seeking to compromise the government on the national question while removing six non-Russian and therefore politically more moderate members from the State Council and replacing them with at least six rightists.[6] Thus the Right Group would have succeeded in embarrassing the government while strengthening its own ranks.

Not surprisingly, pressure to change the electoral rules to the upper chamber was a favorite subject of the nationalist press. *Okrainy rossii*, the weekly paper of the Russian Borderlands Society, stressed the unusual importance of the proposal, seeking to portray the local population of the western provinces as completely dissatisfied with the conditions of State Council representation. Russian residents of Kiev Province complained that in areas where fellow Russians represented the "overwhelming majority" it was impossible for them to elect a Russian to the State Council because of the property qualifications required. The time had come to give local Russians fair representation in the State Council for "not under any circumstances can the Poles . . . be our representatives and defenders."[7]

In the following issue, the editors maintained that Russian nationalists could anticipate little help from Stolypin. During the previous year they explained, Stolypin had been unreceptive to a note from western province representatives pointing out that under his proposed local government reforms there had to be basic alterations in the election procedure to the legislative institutions.[8] Moreover, the Stolypin government's previous record on issues of interest to nationalists had been ambiguous. During the third session of the State Council (1908–1909) the government's noncommittal stand on similar questions had convinced nationalists that Stolypin was not entirely in their camp and that they would have to prepare to move the Pikhno proposal through the legislative chambers without government support.[9]

In the midst of the "politicking" surrounding the Pikhno proposal,[10] on May 2, 1909, the Stolypin government, as a symbol of its new attitude, introduced a bill to separate the Chelm region of Poland and transform it into a separate Russian province—Kholm Province—under the supervision of the Kiev Governor-General.[11] Russian nationalists had been pushing such a plan since the 1860s, but it had always been rejected. This time, however, *Rossiia*, the "official" government newspaper, seemed to indicate otherwise. In an editorial it bemoaned the absence of any Russian representatives to the State Council from the western provinces— an area where Russians comprised over 80 percent of the population. Although the Poles were not to blame for this problem, the paper promised that the government would make every effort to solve the problem of Russian representation fairly, without an anti-Polish bias. Nevertheless, it appeared that the government was much more sympathetic to Russian nationalist arguments than in the past.[12]

In the days prior to the debate on the proposal, various State Council groups discussed their positions regarding the proposed change in the electoral law. The Center Group had originally opposed Pikhno's proposal and had voted unanimously to reject it. On May 4, A. S. Ermolov, one of the Center's founders reported to the group that the government intended to delay State Council elections in the western provinces to introduce a bill guaranteeing the rights of Russians in this region. After long debate the Center voted (thirty-two to eighteen) to alter its position somewhat, deciding to open a discussion of principle at the council's general meeting and to propose rejecting Pikhno's bill. The minority favored sending the Pikhno bill to committee; only two members of the group actually supported the bill itself. The Center argued that it was untimely to restrict Polish electoral rights, but its members were unsure how to communicate their opinion to the government—hence the split vote.[13]

The Union of October 17 also was split in regard to the Pikhno bill. Some feared that it would set a series of dangerous precedents such as elections by national curiae, strengthening the right wing of the State Council to such an extent that "the upper chamber will take on a permanent posture of opposition the lower." Other members of the party fully agreed with Pikhno's position, thus dividing the party on nationalist questions.[14]

On May 8, 1909, the State Council galleries were full, with spectators anticipating an exciting debate over the Pikhno proposal. Indeed, in his speech on behalf of his project, Pikhno argued that representation to the State Council was inherently unfair because all nine representatives were Poles. Not only were Russians unrepresented, but Pikhno made it very clear that if the law was altered to include Russian landowners, the State Council would be rectifying an injustice to the Russian Orthodox population: "[W]e offer our hand, not in order to exclude anyone, but to introduce those who are not here, but who have, we are convinced, the inalienable right and holy obligation to enter here." By emphasizing that Russians would be much more conservative and aid in the formation of a conservative majority as opposed to the existing Polish representatives, Pikhno tried to ally the nationalist elements to those farther on the right.[15]

Stolypin's short reply altered government policy. The prime minister stated that the government had always regarded the electoral law for the nine western provinces as insufficient, but with the introduction of the zemstvo this problem would be rectified. However, the introduction of the zemstvo into the west had been delayed and new elections were at hand. While maintaining that the government "recognized" the acceptability of the fundamental idea behind the bill, Stolypin recommended the creation of a special commission to review the electoral law. In the meantime the government would introduce legislation to extend the mandates of those members already in the State Council from the western provinces for an additional year.[16]

Stolypin's stunning reversal created a new State Council majority—ninety-eight members voted in favor of submitting the Pikhno bill to a special committee as the government proposed, while sixty-four opposed the measure.[17] The new majority consisted of the Right Group, nationalists, and part of the Center Group.

Birzhevye vedomosti related the details of the manipulations in a vivid manner. Apparently when Stolypin had concluded his statement favoring Pikhno's proposal, the "Right . . . was silent." Yet, in a quick recovery from their surprise, when M. G. Akimov, Chairman of the State Council, asked if there were ten members to second the motion to send the bill to committee, "the entire Right" stood.

Some members of the State Council were reluctant to reveal their position publicly. On the first open ballot, the vote was much closer than the final tally. When the chair asked for those opposed to stand, many members rose from their seats to see to it that the vote would be repeated, but this time by secret ballot. *Birzhevye vedomosti* reported that, during the first vote, "nearly half of those present stood against sending the bill to committee. Both halves comprise[d] isolated groups, and it [was] not difficult to see that the difference [was] only several votes for one side or the other."

Those waiting in the halls during the second balloting speculated that the ministers' votes would make the difference since the numbers were so close. To everyone's great surprise the results revealed a clear victory for Stolypin and the Right Group, forcing *Birzhevye vedomosti* to conclude that "under secret voting . . . an important part of the Center which openly had voted against the bill, changed its direction and preferred to go against the Poles."

In its front-page editorial, *Birzhevye vedomosti* proclaimed "*Na pravo!*" ("To the right!"), maintaining that prior to the ministerial crisis over the Naval General Staff, it would have been unthinkable to imagine the Stolypin government pandering to the Right Group. The paper noted that in the past, Minister of Finance V. N. Kokovtsov had rejected the Right Group's opinions decisively. However, the meeting of May "undoubtedly indicated the turn of the . . . government to the right."[18]

The press commentaries on the events in the State Council reflected each newspaper's political leanings. *Rech'*, the Constitutional Democratic paper, condemned May 8 as a "black day," proving that the Right Group had achieved a revolution; the Octobrist paper *Golos Moskvy*, on the other hand, virtually ignored the events in the State Council since the Octobrists had been unable to arrive at any unified decision the government's new nationalist policy.[19] The government paper *Rossiia* concentrated on some of the critics of the policy who had spoken in the State Council arguing that the term "Russian" really applied to anyone who lived in the empire. The paper asked why other national groups should not be forced to accept cultural assimilation, claiming there was nothing wrong with that.[20]

Apparently through this abrupt shift in government policy, Stolypin had succeeded in creating a new alignment in the State Council. During the votes on the Naval General Staff bill preceding the ministerial crisis, Stolypin had learned that he could not rely on the Center Group for sufficient support to guarantee his legislation passage in the upper chamber.[21] By turning to the nationalists who spanned the Center and Right Groups in both the State Council and the Duma, he created a reliable majority to support his legislative initiatives. In the following two years, Stolypin's policy initiatives continued to follow this pattern, combining Great Russian national superiority with legislative initiatives for local government reform and maintenance of internal order.

The Center's leaders were well aware that, in the aftermath of the crisis following the passage of the Naval General Staff bill, their group had lost its preeminent position in the upper chamber. From its founding during the first meetings of the State Council, the Center had been subject to unremitting criticism from its supporters as well as its enemies because of its tendency to fragment. Another danger to the Center was a turnover in members elected by the zemstvos and nobility. During the summer of 1909, when seventy State Council seats were contested, a pessimistic Prince P. N. Trubetskoi, a Center leader and elected noble representative, wrote to his fellow Octobrist A. I. Guchkov that the elections were not going well. Although the results were still incomplete, "the vacillating Center . . . has been wrecked and will suffer still more. The appointments [to the State Council] continue in the same vein, all Akimov's boys (*Akimovskie molodtsy*)."[22]

Because of the three-year time lag between elections, it was only in its fifth session, beginning in the fall of 1909, that the State Council's composition mirrored the general shift toward the right in the zemstvos and other parts of "society." Almost all the "liberal" zemstvo delegates to the upper chamber had been replaced by more conservative representatives. The Left Group in the State Council, which at its most radical paralleled the ideas of the Constitutional Democratic Party (Kadets), sustained a net loss of four zemstvo representatives. Although the Center Group lost only one zemstvo seat, the Right Group had gained four members from the zemstvos. The new composition of the State Council confirmed the zemstvo movement's abandonment of the "constitutionalism" of 1905 for a more conservative position vis-à-vis political reform.[23]

The revised configuration of the State Council raised speculation in the press as to whether the groups within this body would remain intact.

Soon after the new session had begun in October 1909, there was talk of a new alignment in the State Council taking shape around Stolypin's brother-in-law, A. B. Neidgart.[24] Calling itself the "Moderate Right," the group drew its members from the Center and the Right.

In both legislative chambers, Russian nationalists tended to span from the moderate right to the center, reluctant to identify too closely with either the very high-ranking nobility in the capitals or the urban merchant/manufacturing classes. Often nationalists were provincial noble landowners who had learned their political skills in the zemstvo movement.[25] Some nationalists were comfortable within the Center Group of the State Council, a coalition that included zemstvo as well as urban trade and industry interests, in addition to Poles and Baltic Germans. Others focused more on national minority issues. This bifurcation was particularly likely to occur in the State Council because the absence of organized political parties tended to group members around general commonalities while disguising some fundamental differences in outlook. Trade and industry representatives were far less likely to sympathize with overtly nationalistic legislation since their nominal constituency included individuals of a variety of national origins and religious beliefs. Nationalist zemstvo and noble representatives, on the other hand, were critical of the importance of the Polish *kolo* (circle or group) within the faction. Since the zemstvos themselves were located in the provinces of "Great Russia," and their representatives came exclusively from the nobility, these State Council members were more likely to support nationalist policies than were their urban and nonnoble merchant colleagues.

The Center Group encouraged the formation of Neidgart's group as a method of widening its umbrella and retaining its nationalist members. The Right faction, on the other hand, wanted to prevent the new group from taking hold.[26] They feared that since Neidgart's support for his brother-in-law Stolypin was assured, the new group could substantially weaken the Right's antigovernment posture. Ironically, formation of the new coalition was impeded by the fact that Neidgart was reluctant to lead it, apparently fearing it would strengthen the Right and weaken the Center. Forming a moderate right, nationalist group within the State Council was actually the idea of Count D. A. Olsuf'ev of Saratov, a Right Group maverick. He wanted to include as many of the so-called nonparty members of the State Council in the new formation in order to establish a political counterpart to the moderate right, nationalist faction in the Duma, the lower chamber of the parliament.[27] P. N. Krupenskii, leader of the Duma's Moderate Right faction, actually attended the meeting at which organizing a moderate right, nationalist faction in the State Council was discussed, hoping to encourage such a political formation.

But concluding that they felt closer to the Center Group than to their would-be colleagues in the State Council Right Group, Neidgart and his followers elected to remain where they were. As a close relative of the chairman of the Council of Ministers, Neidgart asserted that it would be inappropriate for him to lead a parliamentary group whose members might include prominent Stolypin adversaries such as Count Sergei Iu. Witte who were listed as "nonparty" members of the upper chamber.[28] Although the factional alignment remained unchanged, the dynamic of the Center Group altered considerably.

Once the State Council session had begun, it became clear that the shift rightwards had been at the expense of the small Left Group in the upper chamber. The Center Group's numbers had not really changed as much as Trubetskoi had so pessimistically predicted the previous summer. Yet, the only way the Center could function as any kind of political force in the upper chamber depended on its support of government programs. When Trubetskoi commented to the government "official" newspaper *Rossiia* that his group was becoming more unified, he was compelled to note that it was still not an "exact photograph of the Duma Center."[29]

Significantly, nationalist questions were the issues that continued to cut through the official groupings in the State Council, tending to increase the divisiveness within them. Included among the founders of the All-Russian Nationalist Club of November 1909 were at least five members of the State Council Center Group, as well as six members of the Right Group.[30] During the same period, the first joint meeting of the Right Groups of the Duma and State Council took place at the initiative of the nationalist, conservative *Russkoe sobranie*. In addition to speeches from Prince A. N. Lobanov-Rostovskii, a new noble representative to the upper chamber from Tula, and a response from P. N. Durnovo, an appointed State Council member and leader of the Right Group, the union of the two groups was blessed by Bishop Nikon, a State Council representative elected by the monastic clergy. *Rossiia* reported that the two groups decided to form a coordinating bureau to facilitate their work in the two chambers.[31] By adjournment for the Christmas and New Year's holidays, not only had the State Council and Duma Right heightened their coordination and communication, but nationalist members had become increasingly involved in organizations outside of the State Council where they could discuss areas of common interest.

In their end-of-the-year analyses of the political situation in the legislature, a number of newspapers commented on the new alignment in the State Council. While their conclusions about the direction of the legislative chambers may have differed according to each paper's political leaning, they all echoed similar themes. Unquestionably the elections had created a much more right-wing, conservative State Council majority. To the dismay of papers expecting the legislature to move forward on legislation, and to the delight of those who sought as little movement as possible, all agreed that the current session had produced very little substance.[32]

The press also carefully scrutinized the new appointments to active service in the State Council to see in which political direction the new members would lean. The main focus was on whether the new members would bear the imprint of the reactionary M. G. Akimov, President of the State Council, or of Stolypin, who was rumored to have gained more influence on new appointments as a result of the Naval General Staff Crisis the previous spring. The eight available seats in the upper chamber had been filled by three current government ministers and five former ministers or high-ranking bureaucrats. According to *Birzhevye vedomosti,* none of the new appointees was likely to join the Right Group and work against government policy. The British diplomat Sir Harold Nicolson confirmed that Nicholas had rejected Akimov's list of "Extreme Right party" candidates, but instead had opted for candidates who would join the Center Group, thus facilitating the passage of blocked legislation.[33]

By the end of the month there was quite a commotion brewing regarding the lack of progress of pending legislation from the Duma to the State Council. The Octobrist *Golos Moskvy* accused the State Council of a policy of "conscious obstructionism whose goal was to undermine all the Duma's work." A British observer concurred, noting that the State Council "nullifies, by its obstructive tactics, all the work done by the Duma while the Holy Synod, Ministries of Justice and Public Instruction . . . are undisguisedly hostile to the Duma."[34]

All the commotion apparently had a salutary effect. Rumors spread that if Akimov did not push the upper chamber to speed up its work, he would lose his position. Another rumor claimed that Akimov had received an order to hasten consideration of Duma legislation.[35] Whether the threats were true or not, during the spring of 1910, three major bills were considered by the State Council: Stolypin's agrarian program, originally enacted under the emergency provisions (Article 87) of the Fundamental Laws; the bill extending the rights of Old Believers; and a bill limiting the juridical authority of the Finnish Diet. It is through the debate and issues surrounding the Old Believer and Finnish bills that the new State Council majority came into being. Examination of these two pieces of legislation reveals not only how the government sought to build a majority in the upper chamber, but also how nationalist issues further splintered the Center Group, continuing to prevent unified support of government policies and thus making a new nationalist-based majority even more attractive to the Chairman of the Council of Ministers.

During the early months of 1910, the Center Group was filled with dissent coming largely from the discontent of its urban trade and industry members who thought their interests were being slighted in favor of noble and zemstvo concerns.[36] *Birzhevye vedomosti*, always most vigilant in its reports on the State Council in general, and the Center and its Trade and Industry group in particular, described the Center Group's problems most eloquently.

> Now the so-called Baltic group falls away . . . now the Neidgart group breaks discipline completely, now finally, the small, but very influential and independent Trade and Industry group breaks away because of the faint attention paid by the entire party to its special interests—All these losses have moral and numerical influence [leading] to one and the same lamentable result: they are fatally pushing the party of the Center to the side of the Rightists; they are putting the former in a position of dependence on the latter and the general physiognomy of the State Council is becoming more openly reactionary.

The paper concluded that because of defections the Center Group would have "to adapt itself to the policy of a pendulum: swinging to the right and swinging to the left, whichever suits the subject," forcing the government to create some strange combinations to pass its legislation.[37]

The government's reversal on the Old Believers bill was both an indicator of its pursuit of nationalist policy as well as proof of the accuracy of *Birzhevye vedomosti*'s political acumen. A Duma bill approving and expanding the law governing the rights and privileges of Old Believer communities was brought before the State Council in May 1910. Originally brought into being under Article 87 in October 1906 to extend and normalize the status of Old Believers in the empire, the bill was brought to the Duma in 1909 for retroactive approval.[38] The new legislation extended the rights of Old Believers far beyond the scope originally envisioned by the Stolypin government. Passed by a coalition of Octobrists and Kadets, it granted Old Believers the rights of free preaching, ownership of property, maintenance of schools in areas not directly located within their communities, and exemption of their clergy from military service. The addition of the right of free preaching, meaning the right to proselytize, particularly scandalized the bill's opponents.

The Russian Orthodox Church opposed any extension of privileges to the Old Believers, whom it had always regarded and continued to regard as schismatics. In a speech to *Russkoe sobranie*, the monarchist, cultural group that boasted a number of his fellow State Council representatives among its members, Professor T. I. Butkevich, a seminarian from the white clergy (that is, a member of the Orthodox clergy permitted to be married in contrast to the black Orthodox clergy who remained celibate) attacked the Duma bill as disregarding the interests of the Orthodox Church. Butkevich, claiming to speak in the name of Orthodox Russia, exhorted both the State Council and the Emperor to reject the bill, which he claimed had been promulgated by the Duma for exclusively political purposes. His speech emphasized that the Old Believers continually had worked against sovereign power from the seventeenth century. He maintained that "[t]he Duma found in the Schism [*Raskol*] much that was similar to its own political program. The essence of the Schism is not in its religious foundations, but in its sociopolitical motivations, in its permanent opposition to government power." In this manner Butkevich not only appealed to those who feared revolution, but asserted that recognizing the Old Believers' rights was somehow intrinsically anti-Russian—against the national interests of the Russian state.[39]

Butkevich's appeals to Russian nationalism were echoed in P. N. Durnovo's report to the State Council on the rejection of the Duma's bill by a special committee of the council. In his speech Durnovo stressed that because the Orthodox Church represented the "spiritual consciousness and the spiritual ideals of the Russian people," passage of the bill would degrade the church and separate it from the government. Every other church, Christian or otherwise, could "only be tolerated" in so far as its existence did not infringe on the primacy of the Orthodox Church.[40] He stipulated that every religious organization did indeed enjoy the ability to fulfill its religious obligations. These included the right to juridical identity before the law, the right to own immoveable property, the right to civil representation, the right to educate children, and the right to care for the sick and indigent. These were the only rights to which any religious group, other than the Orthodox Church, was entitled.[41]

Durnovo's criticism of the specific provisions of the legislation asserted that in going beyond the limits set by the government and in seeking to undermine the primacy of the Orthodox Church, the Duma indicated its basic disloyalty to Russia. The special committee therefore opposed both the original—ministerial—and the expanded Duma versions of the bill.[42]

A minority of the special committee consisting of four jurists associated with the Left and Center welcomed the Duma bill. Their speaker, the distinguished attorney A. F. Koni, stressed that Old Believers should have the rights to establish their schools, obtain official recognition for their clergy, and open all types of educational institutions.[43]

Deputy Minister of Internal Affairs S. E. Kryzhanovskii spoke for the government, asserting on the one hand that although the Old Believers were truly a Russian phenomenon whose loyalty to Russia had been proven, the government also had the obligation to protect the Orthodox Church, retaining for it the external symbols of its preeminence. Since the government and the committee majority views were closer to agreement than conflict, Kryzhanovskii maintained that the differences between the two were negligible. Therefore, the government opposed the bill because the Duma amendments endangered the unique position of the Orthodox Church and sought a return to the original government legislation.[44]

Kryzhanovskii's advocacy of the government's version of the Old Believers bill was couched in nationalist terminology. He did not press the government's case very hard, however, since he acknowledged the Old Believers as posing an alternative to the supremacy of the Orthodox Church. In this manner the government had chosen to pacify the majority in the upper chamber by sacrificing reform for the Old Believers.

Despite the forlorn hope by some of the more liberal press for enactment of some semblance of the Duma bill, the State Council accepted the majority redaction and rejected all of the proposed minority amendments. The final version of the bill excluded the right of free preaching and denied Old Believer clergy the right to call themselves clerical officials.[45]

The government position constituted a remarkable turnabout. The bill actually had been in force since October 1906 when it had been issued under the emergency provisions of Article 87. As a sign of his lack of enthusiasm for the Duma bill, Stolypin sent a representative to do battle with the State Council rather than come himself. The prime minister had moved from what could be characterized as a political position akin to that of some of the Kadets and many Octobrists to one much closer to the Right wing of the upper chamber.

The Center's vote was at least as important as Stolypin's change of heart. Very few members of the Center opposed the bill, with the great exception of N. S. Tagantsev, a former Minister of Justice. Other members of the Center who had been expected to express their disappointment remained silent throughout the debate. With the lack of widespread support for the Duma bill, the upper chamber's redaction of the Old Believer bill passed the State Council by virtue of a strong Right-Center majority. Stolypin's stand indicated that he was willing to cooperate with the Right on issues that strengthened Great Russian nationalism, even if it meant abandoning some of his allies by reversing his position on certain issues such as the Old Believers. The Old Believers bill indeed marked a watershed point in the government's policy in the State Council and presaged a new majority on nationalist issues.

The Old Believer legislation was a prelude to the Finnish bill, which constituted an even more blatant example of the new politics at work. The autonomous Grand Duchy of Finland always had maintained its own legislative policy since it had been incorporated into the Russian Empire in 1809. The Finnish Diet, misnamed the Sejm by the Russians,[46] had the right to approve or reject legislation enacted by the Tsar—a privilege of which it often took advantage. Finland's universal manhood suffrage and strong Social Democratic Party disturbed those who feared its example would give Russians too many democratic ideas. Indeed, Russian liberals looked to Finland as a part of the empire that had already achieved many of the goals for which they themselves were striving. In contrast, Russian nationalists regarded Finland as a thorny example of independence that might inspire other minorities, while reactionaries viewed Finland as a cauldron and inspiration for revolutionary activities.

The "assault" began with the formation of the Kharitonov Commission, chaired by State Secretary P. A. Kharitonov, whose mission it was to create a program to settle the problem of Finland. Its initial agenda, worked out by the Ministry of Internal Affairs' "Special Conference on Matters Dealing with the Grand Duchy of Finland," consisted of two sections. The first described the composition of the commission and the second outlined its tasks.[47] The composition of the special commission—five Finns representing three out of four Finnish parties in the Diet (the Old Finns, the Young Finns, and the Swedes; the Social Democrats had been excluded) and five Russians, plus the Russian chair who held the deciding vote—slanted the outcome in favor of the imperial government. The Russian appointees included V. F. Deitrikh, member of the State Council and former Vice Governor of Finland; N. A. Miasoedov, another State Council member; N. N. Korevo, the Chairman of the Imperial Commission for the Systematization of Finnish Legislation; and Lieutenant General M. N. Borodkin and B. M. Iakunchikov, founders of the nationalist *Okrainy Rossii*, the journal of the Russian Borderlands Society. With the exception of Iakunchikov, all the Russian members of the Kharitonov Commission were also members of the Special Conference on Finland.

The commission began its work in June 1909 and completed it the following December. Despite their protestations of loyalty, the Finns were outvoted at every turn.

The Russian members stressed their achievements in reporting back to their nationalist supporters. In January 1910 Deitrikh, speaking to the Russian Borderlands Society, praised his Russian colleagues on the commission for their accomplishments. A month later, in a similar speech to the Council of the United Nobility, Deitrikh thanked that organization for its support of the commission's work. In March at the Congress of the United Nobility, Korevo, Deitrikh, and others spoke again of their success. *Okrainy Rossii* quoted Neidgart as thanking the speakers on behalf of the congress for their work on the Kharitonov Commission and praising their patriotism. Neidgart's words "elicited an enraptured greeting for the members of the Russo-Finnish Commission who were present."[48]

In remarkably rapid fashion, the commission's report curtailing the powers of the Finnish Diet and introducing Finnish representation to the legislative chambers was turned into a bill by the Council of Ministers, which was passed by the Duma in March and brought to the State Council that May. Although the ostensible idea was to bring Finnish representation into the legislative chambers, in reality the bill meant severely curtailing Finnish autonomy and indicated the government's desire to bring Finland under close central control.

Interviews with various members of the State Council revealed the dynamics behind the formation of the majority. The argument behind the bill appealed to nationalist inclinations; in addition, arguments based on the supremacy of the post-1905 legislative system appealed to members who might otherwise have been sympathetic to Finland's historic autonomy. The Center Group's founder, Octobrist P. N. Trubetskoi, favored the legislation because he saw it as an expression of the Tsar's will. A. S. Ermolov, an appointed member, Center leader, and former Minister of Agriculture under Nicholas for twelve years, was more reserved in his opinion, but declared that he thought the general direction taken to solve the Finnish problem was correct. The Diet's decisions could only have the character of "simple inquiries" since he believed that imperial matters had to be approved by imperial institutions. V. M. Andreevskii, noble representative from Tambov, declared that as long as the legislative institutions existed, all matters should be directed through them. He wanted the Finns to have adequate representation in the chambers because the further an area from the center, the greater its tendencies toward independent habits. On the other side, D. A. Olsuf'ev favored compromise policies for Finland; he thought the situation was not as dangerous as portrayed by some and he doubted that measures advocated by the bill would lead to more peaceful relations between Russia and Finland.[49]

The Finnish bill carried Stolypin's name, not that of the Council of Ministers. In effect, Stolypin had made the Finnish bill his own particular cause.[50] Because of this personal attachment, the course of the Finnish bill through the State Council merits special attention as a case study of how Stolypin's association with nationalist policy was supposed to operate.

As we noted earlier, curtailing Finnish autonomy appealed to rightist political figures in both the Duma and State Council because Finland's parliamentary structure represented what they most feared could happen to the empire. Moreover, it was clear that the Tsar favored bringing the Finns under closer central control. Pockets of skepticism remained and the most notable opponent in court circles was Prince Meshcherskii, the influential editor of the right-wing journal, *Grazhdanin*. Meshcherskii was convinced that the Finnish bill was actually part of a conspiracy to discredit the Tsar among the Finns and return Finland to the Swedish crown. "Among the Rightists, I alone do not share their Finnophobia and I am appalled by this fateful, insane rapture with which they who are seemingly devoted to the Tsar, in their blindness do not realize that in inciting the government against Finland, they are making themselves into toys in the hands of those . . . who are trying to incite the feelings of the Finnish people against the Tsar and Russia."[51] It was as yet unclear as to whether Meshcherskii represented anyone but himself.

The nationalists were very anxious to expedite passage of the Finnish bill through the State Council. On April 7, 1910, Deitrikh called for the formation of a special committee to work out a compromise on the Finnish question even prior to the bill's passage in the Duma. Despite the Left's immediate opposition, a large majority composed of the Right and parts of the Center supported Deitrikh and created a committee of twenty.[52]

Because committees were elected on the basis of lists, these election results provide a snapshot of the State Council's political distribution at any given moment. The Special Committee on Finland elected on April 10 consisted of two members of the Left and nine members each of the Center and Right Groups. The leaders of the council's factions were among those elected to the committee and the voting indicated that the Center and Right were approximately equal in size, with the Right's list actually getting two more votes than the Center's. According to one analysis, two of the Center's committee members would vote with the Left, two others would vote with the Right and probably had voted for the Right's list, leaving the Center with only five votes. No more than six members were likely to oppose the Finnish bill. *Birzhevye vedomosti* identified Neidgart and Deitrikh as the culprits weakening the Center and it claimed that the group had put their names on the list in order to retain their followers' votes.[53]

The vote revealed the Center's weakness. The members elected were those most likely to support the Finnish bill, and Trade and Industry group representatives who were likely to oppose the bill were placed so low on the list that it was highly unlikely they would receive a place on the committee. The election resulted in a new round of press speculation on the weakness of the Center and the likelihood of its dissolution.

On the surface it appeared that Stolypin had indeed forged a new majority in connection with the Finnish bill. In attempting to deprive Finland of the remnants of its sovereignty, the bill seemed to suit the Right's antiparliamentary inclinations; however, there were some on the Right who had strong reservations and hoped the bill would fail. Meshcherskii was not alone; according to *Golos Moskvy*, there was an important group in the State Council who strongly opposed the idea that the Finnish problem could be solved by parliamentary action rather than imperial edict. They viewed the "Stolypin bill" as a violation of the emperor's prerogatives, hoping to use the "Finnish question the same way as the naval estimates had been used last year . . . to render a decisive blow to the Stolypin government and bury it under the debris of the Finnish question."

The opportunity to use the Finnish bill to embarrass Stolypin disappeared quickly when it became apparent that the Tsar was as much in favor of the bill as the chairman of the Council of Ministers. According to *Golos Moskvy*, it was at this point that a noticeable change of heart occurred among members of the State Council, producing "a flaming desire to decide the Finnish question immediately." Thus, the quick formation of the special committee for which P. N. Durnovo immediately offered to serve as chairman so there could be no doubt about the immediate passage of the bill.[54]

Bernard Pares, the distinguished British historian, in his observations on Russian political affairs to the Foreign Office, noted that the trend toward nationalism was not as unified as it seemed on the surface. Pares reported a struggle at court for the Tsar's favor between the nationalist faction, "who like Stolypin, wish to keep the Duma, and the Reactionaries, who want to go back to the old regime and undisturbed monopoly of power." According to Pares, the reactionaries were stronger than Stolypin at court and even in the Council of Ministers, but fortunately no one could replace the prime minister. "The Reactionaries always appeal to the Emperor on the issue of personal power, Stolypin can only check them by taking a Nationalist Tory line."

Although Pares personally thought the Finnish bill a disgrace, he described it as exactly the kind of measure necessary to check the "Reactionaries" at court. "The Reactionaries meant to throw it out on their old cry of infringement of the rights of the Sovereign, but here Stolypin beat them at Court, and they were ordered to do nothing of the kind."[55]

In this manner, the Right was forced to go along with the Finnish bill against its will. Its opposition was based not on the content of the bill, but on the fact that Stolypin was using the legislative chambers to strengthen his position and undermining the principles of autocracy that the Right continued to support. Stolypin thus obtained the necessary votes for the passage of his bill, because his enemies on the Right had no choice but to follow the Tsar's will.[56]

By early June the bill was ready for presentation to the State Council. In order to speed its enactment and avoid delay in a compromise committee between the two chambers, the State Council committee decided to adopt the Duma bill. Some of its members were opposed to this proposal because they felt that the State Council would be acting as a rubber stamp. Nevertheless, the need for haste prevailed over independent action. The urgency of passage was based on the need to have the bill in place by mid-

June and the desire of zemstvo representatives to return to their provinces in time for the summer zemstvo elections. Expecting a routine and rapid debate, members were surprised to hear that Stolypin would speak on behalf of the bill.[57]

On the first day of debate, *Golos Moskvy* noted that "[i]t had been a long time since the State Council had lived through such a big day."[58] Deitrikh served as the reporter for the committee majority, stressing that Finland was an integral part of a united and inseparable Russian state and that the bill would establish "once and for all" the manner in which laws concerning Finland within an all-imperial context would be promulgated. The Finnish Diet had the power to pass a law that the Tsar could approve or disapprove without any kind of participation by the legislative chambers. Such a situation violated the Fundamental Laws, he maintained, depriving the Duma and State Council of the right to legislate for the entire empire and interfering with the Tsar's prerogatives on military and naval questions.[59] While the arguments were couched in legal and historical terms, the argument was really about who would control Finnish internal policy—the Russian government or the Finnish Diet.

Stolypin followed Deitrikh to the podium. In ringing nationalist rhetoric he emphasized that there were two paths open to the State Council: "You must choose! . . . Either deny yourselves the rights of imperial legislation for the sake of the Finnish provincial Sejm or demonstrate that Russian legislative institutions [must] . . . protect that which belongs to the entire nation." Stolypin challenged the State Council to prove that Russia could go on her own without the interference of alien cultures and institutions. His nationalist rhetoric reinforced Russian superiority while simultaneously strengthening the Right of the legislative chambers to choose Russia's path, taking that decision out of the Tsar's hands.[60]

Members of the Center who might have been expected to oppose the bill, actually spoke on its behalf. N. S. Tagantsev, professor of law at St. Petersburg University, supported the bill because "strengthening the new state structure" was of the highest priority, overriding secondary interests even if they were worthwhile.[61]

The opposition argued that at issue was Finland's right to sovereignty and that the bill would alter Finland's status to that of an *oblast'* or region much like Turkestan. The Poles in the State Council accused the "young legislative bodies" of destroying the "old pillars" of Finnish culture. Defectors from the Right argued that the bill was illegal because it violated the Tsar's prerogatives.[62]

The maverick Rightist, D. A. Olsuf'ev, provided the most interesting analysis of all in evaluating the new nationalism in the bill against his concept of Russian national identity. He maintained that the Finnish bill was the product of current nationalism, emanating from the Russian defeat in the Russo-Japanese War. For Olsuf'ev, genuine nationalism was similar to Nicholas I's Official Nationality policy. The new nationalism was devoid of the serious content of the past: it lacked "the respectful attitude to the staples of our national existence." Instead it emphasized strong defense and an aggressive struggle against foreigners. Olsuf'ev decried the new nationalism, declaring that "in the course of four generations, the Russian rulers who created our Imperial policies, granting autonomy to Finland by their own free will . . . did not hold to the new nationalism, but held to the old." He argued that Finland possessed all the characteristics of a separate nation and it had more to fear from incorporation by Russia than Russia had to fear from Finnish autonomy. Since Finland, Poland, and the Baltic areas were culturally superior, Russia, which stood on a lower level, had found it difficult to assimilate its western possessions. In Olsuf'ev's opinion, Russia was pursuing a xenophobic policy, violating the tenets of true nationalist philosophy—respect for foreign cultures while upholding the uniqueness of the Russian way of life.[63]

At the second reading, the majority in favor of the Finnish bill was so large it required no head-count. Only votes on amendments revealed the actual extent of the State Council majority. *Birzhevye vedomosti* noted that approximately fifty votes were cast in opposition to the bill. From the Right, only Prince Liven and D. A. Olsuf'ev voted against the bill. At the conclusion of the favorable vote, members of the Right were jubilant at its passage and the paper reported that several rightists ran over to Stolypin to congratulate him on his victory. It was a far cry from Stolypin's other triumphs for which few on the Right displayed any enthusiasm.[64]

The Finnish bill was declared law on June 14, 1910, the same day that the State Council adjourned for the summer. The victory over Finland had served Stolypin well. Not only did he continue to enjoy the Tsar's tacit approval but in following a nationalist policy he actually gained Nicholas's more overt support undermining any incipient opposition from the Right. Moreover, former opponents on the State Council Right, committed to principles of Russification and nationalism and who would have supported the bill in any case, were transformed into allies. Although the Center was no longer the government's mainstay, it had to cling even tighter to its coattails in order retain a reason for its existence. Without its support of the government, there was nothing to keep the Center together. In backing the Finnish bill, the Center relied heavily on its Neidgartist wing while slighting its left flank—Poles and Trade and Industry members.

Nationalist policy had indeed created a new majority in the State Council. Composed of the Right-Center, it put approximately one hundred votes at Stolypin's disposal in the upper chamber, provided he selected his issues carefully so as not to free the extreme Rightists from their unwilling adhesion to his positions. Further, Stolypin's nationalist policy had catapulted him into representing a substantial number of Russians who possessed the right to vote in Duma and State Council elections. While they certainly did not represent a majority of the empire's population, they did constitute a crucial electoral bloc.

During its fifth session Stolypin's position had strengthened in the upper chamber. During March the government had worked hard to pass the Stolypin land reform, first promulgated under the emergency laws in November 1906. In the course of the debate, members of the Right originally expected to oppose the bill had changed their minds and voted for it. That May, the defeat of the Old Believers bill marked the government's retreat from a position damaging to its new nationalist pose. As the session concluded, the Finnish bill had produced the voting combination necessary for Stolypin's success—a new Right-Center majority that no longer depended on Poles and Baltic Germans who might join the Left in opposition.

This new configuration had important consequences for the State Council as well as for Stolypin. In its review of the just-concluded session, *Birzhevye vedomosti* noted that until March, the State Council had met only twenty-four times, sometimes for as little as an hour, while it modified Duma projects, returning them to compromise committees. Since mid-March, the upper chamber had gone to work; it passed the budget, the land reform, and the Finnish bill, while drastically amending the Old Believers bill.

The State Council had begun to act like a real legislative body and it had developed a new configuration. As the Center disintegrated, the Right controlled as many as one hundred votes. "The previously all-powerful Center, since the secession of the national, and Trade and Industry groups, very often walked behind the Right's tail, guaranteeing it 100 to 110 votes. Most serious matters were decided with this majority . . . [but] the absence of a strong and unified Center appears as a poor omen for the State Council's future activities."[65]

Stolypin had apparently succeeded in neutralizing his enemies on the far Right. Although he had not settled his differences with them, he had found an effective formula in nationalism for silencing their opposition and suspending their conspiracies against him. He had chosen to pursue short-range political objectives to stay in power by following nationalist policy with a single-mindedness that necessitated abandoning important elements of his reformist policies. The Old Believers and Finnish bills had provided him the platform necessary to create a reliable majority in the State Council. Unquestionably, pursuit of nationalist policy was a key to transforming the Duma and State Council into a workable legislature, albeit a decidedly unrepresentative and conservative one. Events would prove that his new advantage would not last very long as he badly underestimated his opponents' tenacity and ability to conspire against him and overestimated Nicholas' willingness to cooperate with legislative bodies.

As the summer of 1910 began, Stolypin reached the height of his powers. He had forged a working majority in the Duma and State Council that placed him in a unique position among Russian political figures. While he held power because of the Tsar's approval, he had been able to create a base of support that appeared to exist outside of traditional court circles. His vehicle for reaching this unprecedented position was his use of nationalist policy. In the following legislative session Stolypin planned to press his advantage through the passage of the Western Zemstvo bill, which was to include national curiae. Russian representatives to the Duma and State Council from the western provinces would be indebted to Stolypin's policies and were likely to be reliable supporters of his policies. With secure majorities, Stolypin would be able to pass local government reforms and advance his agenda for Russia's transformation.

Stolypin's enemies were as aware of the significance of his achievement as was the prime minister. Their new task was to find the means to discredit him with the Tsar and the less vehement nationalists among his supporters. Stolypin's success had only temporarily forestalled the reactionary Right. They now directed their energies at breaking his position in the State Council, where the new majority was more precarious than it appeared.

★ ★ ★

The research for this article was made possible through a variety of grants beginning with a Foreign Area Fellowship in 1970. The supplemental research was supported by two Xavier University Summer Research grants in 1991 and 1995, a National Endowment for the Humanities Travel to Collections grant in 1991, and a 1995 IREX Thirty-Day Travel grant.

NOTES

1. The State Council quickly formed three discernible political factions in its first session—aptly named the Right, Center, and Left. The Center group was the first to consciously attempt to organize itself as a political faction with a bureau to orchestrate its policies in the upper chamber. During the second session of the State Council the Right also began a more concerted effort to organize itself while the very small group of "Left" members—roughly approximating the Constitutional Democrats in its platform—was seemingly less concerned with an "organization." By the beginning of the council's third session, however, the groups were forced into a more formal organization with the introduction of voting by lists in order to determine the composition of all State Council committees. Because this chapter deals with the period when the Center group was more structured, it is designated the Center Group. Although there were nationalists in both the Right and Center Groups of the upper chamber, they did not assert themselves through collective action until 1909. This question is particularly important in the case of the Center Group, which was already operating according to subgroups by the council's fourth session in 1908–1909. See Alexandra S. Korros, "Activist Politics in a Conservative Institution: The Formation of Factions in the Russian Imperial State Council, 1906–1907," *Russian Review*, vol. 52, no. 1, pp. 1–19. See also, Gosudarstvennyi arkhiv Rossiskoi Federatsii [hereafter GARF], Moscow, fond 1178, delo 34, list 52 [hereafter f., d., l.]

2. The Center Group already consisted of between four and five subgroups. The largest was the basic subgroup, followed in 1908–1909 by the twenty-one member Neidgart subgroup and then the eighteen members of the Polish subgroup consisting of the representatives from the western provinces and the Kingdom of Poland. There were also at least two others listed from time to time—the Trade and Industry subgroup and the north and southwest subgroup. Each of these elected its own representatives to the Bureau of the Center and each was represented proportionately on the lists for election to Center Group and State Council committees. GARF, f. 1178, d. 39, l. 4 and d. 34, l. 54.

3. For more information in this regard, see Alexandra D. Shecket, "The Russian Imperial State Council and the Policies of P. A. Stolypin, 1906–1911: Bureaucratic and Soslovie Interests versus Reform," Ph. D. Diss., Columbia University, 1974. Also, Alexandra S. Korros, "The Landed Nobility, the State Council and P.A. Stolypin," in Leopold Haimson, ed., *The Politics of Rural Russia, 1905–1914* (Bloomington: Indiana University Press, 1979). See also, Edward Chmielewski, "Stolypin and the Ministerial Crisis of 1909," *California Slavic Studies*, vol. 4 (1967) pp. 1–38.

4. *Birzhevye vedomosti* carefully reported the activities of the State Council Center Group because its membership included the twelve representatives of trade and Industry in the State Council. While often what the paper reported was gossip, its sources were generally very accurate. The paper was a strong advocate for the Center Group and for moderation in the State Council.

5. *Birzhevye vedomosti*, no. 11025, March 24, 1909. See note 1 for a discussion of the Right, Center, and Left Groups in the State Council. The Poles in the State Council almost all belonged to the Center Group, while they formed their own special caucus known as the Polish *kolo*. The paper also noted that the Center Group was less concerned about the seriousness of the attack than were the Polish members of the State Council. The Center felt that the problem was really temporary because with "the upcoming introduction of the zemstvo, the universal electoral law will be spread to the western provinces as well."

6. GARF, f. 1178, d. 39, l. 4 and d. 34, l. 54.

7. *Okrainy rossii*, no. 15, April 11, 1909, pp. 209–216.

8. *Okrainy rossii*, no. 16, April 18, 1909, pp. 227–230.

9. Among the national questions considered in the Duma prior to the fourth session were bills permitting elementary school teachers to study Polish in seminaries located in the border areas of Kholm and Belsk, which the government supported and a bill to separate the Kholm area from Poland, which the government also introduced. The ambiguity of government policy on national questions is clearly evident in these two somewhat contradictory proposals. For more information, see Alexandra D. Shecket, "The Russian Imperial State Council" pp. 190–196.

10. Throughout April 1909 there were numerous efforts to promote the proposal—nine representatives from the western provinces met with members of the two legislative chambers on April 12 to work on passage of the bill. According to *Birzhevye vedomosti*, they set up a permanent council to contact the local population in efforts to mobilize them to support a petition calling for the alleviation of disproportionate Polish representation. *Birzhevye vedomosti*, no. 11054, April 14, 1909.

On May 1, the same paper noted that a deputation from the Orthodox population of the western provinces arrived in St. Petersburg to petition Nicholas II to intervene on behalf of the Pikhno bill as well as on the proposal to separate the Kholm area from Poland. The deputation's members all belonged to monarchical organizations and perhaps hoped to impress the Tsar with their loyalty. *Birzhevye vedomosti*, no. 11084, May 1, 1909.

11. *Birzhevye vedomosti*, no. 10086, May 2, 1909. After the Polish uprising of 1830–1831, the Kingdom of Poland, which had enjoyed autonomy since being attached to the Russian Empire in 1815, was more firmly integrated into the empire, although Poland retained a somewhat separate administration. After the Polish insurrection of 1863–1864, however, Poland gradually was shorn of its political identity. In 1874 the Kingdom of Poland became known as the Vistula Region (*Provislinskii krai*); alternatively, the ten Polish provinces were known as the vistual provinces (*privislinskie gubernii*). For details and more information, see Edward Chmielewski, *The Polish Question in the Russian State Duma* (Knoxville: The University of Tennessee Press, 1970), pp. 3–18.

12. *Rossiia*, May 5, 1909.

13. *Rech'*, May 5, 1909; *Birzhevye vedomosti*, no. 10090, May 5, 1909.

14. *Rech'*, May 5, 1909.

15. *Gosudarstvennyi Sovet, Stenograficheskie otchety* [hereafter *GSSO*], Session 4, meeting 34, May 8, 1909, cols. 1933–1944.

16. Ibid., cols. 1941–1942.

17. Ibid., col. 1949.

18. *Birzhevye vedomosti*, no. 11096, May 9, 1909.

19. *Rech'*, May 9, 1909; *Golos Moskvy*, May 9, 1909. *Golos Moskvy* had actually been much more concerned about a meeting of right-wing associations at the home of Count Sheremetev, but did note that the Polish *kolo* in the Duma had discussed the impact of the Pikhno bill, focusing on how it would affect their representation in the State Council and its impact on the Center Group. According to the paper, the Poles saw the bill as "a symptom of the change in direction of government policy."

20. *Rossiia*, May 10, 1909.

21. The Naval General Staff bill created a major crisis during the fourth session of the State Council because it included both funding and conditions of appointment to the Naval General Staff, which was being reorganized in the wake of the loss of the Russo-Japanese War. The Right maintained that the bill was a major violation of the Tsar's prerogatives and Stolypin was barely able to muster the necessary votes to pass it through the State Council. He managed to do so only with the support of the left wing of the upper chamber. There were many rumors that he would lose his position but he emerged in April-May not only remaining as Chairman of the Council of Ministers, but with a stronger position in nominating appointed members to the upper chamber. The failure of the Center Group to provide Stolypin with a reliable majority and his dependence on the left wing of the State Council—Constitutional Democrats— undermined the Center's credibility with the government. See Alexandra D. Shecket,

"The Russian Imperial State Council," pp. 155–205; and Korros, "The Landed Nobility, the State Council and P. A. Stolypin," pp. 123–141.

22. GARF, f. 115, op. 1, d. 14, l. 200. In April 1907, M. G. Akimov was appointed chairman of the State Council. A former Minister of Justice with comparatively less bureaucratic experience than other possible candidates for a position traditionally held by a very senior, distinguished, and respected bureaucrat, the appointment was regarded as a setback to progressive forces in the upper chamber. Since the State Council chairman traditionally recommended new appointments to the chamber, he could wield important power in determining its political configuration. See Korros, "Activist Politics in a Conservative Institution," pp. 1–19.

23. For a good discussion of the changing character of the zemstvo movement in the aftermath of 1905, see Ruth D. MacNaughton and Roberta T. Manning, "The Crisis of the Third of June System and Political Trends in the Zemstvos, 1907–1914," in Haimson, ed., *The Politics of Rural Russia*, Leopold (Bloomington: Indiana University Press, 1979), pp. 184–218.

24. The Neidgart subgroup had existed in the State Council since at least October 1908; it numbered twenty-one members. GARF, f. 1178, d. 34, l. 52.

25. For more information on the members of the nationalist parties, see Robert Edelman, *Gentry Politics on the Eve of the Russian Revolution: The Nationalist Party, 1907–1917.* (New Brunswick, NJ: Rutgers University Press, 1980).

26. According to *Birzhevye vedomosti*, members of the Right were planning to attend a proposed meeting of the group at Neidgart's home to discredit the group and prevent new members of the State Council from supporting it. *Birzhevye vedomosti*, no. 11357, October 11, 1909.

27. During this period Olsuf'ev was consistently a member of the State Council's Right Group and never a member of the Center. See GARF, f. 1178, d. 51, l. 15 for a financial report dated January 1, 1909, listing all the paid-up members of the Center Group and those who were nominally members who had not paid their 25 rubles in dues.

28. *Birzhevye vedomosti*, no. 11359, October 13, 1909. A variety of reasons can explain this reluctance towards realignment, including fear on the part of the Neidgartists that in joining with the Right, they would fall under its stricter discipline and that they would not receive high listing for election to State Council standing committees. If they formed a separate group, they would have even smaller representation on standing committees. In remaining with the Center, the Neidgartists highlighted the fundamental weakness of the Center Group, whose diverse membership guaranteed no meaningful disciplinary structure, but did indeed guarantee membership in standing committees.

29. *Rossiia*, November 3, 1909.

30. *Pis'ma k blizhnim* (St. Petersburg: Izdatel'stvo M. O. Menshikova, November 1909), pp. 830–832. Neidgart was among those listed from the Center, V. N. Polivanov, N. K. Shaufus, and D. A. Olsuf'ev from among the Right. See also *Rossiia*, December 1, 1909.

31. *Rossiia*, November 22, 1909.

32. *Novoe vremia*, January 1, 1910, and *Birzhevye vedomosti*, no. 11496, January 3, 1910.

33. *Birzhevye vedomosti*, no. 11496, January 3, 1910, p. 5. Also Public Records Office, London, British Diplomatic Correspondence, F. O. 371, vol. 978, no. 3356, Nicolson to Grey, January 11/24, 1910. Nicolson reported on a conversation with Octobrist Duma deputy A. I. Svegintsev from Voronezh who told him that Nicholas had not accepted the New Year's list presented to him by Akimov, that the Tsar's action had "produced an excellent impression," and that he hoped the new appointments would "doubtless greatly facilitate the passage through the Upper House of some important measures now awaiting its approval."

34. *Golos Moskvy*, January 22, 1910. Also, Public Records office, London, British Diplomatic Correspondence, F. O. 371, vol. 977, no. 10427, March 8/21, 1910.

35. *Golos Moskvy*, January 20, 1910; *Golos Moskvy*, January 23, 1910.

36. There were several bills presented to the State Council that concerned commerce and manufacturing including proposals for workers' insurance and a bill enacting new regulations against speculation in sugar. In both cases the Center voted in favor of the government's position despite the strong protests of the Trade and Industry group, which had constituted a subgroup of the Center since the second session of the State Council. In April, frustration led the group to submit a statement to the Center bureau accusing it of conducting a policy inimical to the interests of commerce and manufacturing. Although the statement was supposed to be secret, its contents leaked out and revealed the dissension in the group that was supposed to be Stolypin's strongest ally. See *GSSO*, Session 5, meeting 3, October 20, 1909; meeting 11, December 12, 1909; meeting 41, April 12, 1910, for the debate on the legislation. Also *Birzhevye vedomosti*, no. 11463, April 14, 1910, and *Golos Moskvy*, April 14, 1910.

37. *Birzhevye vedomosti*, no. 11665, April 15, 1910. Strangely enough the Center continued to hold onto most of its members although they obviously felt no need to adhere to any policies the group voted to support. As of January 1910, the Center Group had eighty-one active paid-up members.

38. For the text of the original law approved on October 17, 1906, see *Polnoe Sobranie Zakonov Rossisskoi Imperii* [hereafter *PSZ*], Sobranie tret'e, vol. 264, 1906, pp. 905–914, No. 20424.

39. *Rossiia*, November 15, 1909. The Duma's eagerness to amend the Old Believer legislation by extending them even further rights was probably prompted by the Octobrist effort to disassociate itself as a puppet of the Stolypin government. Moreover, A. I. Guchkov, the Octobrist leader, was one of many Octobrists who, as descendants of Old Believer families, sought to improve the lot of his ancestral coreligionists. Assisted by the Kadets, whose political philosophy was indeed in opposition to the government, the bill was passed by a distinctly left-of-center Duma majority. Butkevich was not entirely off-base in his accusations in terms of the actual political context of the bill.

40. *GSSO*, Session 5, meeting 47, May 12, 1910, col. 2797.

41. Durnovo was in effect endorsing the *Ukaz* or edict on religious toleration issued by Nicholas II on April 17, 1905. See *PSZ*, Sobranie tret'e, vol. 25[1], 1905, No. 26126, pp. 258–262.

42. *GSSO*, Session 5, meeting 47, cols. 2797–2814.

43. Ibid., cols. 2814–2815.

44. Ibid., cols. 2828–2837.

45. *Grazhdanin*, no. 18, May 23, 1910, p. 11.

46. The fact that the Russian government called the Finnish Diet by a Polish term, "the Sejm," is an important indication of the lack of sensitivity and understanding regarding Finland. The Finnish and Polish legislative chambers had nothing in common with one another historically since the Polish Sejm existed until the end of the eighteenth century and was composed of Polish petty gentry and great nobles.

47. "Ob uchrezhdenii russko-finliandskoi kommissi dlia sostavleniia proekta pravil o poriadke izdaniia kasaiushchikhsia finliandii zakonov obshchegosudarstvennago znacheniia," *Zhurnal Soveta ministrov po Finlandii 1909–1911*, no. 35, March 17, 1909, Harvard Law School Library, Special Collections, Pre-Soviet Collections, FIN 766. Section I of the document pertains to the basis of the commission's formation: The five Finnish members of the commission would be named by the Finnish Senate and the five Russian members by the Chairman of the Council of Ministers. The chair would be named by the Chairman of the Council of Ministers and he would hold the tie-breaking vote. All the commission's activities would be conducted in Russian and its conclusions would be reported to the Council of Ministers.

Section II mandated the commission to determine which categories of imperial laws pertained to Finland and how they were formed. How would Finland's laws that fell into the imperial category be formed? Should Finns send their representatives to the legislative bodies? Under what circumstances? How many Finnish representatives would be elected? Would they participate in all matters before the legislature? Do Finnish representatives have to be present on all pending matters pertaining to Finland?

48. A. Ia. Avrekh, *Stolypin i tret'ia duma* (Moscow: *Nauka*, 1968), pp. 23–58, passim.

49. *Birzhevye vedomosti*, no. 111615, March 16, 1910. Note that these interviews occurred prior to the bill's passage by the Duma and two months prior to the bill's submission to the State Council.

50. *Birzhevye vedomosti*, no. 11617, March 17, 1910.

51. *Grazhdanin*, no. 10, March 21, 1910, p. 16. This quote comes from one of Meshcherskii's diaries actually dated March 19.

52. *Golos Moskvy*, April 7, 1910; *Birzhevye vedomosti*, no. 11653, April 8, 1910.

53. *Birzhevye vedomosti*, no. 11659, April 11, 1910. One hundred forty-two members of the State Council participated in the committee election; fourteen voted for the Left, sixty-three for the Center, and sixty-five for the Right.

54. *Golos Moskvy*, no. 99, May 1, 1910. Although the press article was based on rumor and gossip, the Journals of the Council of Ministers on the Finnish Question reveal that Nicholas received copies of many of the documents and actually signed off on several. Clearly, he was informed, if not involved, in this process. See *Osobye zhurnaly Soveta ministrov Rossiiskoi imperii*, Harvard Law School Library, Special Collections, Finland 766, passim.

55. *Golos Moskvy*, January 22, 1910. Also, Public Records office, London, British Diplomatic Correspondence, F.O. 371, vol. 978, No. 19549, May 28 (15), 1910, p. 2. The British observers invariably likened Russian political factions (or fractions, as the

Russians sometimes called them) to British political parties, hence terms like Tory or Conservative in the British sense. Throughout the correspondence, it was clear that Pares and other British observers wanted Stolypin to succeed and that they viewed him as an individual committed to transforming Russia into a parliamentary monarchy. The British were also very fearful of left-wing pressures, had little sympathy for any of the socialist parties, and often appeared skeptical of the Constitutional Democrats as well.

56. There were still some holdouts. For example, Prince Liven informed Durnovo of his total opposition, arguing that because the proposed legislation touched on both the Fundamental Laws of Russia and Finland, the issue was outside the competence of the legislative chambers. He maintained that the Right Group should not even agree to discuss the Finnish bill in such an illegal context. *Birzhevye vedomosti*, no.11696, May 5, 1910.

Meshcherskii did not change his position either. He maintained that any kind of alteration of the relationship between the Tsar and Finland was a matter to be worked out on a personal level; the matter could not be resolved as a nationalist issue. He too viewed legislative action as a violation of tsarist prerogative. *Grazhdanin*, no. 20, June 6, 1910. p. 13. See also *Grazhdanin*, no. 21, June 13, 1910, p. 14.

57. *Birzhevye vedomosti*, nos. 11740, 11742, 11744, June 1–3, 1910.

58. *Golos Moskvy*, June 9, 1910.

59. GSSO, Session 5, meeting 58, June 8, 1910, cols. 3626 and 3640.

60. Ibid., cols. 3640–3641.

61. Ibid., col. 3692.

62. Ibid., cols., 3692, 3720 (M. M. Kovalevskii) and 3742 (M. O. Korvin-Milevskii).

63. Ibid., cols. 3812–3820, passim.

64. *Birzhevye vedomosti*, no. 11763, June 15, 1910.

65. *Birzhevye vedomosti*, no. 11769, June 18, 1910.

The Democratization of the Zemstvo During the First World War

Thomas Porter
North Carolina Agricultural and Technical State University

William Gleason
Doane College

The expansion of the educated public's role in the governance of a changing Russia during the decade preceding the outbreak of the First World War, combined with other positive developments such as the proliferation of cooperatives and myriad other informal groups, poses a fundamental question: was tsarist Russia undergoing a transformation that would have led to the flowering of a civil society? Scholarly consensus on this question is skeptical and for good reason. Russia in 1914 remained an immature and incomplete civil society. Yet one point remains: it must be recalled that modern wars often have proved to be accelerators of change; more than that, and paradoxically, they have sometimes proven to be instruments of modernization.[1]

World War I was no exception. Just as the stresses and strains of modern warfare had inaugurated the era of reforms after Crimea and the semiconstitutional monarchy after the Russo-Japanese fiasco, the First World War would also have brought further political concessions. The increasing irrelevance of the regime was laid bare during this conflict; once again, Russian society demonstrated its vitality as the federated General Zemstvo Organization was merged into the dynamic, centralized All-Russian Zemstvo Union (*Vserossiiskii zemskii soiuz*). This organization, again led, as in the Russo-Japanese War of 1905, by Prince

Georgii L'vov, along with the other voluntary associations established by Russia's increasingly civic-minded entrepreneurial and professional class, would come to play a crucial role in Russia's war effort.[2]

The regime's acceptance of society's [*obshchestva*] proffered hand came none too soon as it quickly became clear that official plans for the evacuation of the wounded and medical supply were virtually nonexistent. Consequently, both the army and the Council of Ministers turned to the union for the purpose of organizing victory in the rear. The response was immediate and staggering. By November, some ninety days after the mobilization order, 1,667 hospital units of varying size and description stood under union aegis.[3] Simultaneously, the army implored the union to outfit and operate the evacuation trains, including those running inside the war zone. By 1915 the union maintained fifty trains spread across European Russia that carried as many as 16,000 sick and wounded at one time.[4]

The nature of the union's activities is of historic note. The government had hoped to limit the union's participation in the war effort to the care of sick and wounded soldiers after their evacuation to the rear. However, the government soon proved to be incapable of meeting its most basic obligations to the Russian people during the war, and was forced to permit the union to expand the scope of its activities to include refugee assistance, food supply, vaccination programs, etc. Society demonstrated its manumission from the grasp of the state by stepping forward and taking responsibility

> not only for a broad expansion of [its] sphere of works formerly planned, not only the extension of the union's activity up to the front as far as the advance positions, but also that [society] take upon itself such functions, the fulfillment of which had been undertaken as purely governmental tasks and which in all preceding wars had been fulfilled exclusively by governmental organs.[5]

In addition, the significance of an umbrella group of tens of thousands of professionals cannot be overstated. National professional associations had formerly been discouraged; typically, professionals met sporadically in so-called congresses (*s'ezdy*) to explore issues of mutual concern. More to our point, however, is the fact that in order to conduct its business at all—whether it came to staffing hospitals, outfitting trains, or coordinating evacuations from front to rear—the union had to range far beyond the narrow limits of the zemstvo class franchise and call in outsiders with technical expertise who were debarred by law from voting in the provincial and county assemblies. Once the union entered the fighting zone, nonnoble consultants hired by the zemstvo—the so-called Third Element—were again placed in positions of authority. Ad hoc committees formed that reflected the de facto transformation of the social composition of local government, a process underscored by the willingness of the regime, usually at the insistence of the army high command, to assign responsibilities to the union that in other combatant countries fell to government bodies.

The regime's dependency upon the liberal component of elected zemstvo delegates (the *zemtsy*) and the zemtsy's dependency upon the Third Element for its professional expertise were magnified several times over by an additional factor—the domestic reverberations of the war. The unanticipated protractedness of the struggle engendered an endless series of problems that defied official solution: nationwide epidemics, millions of displaced persons from the western provinces lost to the Germans in 1915, food and fuel shortages, and inflation. In particular, the challenges of public health care became severe during the Galician campaign of 1915, when hundreds of thousands of people from the western provinces burst into the interior. As with the provisioning of medical supplies and personnel for the soldiers in 1914, the regime now begged the union to take a more significant role in safeguarding the general population against epidemic disease and in instituting welfare programs for refugees that exceeded traditional systems of private charity and government-sponsored philanthropy.

In addition, the municipal counterpart of the zemstvos, the city dumas, had also organized a relief society. The Moscow Duma had convened at the outbreak of hostilities in order to consider a resolution soliciting the support and assistance of municipal dumas throughout provincial Russia; two weeks later the All-Russian Union of Cities (*Vserossiiskii soiuz gorodov*) was born. Together, the Zemstvo Union and the Union of Cities set up *Zemgor*. Headed by Prince Georgii L'vov, Zemgor was to take an active part in the organization of the army's supply needs through the mobilization of industry. Its work included acting as a liaison between the Ministry of War and local enterprises, the evacuation of threatened industries and the construction of new ones. To some extent this duplicated the work of the War Industries Committees set up by Russia's industrialists, and one authority on Zemgor, T. I. Polner, admits that it was only a qualified success.[6]

However, these initiatives brought the union into even closer contact with the military and revealed the dynamism of educated society and its potential for future development. Certainly the authorities needed little convincing; from their perspective the union clearly served as an agent for change in the structure and functioning of the older order of society. Minister of Internal Affairs N. A. Maklakov warned that, unless constrained, both the Union of Zemstvos and the Union of Cities "obviously were preparing themselves for work on the reconstruction of public life which must come, they feel, at the conclusion of the war."[7] By 1916 official concern had deepened. The government was becoming increasingly alarmed at the mushrooming of practical work.

That the regime feared both Zemgor and the politicization of its Third Element is incontrovertible. And the formation of the Progressive Bloc in the State Duma portended precisely the same kind of broad alliance of the inchoate segments of society that had coalesced to wrest reforms from the regime in 1905. B. V. Shtiurmer (Stürmer) had been chair of the Tver' Provincial Zemstvo Board from 1891 to 1894. Now, as Chair of the Council of Ministers, he rightly feared the program of Zemgor that would "lead to the transformation of the zemstvos from institutions dealing with the local economy under the supervision of the government, into organs of local government, independent of the authorities."[8]

Shtiurmer also worried about the loyalty of the Third Element professionals and the influence they had come to wield over the union. He averred that "the zemstvo union was culled from persons of a definite coloration . . . each free unit was saturated with the Third Element . . . moreover, it was impossible to liquidate this problem because the administration could not manage without them."[9]

Shtiurmer's statements are critical in two respects. First of all, they highlight the government's alarm and impotency concerning the transformation of Russian society. That alarm was well placed. By 1916 the union had under its jurisdiction tens of thousands of civilians, it conducted its business at all levels of society, and, unlike the Duma, it operated year round and could not be shut down without an inexcusable increase in human misery. Within the war zone, thanks to the army's control there and its proclivity for union-sponsored programs, the union was quite independent. Nevertheless, and notwithstanding constant accusations by officials of political machinations throughout 1915–1916 and, on a couple of occasions, of rank disloyalty by the Third Element, the government never seriously contemplated disbanding the union.[10]

Secondly, and more to our concern, the history of the union can best be understood as the response of Russia's incipient civil society to the opportunities that crisis provided. The government's incompetence had finally forced society to assume the burden for the conduct of the war. As Prince L'vov wrote:

> The activity of the unions [of zemstvos and of cities] long ago acquired state significance. Public-spirited forces have been attracted to it in very large numbers, and the unions have proven that much of what is unfeasible for the government is feasible [when undertaken] by the people's organized forces. It [the activity of the unions] has proven that the people attracted to state work display the great latent forces hidden within it and that the government mechanism of state administration is far from conforming with the living force of the country.[11]

Thus, from mid-1915 onward union activists—those professionals in charge of medical relief, refugee assistance, and public health care—sought a new role for themselves, one more commensurate with their elevated civic profile. Their initiatives ran in two directions: first, enhancement of the union's status through involvement in the management of the wartime economy; second, exploitation of the union for political ends, namely, decentralization of the Russian state order and enfranchisement of the Third Element in local government.

By this time many zemtsy had also come to understand that Russia could no longer afford to delay the modernization of its social and political relations. L'vov and the other liberal zemtsy had long advocated the destruction of the estate system and the democratization of the zemstvo as being the first steps toward the acculturation of the peasantry to the norms and values of a civil society. But L'vov had not wanted to undertake meaningful reforms until after the war had been concluded as he thought a political struggle would serve only to undermine the war effort. He had advised his colleagues simply "to continue with their work . . . for we believe it is precisely in real action and work that our salvation and the salvation of our country lie."[12] This changed after the Tsar refused to meet with a delegation that represented almost all of society and was headed by Prince L'vov.

This "Progressive Bloc," which included three quarters of the members of the Duma and had ties to the Union of Zemstvos, the Union of Towns, and the War Industries Committee, now demanded the establishment of a government that would be "capable of organizing real cooperation among all citizens. . . ."[13] The time had come to wrest reforms from the regime in connection with the war effort that would necessitate changes in the state structure as well. One problem that continued to impede the zemtsy was the absence of zemstvo institutions at the local level. Polner asserts that the "existing institutions were found to be unsuited for public work." Accordingly, the zemtsy once again demanded the introduction of the volost' or township-level zemstvo as the primary unit of local self-government.[14] Formerly only peasants had paid volost' taxes; now the franchise was to be based upon the amount of taxes paid by all residents of the area irrespective of status, and class distinctions based upon property would be abolished. In sum, the proposal called for the establishment of the all-estate zemstvo. The zemtsy also proposed that the disenfranchised members of the "Third Element" be allowed to participate in volost' elections and be elected as members of the assemblies.

Thus, the leitmotiv of the reform project was the establishment of a more modern and inclusive system of local self-government that would necessarily entail the decentralization of the Russian state political order and allow for the further development of its civil society. But the government responded by creating special volost' committees that were to be completely independent of the zemstvos and under control of appointed provincial governors.[15] The zemtsy complained that the government's action "was inconsistent in principle with the recognized necessity for a volost' zemstvo and at the same time was unsuitable for those volost' organizations which are currently operating."[16]

L'vov and the other zemtsy realized that "a new infrastructure had to be created and this demonstrated that the older zemtvos were too small and limited to handle the tasks; a greater segment of the public had to be mobilized."[17] In a remarkable display of public discourse, L'vov and

N. I. Astrov (the head of the Union of Cities) organized a three-day conference in Moscow that saw workers, tsarist bureaucrats, townspeople, and zemtsy meet to discuss the situation. It was here that the deep fissures in Russian society were made apparent to L'vov and the other members of society. L'vov and Astrov spoke of the need to galvanize Russian society in order to meet the obligations of the unions; however, the workers, represented by Alexander Kerenskii, merely demanded their rights. One delegate went so far as to warn L'vov that "all educated Russia" was on trial and that "the truth must be told, the people are turning away from you. And this must be recognized."[18]

Astrov would later warn L'vov that "the people below us hate us and are irritated."[19] Both L'vov and Astrov fully agreed that it was time to "rectify these ancient wounds," although it should be done in such a way that "the defense of the Fatherland would not be imperiled."[20] L'vov and the other zemtsy had, of course, long demanded that the regime allow for greater public participation in governance in order to hasten the citizenry's acculturation to the norms of a civil society. Reforms now would be in the regime's own best interest because the limitations of the archaic state order were by now manifestly evident, as was the fact that "the regime was not guiding the ship of state."[21] The government also recognized that its superordinate powers were being challenged. Minister of Internal Affairs Maklakov warned Nicholas that the public activists were "systematically moving toward their own goal . . . to black out the light of your glory . . . and to weaken the strength of the significance of the holy, immemorial and in Russia always saving idea of autocracy."[22]

But no matter how much the government wanted to shut down the unions, it was acknowledged that "it was impossible to liquidate this problem because the administration can not manage without them."[23] This was graphically illustrated by Minister of War D. S. Shuvaev's refusal to follow orders from the Tsar himself to cease cooperating with the War Industries Committee. Shuvaev refused to do so because he "did not have enough chinovniki [appointed officials] to replace all the public workers."[24] The regime's fear of the unions reached such proportions that the ministers devoted considerable time to the discussion of their activities and possible responses to the threat to their primacy.

The ministers often expressed their concerns over the "self-abolition" of the government and their helplessness in the face of the dynamism of society. Prince Shcherbatov, acting as Minister of Internal Affairs later during the war, requested instructions on measures to be taken to limit the activities of the unions. He agreed that it was "necessary to tolerate them as an existing fact . . . since their dispersal would create serious complications." However, he also asserted that

> [i]n general, I cannot help but repeat that the zemstvo and city unions, which I found already in full bloom by the time I became minister, are a colossal government mistake. It is impossible to allow such organizations without a statute and determinations as to the limits of their activities. From a philanthropic beginning they have turned into enormous institutions with the most varied functions, in many cases of a purely governmental character, and they are replacing government institutions with themselves.[25]

Thus, by late 1916 the unions had come not only to embody the initiative and public spirit of society, they also well represented the legitimate demands and aspirations of Russian liberalism. The regime recognized that the unions represented a threat to its primacy but was compelled to grant them considerable autonomy in order to address the catastrophic consequences of modern warfare. The exigencies of total war included not only the problems of medical relief and supply for the army but also the uprooted civilian populations that needed to be cared for, along with the resultant economic dislocation that made such endeavors possible only through a massive and coordinated public campaign.

The economic consequences of World War I, in particular the breakdown of the nation's transportation system and the resultant food shortages in the great northern cities, has been well-chronicled.[26] Less is known about the Zemstvo Union's chapter in that story.[27] That chapter was extensive and had its beginnings in August 1915 when, in response to the public clamor for a streamlined apparatus to coordinate the civilian and military sectors of the war effort, the State Duma established four special councils to plan production and supply. Representatives from both the zemstvo and the city unions sat on all four councils. Over the next twelve months attention focused on the Food Council. The unions, both individually and in concert, provided services that the council desperately needed to organize the food market. They made three vital contributions: union members served on executive agencies and commissions; they made policy recommendations; and they supplied administrative-technical assistance. The last item was noteworthy because almost everyone agreed that the rural assemblies could construct an efficient provisioning network based on their experiences during the famine relief campaigns and the fact that they were best able to gather data on grain and livestock reserves for any given area.[28]

By early 1916 special council funds were being allocated to help the villages procure food and food commissioners were appointed to buy grain and coordinate food deliveries. Simultaneously Minister of Agriculture A. N. Naumov appointed zemstvo statisticians to the central statistical commission, an official arm of the Special Food Council. Eight weeks later, in May 1916, the Stavka, the army high command, placed the zemstvos in charge of meat supply within the war zone. By this decision, the rural councils, along with the union, were authorized to fix procurement prices, to requisition, if necessary, and to organize food deliveries. They did their work well. The army, desperately short of meat in 1915, was amply supplied by the fall of 1916, thanks to the expertise of zemstvo professionals.[29]

When the October decrees announcing the formation of the new system of local councils were made public, the unions hailed the decision as a big step forward a and indeed it was. The Union of Zemstvos was especially pleased, for it not only increased the union's autonomy vis-à-vis the central bureaucracy and provincial governors, but extended its jurisdiction beyond the county zemstvo to village Russia itself, a long-cherished objective. Unfortunately, at this late hour society badly overestimated the government's willingness to keep its promises. No sooner had the special council decree been promulgated than rumors began to circulate that the food administration—from top to bottom—was being transferred from the Ministry of Agriculture to the Ministry of Internal Affairs. The Ministry of Agriculture, it will be recalled, had been willing to share power with nonbureaucratic elements and its last two chiefs (A. V. Krivoshein and Naumov) had both expressed their sympathies with the aspirations of the Progressive Bloc. Other ministers, by contrast, were frightened by the possibility that union programs would widen the political arena with perhaps fatal consequences for the power of the imperial bureaucracy.

Thus, in November the Minister of Internal Affairs hinted that "it might be necessary to draw the governors into the whole business" of food supply and that he favored "free trade [in foodstuffs] over fixed prices." A week later the Minister of Agriculture resigned. In December union representatives gathered in Moscow to try, once again, to bring the regime to its senses. Since the ministers would not countenance public participation in the resolution of the food crisis— participation that entailed the devolution of a substantial portion of wartime administration from the state to society—the government resorted to strong-arm police tactics. In a stormy confrontation, the union congress was shut down and the delegates forcibly dispersed.[30]

By 1916 the food supply crisis had dispelled any illusions that the existing order was adequate. In May food riots broke out in Orenburg, followed by similar disorders in Ufa and Krasnoyarsk. From Tiflis came word that 100,000 puds of grain stood undistributed at the nearby train station. Meat rationing was introduced in Khar'kov, and not far away, in Chernigov, meat shipments dropped to 10 percent of their prewar level.[31] By then, clearly, the exigencies of the moment were such as to demand nothing short of a massive and coordinated civic campaign to save Russia from economic collapse.

The response of the union leaders to the problems engendered by the war reflected their belief that the state's power rested on the mobilization of society as demonstrated by the union's history. Prince L'vov stated that the problems of meat supply would be resolved by the unions "from a supreme, state-like point of view."[32] The zemtsy thought reform would be in the state's best interest, and the challenges of inflation and food supply, for example, could not be solved unless more people were brought into the administration. Time after time Prince L'vov claimed that the public organizations, if buttressed by restructured organs of local self-government, would "cement Russian society and channel human resources along useful lines; anarchy," he warned, "was the only alternative." The inescapable conclusion of this argument was that the state's interest was best served by a devolution of power to the zemstvos and the union; "to limit them," L'vov observed, "is to invite disaster."[33]

Unfortunately, it quickly became apparent that the Duma did not have the stomach for the touchy issue of zemstvo and municipal reform. As a political issue, local reorganization should have entailed close cooperation between the union and the legislature. Like the union, the Duma centrist parties had directed their energies at mobilizing the homefront, and by 1915 they too were plainly disillusioned with the political myopia of the regime. But for "liberal Russia," cooperation was frustrated in 1916 by the Duma's inability to act on local government reform. Perhaps, as one writer has suggested, Duma leaders felt in the end that this issue bore little relationship to the fighting, and that Russia could do nothing to improve the zemstvos or municipal organs of local self-government until the war ended.[34]

Whatever the case, in February 1916 L'vov charged that the Duma had done nothing to ameliorate home-front conditions and that greater authority should be given to the unions.[35] In June, at a meeting of the Union of Cities attended by Prince L'vov, N. I. Astrov, a union founder and outspoken liberal, warned that the Duma's indifference "threatened the union's very existence," and that if the liberals declined the imperative of educating the people politically, radicals would become not only the probable, "but the legitimate spokesmen for the future."[36] L'vov did not demur—a single indication that, given his customary disdain for political speechmaking, his confidence in the Duma had eroded badly.

Astrov's intimations of social unrest held a deeper meaning for L'vov, one which brings us to the crux of the final turn of events. By 1916, the Third Element activists were not alone in their drive to democratize the zemstvos.[37] In their campaign for a political voice, the professional intelligentsia of the zemstvos found a powerful ally in the Pirogov Society, which represented Russia's medical community. In April 1916, at its annual meeting attended by 1,500 delegates and numerous union-affiliated physicians, the Pirogov Society appealed for the "politicization of the Third Element and a movement of doctors to the people." The three-day convention ended with an endorsement of the "reconstruction of our rural and urban institutions on the basis of universal suffrage."[38]

Shortly after the Pirogov Congress the cry for change escalated. Frustrated with L'vov, who, convinced that zemstvo work could not be interrupted without disastrous consequences, had largely turned a deaf ear to appeals for work stoppages in the field to prod the Duma, the Third Element took matters into its own hands. In Minsk, along the front, where the Third Element was heavily involved with food supply and refugee relief, doctors and statisticians walked off the job "to protest the class-dominated unions."[39] Momentarily unnerved and under pressure from the regime, L'vov at first threatened to fire the strikers, but soon dispatched an assistant to intercede with the workers. That gesture did not suffice to pacify them because the police intervened and arrested two dozen employees of the Mogilev provincial zemstvo. Three months later, at a conference of consumer cooperatives in Moscow, with union physicians and statisticians in attendance, a resolution was passed condemning the union for its "estrangement from the democratic intelligentsia."[40]

The radicalization of the Third Element was a direct outgrowth of the union's interaction with civilians and soldiers within the war zone. For it was this source, more than any other, that had conferred authority upon the professional intelligentsia. It was here, within the war zone, thanks to the army's control and its pronounced bias for union-sponsored programs, that the intelligentsia had developed considerable autonomy. This was especially true for the Union of Zemstvos because of the magnitude of its medical and relief endeavors. It was here, then, that the Third Element concluded that there could be no return to the status quo ante bellum; Russian society, galvanized in good measure by the unions to win the war because of bureaucratic shortsightedness and incompetence, had been too severely shaken to avoid further modernization of social and political relations. And it was here, at the eleventh hour, that L'vov also acknowledged the legitimacy of the democratic aspirations of the professional intelligentsia; in 1917 the Provisional Government, under L'vov's leadership, radically restructured the zemstvos to accord with the ambitions of the Third Element.

The wartime activities of the Union of Zemstvos and especially the activities of the Third Element highlight the beginning of a new reform tradition, one based on the underpinnings of a civil society. Quite unexpectedly, but decidedly, as a result of the unique size, composition, and function of the Union of Zemstvos, a uniqueness grounded in the nature of modern war and magnified by the existence of a parallel municipal organization, professional specialists took over the war effort. From 1914 to 1917 thousands of doctors, nurses, statisticians, lawyers, and engineers worked for the union, developing associations with rural and urban Russia that went far beyond the purely functional capacities they fulfilled. From this perspective, the story of the zemstvo union illustrates the beginnings of a civil society that might have served to guide the political and economic growth of the country.

Of course, the same process that facilitated the maturation of the middle class—the war—also unleashed other forces, including a savage class struggle and extremist assaults across the home-front. Consequently, the social revolution overwhelmed the middle class and the emerging civil society fell apart before it had time to sink deeper roots. Society's victory over the state proved to be ephemeral when the pleas of Russia's peasant majority went unheeded and the schism between the educated elite and the peasantry widened.

From today's viewpoint, however, the point to be made is that the awakening of Russian society, an awakening drawing on the existence of myriad economic and political groupings, reflects a longer-standing political reality as well. The collapse of the tsarist bureaucracy under the pressure of total war had forced society to carry out many social and economic functions that formerly had been preserved for state action. Similarly, the fall of the Soviet regime largely left the Russian people to their own devices; without directions from the center, citizens were forced to come together and create organizations to promote their various political, social, and economic interests. Today's proliferation of informal groups such as economic cooperatives, cultural associations, and political action networks suggests that the Russians have, as Geoffrey Hosking put it, "lost none of their skill at improvising functioning human institutions under great pressure and stress."[41] Thus, the transformation of Russian society, a process of political, social, and economic change that was readily apparent in the decade before the Great War and then accelerated in the crucible of that war only to be suspended after the Bolshevik takeover in 1917, has now been resumed.

NOTES

1. Thus, writing on the war's impact on the industrial economy, Norman Stone sees the conflict not "as a vast rundown of most accounts, but as a crisis of growth, a modernization crisis in thin disguise." See Norman Stone, *The Eastern Front 1914–1917* (London and New York: Charles Scribener's Sons, 1975), p. 14.

2. There are relatively few published accounts of the union: T. I. Polner, *Russian Local Government During the War and the Union of Zemstvos* (New Haven, CT: Yale University Press, 1930); Mark George, "Liberal Opposition in Wartime Russia: A Case Study of the Town and Zemstvo Unions," *Slavonic and East European Review,* vol. 65 (1987) pp. 371–

390; William Gleason, "The All-Russian Union of Zemstvos and World War I," in Terence Emmons and Wayne Vucinich, eds., *The Zemstvo in Russia: An Experiment in Local Self-Government* (Cambridge: Cambridge University Press, 1982), pp. 365–382; for the only published Soviet assessment, see A. P. Pogrebinskii, "K istorii soiuzov zemstv i gorodov," *Istoricheskie zapiski,* no. 12 (1941) pp. 39–60.

3. *Izvestiia vserossiiskogo zemskogo soiuza* [hereafter *Izvestiia VZS*] (Moscow: Gorodskaia Tipografiia, 1917), no. 26 (1915) p. 19.

4. Ibid., no. 15 (1915) pp. 11–13.

5. *Kratkii ocherk deiatel'nosti vserossiiskogo zemskogo soiuza* (Moscow: Gorodskaia Tipografiia, 1917), p. 8.

6. Polner, *Russian Local Government,* p. 285

7. Gosudarstvennyi arkhiv Rossiiskoi Federatsii [hereafter GARF], fond 102, opis' 17, ed. khr. 343, November 18, 1914, list 10 [hereafter f., op., l.].

8. V. P. Semennikov, *Monarkhiia pered krusheniem, 1914–1917* (Moscow: Gosudarstvennoe izdatel'stvo, 1927), p. 124. B. V. Shtiurmer is called Stürmer in Antti Kujala's Chapter 6. His career in Tver' is chronicled by Charles Timberlake in Chapter 2 of this collection.

9. *Krasnyi arkhiv,* (106 vols.; Moscow, 1922–1941) no. 2 (1929) pp. 150–151.

10. From 1914 to 1916, Empress Alexandra accused the union of seeking to take major credit for relief efforts in order to extract reforms once the fighting stopped. See A. L. Hynes, trans., *Letters of the Tsaritsa to the Tsar, 1914–1916* (London: John Lane, 1923), p. 167.

11. *Kratkii ocherk,* (106 vols.; Moscow, 1922–1941) p. 2.

12. *Izvestiia VZS,* Nos. 35–36, March 15–April 1, 1916, p. 26.

13. *Krasnyi arkhiv,* vol. 50–51, 1932, pp. 133–136.

14. *Izvestiia VZS,* no. 49, p. 154.

15. Polner, *Russian Local Government,* p. 83.

16. *Izvestiia VZS,* no. 49, October 15, 1916, p. 157.

17. Polner, *Russian Local Government,* p. 80.

18. *Vserossiisskii soiuz gorodov, Trudy ekonomicheskogo soveshchaniia 3–4 ianvaria 1916 goda,* p. 48.

19. *Krasnyi arkhiv,* vol. 52, 1932, p. 145.

20. *Vserossiiskaii soiuz gorodov, Trudy ekonomicheskogo soveshchaniia,* p. 69.

21. *Izvestiia VZS,* nos. 35–36, March 15–April 1, 1916, p. 25.

22. Semmenikov, *Monarkhiia pered krusheniem,* pp. 95–96.

23. "Soveshchanie gubernatorov v 1916 godu," *Krasnyi arkhiv,* vol. 33, part 2, p. 152.

24. Semmenikov, *Monarkhiia pered krusheniem,* pp. 144–145.

25. A. N. Iakhontov, "Tiazhelye dni," *Arkhiv russkoi revoliutsii,* vol. 18 (Berlin, 1926), p. 33.

26. See, for example, A. I. Sidorov, *Ekonomicheskoe polozhenie Rossii v gody pervoi mirovoi voiny* (Moscow, 1973).

27. One source for this account is Thomas Fallows, "Politics and the War Effort in Russia: The Union of Zemstvos and the Organization of Food Supply, 1914–1916," *Slavic Review,* vol. 37, no. 1 (1978) pp. 70–90.

28. *Izvestiia VZS,* no. 50, 1916, p. 100.

29. Naumov's memoirs are clear on this point. He notes that when he came into office in November 1915 there was no meat-provisioning plan for the army and that "only in the spring of 1916, due to the statistical and organizational endeavors of the zemstvos, were improvements made." See A. N. Naumov, *Iz utelevshikh vospominanii 1868–1917 g.* (New York, Izdanie A.K. Naumova O.A. Kusevitskoi, 1955), p. 471.

30. GARF, f. 102, op. 17, ed. khr. 343 (3c), v. 4, ll. 31–34.

31. *Izvestiia vserossiiskogo soiuza gorodov* [hereafter *Izvestiia VSG*], no. 33, 1916, pp. 220–227. Like its rural counterpart, the Union of Cities published a monthly journal that frequently ran to several hundred pages and contained lengthy articles on every phase of the wartime economy. A pud equals approximately 36 pounds.

32. *Izvestiia VZS,* no. 39, May 1, 1916, p. 2.

33. Ibid., no. 47, 1916, p. 2.

34. Michael Hamm, "Russia's Fourth State Duma: The Progressive Bloc," Ph. D. Diss., Indiana University, 1971, pp. 136–139.

35. N. N. Lapin, ed., "Progressivnyi blok v 1916–1917 gg.," *Krasnyi arkhiv,* vol. 52, 1932, pp. 189–194.

36. *Izvestiia VSG,* no. 33, 1916, p. 87.

37. As early as 1914, union doctors and statisticians had formed a clandestine body within the Moscow provincial zemstvo "to mobilize and unify the Third Element of the All-Russian Union of Zemstvos." See GARF, f. 102, op. 17, ed. khr. 343, t. 4, l. 305.

38. Ibid., ed. khr. 338, ll. 83–84.

39. Ibid., ed. khr. 343, t. 4, l. 99.

40. Ibid., l. 94.

41. Geoffrey Hosking, *The Awakening of the Soviet Union* (Cambridge: Harvard University Press, 1990), p. 75

Interregional Conflicts and the Collapse of Tsarism: The Real Reason for the Food Crisis in Russia After the Autumn of 1916

Kimitaka Matsuzato
Hokkaido University

Historians during the last twenty years have given little attention to the reasons for the collapse of the Russian Empire, one of the most important empires in history. In a sense, this is a natural result of the predominance of so-called revisionism in historical studies of Russia, according to which tsarism was structurally inviable because of its failure in nation-state building or because of insurmountable frictions in Russian society. However, this essentialist/ontologist understanding of tsarism's inviability does not release historians from the responsibility of analyzing the actual process of the collapse of tsarism. As for the Russian countryside on which this study focuses, with the exception of such rare studies as *The Politics of Rural Russia, 1905–1914*,[1] which overemphasizes the "polarization" and "crises" in rural politics on the eve of World War I, most agrarian studies confirm that the economic and political situation of the Russian peasantry prior to World War I was relatively favorable and, moreover, there was almost no peasant violence during the tsarist period of World War I.[2] Therefore, even convinced revisionists would hardly be surprised to find the testimony by I. F. Koshko, former Penza governor and an inspector of procurement activities for the Ministry of Agriculture on the eve of the February Revolution, that "the situation was far worse in 1905 [than at the beginning of 1917]."[3]

The February Revolution was a peculiar historical phenomenon. The small scale of the popular uprising might barely have caused the abdication of the Tsar, had there been the slightest political will among the ruling elites to defend the monarchy. The February Revolution cannot be attributed to the general revolutionary situation that commenced *after* February. Aware of this, some historians have directed attention to such court scandals as the Rasputin issue, which generated aversion among the ruling elites toward the imperial family and the Tsar.[4]

This study provides another version of a conjuncturist (anti-essentialist) approach to the February Revolution by seeking the reason for the urban food crisis after the autumn of 1916, that is, the prelude to the February Revolution.

If this urban food crisis was, as traditionally believed in historiography, caused by peasants' resistance to the government's procurement policy, the revisionists' argument can be partially justified, for it leads to the assertion that the socially and judicially segregated Russian peasants, unlike their German and French counterparts, could not understand the meaning of total war and, although the peasants themselves did not rebel until the February Revolution, they provided political fuel for urban discontent. Unfortunately for the revisionists, statistics of public grain procurement testify that the tempo of grain procurement was accelerated by the improvement of weather conditions in October 1916,[5] in addition to the grain levy introduced at the end of November by Minister of Agriculture A. A. Rittikh.[6] As a result, the Romanov dynasty collapsed, while the equivalent of 18,000 carloads of grain remained on sidetracks or in railroad storehouses in agrarian regions.[7]

This disarray in railroad transportation appears to have been the main reason for the urban food shortage. But this chapter purports to demonstrate that this railroad disarray was caused not by some technical or material limitations but by protectionist transport regulations imposed by local procurement organs, that is, zemstvos. In short, the tsarist regime collapsed because of interregional conflicts.

TOTAL WARS AND DECENTRALIZATION

Western studies of the Soviet war regime during World War II have countered the stereotype that total-war regimes can only be highly centralized. Sanford Lieberman was the first to break with this theory in 1983. Analyzing the evacuation of Soviet industry during World War II, he argued that an essential requisite for total-war regimes was not simple centralism but, rather, a combination of centralism with "operative leadership" that requires decentralized decision making. From this vantage, Lieberman evaluated positively the performance of Stalinist war efforts.[8]

Analyzing Soviet food policies during World War II, William Moskoff also highlighted the de facto decentralization of the Stalinist regime during the war. In his opinion, central planning could not totally organize a national economy even in peacetime. Rather, it was adept only at channeling resources "to areas that have been given priority status." During the war, therefore, central planning functioned mainly to allocate scarce food resources to the military. As for the civilian population, "a decision was made early in the war to decentralize production and distribution and to require the population explicitly to rely on local resources for most of its food." For this purpose, authorities could not but legalize private initiatives such as *kolkhoz* markets and garden agriculture to a scale considered inconceivable in the 1930s.[9]

The Soviet Home Front 1941–1945, by John Barber and Mark Harrison, presented a more general model of this de facto decentralization. During World War II immense new administrative tasks emerged, while on the other hand vast numbers of communists and administrators were mobilized for war efforts. As a result, a significant share of decision making was transferred to local leaders.[10] Moreover, not only in food administration, which Moskoff analyzed, but also in manufacturing, resources were funneled into strategic areas, while nonstrategic enterprises were required to be self-reliant. As a result, sideline production grew on an unprecedented scale: "[M]unitions and civilian engineering factories learnt to make their own construction brigades; the latter in turn learnt self-reliance in supply of building materials and tools."[11]

It is necessary to emphasize here that the foregoing discussions are related to the Stalinist war regime, which is supposed to have been much more centralized than the tsarist one.

According to George Yaney, despite Russians' inferiority complex with respect to the "organizational instrumentality" supposedly enjoyed by developed nations, modern organizations are distinguished by the fact that "statements of plan and policy do not determine the action of participants." Rather, "these apparent structures take their meaning from individual behavior as the participants use them to interact." Modern managerial activities are aimed mainly at coping "with the confusion that systems continually ferment." This is the theoretical basis on which Yaney analyzes food management in Berlin during World War I.[12] If his opinion is valid, then we should not be surprised at the success of the Soviet evacuation at the beginning of World War II despite the collapse of the central leadership.

I wish to add another dimension to the theory of de facto decentralization during total wars: the unavoidable conversion of existing peacetime institutions to war management. Historians of World War I have been caught up in the myth that "total war" was not foreseen in that conflict. On the basis of memoirs or statements referring to the first days of hostilities, historians have condemned the leaders of belligerent countries for optimistically thinking that the war would end by Christmas. Strangely, historians have not noticed that the war, which was expected to involve great powers and to last half a year ("until Christmas"), was recognized as an unprecedented war categorically different from wars in the previous centuries. It was natural that European nations did not fully know what total war would be like, but they did foresee that the coming war would be record-breaking in scale and cruelty. With this in mind, the key issue for European governments during their war preparations and in the initial stage of World War I was how to exploit existing institutions for military needs. This need for "conversion" contained a potential momentum toward decentralization.

This phenomenon is illustrated by Russia's food policy during World War I. On the eve of the war, two kinds of "social" grain procurement were in operation: public or cooperative collection of grain that had been established in agrarian provinces to protect peasants from exploitation by rural middlemen; and municipal grain procurement that occurred in times of famine. Wartime food management in Russia could rapidly and inexpensively be organized by converting these two social forms of grain collection. Enhancement of local food procurement, however, ipso facto hindered the emergence of centralized, well-coordinated food management. Russian wartime food administration not only absorbed regionalist tendencies inherent in prewar social grain procurement but also reinforced regionalist tendencies by entrusting local grain procurement institutions with some portion of state power—in particular, railway regulation. The irony of tsarist war management was that "in order to be militarized, it had to be decentralized."

WARTIME CONVERSION OF PUBLIC GRAIN COLLECTION

Devolution of Purchase, Receiving, and Shipment of Grain to Zemstvos

Public collection of agricultural products occurred not only in Russia but also in many other countries at a certain stage of development of agrarian capitalism. Public collection of agricultural products rested on the assumption that if collection and marketing of agricultural products were dominated by rural middlemen, peasants would be dependent on those middlemen, even with a significant development of other kinds of cooperative movements. Unfortunately, collection and marketing of agricultural products is a complicated sphere of endeavor that requires experience, information, intuition, and flexible organization. Lack of these qualities on the part of rural cooperators and intelligentsia usually turned attempts at "public collection" into "samurai commerce"—impractical, bureaucratic commerce. But during wartime the huge need of food for the military and other exigencies elevated the status of "samurai commerce." In Japan, for example, a system of state control of the rice market based on monopolistic agricultural cooperatives took shape during the Sino-Japanese War in the 1930s. A similar phenomenon appeared in Russia during World War I.

On the eve of the war, in contrast to market-oriented products such as flax and dairy products, public collection of grain was still regarded as risky by zemstvo-cooperative leaders. Yet it was in this period that various infrastructures for the public collection of grain were prepared: rural credit cooperatives, zemstvo district (*uchastkovye*) agronomists, and grain elevators built by the State Bank. In addition, even small experiments contributed to legitimizing the idea of public grain collection not only within zemstvo-cooperatives but also government circles.[13]

On August 1, 1914, the Council of Ministers decided to authorize A. V. Krivoshein, Chief of the Main Administration of Land Settlement and Agriculture (*Glavnoe upravlenie zemleustroistva i zemledeliia*) to purchase grain for the military, establish the principle of "direct purchases from grain producers," and mobilize zemstvos for this purpose. The Vice-Chief of the Main Land Settlement and Agriculture Administration, G. V. Glinka, was appointed Central Agent of Grain Purchase for the Army.[14] In most cases, the Main Agriculture Administration appointed chairmen of provincial zemstvo boards as Local Plenipotentiary Agents of Grain Purchase for the Army (*upolnomochennye po zakupke khleba dlia armii*: hereafter, Local Grain-Purchasing Agents for the Army).

Before long, it became apparent that, given the scale of the war, not only purchasing but also receiving (*priem*) grain and grain shipment to the front were beyond reach of the Ministry of War's existing logistic organization, the staff of which numbered only about 2,000 in the entire empire.[15] Therefore, these duties also were to be transferred to the control of Local Grain-Purchasing Agents for the Army, who in practice were frequently zemstvo leaders. Krivoshein's Instruction of August 11, 1914, authorizing military logistic officials to receive grain from the Local Grain-Purchasing Agents for the Army,[16] was virtually abolished as early as August 24.[17] At the beginning of September, D. S. Shuvaev, Chief of the Main Logistic Administration (*Glavnoe intendantskoe upravlenie*), ordered that logistic officials should be present at receiving locations "if possible." Thus logistic staff became merely receivers and distributors of grain at the front and lacked any authority to inspect the quality of the grain.[18]

In the prewar period, excessively strict quality standards for grain required by logistic organizations, coupled with their bureaucratic attitude toward agrarian interests, hindered public collection of grain from supplying the military; as a result only a handful of zemstvos participated in this activity.[19] During the war, devolution of grain-receiving duties to zemstvos facilitated agrarian interests in procurement operations but, on the other hand, caused disarray in railway transportation.

At the onset of the war, railway transportation to the front was incorporated into its ordinary (peacetime) regulation system headed by the Central Committee for the Regulation of Massive Transport of Freight by Railways (*Tsentral'nyi komitet po regulirovaniiu massovykh perevozok gruzov po zheleznym dorogam*: hereafter, the Central Railway Committee), attached to the Ministry of Transport and its local committees.[20] The following route of communication was to be established: first, grain was to be brought to the receiving commissions (*priemnye komissii*), organized, as a rule, near relatively large railway stations. Logistic officials, who were supposed to be part of the commissions, were to transmit information on supplies to the Main Logistic Administration. The Main Logistic Administration, in turn, was to convey information to the Department of Military Communication of the General Staff Office. This department then was to issue shipment orders to the Central Railway Committee, which was to transmit them through local committees and local railway administrations (branch offices) to each railway station. Upon receiving these orders, the stations were to ship grain toward the front.

Any break in the numerous links in this chain of communication would have disrupted the operative issue of shipment orders. But this problematic route of communication was precluded from operating at all because logistic officials, who were supposed to play the role of neurons in this system, were removed from it. As a result, the brain—the Main Logistic Administration and the Department of Military Communication—was severed from its sense organs—the receiving commissions—and could not issue adequate shipment orders.[21] Through trial and error during the autumn of 1914, the following route of communication was improvised: from receiving commissions to Local Grain-Purchasing Agents for the Army, from these agents to the Central Agent of Grain Purchase for the Army, Glinka, then to the Main Logistic Administration, and finally to the Department of Military Communication. Shipment orders were issued and transmitted according to the original scheme previously mentioned.[22] The communication route was thus relinked, but its complex tiers of stages became even more extreme.

To overcome these excessive multiple stages, on December 16, 1914, the Railway Department of the Ministry of Transport sent a circular to stationmasters. It demanded that decision making regarding shipment of grain to the front be concentrated in local railway administrations. This deprived Local Grain-Purchasing Agents for the Army of the authority to determine the destination of grain shipments. Shipment orders were to be distributed among the stations by local railway administrations, which were simultaneously to supply freight cars to each station according to the distribution of orders.[23] Since this circular only exacerbated the disorganization of grain shipment to the front and was harshly criticized by Local Grain-Purchasing Agents for the Army,[24] it was replaced with another system. In February 1915, a special commission comprised of representatives from Glinka, the Department of Military Communication, and the Railway Department was established in Petrograd by the Main Logistic Administration. All information about grain-receiving was channeled directly from the Local Grain-Purchasing Agents for the Army to this special commission, which in turn issued shipment orders directly to local railway administrations. In other words, the Central Railway Committee and its local committees were removed from the transmission of shipment orders.[25] Thus excessive multiple stages of communication were simplified and shipment of grain to the front proceeded more smoothly.

As a whole, the general tendency in railway reorganization during the first seven months of the war involved removing peacetime authorities (the Central Railway Committee and its local committees) from military transportation and entrusting substantial regulatory power to Local Grain-Purchasing Agents for the Army. Thus railway regulation was significantly decentralized. This trend was enthusiastically supported by the National Convention of Local Grain-Purchasing Agents for the Army, held in Petrograd July 1–3, 1915, which passed a resolution to develop "constant contact" between Local Grain-Purchasing Agents for the Army and local railway administrations.[26] Railway crises after the retreat of the Russian army from Galicia during the summer and autumn of 1915 modified this system to some extent,[27] but its basic structure was maintained until the October Revolution.

Compulsory Procurement and Fragmentation of the Grain Market

At the onset of the war, nearly a third of the territory of European Russia, which was declared the "territory for military operations," was separated from civilian administration and entrusted to the General Staff Headquarters. Within this territory, resources were mobilized by compulsory measures in contrast to the territory under the civilian government in which resource mobilization was purely commercial. At the beginning of 1915, however, food resources in the "territory of military operations" were nearly exhausted, while inflation made food procurement within the home front difficult. As a result, the Decree of February 17, 1915, allowed adoption of three kinds of compulsory measures for food procurement also within the home front: fixed prices (*tverdye tseny*), requisitions, and food embargoes from certain areas.[28]

Of the three compulsory measures, food embargoes directly intensified the autarkic (self-protective) tendency of local procurement organs, which, as stated above, were mainly zemstvos. Embargoes in particular hurt villages and townships (*volosti*) adjacent to provincial boundaries by rupturing their long-established commercial relations with neighboring areas belonging to other provinces. The newly created public distribution centers in county (*uezdnye*) seats were too distant from border villages. Aggrieved by this situation, the governor of Vladimir requested in January 1917 that imposition of embargoes be restricted to large-scale commercial trade and "small-scale purchases by the population themselves not be subject to embargoes."[29]

Interregional conflicts revolving around embargoes became particularly serious when administrative-territorial divisions significantly contradicted actual economic affinities. In November 1916, for example, the Executive Committee for the Struggle with the High Cost of Living in the city of Astrakhan' passed a resolution petitioning the authorities to modify the jurisdictional boundary of the regional food councils with neighboring Samara Province. The resolution related that the city of Astrakhan' was supplied with grain by the Astrakhan' railroad branch line, which emanated from the Riazan'-Uralsk line at Urbakh station in Novouzensk County in southern Samara Province. Although the entire territory attached to the Astrakhan' branch line was under the economic influence of the city of Astrakhan', the fact that Urbakh lay in Samara Province placed the branch line under the control of the Plenipotentiary Agent of the Chairman of the Special Council on Food (*upolnomochennyi predsedatelia Osobogo soveshchaniia po prodovol'stvennomu delu*)[30] for Samara Province. This individual was dismissing Astrakhaners' interests. The Executive Committee for the Struggle with the High Cost of Living demanded that the area around the Astrakhan' branch line be transferred to the jurisdiction of the contractor for civilian food purchase for Astrakhan' Province.[31] This resolution was aimed at benefiting the city of Astrakhan' since its grain purchases had often been hampered by embargoes issued by the Samara Grain-Purchasing Agent for the Army. In all probability, Astrakhaners wished to obtain purchasing freedom in the neighboring province by having the Urbakh area transferred to their jurisdiction.

Requisitions were originally aimed at regulating relations between grain dealers (or producers) and procurement organs, but not between regions. In addition, requisitioning was intended to intimidate, not

actually force, dealers or producers to sell food products. If they refused to sell, Local Grain-Purchasing Agents for the Army could compel the sale of grain at requisition prices, which were 15 percent less
than the ordinary fixed prices. But few people are so stubborn as to
incur willingly a 15 percent loss. Thus, in fact, the portion of grain obtained by requisitions during the first year of the procurement campaign (1914–1915) was only 1.1 percent of the total.[32]

During the second procurement year, however, a variant of requisitioning became popular among Local Grain-Purchasing Agents for
the Army who wished to paralyze activities of contractors for civilian
food purchase dispatched or hired by merchants or municipalities in
grain-consuming areas.[33] If the contractors bought grain at higher than
fixed prices, Local Grain-Purchasing Agents for the Army requisitioned
the grain at railway stations. The previous grain owners, that is, merchants or municipalities, then demanded that the Local Grain-Purchasing Agent for the Army who had seized the grain release it. The local
agent in turn acceded to such demands if he was able to find a surplus
after completing grain shipment to the front. Although buyers in consuming provinces had no guarantee of receiving the grain, they seldom
offered to settle their claims with cash. Since these claims were to be settled according to fixed prices, they would receive less than they had paid
if they had paid more than the fixed price. Moreover, even after settling,
they would have had no choice but to try the same process in another
agrarian province and there was little probability that another Local
Grain-Purchasing Agent for the Army would tolerate it. This version of
requisitioning was devised by Iu. V. Davydov, the Tambov Grain-Purchasing Agent who was chairman of the provincial zemstvo board during the first procurement year.[34] Chief Agent of Grain Purchase for the
Army, Glinka, recommended it to all Local Grain-Purchasing Agents
for the Army in the second procurement year.

Remarkably, food embargoes contributed more to improving grain
procurement from February to June 1915, than requisitioning. As described above, the requisitioning that actually began to be adopted in the
second procurement year, in contrast to the original version of requisitioning, aimed to paralyze grain purchasing by contractors of consuming
regions. In other words, not only embargoes but also requisitioning was
targeted at regulating interregional commerce in order to encourage

procurement by Local Grain-Purchasing Agents. Requisitioning thus strengthened regionalist tendencies.

At a glance, fixed prices seemed to have nothing to do with zemstvo regionalism. However, they also damaged natural market relations because their geographic jurisdictions could only be administrative territories, that is, provinces or counties. A conference of representatives of commodity exchange committees (*birzhevye komitety*) of the Volga-Kama region, held in Rybinsk in February 1916 (hereafter, the Rybinsk Conference), criticized this situation, citing the abnormal relationship between Samara and Saratov Provinces. According to a report presented at the conference, the normal flow of the *russkaia* strain of wheat (Samara to Saratov or east to west) had been disrupted because the Special Council on Food established for this strain a fixed price common for both provinces. As a result, if a dealer had carried the russkaia wheat from the hinterlands of Samara Province to Saratov City and then faced the Saratov Grain-Purchasing Agent's demand for requisition, he would have suffered a great loss.[35]

As the Special Council on Food became more skillful at price regulation, inequities of this sort became rare, but problems caused by the basic structure of Russia's wartime food management based on administrative-territorial demarcations were, by nature, insurmountable. The Plenipotentiary Agent of the Chairman of the Special Council on Food for Kiev Province, who was the chairman of the provincial zemstvo board, presented a memorandum to the Minister of Agriculture in November 1916, calculating (on the basis of prewar railway statistics) that the city of Kiev had been supplied with only 38.4 percent of its food from within the province. For the remainder of its food, Kiev turned to neighboring provinces. Only fifty-eight stations in Kiev Province dispatching food supplied freight to the city of Kiev, whereas sixty stations in Poltava Province did so, forty-one in Podoliia Province did so, and twenty-six in Chernigov Province did so. Given this interprovincial dependency, the Kiev Agent of the Chairman of the Special Council on Food concluded that "giving each Plenipotentiary Agent the authority to distribute products for each province is creating serious obstacles to supplying each consuming center." The Kiev Agent of the Special Council on Food proposed that a new official called "Broad-Area Plenipotentiary Agent" be created. This official would have sufficiently strong authority to coordinate the activities of several neighboring Agents of the Special Council on Food.[36] The proposal highlighted the hardships the city of Kiev, which, as one of the largest consuming centers in Russia, was suffering due to increasingly regionalist tendencies on the part of neighboring Grain-Purchasing Agents for the Army. It seems unlikely, however, that the proposed "Broad-Area Plenipotentiary Agents" could have rectified the situation, for the system of provincial Grain-Purchasing Agents for the Army and Agents of the Special Council on Food could function more or less effectively precisely because it was organized on the basis of zemstvo institutions.

Ironically, the contradictions between administrative units and real economic alignments made the concept of "economic affinity" (*ekonomicheskoe tiagotenie*) quite popular among local leaders during World War I. This concept was retained by the Soviet government as a criterion for its administrative-territorial division.

The Failure of the Corporatist Mobilization of Commerce

Beginning in June 1915, the last month of the first procurement year, the grain procured by Local Grain-Purchasing Agents for the Army began to be released not only to the military but also to the civilian population. As a result, procurement norms became almost unlimited. It appeared impossible to purchase such an amount of grain only through public collection. The Ministry of Agriculture (reorganized from the Main Administration of Land Settlement and Agriculture in November 1915) began to demand that Local Grain-Purchasing Agents for the Army mobilize commercial sectors of their provinces.[37] However, irritated by the obstacles erected by Local Grain-Purchasing Agents for the Army to municipal grain-purchasing, some leaders of the All-Russian Union of Cities[38] began to seek an alternative method of nationwide food management, while also considering complaints from grain dealers and commodity exchange committees.

Thus, a "popular front" strategy for social organizations (agrarian, urban, and commercial) was promulgated by leaders of the All-Russian Union of Cities at the Second Convention of the War Industries Committees (February 26–29, 1916)[39] and given organizational formulation at the Fourth Convention of the All-Russian Union of Cities (March 12–14).[40] Merchants responded to this call at the Second Extraordinary

Congress of Representatives of Commodity and Agriculture Exchanges (April 24–28). A public resolution adopted by this extraordinary congress proclaimed that "the absence of a solid organization of merchants" was one reason for the high cost of living, and elected three delegates to the Central Committee of proposed "United Social Organizations."[41] However, a private missive sent by V. I. Timiriazev, chairman of the executive board of the congress, to a high official of the Ministry of Agriculture revealed that the debate held at this congress was not constructive. Moreover, although the congress opened with more than 300 representatives present, this number dwindled to only thirty-seven at the time of election of delegates to the Central Committee of the United Social Organizations. Timiriazev lamented that "the mountains have brought forth a mouse."[42] At the beginning of July 1916, a Central Committee of the United Social Organizations was established under the aegis of the All-Russian Union of Cities[43] but this committee was unable to organize even its executive and local organs.

Another form of "commercial mobilization," the Central Bureau of Flour Millers, was established in June 1916. The initiators of this institution were Samara millers, although its final plan was deliberated in Petrograd. A convention of millers of the Volga region held in Samara April 16–17, 1916, diverged from the hard-line criticism of the existing grain-procurement system voiced two months earlier in the Rybinsk Conference and advocated instead that millers be corporatively organized.[44] Why the millers at Samara adopted such a "statist" orientation—which was exceptional in Russian commercial circles—is unknown. This innovativeness might have been fermented by experiments of wartime state capitalism carried out under Samara Grain-Purchasing Agent for the Army V. N. Bashkirov, chairman of the Samara Commodity Exchange Committee, who mobilized both cooperative and commercial sectors by utilizing the grain elevators of the State Bank.

In any case, soon after its establishment, the Central Bureau of Flour Millers was faced with two questions: how to simplify grain classification, that is, how to reduce the number of strains and grades of grain; and how to organize local branches of the bureau. With regard to the latter issue, to give each local branch jurisdiction over a broad region and multiple functions might be most tolerant of merchant corporatism. On the contrary, if branches were organized according to provincial demarcations and their functions confined to the distribution of orders for flour, they might serve as hardly more than factotums for Local Grain-Purchasing Agents for the Army. The Central Bureau could not resolve these questions by itself; hence it placed them on the agenda for the All-Russian Congress of Flour Millers held on August 10, 1916. The congress demonstrated that the innovativeness exhibited at Samara was an exception among Russian flour millers. Delegates supported the three-grade classification of flour (only because three was the most numerous among various proposals) and refused even to deliberate the question of local branches of the bureau.[45]

Unfortunately, these developments confirmed the conventional view that Russian merchants were too avaricious to assume civic responsibility and adopt a national perspective, even during war. Thus it appeared that grain dealers and millers could be mobilized only individually (not corporatively) by each Local Grain-Purchasing Agent for the Army in each province. As a result, during the third procurement year (1916–1917) Local Grain-Purchasing Agents were authorized to regulate the flour-milling industry. They were required to supervise fixed price classifications for flour, to mediate between mills and Agents of the Special Council on Food, to monitor the productivity of mills, to supply mills with grain and fuel, and to review the monthly reports submitted by millers.[46] This method of provincial mobilization of millers generated such a regionalist tendency that Grain-Purchasing Agents for the Army often tried to fulfill supply norms for other provinces as much as possible in flour, rather than in grain, in order to make the milling industry of their own provinces work at full force.[47] These measures, in turn, hampered the rational use of national milling potential.

As a whole, attempts at converting public collection of grain into government procurement strengthened the regionalist tendencies of the Local Grain-Purchasing Agents for the Army, who in practice were often zemstvo leaders. Regionalism became more pronounced by entrusting Local Grain-Purchasing Agents for the Army with railway regulation, granting zemstvos the right to employ compulsory measures, and allowing each Local Grain-Purchasing Agent for the Army to mobilize local commercial sectors.

THE CONVERSION OF MUNICIPAL FOOD PURCHASING

Statutory Prices, Purchases, and Railway Regulation

In regard to famine relief in urban areas, prewar Russian legislation pre-scribed only administrative price control of meat and grain by city mu-nicipalities.[48] The ceiling on consumer prices was called the *taksa* or Table of Statutory Prices. The exigencies of World War I required en-larging the number of items controlled by the Table of Prices. This was done by relying upon the authority that governors or military district commanders were allocated under the provisions of "emergency laws." Rural Russia had a system of communal grain storage, as was the case with many early modern countries. In both urban and rural areas, how-ever, famine relief became significantly commercialized before the fam-ine of 1891; municipal food purchases and distribution proved to be the main weapon in the fight against famine.[49] Unfortunately, fighting famine through municipal food purchases led to competition among municipalities and price rises that in turn made the consequences of famines more serious. This was one reason why zemstvos, which were condemned by the Ministry of Internal Affairs for being unable to co-ordinate their activities,[50] were deprived in 1901 of the authority to su-pervise communal grain storage,[51] although commercial measures for famine relief were still left in their hands.[52] World War I did not dimin-ish interregional competition in grain procurement but, rather, added a new aspect to it: competition for scarce transportation resources. In view of this, it was hardly surprising that food-purchasing municipali-ties and zemstvos demanded that the government create a nationwide body to coordinate railway transportation, a body that, moreover, would reflect their own priorities regarding each separate shipment. Without such a system food shipments might rot at railway sidetracks in agricultural regions.

The desire of zemstvos and cities to access railway regulation had an-other motive: by exploiting this authority, they could control merchants within their jurisdictions. If zemstvos and cities monopolized access to railway regulations, merchants would have no other recourse but to ask these bodies to include their freight in the lists for preferential shipment. Zemstvos and cities, in return for these favors, could compel merchants to observe statutory prices and other commercial regulations.

Among the three methods of local food management, that of imposing statutory prices was the most popular in the early stage of the war. In most cases, the the statutory prices were calculated by municipal food organs and sanctioned by the provincial governor or the military district commander concerned.[53] Before long, however, the flaws in this method became apparent. Since statutory prices were not geographically coordinated, goods "escaped" from cities or counties where authorities had introduced strict (and low) statutory prices. These authorities then had no alternative but to raise statutory prices to attract goods. Moreover, statutory prices did not correspond to the actual availability of regulated commodities. Thus there was no guarantee that the population could obtain commodities at statutory prices.[54]

Since municipal food purchases, in contrast to the imposition of statutory prices, required money and specialized staff, they developed relatively slowly. According to a questionnaire carried out by the All-Russian Union of Cities in May–June 1915, of 214 cities responding, 65 (30.4 percent) were engaged in municipal purchasing and 34 (15.4 percent) were preparing to do so. In November–December of the same year, of 94 cities responding, 62 (65.9 percent) were engaged in municipal purchasing and 8 (8.5 percent) were about to.[55]

The government provided two kinds of financial assistance for local food purchases. Municipalities were granted loans and guarantees to cover debts they might incur to private banks. Zemstvos were treated differently from cities. They were allowed to request financial aid from the Imperial Food Capital (the central financial fund of the communal grain storage system under the jurisdiction of the Ministry of Internal Affairs) when they prepared to purchase grain. When zemstvos purchased sugar, salt, meat, and other nongrain foodstuffs, they were permitted to ask for financial aid only from the Wartime Fund (which was under the jurisdiction of the Council of Ministers), as was the case with municipalities. The zemstvos that had been financed on the eve of the war from the Imperial Food Capital for their fodder campaigns of 1914 repeatedly submitted petitions for extension each time the payment deadline approached, thus virtually transforming this fund into permanently circulating capital for wartime food procurement.[56]

In October 1915, the Council of Ministers approved the allocation of 30 million rubles for subsidizing municipal food procurement. By

February 17, 1916, the Special Council on Food had lent 15,620,000 rubles and guaranteed municipal debts of 2,770,000 rubles.[57] Assuming that the average price of rye grain throughout this period was 1.2 rubles per pud and all the released funds were expended on rye, it would appear that 15,000,000 puds (about 250,000 tons) of rye could be bought with government funds. Concomitantly, from August 1915 to January 1916 the government released 4,680,000 puds (about 77,000 tons) of grain from storage facilities of the Local Grain-Purchasing Agents for the Army to municipalities.[58] Thus, if we accept the foregoing calculations, the relative amount of the government's monetary aid to zemstvos and cities was about *three times* more than the direct release of grain to the localities.

In 1916, recognizing the danger of concurrent purchases by zemstvo and city authorities, the Special Council on Food began to assume a cautious attitude toward monetary aid. This caution, however, was only related to loans to municipalities, the total of which increased only slightly from the already cited 15,620,000 rubles lent before February 17 to 18,080,000 rubles lent during the whole period until May 17, 1916. In contrast, guarantees for municipal debts increased astronomically from the already cited 2,770,000 rubles (before February 17) to 36,950,000 rubles (prior to May 17).[59] If we combine the amount of state guarantees and loans, total government monetary aid to municipalities during this period was 55,030,000 rubles. Assuming that the average price of rye grain throughout the period was 1.3 rubles per pud and that all the released money was spent for rye, 42,000,000 puds (about 690,000 tons) of rye could be bought on the basis of this aid. Meanwhile, direct release of grain from Local Grain-Purchasing Agents' storage facilities to municipalities between August 1915 and May 17, 1916 (except for a short unknown period from February 1 to 17, 1916), totaled 6,010,000 puds (about 98,000 tons).[60] Thus, despite the change in government policy toward monetary aid, the gap between monetary aid and direct release of grain increased from three times to nearly *seven times* during the period.

The main form of government assistance to municipal food procurement agencies was to disburse money and rely on local authorities to procure grain by themselves. Direct release of grain from Grain-Purchasing Agents' reserves played only a subordinate role. This tendency increased with the passage of time, although the government realized the dangers of passively relying on municipal food purchasing.

Railway Regulation and Local Food Organs

The development of local food procurement organs in wartime Russia can be divided into three periods: the spring of 1915, when the Central Food Committee was introduced; the autumn of 1915, when the provincial and county food councils were established and Plenipotentiary Agents of the Chairman of the Council on Food were appointed; and the spring of 1916, when the introduction of the Permit System for Preferential Transport prompted the formation of small-area (*raionnye*) food councils.

The Central Food Committee, the first central food organ in Russia during World War I, was established at the end of March 1915 under the chairmanship of Minister of Commerce and Industry V. N. Shakhovskoi.[61] Although previous studies have given a negative evaluation to this institution's performance,[62] we should not ignore the fact that the Central Food Committee played an important role in ironing out interregional and civil-military frictions,[63] which had become extreme after the promulgation of the Decree of February 17, 1915. Moreover, the Central Food Committee began to deliberate numerous policies and projects, subsequently realized several months later by the Special Council on Food.[64] Most important, a prototype of local railway regulation in wartime took shape under the Central Food Committee: the committee proposed that provincial governors convene meetings of municipal representatives, collect demands for preferential shipment, and using these materials, enter into negotiations with Local Committees for Railway Regulations.[65] With this in mind, a circular sent on April 30 by the Minister of Internal Affairs ordered governors to establish provincial food committees under their chairmanship.[66] In reality, provincial committees were not organized in most provinces until the abolition of the Central Food Committee in August 1915, but nevertheless railway regulation and the formation of local food institutions were closely connected from the very beginning.

The Central Food Committee and its provincial committees were abolished when the Special Council on Food was established by the Law of August 17, 1915. New local food organs, however, were not introduced except that the special mayors (*gradonachal'niki*) of the two capitals were appointed as Agents of the Chairman of the Special Council. As the legal provisions in the Law of August 17 regarding Agents of the Chairman of the Special Council on Food and local food councils were too brief and vague, it was necessary to wait for the Provision on Agents of the Chairman of the Special Council on Food, approved by the Tsar on October 25.[67] From then to November, these agents were appointed in nearly all regions of the empire.

In most agrarian/zemstvo provinces, the existing Local Grain-Purchasing Agents for the Army were appointed as Agents of the Chairman of the Special Council on Food, since the Ministry of Agriculture intended to organize the latter institutions promptly and inexpensively by converting the former institutions.[68] As a result, a "monolithic zemstvo system" was established in sixteen of thirty agrarian/zemstvo provinces of European Russia. If we add three members of the State Duma and the State Council who were serving as Grain-Purchasing Agents for the Army and were appointed as Agents of the Chairman of the Special Council on Food, a "monolithic system of social representatives" was established in nineteen of thirty grain-*producing* provinces, while governors, appointed by the Tsar and representing the government, were designated Agents of the Special Council on Food in only nine of these same provinces. In contrast, in most grain-*consuming* provinces of European Russia, governors were appointed as Agents of the Chairman of the Special Council on Food. The only exceptions were Moscow, Kostroma, and Olonets Provinces.[69] This organizational structure is illustrated in Figure 9–1.

The Provision on Agents of the Chairman of the Special Council on Food was prepared by the Commission for the Struggle with the High Cost of Living, a subcommittee of the Special Council on Food, amid a tense atmosphere caused by railway crises after the retreat from Galicia and by the flood into Petrograd of innumerable petitions for preferential shipment. As a result of this critical situation the provision had two, potentially contradictory, purposes. It was to incorporate municipal food purchasing into the national food administration and also to forestall competitive food purchasing. To facilitate the incorporation of municipal food purchasing, the provision authorized Agents of the Chairman of the Special Food Council to "enter into negotiations with organs of the

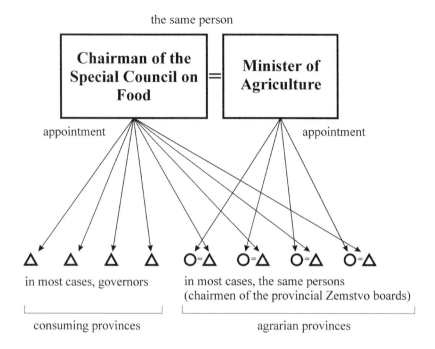

○   Grain-Purchasing Agent for the Army
△   Agent of the Chairman of the Special Council on Food

FIGURE 9-1   The Structure of the Wartime Food Institutions in Russia

Ministry of Transport" and to "demand urgent transport" from railway administrations. These articles provoked a furious protest from the Ministry of Transport, which regarded the provision as "nothing but the establishment of another authority [controlling railway transportation] along with the Ministry of Transport."[70]

In February 1915, as previously noted, significant authority to regulate railway transportation to the front was granted to Local Grain-Purchasing Agents for the Army—frequently zemstvo leaders. In addition, that October, the power of Agents of the Chairman of the Special Council on Food to regulate food transportation destined for the civilian population began to be consolidated. Grain-consuming provinces became eager to have their own Agents of the Chairman of the

Special Food Council authorized to decide the question of preferential shipment. An extraordinary provincial zemstvo assembly of Moscow Province resolved in October 1915 that only the appointment of an Agent of the Chairman of the Special Council on Food to Moscow Province could enable Muscovites "to utilize the entire solid and powerful food-transport apparatus" because only such an institution as the Special Council on Food could improve the food supply to Moscow "by directing its authority and power mainly toward the solution of transport problems."[71]

Although the Provision on Agents of the Chairman of the Special Council on Food contained only prescripts for "provincial, regional (*oblast'*), and city" food councils, county food councils also began to be established. It was impossible for Agents of the Chairman of the Special Council on Food to receive petitions for preferential shipment directly from numerous dealers and public food organs in their provinces. Simultaneously, county zemstvos and cities needed to establish county food councils in charge of collecting those petitions and distributing commodities thus obtained.[72]

In Volyn' Province, which was particularly exhausted because of its geographical proximity to the front, the provincial zemstvo board convened a food conference attended by mayors and chairmen of county zemstvo boards in September 1915, before the province had its Agent of the Chairman of the Special Council on Food. This conference resolved that each city and county zemstvo should establish its own food councils to calculate the necessary number of freight cars, negotiate this matter with government organs, distribute goods thus obtained among cooperatives and merchants of their own locales, and supervise their fair trade and sale.[73] We can envision a picture in which the basic framework for municipal food management ("to supervise fair trade by controlling preferential shipment") was being absorbed into the system of local food councils, which would be integrated into a national hierarchy a few months later by the appointment of Agents of the Chairman of the Special Council on Food.

In Poltava Province, because of its abundant food resources, county food councils were not introduced until April 1916. The session of the provincial food council that resolved to establish county food councils also requested that the Local Committees for Railway Regulation

should issue shipment orders "only in response to the petitions presented by the county food councils."[74] The food council of Kremenchug
County (southern Poltava Province) was convened eight times during
the two months following its establishment on April 14. Most of the deliberations of this council were concerned with permits to transport
commodities into or out of the county. The council, "in most cases,"
prohibited the outflow of commodities because "the data collected by
our council indicate that permission for the export of the goods out of
our county will result in shortages." On the other hand, there were cases where the council rejected requests for freight cars to import goods
on the grounds that inventories of these goods in the county seemed to
be adequate. One member of the council noted in self-congratulatory
fashion that the council paid attention not only to the "interest of the
local population" but also to the "national interest" in using freight
cars.[75] However, the Kremenchug experience demonstrates how the
organizational policy of allowing county food councils to exert control
over local railways made the front line of regionalism proceed forward
from provinces to counties.

   Despite resistance on the part of the Ministry of Transport, newly
appointed contractors for civilian food purchase steadily implemented
direct control over railway transportation, employing such methods as
deliberating on stationmasters' daily (or weekly) reports and monitoring arrivals and departures of freight cars with the help of zemstvo statistical organs.[76] Generally, the statistics–obsessed zemstvos (for
example, those in Moscow, Nizhegorod, and Samara) were also eager
to initiate direct control over railways. Simultaneously, technocrats in
the Special Council on Food prepared a plan to overcome weaknesses
in existing municipal food management, in particular, statutory prices.
This plan was summarized in a pamphlet entitled "The Current Situation of Statutory Prices in Russia and Measures for Their Normaliza-
tion," published by the secretariat of the Special Council in December
1915. This pamphlet reiterated criticism voiced by municipal activists
that "statutory prices" were neither geographically integrated nor supported by actual supplies of food. To overcome these problems, the
pamphlet stipulated that "transport regulation should be concentrated
in the hands of local contractors for civilian food purchase."[77] Referring
to such local experiences as those in Volnynia Province, the pamphlet

proposed the following system: each consuming area would calculate minimum supply levels and be assigned areas within which to conduct its procurement operations. Transport plans (deliberated with the consent of the Ministry of Transport) should aim at making optimum use of national transport capacity. Contractors for civilian food purchase should monopolize the authority to decide to whom to assign rights for preferential shipment and how to distribute goods through preferential means. Permits for preferential shipment were to be granted only to those who agreed with the newly determined statutory prices in accordance with the actual cost of the goods in the regions where they were produced.[78]

This ambitious plan met with resistance even in the Special Council on Food, the central authority for the contractors. The majority of its members were wary of excessively strengthening state regulations over the economy. Only uncompromising support of the plan on the part of the council chair, Minister of Agriculture A. N. Naumov, and Vice-Minister G. V. Glinka enabled it to be published as the ordinance of the Ministry of Agriculture on February 12, 1916.[79] According to this ordinance, local contractors for civilian food purchase had complete authority to permit preferential shipment. As a result all merchants, cooperatives, and municipalities procuring food were placed under the control of the local contractors for civilian food purchase. This was the first purpose of the ordinance. A second was to systematize statutory prices geographically by combining three elements of public food policy: fixed prices for government procurement in agricultural regions, railway regulation, and statutory prices in consuming areas. A third purpose of the ordinance was to shift the main style of railway regulation from "arbitrary" embargoes to the "more organic" Permit System of Preferential Shipment. To what extent were these purposes realized?

As for the first purpose, freight transport for the civilian population was actually normalized to some extent after the promulgation of the ordinance on February 12, 1916, and this relatively favorable situation continued until the summer when the regionalist tendencies of Local Grain-Purchasing Agents for the Army intensified.[80] On the other hand, precisely because the permit system made local contractors for civilian food purchase the keystone of railway control, it soon became apparent that they did not always have adequate information about transportation, demand, and supply. Local contractors for civilian food purchase often issued permits, the total of which exceeded the total transport capacity of the railway concerned. In other dishonorable cases, since unfulfilled permits for preferential shipment constantly accumulated, the contractors voided them, questioning the municipalities as to how urgently they needed each freight shipment, and issued new, stricter permits.[81]

Recognizing that local food councils lacked sufficient information, in his circular of April 4, 1916, Minister of Agriculture A. N. Naumov suggested that local food councils introduce "organizations" that would "stand alongside the population and manifest a social character" to supervise dealers who had enjoyed preferential shipment. In Naumov's opinion, without such organizations the permit system was "not only ineffective but also in danger of leading transport into unnecessary disorder."[82] Thus the new public food system that emerged in the spring of 1916 was comprised of three elements: the permit system for preferential shipment, local food councils' domination over transport information, and the introduction of small-area (raionnye) food organs with "a social character."

Since small-area food councils were organized according to "economic gravities" of large railroad stations, they did not always enter into hierarchical subordination to county food councils. Rather, there appeared three general patterns in the formation of county and small-area food councils: (1) food councils with a jurisdiction including an entire county (county councils in the true sense); (2) food councils organized in one part of a county; and (3) food councils with jurisdictions straddling county boundaries. Map 9–1 shows the approximate jurisdictions of county and small-area food councils organized in Tver' Province in the spring of 1916. Remarkably, this map shows the development of new economic centers outside county seats. Nearly all of these newly developing centers (except for Smerdyn) were situated at junctions of railway or river transport. It should be added that all of them subsequently developed into the raion seats in the Soviet era, although Tordom now belongs to Moscow oblast' and Smerdyn has changed its name to Lesnoe. Thus wartime food management brought a new concept of "economic affinity" into the tsarist regionalization policies that had been, as with any autocratic state, purely demographic.[83]

Combining railway regulation with supervision over commerce enjoyed modest success. In contrast, the second purpose of the ordinance

MAP 9-1 Tver' Province

of February 12, 1916, that is, geographical systematization of statutory prices, ended in a miserable failure. Fair prices in consuming regions could not be calculated by the simple addition suggested in this ordinance ("costs of procurement and transportation plus a fair profit for merchants"), except for products with a very simple geographic marketing structure such as sugar and salt. As for grain, very few municipalities, complying with the ordinance, reexamined their statutory prices. On the contrary, many of them began to argue that "if we have gained leverage on actual supply (the permit system), why are statutory prices necessary?" In Ufa Province, for example, nearly all county seats requested the abolition of statutory prices for various commodities, despite resistance from the Ufa governor.[84]

As for the third purpose of the ordinance of February 12, 1916, that is, systematization of railway regulation, it is true that after its promulgation, the Ministry of Agriculture and the Special Council on Food began to strictly investigate the imposition of embargoes by local authorities. Such scrutiny, however, could not be consistent because during the spring of 1916 competitive municipal food purchasing gained momentum. Due to guarantees on shipment of goods procured by municipalities, rivalry between Local Grain-Purchasing Agents for the Army and food-purchasing municipalities intensified even further. In addition, there were two specific reasons for embargo-frenzy in this period. The first was introduction of a levy on livestock and meat. Generally, levies determine the total quantity of a resource in each region and commandeer a certain portion of it. This usually leads local authorities to restrict commercial outflow of the resource. Additionally, there was danger that statistical surveys of livestock as a preparation for commandeering would prompt peasants into hasty sale or illegal export of livestock. For this reason as well, embargoes of livestock were necessary.

The second reason for embargo mania in the spring of 1916 was the flour-milling crisis in the mid-Volga region during the preceding winter. Because of this crisis, the responsibility to supply central Russia with flour was shifted to the Left-Bank Ukraine.[85] Consequently, various embargoes imposed on the Odessa Military District were lifted, and nearly 210,000 tons of grain and flour immediately flowed out of the district. As a result, according to a telegram sent by S. N. Gerbel', Grain-Purchasing Agent for the Army in the military district, "a critical situation for the army and the population" was developing.[86] Moreover, during the same spring, the provincial Grain-Purchasing Agents for the Army from the Odessa Military District also were burdened with the duty of procuring food for coal miners of the Donets Basin. This measure further tempted the Local Grain-Purchasing Agents for the Army to declare embargoes.

The Ministry of Agriculture criticized both kinds of embargo. In a telegram sent on March 8 to governor of Viatka Province, who demanded an embargo on livestock from the province as a prerequisite for complying with the levy of livestock from the province, Vice-Minister Glinka suggested that the governor should rely, in lieu of embargoes, upon "more substantial and organic measures such as purposeful organization of private commerce combined with the permit system for food transportation, overall assistance to cooperatives, and massive food purchases by cities and zemstvos."[87] A circular sent out by Naumov on

April 4 emphasized that "burdening zemstvos with the responsibility for levies of livestock is not meant to legitimize embargoes by zemstvos,"[88,] [89] although this circular was met with a storm of protest from zemstvos. As for the request for embargoes by Local Grain-Purchasing Agents for the Army from the Odessa Military District, Glinka presented the following argument in his telegram on March 25 addressed to District Grain-Purchasing Agent Gerbel':

> Under such conditions [political instability in central Russia, complete embargoes from your military district can be tolerated only when all the wheat and flour have been purchased by our organization. Considering, however, the abundance of wheat in south Russia, despite strenuous efforts by our plenipotentiary agents, such a result cannot be expected. In addition, the very petitions requesting export of grain testify the existence of a large surplus. . . . Although plenipotentiary agents expressed their readiness to bear the supply for regions suffering from deficits in order to eliminate competitive purchases, it has hitherto been the usual case that plenipotentiary agents reject demands to supply cities on the grounds that it is difficult for them to even fulfill procurement orders for the military. Thus, it is no other than Local Grain-Purchasing Agents for the Army that are creating the inevitability for cities to buy grain through private merchants and to struggle to carry it out.[90]

This telegram reveals that the nature of the disagreement between the Ministry of Agriculture and Local Grain-Purchasing Agents for the Army can be expressed with the proverbial question, which came first, the chicken or the egg? Local Grain-Purchasing Agents for the Army wished, before everything else, to monopolize their own provincial grain market by means of embargoes. If they found extra grain after fulfilling supply norms for the military, they might consider somehow helping consuming provinces. Glinka, on the contrary, argued that the autarky of agrarian provinces could be tolerated only if each Grain-Purchasing Agent was already a monopolist, having bought a sufficient amount of grain to feed not only the military but also the population of food-consuming provinces. Since such a situation had not been realized, in Glinka's opinion, concurrent purchases by agents of consuming provinces should not be prohibited. Thus, the ordinance of

February 12, 1916, could not restrain Local Grain-Purchasing Agents for the army from invoking food embargoes.

Mobilization of Zemstvo Statistics

It was hardly surprising that the government tried to use zemstvo statistics, which had been praised as among the most comprehensive statistics in the world, for military purposes. Zemstvos also found merit in being useful to the government. Wartime conditions—such as drastic decrease in labor power and livestock herds, reduction of sown areas, and changes in market conditions due to Russia's isolation from the world market—devalued prewar statistical bases and made it difficult to correct them by current (*tekushchie*) surveys.[91] Moreover, current surveys also became difficult due to the decline in the number of correspondents after the outbreak of the war.[92]

Zemstvos needed to carry out another general agricultural survey, the budget for which could only be obtained through cooperation with the government. The need for a general agricultural survey became widely recognized within zemstvo circles in the autumn of 1915, when a possible reduction in sown areas in the coming spring was a matter of serious concern.[93] Until the end of 1915, however, the Special Council on Food used zemstvo statistical institutions only for comparatively simple surveys such as inventory and current railway statistics. This passive approach was abandoned in January 1916 when the Special Council decided to introduce a levy on livestock.

In prewar Russia, meat diets were limited to festival days, and the annual per capita consumption of meat in rural areas was only about five kilograms. The annual percentage of cattle slaughtered amounted to only 11.5 percent in Russia, as contrasted with 20 percent in Australia or Argentina. The main purpose of Russian stockbreeding was expressed as "manure and dairying in the north and draft cattle in the south."[94] Between the onset of the war and October 1915, however, European Russia had lost almost a fourth of its livestock. The total of all livestock decreased from about 40 million to about 31 million head because of military demands, increase in meat diets in rural areas, bad fodder harvest in 1914, and the massive slaughter of livestock during the retreat from Galicia.[95]

In contrast to grain, which was procured on the principle of public collection from the beginning of the war, meat and livestock were purchased by contractors. To fulfill the procurement norms of 4 million head of livestock in 1916[96] without unduly harming Russian agriculture, a new method of obtaining livestock was needed. The Special Council on Food decided on January 25, 1916, to entrust the levy in livestock to zemstvos, which were regarded as well versed in local economies.[97] For the same reason, the Special Council also decided to conduct a nationwide survey of livestock by mobilizing zemstvo statistical staff. Since livestock was a key factor in agriculture, data on the existing number of livestock alone were obviously insufficient as a basis for reasonable procurement norms. The Special Council on Food hence decided on March 1 to conduct a nationwide survey of food reserves and sown areas after the projected livestock survey.[98] However, a conference of statisticians organized by the All-Russian Union of Zemstvos and Cities on March 5–8 resolved that the livestock survey should be conducted simultaneously with other agricultural surveys. This proposal was supported by a conference of the All-Russian Zemstvo Union held on March 14, as well as by a number of zemstvo assemblies.[99] The Minister of Agriculture finally issued an ordinance on April 3 for a comprehensive agricultural survey of labor power, livestock, sown areas, and food and fodder reserves.[100] Thus, attempts to mobilize zemstvos for the livestock levy resulted in the all-Russian agricultural survey, which was unprecedented in Russian history.

The government's reliance on zemstvo statistics gave zemstvos an opportunity to outshine the government. As early as May 1915, the Moscow provincial zemstvo board had remarked on the need for a nationwide survey of sown areas and harvest volumes to provide a statistical basis for food management. At that time, however, this suggestion was rejected by Krivoshein, Chief of the Main Administration of Land Settlement and Agriculture.[101] A year later, implementation of the all-Russian agricultural survey convinced zemstvos that they were more skillful than the government at statistical surveys.[102] Most conflicts between the center and regions during the war were affected by varying interpretations of statistical data. Contractors for civilian food purchase from consuming provinces were inclined to overestimate their food requirements to receive as many supply orders as possible, while Local

Grain-Purchasing Agents for the Army were liable to underestimate grain surpluses in their provinces to resist procurement norms set by the Ministry of Agriculture. This "war of statistics" intensified with the passage of time because the commitment of the zemstvos to government surveys gave them independent sources of information and alternative methods of interpretation. Zemstvos began to dismiss government data.

If zemstvos needed to take the initiative in interpreting statistical data to defend their local economies, it was hardly surprising that they did not wish to relinquish automatically the results of the agricultural survey to the government but, rather, tried to appraise the data by themselves. A conference of chairmen of provincial zemstvo boards and local contractors for civilian food purchase held in Moscow on August 22–23, 1916, proposed to have the agricultural surveys appraised "in the localities." At the end of October, another conference of chairmen of provincial zemstvo boards presented an alternative method of appraising data in opposition to the method adopted by the Ministry of Agriculture. This parallel appraisal method demanded that the ministry return provincial data to each zemstvo, if the zemstvo had sent the data to the ministry without copying it.[103]

Remedies Against Competitive Purchases

During World War I, Grain-Purchasing Agents for the Army entered into a competitive relationship with four types of public grain buyers: (1) the army; (2) the Department of Rural Food Administration of the Ministry of Internal Affairs; (3) contractors dispatched from grain-consuming provinces; and (4) other Grain-Purchasing Agents for the Army. From an official, legislative point of view, the competition of the first, second, and fourth types was eliminated in 1915. In practice also, these types did not pose insurmountable obstacles to wartime food management. Only the competition of the third type could not be eliminated even officially and, in practice, was the most damaging among the four. It was because of this competition that the tsarist regime collapsed.

Until the end of 1915, the government was passively dependent upon municipalities to supply the civilian population with food. During this period, food purchases made by consuming municipalities were not regarded as harmful unless they directly disrupted grain purchases for the army. Therefore, the formula for avoiding competitive purchases in agrarian provinces was relatively simple: food purchases by municipalities should be entrusted to the Grain-Purchasing Agents for the Army of the province or made by municipalities themselves with Grain-Purchasing Agents' consent regarding prices and other procurement conditions.[104] Let us shorten this formula to "via the Grain-Purchasing Agent for the Army or with his consent." Although this formula was not abandoned throughout the war's duration (or until, it would seem, the onset of the Bolshevik food dictatorship), new circumstances in early 1916 made the formula unsatisfactory. The widening gap between fixed and market prices convinced Grain-Purchasing Agents for the Army and the Ministry of Agriculture that competitive purchases by municipalities should be regulated more systematically. Additionally, weakened transport capability following the retreat from Galicia made it appear that free selection of agricultural provinces by food-purchasing municipalities was an unaffordable luxury—a waste of transport capabilities—and that local food purchases should be regulated. Moreover, growing autarky on the part of Grain-Purchasing Agents for the Army in the second procurement year (1915–1916) induced food-purchasing municipalities to request legitimately that "if you restrict our activity in such a way, then supply us from *your* grain reserves." As already mentioned, it was in this procurement year that government food purchasing began to assume the moral responsibility of supplying the civilian population.

Under this situation, two approaches to preventing competitive purchases between Grain-Purchasing Agents for the Army and municipalities emerged. One suggested that *all* grain requested by municipalities be supplied from Grain-Purchasing Agents' reserves. Objectively, this proposal was a big step toward "state monopoly of grain." If this state monopoly had become a reality, each producing province might have been assigned to a few food-consuming provinces in a simple, arithmetic way to ensure the most rational use of transport capacity. The Ministry of Agriculture headed by A. N. Naumov at first tried to achieve this radical approach and gained Grain-Purchasing Agents' agreement for it at a conference of Grain-Purchasing Agents held in Petrograd on February 10–11, 1916. However, except for such active

Grain-Purchasing Agents as Davydov in Tambov and Gerbel' in Kherson, the consent was only lip service. Most agents believed that "when even the norms for the military are so hard to fulfill, how can we handle additional norms for the civilian population?" As already mentioned, in the spring of 1916, the portion of grain released from Grain-Purchasing Agents' reserves within the entire government aid to municipal food management *decreased*. Naumov and Glinka in vain sent telegrams and circulars to Local Grain-Purchasing Agents criticizing their passive attitude toward the urgent needs of the civilian population.[105]

Faced with tacit resistance from Local Grain-Purchasing Agents for the Army, the Ministry of Agriculture shifted its emphasis to another, more realistic approach: it tried to deprive municipalities of the freedom to select agrarian provinces for their procurement activities and to assign each municipality certain provinces within which to procure. One preparatory step for this policy was the aforementioned all-Russian agriculture survey. Because of the delay of its appraisal, however, the imperial supply plan based on these newly obtained statistical data was not ready in time for the third procurement year (1916–1917) and was adopted only in mid-November. Moreover, it already had become unrealistic when it was adopted. Another preparatory step was the founding of the Central Bureau of Flour Millers. The ordinance of the Minister of Agriculture on June 30, 1916, which established this bureau, assigned to it the task of geographically relating flour supply to consuming centers, on the one hand, and grain supply from agrarian regions to milling centers, on the other. One leader of the Special Council on Food remarked that one of the most important duties of the bureau was to "establish the most rational relationship between producing and consuming areas." If "historically constituted relationships" contravened the need for rational use of transport capacity, the bureau was expected to attempt to change them.[106] Since the Central Bureau of Flour Millers failed to mobilize millers corporatively, this geographic coordination became nearly its sole raison d'être. Yet the actual shipment of flour, as well as grain, depended totally on Local Grain-Purchasing Agents for the Army.

Two ordinances of the Minister of Agriculture issued on September 9 and October 10, 1916, introduced a system in which the Central Agent of Grain Purchase for the Army and the Central Bureau of Flour Millers were in charge of assigning several provinces for procurement to each Agent of the Chairman of the Special Council on Food in consuming provinces. According to these ordinances, any Local Grain-Purchasing Agent for the Army having norms for consuming provinces was obliged to choose between, first, releasing grain from his reserves or, second, permitting contractors dispatched by Agents of the Chairman of the Special Council on Food of the consuming provinces to purchase grain by themselves, yet assisting them with compulsory measures.[107] The first option was the successor to the previously noted radical remedy against competitive purchases, whereas the second option took the place of the realistic one. In what follows the system prescribed by the two ordinances is called the "planned supply system."

A decisive flaw in the planned supply system was that it did not prescribe what should be done if a Local Grain-Purchasing Agent for the Army refused both to release grain and to permit contractors of consuming provinces to purchase. Rather, this system was based on the fragile assumption that Local Grain-Purchasing Agents for the Army (that is, zemstvo leaders of agrarian provinces) would respect statistical data offered by the Ministry of Agriculture. If a Local Grain-Purchasing Agent for the Army argued against the ministry that the latter's data were inaccurate and that the grain surplus in his province was being depleted, the ministry could not force him to release grain to the civilian population. Even more decisive would be the assertion that not only release of grain from the agent's reserve but also any permit for municipal purchases in the agent's province would impede shipment quotas to the front. Thus, despite its original motives and outward appearances, the planned supply system guaranteed the priority of agrarian provinces.

This situation is exemplified by a telegram sent at the end of September 1916 by the Grain-Purchasing Agent for the Army of the Elets procurement district, K. N. Lopatin (chair of the Elets County zemstvo board) to the Moscow provincial Agent of the Chairman of the Special Council on Food, in which Lopatin not only refused to supply Moscow with flour but also asserted that "it is useless to dispatch your agents. If circumstances were not like this, I would have gladly permitted their purchases."[108] In January 1917, all Grain-Purchasing Agents for the Army from Taurida, Voronezh, and Kursk Provinces, who were duty-bound by the imperial plan to supply Tula Province with wheat, unanimously informed contractors dispatched from Tula: "Why did you come to us? The people of our provinces are themselves suffering from a grain short- age and we cannot fulfill even shipment orders to the front. Therefore, we cannot give you anything."[109] In December 1916, N. A. Gavrilov, the Deputy-Central Agent of Grain Purchase for the Army, ordered the pre- viously cited Lopatin in Elets to release two freight cars of grain from embargo to improve the food situation in Kaluga Province. Lopatin an- swered in his telegraph:

> I am purchasing rye and flour commercially and compulsorily only for the purpose of fulfilling your supply orders for the Orel and Elets garrisons and for marshalling freight trains toward the front. I will never permit purchases by consumer contractors, because they are secretly violating fixed prices and have the possibility to completely stop delivery of food to me.[110]

This telegram reveals Lopatin's view of priorities: the interest of the front above all and then of the local garrisons. After these, the interest of the population of his own province implicitly follows, while consum- ers of other provinces were put in the lowest place.

In October 1916, A. E. Gruzinov, Agent of the Chairman of the Special Council on Food and chair of the Moscow provincial zemstvo board, protested to the Ministry of Agriculture that even the grain Muscovites bought *before* the introduction of the planned supply system was being sent by Local Grain-Purchasing Agents for the Army to other provinces. Gruzinov insisted that "it can never be tolerated that Local Grain-Purchasing Agents for the Army declare embargoes on grain shipments which, according to the 'imperial supply plan,' were to be sent to Moscow Province and, on the other hand, refuse to replace them with their own grain. . . . Embargoes can be declared only when the procurement organization is by itself able to supply consuming provinc- es completely."[111] Thus, we again face the paradox: Which came first, the chicken or the egg?

Since the Ministry of Agriculture could not make Local Grain- Purchasing Agents obey, the planned supply system was a fiction. Of course, the Minister of Agriculture could remove defiant Grain-Purchas- ing Agents from their positions. But such formal authority was meaning- less, since the Ministry was unable to organize grain procurement without the assistance of the zemstvos. If the Minister of Agriculture dismissed a chairman of a provincial zemstvo board as Local Grain-Purchasing Agent for the Army, the Minister probably would have no alternative but to replace him with another member of the same zemstvo board and the latter could well be as "regionalist." Probably because of this consideration, throughout the period of harsh conflicts between central and local authorities after the autumn of 1916, not a single Local Grain-Purchasing Agent for the Army was dismissed. This was the extent to which the tsarist government had become dependent on zemstvos.

Although the planned supply system prescribed the option to release grain from Local Grain-Purchasing Agents' storage to municipalities and Local Agents of the Chairman of the Special Council on Food, the latter nevertheless needed to dispatch their contractors (with the supply orders issued by the Ministry of Agriculture in hand) to Local Grain-Purchasing Agents for the Army to negotiate. The progress of these negotiations was to be conveyed to local railway administrations by the Local Agents of the Chairman of the Special Council on Food concerned. In other words, that Local Grain-Purchasing Agents for the Army would fulfill supply orders was *not* taken for granted when transport plans were being made. Moreover, if a Local Grain-Purchasing Agent agreed to release grain from his reserve, he demanded payment in advance. Given the railway disarray at that time, it was not unusual that freight trains arrived long after the time of purchase, thus keeping municipal floating capital inoperative. Sometimes, Local Grain-Purchasing Agents for the Army did not even ship grain after having received money.[112] In short, the planned supply system did not rescue Local Agents of the Chairman of the Special Council on Food and municipalities either from troublesome negotiations or from risks. Rather, they had to continue to keep numerous contractors operating in agrarian provinces.[113] In this respect, there had been no significant improvement from the period when provinces could be freely selected for procurement.

The introduction of the imperial supply plan in mid-November did not ameliorate the regionalist tendencies of Local Grain-Purchasing Agents for the Army, as admitted in a telegram sent December 22 by the Secretariat of the Special Council on Food to the Chief of the Imperial Food Administration (a senior official of the Ministry of Internal Affairs). This telegram remarked that planned supply is especially difficult in the first months of its operation because local plenipotentiary agents [of grain purchase for the army], *for understandable reasons*, have not changed their attitude—not only to meet the demands of their own provinces in the near future but also to supply their own provinces with food *as completely as possible and as long as possible.*[114] [italics added].

THE FATEFUL AUTUMN OF 1916:
THE "SHTIURMER (STÜRMER) DICTATORSHIP" AND
THE MINISTRY OF AGRICULTURE

Previous studies have posited a direct causal relationship between the procurement crisis in the autumn of 1916 and the February Revolution. However, as mentioned in the foregoing, the performance of government grain procurement improved after October, although it did not alleviate the food crisis in urban Russia. In my opinion, the procurement crisis in the autumn of 1916 only "switched on" an accelerator of more serious, intertwined crises. What, then, was this "accelerator"? My answer is ironical: public food institutions and food statistics, which had developed in the preceding eighteen months, facilitated increased panic among local leaders and the population. The hierarchy of public food institutions, having penetrated down to the level of "small areas" or even townships, not only amplified uneasiness but also became a mechanism for sealing off local markets from within. For example, a food activist in Tambov Province reminisced that "due to poorly organized statistics, it was impossible to gauge the existing surplus of food accurately. Due to the disarray of transport, acute deficits of certain commodities developed . . . right alongside the areas of their abundance. Such a situation led to the opinion that we are experiencing a general deficit and food export from our province was prohibited."[115]

In this process of converting the autumnal procurement crisis into an acute interregional conflict, the so-called Shtiurmer dictatorship and the reshuffling of ministers and vice-ministers played an important role. Born in 1852 into a distinguished aristocratic family, Aleksei Aleksandrovich Bobrinskii had neither learned agronomy nor worked in agricultural ministries. As a nobleman who owned sugar refineries in Kiev Province, Bobrinskii had spent much of his time in archeological pursuits and philanthropy. After the 1905 Revolution, he cut a conspicuous figure in the political movement representing the landed nobility, and became a leader of the Right Group of the State Council after the death of P. N. Durnovo. In March 1916, when B. V. Shtiurmer—the same Shtiurmer (or Stürmer) who had occupied the post of chair of the Tver' provincial zemstvo board in the 1890s—having served as Chair of the Council of Ministers since January 1916, was appointed Minister of Internal Affairs, Bobrinskii was selected as Vice-Minister of Internal Affairs. Bobrinskii eventually took the place of A. N. Naumov as Minister of Agriculture in July 1916.[116] Naumov was forty-eight years old when he was dismissed. Bobrinskii was sixty-four when he succeeded Naumov.

On September 21, 1916, Local Food-Purchasing Agents for the Army were astonished by a circular that appeared with joint signatures of new Minister of Internal Affairs A. D. Protopopov and new Minister of Agriculture A. A. Bobrinskii demanding that governors supervise food embargoes. This circular ordered that if any Local Grain-Purchasing Agents for the Army issued an embargo against a governor's will, the governor should inform the ministers of Internal Affairs and Agriculture and that embargo issues in general should be deliberated at meetings presided over by governors.[117] Since a significant number of governors were already as parochial as zemstvos, this circular was not always observed, but there were cases in which governors lifted embargoes without the consent of Local Grain-Purchasing Agents for the Army.

The Grain-Purchasing Agent for the Army of the Odessa Military District, S. N. Gerbel', furiously protested against this circular. Even when he had been in conflict with Glinka in the spring of that year, it was taken for granted that Gerbel' was the only coordinator regarding embargoes in the district. Now, however, he perceived that this role was being usurped. On the very day Gerbel' received the circular, he telegraphed Bobrinskii that "it is impossible to fulfill such a vast amount of procurement orders without embargoes and requisition and you make it impossible, instead of helping." In the same telegraph, Gerbel' threatened to resign as the Military District Grain-Purchasing Agent unless the circular was rescinded.[118] Bobrinskii explained apologetically to Gerbel' that the circular intended that governors should "grasp," but not "control," the imposition of embargoes.[119] At the beginning of October Gerbel' again telegraphed that the poor progress in grain procurement was caused by the fact that "circulars sent out by ministers contradict each other."[120] In the same month, denouncing the defiant governor of Bessarabia, Gerbel' remarked that "It is difficult to overcome this bad situation because the ministry itself is creating it."[121]

A. N. Neverov, born in 1862, served as governor of Akmolinsk from 1910 to August 1915, then as governor of Volynynia Province for just two months, and was selected to be director of the Peasant Department (*zemskii otdel*) under newly appointed Minister of Internal Affairs A. N. Khvostov.[122] Ten months later, on August 28, 1916, to reinforce the "Shtiurmer dictatorship," Neverov replaced Glinka as the Vice-Minister of Agriculture and as Central Agent of Grain Purchase for the Army.[123] In other words, without any experience in the Ministry or in national food management, Neverov was placed in charge of assigning procurement provinces to consuming provinces, that is, to their Local Agents of the Chairman of the Special Council on Food, a duty upon which the fate of the empire depended, and confronting the procurement crisis.

Historical science dislikes hypotheses. But such a counterfactual assumption as "if Shtiurmer's camarilla had been satisfied with the resignation of Naumov and had not removed Glinka from his post, what would have become of the tsarist regime?" is too close at hand to remain a forbidden fruit. In any case, "shaken by endless rumors about food crises and shocked by reports about the general plight of procurement,"[124] Neverov retreated from the idea of planned supply. In October, he sent "exceptional" shipment orders to any station that had accumulated a certain quantity of food. The specter of arbitrary transportation caused by Neverov's countless telegrams reminds us of a billiard game. On October 16, 1916, the Tambov Grain-Purchasing Agent for the Army, Iu. V. Davydov, criticizing the absence of systematization in Neverov's leadership, telegraphed that "the shipment orders given to Tambov Province accumulated to more than 50,000 puds [about 800 tons] per station. If any more orders are issued, all internal transportation will definitely collapse, and mills and grain-drying stations will cease to function."[125]

The excessive dispatch of shipment orders altered the geographic distribution of food resources of the empire, thus making it difficult to return to a planned system of food supply. Moreover, it "shook" the hierarchy of food organs, provoking from above a panic that reached the township level. Food organs at all levels began to exert themselves "to import as much as possible, and to permit as little export as possible."

The Bobrinskii-Neverov leadership of the Ministry of Agriculture, disliked by zemstvos from the beginning because of these individuals' connection with Rasputin, discredited irrevocably the ministry's authority by their billiardlike shipment orders. A telegram sent by Gerbel' at the end of October to answer Neverov's inquiry about the reasons for the procurement crisis seems representative of the general mood among Grain-Purchasing Agents for the Army: "What is incompetent is your organization, not mine. I always supply both the front and cities with more food than ordered."[126]

Political crises in November delivered the coup de grâce to "Shtiurmer's dictatorship." A. A. Rittikh, a career bureaucrat in agricultural ministries, took Bobrinskii's place. Although Neverov kept his post until January 1917,[127] N. A. Gavrilov (also a career agricultural bureaucrat)[128] began to control the assignment of procurement provinces and the imperial supply plan was introduced at long last. However, the self-protective mood and distrust of Petrograd among zemstvo leaders did not dissipate even after Bobrinskii left the scene.

A Case Study: The Collapse of Planned Supply in Central Russia

In this section, I will describe the process of the collapse of the planned supply system, focusing on central Russia. In terms of grain transactions, provinces in central Russia could be classified into four zones: (1) provinces that, as exclusive consumers, imported both rye and wheat (Moscow, Kaluga, and Vladimir); (2) provinces which exported rye but imported wheat (Riazan', Tula, Orel, Tambov, and Penza); (3) provinces that were full producers, exporting both rye and wheat (Kursk, Voronezh, and Saratov); and (4) provinces that were milling centers (Nizhegorod and Simbirsk). Because of the market gravity of Moscow and the northern limit of wheat cultivation at that time, zones 1, 2, and 3 form concentric sectors around Moscow. These are depicted in Map 9–2.

Among provinces in zone 2, Riazan' and Tula in particular were exposed to market gravity from zone 1. Given the widening gap between fixed and market prices in the autumn of 1916, market gravity was an enticement to illegally cart or transport grain out of these provinces. As of February 1917, if a peasant of Riazan' Province carried oats to Moscow or Vladimir Provinces, he could make a profit of 150 or

MAP 9-2   Provinces analyzed

even 200 rubles per cartload.[129] If he delivered the same amount of oats
to the Grain-Purchasing Agent for the Army, his profit was only 40 or
50 rubles per cart. Under such circumstances, it was impossible for
Riazan' and Tula Grain-Purchasing Agents to buy grain unless they
strictly imposed embargoes.

As mentioned above, the Moscow provincial zemstvo was one of the
originators of the idea of planned supply. From January 1916, each month
the provincial zemstvo board prepared a broad-area plan (covering twenty-four provinces and an oblast' as sources of supply) for shipment toward Moscow.[130] Muscovites welcomed the long-awaited planned

supply system, but the performance of Grain-Purchasing Agents for the Army assigned to Moscow Province in the first months under the new system (September and October) disappointed the Moscow Agent of the Chairman of the Special Council on Food, A. E. Gruzinov.[131] At the end of October, he demanded that the Ministry of Agriculture assign provinces which were actually capable of fulfilling supply orders for Moscow Province.[132] Since the ministry was impeded from responding to this demand, the Moscow zemstvo board entered November without any supply plan, being driven to telegraph randomly to numbers of Grain-Purchasing Agents for the Army in search of supply.[133] Ironically, the introduction of the imperial supply plan forced the Moscow zemstvo to retreat from a concept of planned supply.

Gruzinov's agents negotiating with Grain-Purchasing Agents for the Army in agrarian provinces informed him of actual harvest volumes and other details, which convinced Gruzinov that grain surpluses did exist in Taurida, Saratov, Poltava, and other provinces, and that the Simbirsk Grain-Purchasing Agent for the Army was sabotaging, while winking at illegal exports of food from the province.[134] Gruzinov never explicitly neglected the idea of planned supply, but realizing that interprovincial solidarity between zemstvos could not be expected, he shifted the emphasis of his requests addressed to the Ministry of Agriculture from "strict enforcement of the imperial plan" to "elimination of obstructions erected by Grain-Purchasing Agents for the Army to food export." On December 10 when Gruzinov still persisted in planned supply, he telegraphed: "[M]inistries neither took any practical measures to supply our province with food, nor did they force the plenipotentiary agents [purchasing grain for the army] to permit the purchase and export of food by my agents, although that is included in the supply orders.[135] On the eve of the February Revolution, however, the nuance of his requests changed: "I have convincing evidence that there is sufficient flour in Saratov and Poltava Provinces. . . . October, November, December, and January showed that plenipotentiary agents cannot purchase by themselves. Give me the right to purchase by myself there and to release the purchased grain from the authority of plenipotentiary agents."[136]

Kaluga Province had already suffered from food shortages as early as October 1916. The Agent of the Chairman of the Special Council on Food of that province, Governor Chernykaev, ignored the official assignment of procurement provinces from the beginning. So did the provincial zemstvo, which kept its contractors active in various provinces, ignoring the official assignment. Confronting food crises in October, municipalities and Governor Chernykaev purchased haphazardly in Voronezh, Samara, Taurida, Riazan', Tula, Kursk, and other provinces, all the while bombarding the Ministry of Agriculture with telegrams. "Considering the situation of the province," Neverov ordered Grain-Purchasing Agents for the Army of those regions to permit Kaluga agents to carry out grain "as an exceptional measure," even if the province was not assigned to Kaluga Province.[137] Concurrent purchases by Kaluga municipalities were one of the causes of the billiard-ball–like transport syndrome previously described.

Nevertheless, the result of such desperate activities was not significant: according to Chernykaev, from November 1916 to January 1917, Kaluga Province received only 112 freight carloads of grain (or 11 percent) of the 1,061 the imperial supply plan had guaranteed.[138] According to the chairman of the provincial zemstvo board, of 761 freight carloads of rye the provincial zemstvo had purchased in other provinces, only 95 were actually dispatched and of these 61 reached Kaluga Province.[139] Kaluga Province needed about 110,000 tons of rye imported each year, but it received only about 5,000 tons throughout July to December 1916, and only about 560 tons in January 1917.[140] In February, some symptoms of epidemics, which often accompanied starvation, were observed in the province.[141]

Given this situation, the Ministry of Agriculture generously allotted Kaluga Province the grain supply norms for February, totaling five hundred freight carloads. These norms were, however, imposed on Tambov, Orel, Voronezh, Ufa, and Penza Provinces and this worried Chernykaev since he realized that, given the disarray in railway transportation at that time, norms assigned to distant provinces would be meaningless. Therefore, Chernykaev requested that the norms be imposed on neighboring Orel and Tula Provinces and that carting of grain by Kaluga inhabitants out of those provinces should be permitted.[142] The fact is that Chernykaev intended to assist Kaluga zemstvos, which were organizing illegal cart export of grain from these southern neighbors. The Ministry of Agriculture was again forced to compromise, and ordered Orel and Tula governors to permit cart export of grain to Kaluga Province out of their northern territories, if the grain was proved to be intended for household consumption but not for commercial purposes.[143] Since Tula Province itself suffered from a food shortage in its nonblack-soil northern counties, the Tula governor (who was simultaneously the Agent of the Chairman of the Special Council on Food) had never moderated his attitude that grain should not be exported even for household consumption.[144] Given the existence of strong market gravity, however, it was difficult to prohibit cart export. The chairman of the Kaluga provincial zemstvo board triumphantly remarked that "such prohibitive measures [adopted by the Tula and Orel governors] cannot eliminate the necessity for completely natural and historically formed commodity circulation and gravity toward local markets."[145]

According to a calculation by the Ministry of Agriculture, Riazan' Province might have 16,000 tons of surplus rye in 1916–1917 even after supplying its population entirely. The ministry ordered Riazan' Province to supply Moscow and Vladimir Provinces with rye,[146] while imposing upon Saratov and Simbirsk Provinces the responsibility to supply Riazan' Province with wheat. However, the Saratov and Simbirsk Grain-Purchasing Agents for the Army did not fulfill the supply norms, while the Riazan' procurement organization (that is, the zemstvos) could not control food exports to Moscow and Vladimir Provinces. As early as October 3, 1916, the Riazan' provincial food council petitioned to release grain to the local people from the storage facilities of the provincial Grain-Purchasing Agents for the Army.[147] While such strong provincial procurement organizations as those in Tambov and Saratov improved their procurement activities in October, the procurement of rye in Riazan' Province remained in a desperate situation.[148] Before long, V. F. Eman, the provincial Grain-Purchasing Agent for the Army and chair of the provincial zemstvo board, fell ill.

On the other hand, the Riazan' city council, as well as Kaluga municipalities, never believed in the planned supply system and requested a return to free procurement. The Riazan' city mayor claimed the planned supply system was a sham in a telegraph sent on November 29, 1916, to the Ministry of Agriculture:

> If there is no possibility to supply us with urgently needed commodities, why do you reassure us and direct us to another plenipotentiary agent

[of grain purchase for the army], thus making us waste time and money? If plenipotentiary agents are incapable of fulfilling supply-orders given by the Special Council on Food, why were you so hasty as to deprive us of the right to make independent purchases, thus leading us to the current terrible disruption of the food supply? Thus far, our city board has by itself supplied the population with all necessary goods, by employing men of experience and utilizing widely cooperatives and representatives of private commerce. We have managed somehow to survive. Now, while depriving us of our independence, the Special Council has given us nothing, except such promises as have never been fulfilled by the plenipotentiary agents.[149]

In fairness, I am obliged to add that the Riazan' Grain-Purchasing Agent for the Army, Eman, categorically refused to permit "parallel purchases by private individuals" in his provinces.[150] Thus, municipal leaders of Riazan' Province requested from other people what they would never permit others to do.

The responsibility for supplying Tula Province with wheat during November and December 1916 was imposed on Voronezh, Khar'kov, and Kursk Provinces, but only 34 percent of the planned volume could be obtained (165 freight cars arrived, compared with the projected 490).[151] Tula city and the northern counties of the province began to suffer from food shortages. The January plan assigned Voronezh, Kursk, and Taurida Grain-Purchasing Agents for the Army to Tula Province but, according to a letter sent on January 31, 1917, by the Tula governor (who simultaneously was the agent of the Chairman of the Special Council on Food) to the Ministry of Agriculture, the Grain-Purchasing Agents for the Army refused to send grain to Tula. Only ten freight cars reached the province—6 percent of the planned number. Warning that local garrison soldiers might possibly join the "hungry crowds," the Tula governor requested that his province be released from the obligation to supply the army, retaining only the duty to supply the local garrison and that the remaining grain, after supplying the garrison, be transferred from the Grain-Purchasing Agent for the Army to his (that is, the Agent of the Chairman of the Special Council on Food) control.[152] Before long, the Ministry of Agriculture agreed to this petition.[153]

A similar resolution was adopted at the food council of Penza Province on February 18, 1917. On the grounds that the supply plan for the province had not been realized at all, the council resolved to immediately release a sufficient volume of rye flour from the reserves of the Grain-Purchasing Agent for the Army to the urban and nonagricultural population of the province so that they might survive the approaching two months of "spring's bad transportation (*rasputitsa*)." For this purpose, the provincial Grain-Purchasing Agent for the Army (chairman of the provincial zemstvo board) asked the Ministry of Agriculture to permit him to suspend the shipment of flour to the front and other provinces until late spring.[154]

The western part of Orel Province was part of the nonblack-soil region and contained the industrial city of Briansk, which was also a garrison post. Therefore, the food situation of this area was similar to that of Kaluga and northern Tula Provinces. More critically, the war had severed the Briansk area from its natural agricultural hinterland such as Chernigov, Poltava, and Kiev Provinces, for these southwestern provinces had been placed under military rule or had become important supply bases for the army. Food crises in Briansk had already commenced in October 1916 and by the end of the year "epidemics among children" were observed.[155] As was the case with the Kaluga municipalities, the city of Briansk haphazardly purchased food, ignoring the imperial plan and often violating fixed prices as well.[156] Not only the Ministry of Agriculture but also the Special Council on State Defense (attached to the Ministry of War) had no alternative but to repeatedly grant "exceptional" permission, considering that the food crisis in Briansk might easily provoke riots by workers and garrison soldiers.[157]

Another food crisis in Orel Province was related to the flour-milling industry in its central and eastern counties. Considering the natural flow of grain and flour, the imperial plan obliged the Grain-Purchasing Agents for the Army of "outer" Voronezh and Kursk Provinces to supply Orel flour-millers with wheat, but these Local Grain-Purchasing Agents for the Army sabotaged their responsibility.[158] The Ministry of Agriculture requested that the Orel Grain-Purchasing Agent for the Army (chair of the provincial zemstvo board) alleviate the shortage of wheat by relying on Orel's own agricultural riches[159] and thus provided the Orel Grain-Purchasing Agent with an excuse for rejecting supply orders for its "inner" provinces such as Tula, Kaluga, and Moscow.

The Tambov Agent of the Chairman of the Special Council on Food, Davydov, also charged the Voronezh Grain-Purchasing Agent for the Army (chair of the provincial zemstvo board), V. N. Tomanovskii, with sabotaging grain purchasing. Tomanovskii was responsible for supplying Tambov Province with 13,000 tons of wheat and wheat flour during November and December 1916 but "not a wagon was sent" to Tambov. Moreover, Tomanovskii refused to assist Davydov's contractors. Correspondence with Tomanovskii convinced Davydov that in Voronezh Province, "wheat had not been obtained from large estates as late as December."[160] The Borisoglebsk city board (southern Tambov Province) also remarked that the unsuccessful procurement in Voronezh Province could not be justified, since grain surplus in the province was estimated at nearly 200,000 tons.[161]

The Nizhegorod flour-milling industry was seriously damaged by the growing autarky of Grain-Purchasing Agents for the Army in the autumn of 1916 since Nizhegorod millers, in contrast to those in Samara, did have their own agrarian hinterland. According to the November plan, Nizhegorod Province should have received 1,000 freight cars of grain mainly from Khar'kov and Taurida Provinces, but in fact it received only "seven wagons."[162] while Nizhegorod millers curtailed production due to the grain shortage, flour export to Moscow and neighboring Vladimir Province was gathering momentum. As early as September 1916, the Nizhni-Novogorod city council passed a resolution petitioning the prohibition of flour exports from the province. The miserable fulfillment of the grain supply plan to Nizhegorod Province in November convinced D. V. Sirotkin, provincial Grain-Purchasing Agent for the Army and chair of the Exchange Committee, that it was necessary to "temporarily suspend supply orders for other cities until the arrival of a sufficient volume of grain." In accordance with Sirotkin's action, the Vice-Agent of the Chairman of the Special Council on Food, chairman of the provincial zemstvo board P. A. Demidov, was sent to Petrograd and tried in vain to persuade Central Agent of Grain Purchase for the Army Neverov to agree with this measure. Repeated refusals by the Ministry of Agriculture gave Nizhegoroders the impression that it was meaningless to petition the government any further.[163] On November 20, 1916, the governor of Nizhegorod convened a provincial food conference that was attended by Sirotkin, Demidov, high officials of the provincial administration, and representatives of cities, zemstvos, and flour millers. This conference unanimously declared the need for provincial self-protection. According to Sirotkin, if Nizhegorod Province continued to supply other provinces with flour, mills in the province would have to cease production after December: "[T]he local people will pour out into the streets with demands for bread. We do not have the right to drive our people into such a situation."[164] Demidov echoed: "We do not have sufficient grounds for thinking that we must sacrifice the people of our own province for the national interest. If export of the remainder of our flour is really dictated by some higher interests, let them prove it in front of us. In that case, we will bear the sacrifice."[165]

The provincial conference requested that 600,000 puds (about 10,000 tons) of wheat flour be left in Nizhegorod Province, justifying this volume on the basis of zemstvo statistics.[166] The attendees approved the governor's proposal that he would enforce the resolution, relying upon his competence prescribed in emergency laws.[167] This conference also deliberated the question of an embargo on rye flour but, "considering that rye flour is being exported out of our province to supply troops," it voted against the embargo.[168] Here again, we see local leaders' priorities: first, demands of the military; next, civilian needs of the home province; and least of all, civilian needs of other provinces.

The flour embargo adopted by Nizhegorod Province immediately devastated the food situation of its "inner" neighbor, Vladimir Province. This is why Minister of Agriculture A. A. Rittikh sent a telegram to Nizhni-Novgorod just one week after the conference that introduced the embargo. Rittikh argued that Nizhegoroders' desire for 600,000 puds of flour reserve was ill-founded and, moreover, criticized the governor of Nizhegorod who introduced the embargo without first consulting Rittikh, "against the joint telegram by my predecessor [Bobrinskii] and the Minister of Internal Affairs [Protopopov]."[169]

Grain and flour procurement in Simbirsk Province was thwarted by the transfer of the area adjacent to the Volga-Bugul'ma branch line to the jurisdiction of the Samara Grain-Purchasing Agent for the Army, Bashkirov. It was Bashkirov who lobbied the Ministry of Agriculture for this reorganization. When this lobbying was made public at the beginning of November 1916, not only the Simbirsk Grain-Purchasing Agent for the Army, chairman of the provincial zemstvo board N. F.

Beliakov, and Simbirsk zemstvos, but also local grain dealers in Bug-ul'ma County (such as grain elevators of the State Bank and the Bug-ul'ma Exchange Committee) protested. On November 5, the director of State Bank grain storehouses of the Simbirsk-Penza district tele-graphed to the State Bank that "such a transfer [of jurisdiction] does not correspond to the natural affinity and actual interests of the area adja-cent to the Volga-Bugul'ma line, which is bent to the Simbirsk side, and partly to the upper Volga, but not at all to Samara. . . . Removal of grain by railways to Samara will assume an exclusively compulsory charac-ter."[170] Despite these protests, the reorganization was carried out in the "midst" of procurement operations.

At that time, a provincial convention of grain dealers sponsored by the Simbirsk Exchange Committee resolved to organize a merchant as-sociation that would monopolize grain purchase and processing in order to realize "successful and planned supply of products to the army and the population."[171] Simbirsk Grain-Purchasing Agent for the Army Be-liakov opposed the transfer of the Bugul'ma area, referring to this mer-chant association as one that "completely abandoned private commerce and is ready to work as a single firm, supplying me with all commodities thus purchased." However, Beliakov warned, given the significant weight of the Bugul'ma area in the whole Simbirsk grain market, trans-fer of it to Bashkirov would make the merchant association meaning-less.[172] Dismissing this warning, Rittikh resolutely reorganized the geographical jurisdictions between the Grain-Purchasing Agents for the Army but, on the other hand, did not hesitate to suggest that Belia-kov assist the fledgling merchant association to develop.[173] In Decem-ber, Beliakov replied curtly that the association was already disunited, and "speculators" were hailing this fact.[174]

Completing analysis of this section, we can see that the foundations of planned supply collapsed at the following four points:

(1) Such secondary municipalities as Kaluga zemstvo and the cities of Riazan' and Briansk, that is, onlookers en route to the planned sup-ply system—did not believe in the system from its inception, pro-tested against it, or defiantly continued free purchases. Muscovites, the earliest advocates of planned supply, never officially abandoned this idea. As they recognized, however, that there could be no in-terregional solidarity among zemstvo leaders, their requests to the

government degenerated from decisive imposition of the plan to irritated cries to eliminate, at least, obstructions to food exports to Moscow erected by Grain-Purchasing Agents for the Army from agricultural provinces.

(2) Inflow of wheat and wheat flour from zone 3 to zone 2 (see Map 9-2) decreased. Suggestions given by the Ministry of Agriculture to zone 2 provinces (Riazan', Tula, Penza, and Orel) to alleviate the situation by depending upon their own food resources naturally resulted in disrupting the inflow of rye and rye flour from zone 2 to zone 1, thus putting zone 1 provinces (Moscow, Kaluga, and Vladimir) in a desperate condition.

(3) Idle procurement organizations such as Voronezh used compulsory measures only for self-protection. Weak procurement organizations such as Riazan' could not even establish an embargo regime and were easily crushed when confronting the strong market gravity from zone 1.

(4) The Nizhegorod flour-milling industry was seriously damaged by the growing autarky of Grain-Purchasing Agents for the Army because this province did not have its own agrarian hinterland. This made the province inclined toward a strong embargo regime. The collapse of the Simbirsk flour-milling industry caused by the transfer of its Bugul'ma area to the jurisdiction of the Samara Grain-Purchasing Agent for the Army resulted in the flour shortages in central Russia, a general background of the crises mentioned in 1, 2, and 3.

CONCLUSION

The real reason for the collapse of the tsarist regime was interregional conflict and this was generated by organizational policies adopted by tsarist officials to incorporate municipal social movements into the total-war regime. To convert public collection of grain conducted by zemstvos and cooperatives into procurement for the military, the government endowed zemstvos with the authority not only to purchase grain, but also to regulate railway transportation, seal off local markets from within by compulsory measures, and mobilize local merchants and flour millers. To convert municipal food purchases into wartime food policy, the government encouraged municipalities to establish local food councils, motivating them by granting, again, authority over railway regulation. The government's dependence on municipal statistics gave municipalities independent sources of information and alternative methods of interpretation. This resulted in a "war of statistics" between the government and municipalities. The war of statistics and embargo syndrome of zemstvos put an end to the planned supply system, the lifeline for the tsarist war regime.

Despite the self-image of Russians, Russian (and Soviet) public administration has been and will continue to be characterized by the underdevelopment of professional bureaucracy and direct dependence on social resources. This study was an attempt to clarify how and to what extent the tsarist state could cope with total-war management, which requires an optimum combination of centrism with operative, decentralized leadership.

NOTES

1. Leopold Haimson, ed., *The Politics of Rural Russia, 1905–1914* (Bloomington: University of Indiana Press, 1979).

2. See the conclusion of my "The Fate of Agronomists in Russia, 1911–1916: Their Quantitative Dynamics from 1911 to 1916," *The Russian Review*, vol. 55 (April 1996) pp. 195–196.

3. I. F. Koshko, "Vremennoe pravitel'stvo i uzhasy bol'shevizma: perezhivaniia byvshego gubernatora Imperii 1917–1924," Bakhmeteff Archive (Columbia University, New York), Koshko Family Collection, Box 1.

4. Haruki Wada, "Tsuari no rekishigakuteki kenkyu no tameni (For the Historical Studies of the Tsar)," *Rosiasi Kenkyu*, no. 41 (1985) pp. 48–54. Koshko's memoir shows that the frequent reshuffling of higher officials (in particular, governors) under the influence of Rasputin humiliated those who were removed and made them a potential opposition to Nicholas II. Moreover, it demoralized even those who fortunately retained their position by depriving them of their conviction in their own authority and power. This seems to be one of the reasons why the upper elites were barely resistant to the February Revolution.

5. Rossiiskii gosudarstvennyi voenno-istoricheskii arkhiv [hereafter RGVIA], f. 499, op. 3, d. 1644, l. 60; Rossiiskii gosudarstvennyi istoricheskii arkhiv [hereafter RGIA], f. 456, op. 1, d. 156, l. 165; *Sel'skokhoziaistvennaia zhizn'* (Izdanie Tambovskogo sel'skokhoziaistvennogo obshchestva) [hereafter *SZh*], no. 21/24, 1916, p. 268.

6. See my "Prodrazverstka A. A. Rittikha," *Acta Slavica Iaponica*, no. 13 (1995) pp. 168–170.

7. RGIA, f. 273, op. 10, d. 3677, l. 39.

8. Sanford R. Lieberman, "The Evacuation of Industry in the Soviet Union During World War II," *Soviet Studies*, vol. 35, no. 1 (1983) pp. 90–102. See also his "Crisis Management in the USSR: The Wartime System of Administration and Control" in Suzan J. Linz, ed., *The Impact of World War II on the Soviet Union* (Lanham, MD: Roman–Littlefield, Pubs., Inc., 1985), pp. 59–76.

9. William Moskoff, *The Bread of Affliction: The Food Supply in the USSR During World War II* (Cambridge, UK, and New York: Cambridge University Press, 1990).

10. John Barber and Mark Harrison, *The Soviet Home Front 1941–1945: A Social and Economic History of the USSR in World War II* (London, and New York: Longman, 1991), pp. 48–50.

11. Ibid., pp. 82, 203–205.

12. George Yaney, *The World of Manager: Food Administration in Berlin During World War I* (NY: Peter Lang, 1994).

13. See my "'Obshchestvennaia ssypka' i voenno-prodovol'stvennaia sistema Rossii v gody pervoi mirovoi voiny," forthcoming in T. Shanin and V. P. Danilov, eds., *Ezhegodnik krest'ianovedeniia*.

14. *Izvestiia glavnogo upravleniia zemleustroistva i zemledeliia* [hereafter *IGUZZ*], no. 45 (1914) p. 1160.

15. RGIA, f. 456, op. 1, d. 18, l. 4.

16. *IGUZZ*, no. 33 (1914) p. 810.

17. Ibid., no. 35 (1914) p. 849; RGIA, f. 456, op. 1, d. 26, ll. 1–2.

18. RGVIA, f. 499, op. 3, d. 1255, ll. 188, 236 and 338–339; Ibid., d. 1252, l. 530; RGIA, f. 456, op. 1, d. 26, ll. 1–2.

19. T. M. Kitanina, *Khlebnaia torgovlia Rossii v 1875–1914 gg. (Ocherki pravitel'stvennoi politiki)* (Leningrad, 1978), pp. 264–265.

20. Local Committees for the Regulation of Railway Transportation were intermediate organs between the Central Railway Committeeand local railway administrations. As they totaled only ten in the entire empire in 1915 (*IGUZZ*, no. 11 [1915] p. 255), their geographical jurisdictions were extremely broad.

21. RGVIA, f. 499, op. 3, d. 1252, l. 266.

22. Ibid., ll. 340–343; Ibid., d. 1255, l. 45.

23. RGIA, f. 456, op. 1, d. 24, ll. 16–17.

24. Ibid., d. 19, l. 72.

25. Ibid., d. 24, l. 35–38.

26. *IGUZZ*, no. 28 (1915) p. 691.

27. Upravlenie delami osobogo soveshchaniia dlia obsuzhdeniia i ob"edineniia meropriiatii po prodovol'stvennomu delu [hereafter UD OSPD], *Obzor deiatel'nosti osobogo soveshchaniia dlia obsuzhdeniia i ob"edineniia meropriiatii po prodovol'stvennomu delu za 17 avgusta 1915 g.–17 fevralia 1916 g.* (Petrograd, 1916), p. 125.

28. *Sobranie uzakonenii i rasporiazhenii pravitel'stva, izdavaemoe pri pravitel'stvuiushchem senate* [hereafter *SU*], no. 64 (1915) art. 551.

29. RGIA, f. 1276, op. 12, d. 1816, l. 12.

30. The Special Council on Food was one of four wartime councils established by laws that the Tsar confirmed August 17, 1915. The main tasks of the council were to assist in procuring food for the army and to regulate food supply for the civilian population.

31. RGIA, f. 457, op. 1, d. 15, l. 315.

32. Ibid., f. 456, op. 1, d. 19, l. 67.

33. They were not always dispatched from food-consuming regions. Rather, municipalities of these regions often contracted with grain dealers in agrarian provinces.

34. Glavnyi komitet, Vserossiiskii soiuz gorodov [GK VSG], Ekonomicheskii otdel, *Materialy po voprosam organizatsii prodovol'stvennogo dela*, vol. 3, *Organizatsiia zagotovki khlebov v tambovskoi gubernii* (Moscow, 1917), p. 22.

35. "Doklad soveshchaniia predstavitelei birzhevikh komitetov volzhsko-kamskogo raiona o polozhenii khlebotorgovogo dela v sviazi s voprosom prodovol'stviia armii i naseleniia strany" (1916), pp. 2–3.

36. RGIA, f. 457, op. 1, d. 15, ll. 106–108.

37. Ibid., f. 456, op. 1, d. 156, ll. 29, 46–47.

38. For this organization, see Gleason and Porter, chapter 8.

39. Tsentral'nyi voenno-promyshlennyi komitet, *Trudy 2-go s"ezda predstavitelei voenno-promyshlennykh komitetov, 26–29 fevralia 1916 g.* (Petrograd, 1916), vol. 1, pp. 187–207, 223–226, 278.

40. *Izvestiia vserossiiskogo soiuza gorodov* [hereafter *IVSG*], no. 29/30 (1916) pp. 165–168.

41. *Svod postanovlenii 2-go chrezvychainogo vserossiiskogo s"ezda predstavitelei birzhevoi torgovli i sel'skogo khoziaistva v Petrograde s 24 po 28 aprelia 1916 g.* (Petrograd, 1916), p. 33.

42. RGIA, f. 456, op. 1, d. 63, ll. 7–12.

43. *Izvestiia vserossiiskogo zemskogo soiuza*, no. 45/46 (1916) pp. 6–9.

44. RGIA, f. 457, op. 1, d. 88, ll. 1–2; Ibid., d. 105, ll. 49–50.

45. Ibid., d. 94, ll. 60–69, 75–78.

46. Ibid., d. 78, l. 32; Ibid., d. 95, l. 95.

47. For an example of the application of these measures in Orenburg Province, see Gosudarstvennyi arkhiv Rossiiskoi Federatsii [hereafter GARF], f. 6809, op. 1, d. 108, l. 6.

48. N. D. Kondrat'ev, *Rynok khlebov i ego regulirovanie vo vremia voiny i revoliutsii* (Moscow, 1922), p. 135.

49. G. P. Sazonov, *Obzor deiatel'nosti zemstv po narodnomu prodovol'stviiu 1865–1892*, vol. 1 (St. Petersburg, 1893), pp. 1–191.

50. G. G. Savich, *Sbornik pravil po obespecheniiu narodnogo prodovol'stviia*, vol. 1 (St. Petersburg, 1900), pp. 87–88.

51. This reform was implemented under the "Temporary Regulation for Guaranteeing the Food Needs of Rural Inhabitants" ("Vremennye pravila po obespecheniiu prodovol'stvennykh potrebnostei sel'skikh obyvatelei"), *SU*, 1900, art. 1620.

52. A series of ordinances issued by the Ministry of Internal Affairs soon after this reform suggested zemstvos intensify these "economic measures." See B. B. Veselovskii, *Istoriia zemstva za sorok let*, vol. 2 (St.Petersburg, 1909), pp. 333–334.

53. UD OSPD, *Sovremennoe polozhenie takasirovki predmetov prodovol'stviia v Rossii i mery k ee uporiadocheniiu* (Petrograd, 1915), pp. 22–24; and Kondrat'ev, *Rynok khlebov*, pp. 135–136.

54. *IVSG*, no. 27/28 (1916) pp. 131–132.

55. Ibid., p. 136.

56. For Moscow Province, see Moskovskoe gubernskoe zemskoe sobranie [hereafter MGZS], Ekstrenniaia sessiia (May 1915), "Doklad o merakh obezpecheniia naseleniia Moskovskoi gubernii prodovol'stviem," p. 7.

57. UD OSPD, *Obzor deiatel'nosti,* p. 142.

58. Ibid., pp. 138–139.

59. UD OSPD, *Dopolnenie k obzoru deiatel'nosti osobogo soveshchaniia dlia obsuzhdeniia i ob"edineniia meropriiatii po prodovol'stvennomu delu za 17 avgusta 1915 g.–17 fevralia 1916 g., 17 fevralia–17 maia 1916 g.* (Petrograd, 1916), p. 4.

60. Ibid., *Obzor deiatel'nosti . . .* , pp. 138–139; Ibid., *Dopolnenie k obzoru . . .* , p. 7.

61. UD OSPD, *Obzor deiatel'nosti . . .* , pp. 2–3; RGIA, f. 1276, op. 1, d. 980, ll. 21–27.

62. V. Ia. Laverychev, "Prodovol'stvennaia politika tsarizma i burzhuazii v gody pervoi mirovoi voiny (1914–1917 gg.)," *Vestnik moskovskogo universiteta*, no. 1 (1956) p. 151; idem, "Gosudarstvenno-monopolisticheskie tendentsii pri organizatsii prodovol'stvennogo dela v Rossii (1914-fevral' 1917)," *Istoricheskie zapiski*, no. 101 (1978) p. 104.

63. *IGUZZ*, no. 16 (1915) p. 387; RGIA, f. 456, op. 1, d. 9, ll. 20–22, 29; RGVIA, f. 499, op. 3, d. 1401, ll. 122–124, 129, 132, 134–135.

64. *IGUZZ*, no. 37 (1915) pp. 917–918; RGIA, f. 457, op. 1, d. 23, ll. 55, 58–59.

65. RGVIA, f. 499, op. 3, d. 1401, l. 123.

66. GK VSG, *Trudy soveshchaniia po ekonomicheskim voprosam, sviazannym s dorogoviznoi i snabzheniem armii, Moskva, 11–13 iiulia 1915 g.* (Moscow, 1915), p. 32.

67. *SU*, no. 318 (1915) art. 2356.

68. In Perm' Province, a provincial zemstvo assembly held in June 1915 resolved that the provincial Grain-Purchasing Agent for the Army should also be in charge of supplying factories with food and fodder "lest rivalry [between military and civilian procurements] occur." In October of that year, a session of the provincial food council stated its wish to conduct food procurement for the local population through the "existing" organization of grain-purchasing for the army. It was immediately after this session that the Ministry of Agriculture appointed the Grain-Purchasing Agent for the Army (who was simultaneously a member of provincial zemstvo board), E. D. Kalugin, to the additional post of agent of the Special Council on Food. See: *Zhurnaly permskogo*

gubernskogo zemskogo sobraniia 53-i chrezvychainoi sessii i doklady upravy semu sobraniiu, 16–17 iiunia 1915 g. (Perm', 1915), "Zhurnal za 16 iiunia 1915 g.," p. 11; Gosudarstvennyi arkhiv permskoi oblasti, f. 43, op. 1, d. 1376, l. 5.

69. *Spisok upolnomochennykh predsedatelia osobogo soveshchaniia po prodovol'stvennomu delu i upolnomochennykh ministerstva zemledeliia po zakupkam dlia armii (30 ianvaria 1916).*

70. RGIA, f. 457, op. 1, d. 8, l. 30.

71. MGZS, ekstrenniaia sessiia 1915 g. (Oktiabr'), "Doklad upravy o meropriiatiiakh po prodovol'stviiu naseleniia gubernii," pp. 4–5.

72. For examples of Lipetsk County (Tambov Province) and of Moscow Province, see Gosudarstvennyi arkhiv tambovskoi oblasti [hereafter GATO], f. 24, op. 3, d. 1, l. 12 and *Izvestiia osobogo soveshchaniia dlia obsuzhdeniia i ob"edineniia meropriiatii po prodovol'stvennomu delu* [hereafter *IOSPD*], no. 25/26 (1916) p. 1.

73. UD OSPD, *Sovremennoe polozhenie taksirovki*, pp. 67, 132–133.

74. *Poltavskaia agronomicheskaia izvestiia*, no. 2 (1916) p. 39.

75. Ibid., no. 3 (1916) pp. 38.

76. For Moscow, Ufa, Nizhegorod, and Samara Provinces, see: MGZS, Ocherednaia sessia 1915 g., "Doklad o perepisi posevnykh ploshchadei i tekushchei prodovol'stvennoi statistike," pp. 11–12; Gosudarstvennyi arkhiv Bashkirskoi respubliki [hereafter GABR], f. I-96, op. 1, d. 8, ll. 55, 58; *Svedeniia o polozhenii prodovol'stvennogo dela v Petrograde, Moskve i drugikh mestnostiakh Imperii, a takzhe v innostrannykh gosudarstvakh*, no. 18 (1916) p. 21; *Svedeniia o polozhenii prodovol'stvennogo dela v Petrograde, Moskve i drugikh mestnostiakh Imperii*, no. 13 (1915) p. 30; *Trudy soveshchaniia statistikov 24 gubernii pri upolnomochennom predsedatelia osobogo soveshchaniia po prodovol'stvennomu delu po moskovskoi gubernii, 27–29 dekabria 1915 g.* (Moscow, 1916), pp. 16–17; *IOSPD*, no. 22 (1916) pp. 49–50.

77. UD OSPD, *Sovremennoe polozhenie taksirovki*, pp. 42–62.

78. Ibid., pp. 68–69.

79. *SU*, no. 53 (1916) art. 355.

80. For an example of this phenomenon in Tver' Province, see *Doklad upolnomochennogo osobogo soveshchaniia po prodovol'stvennomu delu tverskoi gubernii, ocherednomu gubernskomu zemskomu sobraniiu sessii 1916 g.* (Tver', 1916), p. 2.

81. Such phenomena were even seen in Perm' Province, where the prototype of the Permit System of Railway Transportation had been introduced as early as the autumn of 1914. Gosudarstvennyi arkhiv sverdlovskoi oblasti, f. 18, op. 1, d. 467, l. 262.

82. *IOSPD*, no. 23/24 (1916) pp. 19–20.

83. See my "The Concept of 'Space' in Russian History: Regionalization from the Late Imperial Period to the Present," in the Teruyuki Hara, ed., *Empire and Society: New Approaches to Russian History* (Sapporo, forthcoming). In the early 1930s *oblasty* replaced *gubernii* or provinces, the tsarist administrative divisions that had been established under Catherine the Great in the 1770s.

84. GABR, f. I-421, op. 1, d. 7, ll. 18–19; Ibid., f. I-96, op. 1, d. 8, ll. 89–90. According to a questionnaire survey carried out by the Ufa provincial food council in March-April

1916, only one city board (Birsk's) of all district seats in the province affirmed the need for statutory prices (Ibid., ll. 112–114).

85. RGIA, f. 456, op. 1, d. 244, l. 38.

86. Ibid., ll. 34–35.

87. Ibid., f. 457, op. 1, d. 248, l. 18.

88. This circular is not to be confused with the one proposing the small-area food organs on p. 266 of this chapter.

89. RGIA, f. 457, op. 1, d. 248, l. 206.

90. Ibid., f. 456, op. 1, d. 244, l. 38.

91. Many participants in a conference of statisticians convened by the Moscow zemstvo in December 1915 remarked on this problem. See in particular a speech by a statistician from the Ekaterinoslav provincial zemstvo: *Trudy soveshechaniia statistikov . . . po moskovskoi gubernii,* pp. 24–25.

92. "Zhurnaly Khersonskogo gubernskogo zemskogo sobraniia chrezvychainoi sessii 1916 g., Zasedanie 18 marta," p. 47.

93. Viatskoe gubernskoe zemstvo, "Zhurnal zasedaniia statisticheskogo soveta 25 oktiabria 1915 g.," pp. 14–17; Gosudarstvennyi arkhiv kirovskoi oblasti [hereafter GAKO], f. 616, op. 1, d. 236, ll. 50–51; and *Trudy soveshchaniia statistikov . . . po moskovskoi gubernii,* p. 17.

94. UP OSPD, *Obzor deiatel'nosti,* pp. 90–91.

95. Ibid., pp. 92–93.

96. Ibid., p. 90.

97. Ibid., p. 95.

98. *IOSPD,* no. 21 (1916) pp. 4–8.

99. P. A. Vikhliaev, *O rabotakh, vypolnennykh statisticheskim otdeleniem v 1916 g. i predpolagaemykh k vypolneniiu v 1917 g.* (n.d.), p. 22; GAKO, f. 616, op. 7, d. 278, l. 17; "Zhurnaly Khersonskogo . . . Zasedanie 18 marta," p. 42.

100. *IOSPD,* no.23/24, 1916, pp. 16–17.

101. MGZS, Ocherednaia sessiia 1915 g., "Doklad o perepisi," pp. 1–9.

102. See reports by the Kazan' and Poltava provincial zemstvo boards; "Otchet kazanskoi gubernskoi zemskoi upravy po proizvodstvu sel'skokhoziaistvennoi perepisi 1916 goda," pp. 6–10, 15; and "O rabotakh, provedennykh statisticheskim biuro v 1916 g. i predpolozhennykh na 1917 g.," in *Doklad poltavskoi gubernskoi zemskoi upravy 52 ocherednomu gubernskomu zemskomu sobraniiu* (Poltava, 1917), pp. 16–33.

103. Vikhliaev, *O rabotakh,* p. 24; *Zhurnaly ekaterinoslavskogo gubernskogo zemskogo sobraniia 51-i ocherednoi sessii 1916 goda s prilozheniem* (Ekaterinoslav, 1917), pp. 603–605; *Khersonskoe gubernskoe zemskoe sobranie 51-i ocherednoi sessii 1916 g., doklady upravy i komissii, zhurnaly sobraniia* (Kherson, 1916), pp. 143–146; GAKO, f. 728, op. 1, d. 4, ll. 277–278; Gosudarstvennyi arkhiv khar'kovskoi oblasti, f. 304, op. 1, d. 2834, l. 7.

104. This formula was adopted by the Council of Ministers at the end of December, 1915 (RGIA, f. 456, op. 1, d. 931, l. 1).

105. *IOSPD*, no. 23/24 (1916) pp. 18–19.

106. Ibid., no. 27 (1916) p. 115.

107. Ibid., no. 28 (1916) pp. 2–3.

108. RGIA, f. 457, op. 1, d. 571, l. 33.

109. Ibid., d. 576, l. 235.

110. Ibid., d. 574, l. 256.

111. Ibid., d. 571, l. 73.

112. Ibid., f. 575, ll. 129–130.

113. For an example of Tula city, see: RGIA, f. 457, op. 1, d. 575, l. 129.

114. RGIA, f. 457, op. 1, d. 575, l. 299.

115. GATO, f. 207, op. 1, d. 134, l. 3.

116. *Padenie tsarskogo rezhima* [hereafter *PTsR*], vol. 7 (Moscow-Leningrad, 1927), p. 309. Charles Timberlake describes B. V. Shtiurmer's career in Tver' Province in chapter 2. As chair of the Tver' provincial zemstvo board in the 1890s, Shtiurmer asked advice from liberal zemstvo delegates and began to form a "center group" opposing the authoritarian governor of Tver' Province. After serving in Tver', Shtiurmer was appointed governor of Yaroslavl' Province, just east of Tver'. Shtiurmer's name is often cited as Stürmer in English-language histories of Russia dealing with World War I. As this is familiar to English-speaking readers, both versions of his name are given here. In chapter 6 Antti Kujala uses the version Stürmer.

117. RGIA, f. 456, op. 1, d. 23, l. 130.

118. Ibid., d. 244, l. 152.

119. Ibid., l. 223.

120. Ibid., d. 156. l. 137.

121. Ibid., l. 184.

122. *PTsR*, vol. 7, p. 387.

123. *Izvestiia ministerstva zemledeliia*, no. 36 (1916) p. 747.

124. *SZh*, no. 21/24, 1916, pp. 268–269.

125. RGIA, f. 457, op. 1, f. 572, l. 89.

126. Ibid., f. 456, op. 1, d. 156, l. 214.

127. *PTsR*, vol. 4 (Leningrad, 1925), p. 75.

128. Ibid., vol. 7, p. 321.

129. RGIA, f. 456, op. 1, d. 126, l. 62.

130. *IOSPD*, no. 25/26, (1916) p. 2; *Izvestiia moskovskoi gubernskoi zemskoi upravy*, no. 2/3 (1916) pp. 14–15; *Trudy soveshchaniia statistikov . . . po moskovskoi gubernii*, pp. 12, 22, 57.

131. Norms for Moscow Province for September and October 1916 were imposed on the following agrarian provinces: Tambov, Kursk, Orel, Voronezh, Saratov, and Taurida; and additionally, Khar'kov and Simbirsk. According to Gruzinov, however, among those only the Tambov Grain-Purchasing Agent for the Army fulfilled the September norm. The others sent Moscow less than half of their norms; the worst was the Simbirsk Grain-Purchasing Agent for the Army, who did not send a single wagon to Moscow Province (RGIA, f. 457, op. 1, d. 571, l. 2; Ibid., d. 572, ll. 74–75, 272).

132. RGIA, f. 457, op. 1, d. 572, ll. 90–93.

133. Ibid., l. 311.

134. Ibid., d. 573, l. 389; Ibid., d. 576, ll. 255–256; Ibid., d. 577, l. 111.

135. Ibid., d. 575, ll. 61–62.

136. Ibid., d. 577, ll. 111–112.

137. Ibid., d. 574, ll. 181, 230, 231; Ibid., d. 575, ll. 116, 117.

138. Ibid., d. 576, l. 267.

139. Ibid., l. 416.

140. Ibid.

141. Ibid., l. 269.

142. Ibid.

143. Ibid., ll. 191.

144. Ibid., d. 577, l. 74.

145. Ibid., d. 576, l. 416.

146. Ibid., l. 37.

147. Ibid., d. 572, l. 164.

148. Ibid., l. 341.

149. Ibid., d. 575, l. 48.

150. Ibid., d. 572, ll. 102, 318.

151. Ibid., d. 576, l. 4.

152. Ibid., ll. 234–236.

153. Ibid.

154. Ibid., d. 566, ll. 202–206.

155. Ibid., d. 576, l. 380.

156. Ibid., d. 572, ll. 128, 313.

157. Ibid., ll. 128, 314–315.

158. Ibid., d. 574, ll. 248–249; Ibid., d. 575, ll. 53, 250.

159. Ibid., d. 573, l. 323; Ibid., d. 576, ll. 358–359.

160. Ibid., d. 564, ll. 192–193.

161. Ibid., l. 263.

162. Ibid., d. 563, ll. 68, 70.

163. Ibid., ll. 68–69.

164. Ibid., l. 68.

165. Ibid., l. 69.

166. Ibid.

167. Ibid., l. 70.

168. Ibid.

169. Ibid., l. 74.

170. Gosudarstvennyi arkhiv samarskoi oblasti [hereafter GASO], f. 230, op. 1, f. 209, ll. 113–114.

171. RGIA, f. 457, op. 1, d. 18, l. 30.

172. GASO, f. 230, op. 1, d. 209, l. 158.

173. RGIA, f. 457, op. 1, d. 18, l. 33.

174. Ibid., l. 35.

INDEX